ON SPEAKING TERMS

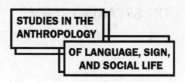

Studies in the Anthropology of Language, Sign, and Social Life focuses on cutting-edge developments in the analysis of linguistic and semiotic processes within a comparative, ethnographic, and socio-historical context. The series provides a home for innovative, boundary-pushing scholarship in linguistic anthropology, as well as work in sociolinguistics, the sociology of interaction, and semiotics. Including both ethnographic monographs and theoretical explorations, books in this series present new ways of understanding the centrality of language and other sign systems to social and cultural life.

Editor: Jack Sidnell, University of Toronto

On Speaking Terms

Avoidance Registers and the Sociolinguistics of Kinship

LUKE OWLES FLEMING

UNIVERSITY OF TORONTO PRESS
Toronto Buffalo London

© University of Toronto Press 2024
Toronto Buffalo London
utorontopress.com
Printed in Canada

ISBN 978-1-4875-4970-1 (cloth)   ISBN 978-1-4875-5302-9 (EPUB)
                                 ISBN 978-1-4875-5091-2 (PDF)

Studies in the Anthropology of Language, Sign, and Social Life

Library and Archives Canada Cataloguing in Publication

Title: On speaking terms : avoidance registers and the sociolinguistics
of kinship / Luke Owles Fleming.
Names: Fleming, Luke Owles, author.
Description: Series statement: Studies in the anthropology of language,
sign, and social life | Includes bibliographical references and index.
Identifiers: Canadiana (print) 20240475615 | Canadiana (ebook) 20240475623 |
ISBN 9781487549701 (cloth) | ISBN 9781487553029 (EPUB) |
ISBN 9781487550912 (PDF)
Subjects: LCSH: Language in families – Cross-cultural studies. | LCSH: Joking
relationships – Cross-cultural studies. | LCSH: Nonverbal communication –
Cross-cultural studies. | LCSH: Avoidance (Psychology) – Cross-cultural
studies. | LCSH: Kinship – Cross-cultural studies. | LCSH: Sociolinguistics –
Cross-cultural studies.
Classification: LCC P40.5.F36 F54 2025 | DDC 306.44 – dc23

Cover design: Liz Harasymczuk
Cover images: Julien Posture

We wish to acknowledge the land on which the University of Toronto Press
operates. This land is the traditional territory of the Wendat, the Anishnaabeg,
the Haudenosaunee, the Métis, and the Mississaugas of the Credit First Nation.

This book has been published with the help of a grant from the Federation
for the Humanities and Social Sciences, through the Awards to Scholarly
Publications Program, using funds provided by the Social Sciences and
Humanities Research Council of Canada.

University of Toronto Press acknowledges the financial support of the
Government of Canada, the Canada Council for the Arts, and the Ontario Arts
Council, an agency of the Government of Ontario, for its publishing activities.

   Canada Council   Conseil des Arts
                       for the Arts   du Canada

   ONTARIO ARTS COUNCIL
                       CONSEIL DES ARTS DE L'ONTARIO
                       an Ontario government agency
                       un organisme du gouvernement de l'Ontario

Funded by the   Financé par le
Government   gouvernement   Canadä
of Canada   du Canada

*To my mother and father,
Joan E. Fleming and John V. Fleming,
with love and thanksgiving*

Contents

List of Figures, Tables, and Boxes ix

Acknowledgments xiii

Introduction: The Total Orientation 3

Part One – Proscriptive Regimes of Language and Avoidance Registers

1 Avoidance Lexicon, Everyday Grammar: Why Words Are Good to Proscribe 35

2 Many to One: Lexicon Asymmetries in Avoidance Registers 51

Part Two – The Sounds of Reference: Name Taboos

3 Name Registers: A Sociolinguistic Kind 83

4 Rigid Performativity: Cross-Cultural Convergences in Name Registers 107

Part Three – The Anti-Phatic Function: Interactional Avoidances

5 Not on Speaking Terms: Closing and Rerouting Channels of Communication 137

6 Out of Touch: Sensory Avoidances and the Multimodality of Mutuality 162

Part Four – The Pattern Which Connects: Avoidance Registers as Scalar Honorific Formations

7 The Pragmatic Suspension of Semantic Distinctions: Honorific Pronouns in Kinship Avoidance   191
8 Degrees of Unfreedom: From Pragmatic Structures to Intensities of Experience   218

Conclusion: The Mutuality of Being Apart   253

Notes   273

References   309

Index   347

Figures, Tables, and Boxes

Figures

0.1 Kobon kinship taboos and their organization into avoidance levels 24
4.1 Tropes of kin address between namesakes in Ju | 'hoan 126
4.2 Formal-functional diagrammatic structure which produces honorifically graded avoidance levels in name registers 129
4.3 Nested negative repertoires characteristic of the speech of some Zulu married women 132
5.1 Two communicative infrastructures conditioned by affinal avoidance relationships 146
7.1 Kobon pronominal honorifics 205
7.2 Manus in-law relationships by the numbers 206
7.3 Temiar honorific number in addressee-reference 210
7.4 Jahai number skewing in pronouns employed in addressee-reference (above) and non-participant-reference (below) 211
7.5 Inferred recursive suspension of number values in Manus avoidance register 214
8.1 Avoidance levels in Sidaama name register 220
8.2 Encompassment relations between name avoidances in Motuna 222
8.3 Stereotypical cross-gender uses of kinship respect vocabulary (*Uw Ilbmbandiy/Olkel-Ilmbanhthi*) among Kunjen speakers; male origo, female target 237
8.4 Three levels of *maddiyali* "mother-in-law" avoidance in Gooniyandi 238
8.5 Avoidance levels determined by indexical focus type in mother-in-law languages 239
8.6 Layers in the (meta)pragmatic structuring of avoidance repertoires 247
C.1 Spheres of (un)shareable experience 269

Tables

0.1 Norms of Chiricahua Apache in-law avoidance 19
0.2. Implicational relationships between joking-avoidance comportments in Tikopia 22
0.3 Implicational relationships between kinship avoidances in Kobon (Papua New Guinea) 23
1.1 Complementarity in the loci of the social indexing of speaker gender and speaker-addressee kin relationship in Yanyuwa 43
2.1 Many-to-one correspondence in verbs of motion between everyday Guugu Yimidhirr and brother-in-law language 52
2.2 Many-to-one relations between everyday Kalam words and pandanus language vocabulary items 57
2.3 One-to-many relations between pandanus register entries and everyday Kewa words 58
2.4 Many-to-one relations between everyday Buru lexicon and Li Garan avoidance terms 59
2.5 Descriptive paraphrases used for "non-nuclear" meanings in Dyirbal mother-in-law language (Jalnguy) 64
2.6 Comparison of ethnobiological nomenclature across everyday and avoidance registers of Uradhi, Guugu Yimidhirr, Lardil, and Gbaya 66
2.7 Noun formation in the alternate sign language employed at St. Joseph's Abbey in Massachusetts 69
3.1 Some examples of name and homophone taboos in Mongolian 84
3.2 Sociopragmatic markedness of avoidance vocabulary in V'ënen Taut 89
3.3 True homophone avoidance on the Xingu River (Brazil) 95
3.4 Global survey of affinal name and homophone avoidance registers 97
4.1 Distinction between joking (or k"ãi "to joke"/"to play") and avoidance (or kwa "to fear"/"to respect") relationships in Ju|'hoan, depicted from the perspective of a female ego 125
4.2 Examples of near-homophone avoidance in in-law name registers 128
6.1 Portable technologies of visual avoidance employed between in-laws in Melanesia and Aboriginal Australia 177
7.1 Examples of kinship-restricted T-V systems 195
8.1 Different veiling styles among Hindu women in rural Saurashtra, Gujarat, India 244

C.1 Joking and avoidance symbolized through their association with dimensions of social categorical identity and difference 268

Boxes

8.1 Accounts of fluid referent/recipient targeting in use of Aboriginal Australian affinal avoidance registers 230
8.2 Accounts where only recipient-targeting use of avoidance registers is discussed 232

Acknowledgments

Were I even capable of giving a proper accounting, the intellectual supports upon which this book are built would be too numerous to be named. Here I single out only a few of the many people who have helped me during what have been many years of researching and writing this book.

Rupert Stasch carefully reviewed the manuscript, and his editorial feedback crucially informed major revisions (including the drafting of a completely new Introduction and Conclusion). As will be seen throughout, Stasch's Korowai ethnography was a major intellectual influence on the approach to the problem of kinship avoidance taken here.

Francesca Merlan was another important inspiration for me. Her 1997 essay on the "mother-in-law taboo" is a touchstone for this topic, as is the 1983 volume *Languages of Kinship in Aboriginal Australia*, which she edited with Jeffrey Heath and Alan Rumsey. Beyond their rich ethnographic and theoretical interventions, I thank Francesca and Alan for their kindness to me when I visited the AIATSIS archive in Canberra in 2019. They graciously welcomed me at the Australian National University; Francesca even lent me her bicycle for that glorious week!

At the University of Montreal, I wish to express my thanks to graduate research assistants paid through the generous support of the SSHRC: Amal Haroun, Robbie Penman, Raphaël Preux, Adèle Raux-Copin, and Étienne Rougier. My thanks also to Miriam Guilbeault, with whom I read a sampling of Roy Wagner's oeuvre in the context of an independent study; Wagner, especially as I realized his close connection to Gregory Bateson, turned out to have a major influence on the argument. Finally, I wish to express my gratitude to Julien Porquet for the beautiful cover-art.

Other figures important in bringing this book into being include James Slotta, who – in Austin in 2019 – urged me to write the book after

I had given up following an earlier failed attempt; Jack Sidnell, who has been so supportive of me over the years, for including this manuscript in his wonderful series; Paul Kockelman, who wrote up a long and rich set of notes and suggestions after reading the book proposal; Chip Zuckerman, who offered very helpful feedback on a draft of Part 3. As will be recognizable to those well-versed in the field of linguistic anthropology, the theoretical armature of the book is deeply indebted to Michael Silverstein and Asif Agha, my undergraduate and graduate-school mentors, respectively.

Finally, I thank my wife, Melanie Dean, and our wonderful children, Hazel and John-Henry, for suffering (the specter of) "my book" for so long. The realization of this project would have been impossible without their forbearance, support, and encouragement.

ON SPEAKING TERMS

Introduction

The Total Orientation

In an essay entitled "An Outline of Chiricahua Apache Social Organization," Morris Opler (1937) recounts an informant's testimony concerning events that

> occurred a few days after [the informant's] marriage. He had gone with his wife to visit some friends. As he entered the dwelling, he came face to face with his father-in-law's cousin. This woman said, "It's too bad we have met face to face. I was going to avoid this man, but now it has been spoiled. Hereafter we will use the polite form." The informant expressed his surprise and pleasure at hearing the venerable lady say that she had intended to avoid him. "I never knew she thought so much of me," he said. (p. 220)

This passage concerns the practices of interpersonal avoidance mutually maintained between Chiricahua Apache in-laws – specifically, the use of the indefinite or "fourth person" pronoun as a polite form of reference and address, and the reciprocal practice of not looking at or being seen by the affinal other.[1] The informant's account highlights that "avoidance" between in-laws, far from being experienced as ostracizing, was interpreted as a sign of respect. The informant is flattered that his wife's cousin, the "venerable lady," should have even considered engaging in sight-avoidance with him! Interpretations like these contrast markedly with those suggested by English expressions such as "to cut off contact" or "to not be on speaking terms," idioms that imbue the studious interpersonal avoidance of social others with relationship-rupturing force. And yet, all over the world, particular categories of kin enact respect toward one another in essentially the same way – by avoiding mutually ratified sensorial and semiotic exchanges.

How has it come to be that, in so many far-flung places, particular kin enact respect toward one another through avoidance? In this book I seek to answer that question. The question itself is not new, but the kind of answer that I give to it is. Earlier scholarship invariably understood cross-cultural convergences in kinship avoidances to be a function of common exogenous causes, like conflict mitigation (Radcliffe-Brown, 1949; Tylor, 1889) or sex regulation (Freud, 1918; Murdock, 1967). Drawing upon a broad sample of rich ethnographic studies of kinship avoidance, I show that this approach is fundamentally misguided. I will argue that it is only when we grasp the internal and *sui generis* character of kinship avoidance as an indexical or pragmatic sign system that we can render intelligible its cross-cultural comparability. Grappling with kinship avoidance as a comparative phenomenon requires rematerializing kinship as a reflexively appreciated, internally coherent, and semiotically rich practice of relationship.

The Total Orientation

Kinship avoidances like those of the Chiricahua Apache are documented in communities from all over the world. Again and again, the ethnographic archive presents "avoidance" as a highly significant relational practice, densely emblematic of other-oriented kinship morality and actualized as an intense phenomenological experience of being-toward-others.

How should we understand kinship avoidance as a cross-culturally convergent and recurrent phenomenon? The best place to start our investigation is with the state of the art in thinking concerning the topic. Crucial here is Francesca Merlan's (1997) and Rupert Stasch's (2003, 2009) understanding of the most focal and intense forms of kinship avoidance as implying a "total orientation" toward the other in interaction (Merlan, 1997, p. 106). Stasch (2003) writes of Korowai mother-in-law/son-in-law avoidance:

> The practices of separation upheld by a mother-in-law and a son-in-law brusquely intrude on everything else in the social scene. Any other activities that the two undertake in each other's presence are dominated by the care they have to take over such things as staying out of each other's sight. ... When they are in each other's vicinity, the voice and abstract presence of each surrounds the other, and the affinal relationship surrounds each of them as an intangible, invisible, and transcendent condition of their lives. (p. 325)

Merlan (1997), working from her own Mangarayi ethnography, but also from the wider scholarship documenting Aboriginal Australian cultures of kinship, underscores the "univocal" character of speech and action in the presence of a mother-in-law.

> [T]he mother-in-law avoidance taboo, in which the highly prescribed and institutionalised forms – aversion of gaze, relative taciturnity, special proxemics, and so on – tend to give *one* aspect of the relationship between people overriding determination of their conduct in each other's presence. Thus, a man in his mother-in-law's presence finds it difficult to behave towards her in any way other than as her son-in-law; and further, his conduct towards everyone else on the scene is very strongly shaped by their co-presence, and the social emphasis placed on it. (p. 108)

I want to highlight two themes in these passages. I cannot explore them in depth here; their richer exploration is a concern throughout the book. But I do want to flag them as crucial dimensions of the total social fact that should direct our enquiry. First, the concept of univocality: Avoidance involves a privileging of one mode or manner of communicating over others. One reason that doing avoidance is culturally interpreted as enacting respect is that it involves the suspension of other possible ways of talking, looking, interacting, and so on – in the presence of a mother-in-law, a man cannot act "in any way other than as her son-in-law." Second, the intense and enveloping phenomenological experience of the other: Sartre (2003) argues that the loss of the world as for me is always an effect of the coming onto the scene of an other. Ritualized avoidance hypertrophies this effect. (Think of times when you have experienced intense embarrassment, shame, or self-consciousness in the presence of some particular person.) In avoidance, one is "for the other" (Sartre, 2003) in a continuous and conscious manner. In the Korowai and Chiricahua Apache examples, the specter of the presence of the affinal other is heightened by constraints on sensorial contact with them. When one is unable to look directly at the other, the "abstract presence of each surrounds the other" (Stasch, 2003, p. 325).

Remarkably, this total orientation *toward* the other – which is, at one and the same time, an interactional practice and a subjective experience – is enacted and experienced by circumscribing and attenuating contacts: by not speaking to, by not referring to, by not seeing that other. That is, the total orientation toward the other is enacted by turning away, by abstaining from contact. The cultural sentiments and qualities of experience – often translated as "shame" and "respect" – which the total orientation instantiates vary cross-culturally. Nevertheless, in culture after culture, focal avoidance involves a hypertrophic intensification of the experience of the other's (always deferred and refracted) presence as a sensorially accessible or semiotically invokable other in interaction.

A deeper understanding of the total orientation characteristic of focal avoidance relationships, like the mother-in-law/son-in-law relationships that Merlan and Stasch document among Mangarayi and Korowai, is a central goal of this book. I contribute to an account of this important dimension of social relationship by offering a close analysis of the sign systems – we will call them "avoidance registers" – through which these kinship relationships are both enacted and reflexively apprehended. The different chapters of the book focus on distinct linguistic and semiotic media in which kinship avoidance is registered, seeking to account for cross-cultural convergences in their patterning. The Conclusion returns to questions of the collective representation and the subjective experience of avoidance.

Grand Theories and the Driftwood Thereof

Avoidance relationships, often where structurally opposed to joking relationships, have been a long-standing topic of ethnographic and comparative ethnological study (Eggan, 1937; Freud, 1918; Lowie, 1920; Radcliffe-Brown, 1949; Rivers, 1914; Tylor, 1889, etc.). The problem of "avoidance" – why do particular classes of kin ceremoniously avoid one another? – has been with anthropology for such a long time that influential accounts of the phenomenon have been proposed within each of its major schools of thought.

Tylor (1889) and Rivers (1914) interpreted avoidance through an evolutionary lens. Tylor, for instance, saw affinal avoidance as the "survival" of the hostile attitude that historically must have reigned between warring groups that, now converted into exogamous moieties, maintain the peace through marriage. From the functionalist school, it is Alfred Radcliffe-Brown's (1924, 1940, 1949) theorization of the topic that is justifiably the most well respected. His thought on the topic evolved from his early writings on the avunculate (the special and intimate relationship of licence with the mother's brother) through to his later writings on the joking relationship – a "relation between two persons in which one is by custom permitted, and in some instances required, to tease or make fun of the other, who in turn is required to take no offence" (Radcliffe-Brown, 1940, p. 195). But his reflections never culminated in a single programmatic statement where all the loose ends got tied up. He argues that affinal relationships involve both "conjunctive" and "disjunctive" elements. Inasmuch as spouses come from distinct families of origin, their allegiances and interests are divergent. But inasmuch as the two form a new nuclear family within which their parents can envision their own biosocial continuation, the interests of in-laws are aligned. Avoidance, from this perspective, functions to temper tensions and cut off possible conflicts before they can begin.

As these examples illustrate, the functionalist and evolutionist literatures are obsessively concerned with the question of "the" cause of avoidance.[2] Unfortunately, the question doesn't really make sense. Any explanation that posits a unifunctionalist cause must treat avoidance as an automatic, almost autonomous, activity – an instinctual response, like the "flight" in "fight or flight." But this misrecognizes what is going on. Kinship avoidance can't be given a neat, causally reductive explanation because it isn't one "thing." It certainly isn't some primitive or innate response, leaving only its stimulus to be discovered.

Kinship avoidance is a *sui generis* system. It is only when it is approached as such that one can gain traction on questions concerning its cross-culturally convergent properties. These systems are composed, minimally, of the following moving parts, all of which are discussed in more depth as we go along. Avoidance involves particular acts (e.g., not saying someone's name, not eating food in the other's presence), fashioned from diverse semiotic media, which are registered as respectful signs of relationship. The ensemble of such signs (what I call the "register repertoire") is itself elaborately structured, such that distinct sub-repertoires (or "avoidance levels") are stereotypically keyed to particular kin categories. (Korowai sight-avoidance, for instance, is stereotypically associated with the mother-in-law/son-in-law relation.) Further, because the signs in question involve specific and embodied modes of (not) making contact with the other, the enactment of these signs in interaction instantiates "phatic infrastructures" – patterned openings and closures of communicative channels across the kinship field.[3] These modes of phatic contact are themselves reflexively apprehended through the mediation of cultural ideologies. (The Daribi say, for example, "To look at one's mother-in-law is like looking at the sun" [Wagner, 1967, p. 173].) This cultural symbolization of contact feeds back into the actual experience of being in avoidance relationship, into the experience of contact, and its attenuation (after Russell, 2020), as qualities and intensities of relationship.

It was perhaps Claude Lévi-Strauss who first gestured toward an understanding of joking-avoidance as a *sui generis* phenomenon. Framed as a critique of Radcliffe-Brown's theory of the avunculate, Lévi-Strauss (1958) argued that joking (*relation familière*) and avoidance (*relation rigoureuse*) constituted a structural opposition. Radcliffe-Brown (1924), drawing on Junod's BaThonga ethnography, had interpreted the affectionate relationship with the mother's brother (the "male mother") and the restrained relationship with the father's sister (the "female father") as involving the extension of feelings of affection and respect which naturally attach to the mother and father, respectively, in a patrilineal system. Lévi-Strauss demurred. Drawing on enough examples to illustrate all possible permutations, he showed that the BaThonga configuration was just one among a number of attested ways in which styles of interpersonal comportment become structurally opposed in the mediation of the "elementary" set of kinship relations. Unfortunately, Lévi-Strauss's analysis – like those of so many other mid-century comparativists – abstracted away from the material practices and the semiotic media through which relationship is enacted. His concern for uncovering digital or binary oppositions meant that he gave no attention to the analogue intensities and gradients of joking and avoidance as lived experience and embodied practice. And yet it is precisely this dimension that must be theorized in order to grasp avoidance as a total orientation.

Rematerializing Avoidance: Ethnographic Details

While some of the biggest names in the anthropological canon were busy trying their hand at reducing avoidance – whether to an evolutionary "survival," to being the guarantor of inter-family equilibrium, or as the playing out of a universal principle of structural binarism – ethnographers were busy writing rich accounts of avoidance practices as encountered in specific cultures. Sometimes avoidance had a starring role! So, for instance, in Monica Wilson's (1951) *Good Company*, the total avoidance between father-in-law and daughter-in-law is the initial condition generative of the residential segregation of adjacent generation kin – the central empirical object of Wilson's magisterial study of the Nyakyusa (Bantu; Tanzania). As Meyer Fortes (1953, p. 19) observed, "the whole scheme of local organization in age villages turns on such avoidances." Similarly, in Jane Goodale's (1995) *To Sing with Pigs Is Human*, in-law avoidance is revelatory of the orienting concerns of Kaulong (New Britain) social life. Beginning with marriage, one avoids all of the cognatic kin (both living and dead) of one's spouse. Linguistically, this entails the avoidance of the names and homophones of the names of these persons; the substitute vocabulary employed for replacing the taboo homophones of one's in-laws' names is called the "language of the married" (Tok Pisin, *marid tok*). These avoidances saliently underscore that the primary ontological division for Kaulong is not one between nature and culture or male and female or even affine and consanguine.

Rather, it is one between the sexually active (and thus impure) and the virginal (Goodale, 1980). Sex is understood to cause the wasting away and eventual death of the body. Avoidance practice functions here as an emblem of the impure state of the married. To speak *marid tok* is to have entered a life-stage – marriage and parenthood – of ritual impurity.

I have highlighted these two ethnographies because avoidance plays a particularly important role in them. But they are also metonyms for the ethnographic record – our problematic, but nevertheless vital, disciplinary inheritance. It is this record which I will draw upon, time and again, in trying to formulate an understanding of kinship avoidance as recognizable (that is, registered) relational practice. But immediately some caveats are in order. Ethnographies have the tendency to conflate and collapse the distinction between norm and practice. They employ nomothetic statements – "A man gives food and valuables to his sister's children" – that paper over the distinction between the two. Further, in many instances, field research was part and parcel of colonial and nation-building projects that fundamentally transformed the material conditions of people's lives. For instance, most of the linguistic descriptions of Aboriginal Australian "mother-in-law languages" are drawn from the testimonials of older informants concerning life as they remembered it from their youth. The portraits of affinal avoidance from Native Californian communities – which I draw on in Chapter 7 – are similarly sourced from remembered and reconstructed practices (see the compilation in Gifford, 1922).

Rather than seek out only the most thorough descriptions, I have drawn upon a wide range of sources. Invariably, these are of varying quality and comprehensiveness. In some cases, researchers lacked competency in local languages, relied on contact languages or translators, and spent only a short time in the relevant communities. In other cases, researchers had long and lasting relationships. In still others, we are lucky enough to have pieces co-authored with native fieldworkers (see, for example, Keesing & Fifi'i, 1969; Majnep & Bulmer, 1977), or even to have rich autobiographical sources to draw upon (see, for example, Boyer & Gayton 1992; Roughsey, 1971; Villa & Matossian, 1982). My conclusions must necessarily be tempered by the variable quality of my sources. This problem applies in particular to my inferences concerning avoidance as dynamic intersubjective practice. And it applies most profoundly to my speculations concerning difficult-to-access kinds of meaning, like the qualities of the phenomenological experience of avoidance. Throughout, I try to underscore when I am making inferences and what my bases for them are. Even if you are not wholly convinced by my arguments, I hope that this book will serve as a source text for scholars interested in the sociolinguistics of kinship.

Despite these caveats, my goal is to make ethnographic detail speak in a way that it has not in previous comparative treatments of kinship avoidance. It is counterintuitive, but in order to understand cross-cultural convergences in the patterning of kinship communication we must look deeper "inside" culture-specific systems of avoidances rather than look for some exogenous causal precondition "outside" of them. We must take a deep dive into the ethnographic details of avoidance rather than abstract away from them.

Scale without a Measure: The Joking-Avoidance "Continuum"

If one reads enough ethnographic descriptions of kinship "codes of conduct," one will run into numerous descriptions like the following, from Tonkinson's (1978) ethnography of life in the Western Desert of Australia: "Although the Mardudjara themselves do not describe kinship patterning in terms of a continuum, it may be helpful to consider the different gradations of patterned kin behavior as falling between two extremes: complete avoidance and uninhibited joking" (p. 47). Descriptions invoking poles of "absolute avoidance and extreme familiarity" (Gilbert, 1937, p. 324) could be multiplied. In his incredibly detailed account of Oykangand kinship registers, Bruce Sommer (2006, p. 105) describes both "a cline or gradation in ... instances of obscene joking" as well as "shades of difference in avoidance or respect," in both instances normatively keyed to "kinship category." To take one last example, Fred Eggan (1937) wrote an insightful piece on Cheyenne and Arapaho kinship in which the language of gradience is pervasive: "Respect and joking relationships seem to represent mutually exclusive forms of social behavior which stand at opposite *poles* of conduct. Each of these relationships may vary in *intensity*. Thus avoidance seems to represent an *intensification* of the respect relationship, while 'rough joking' seems to be an *extreme* form of the 'mild joking' relationship" (p. 76; italics added). Eggan was strongly influenced by Radcliffe-Brown, with whom he worked at the University of Chicago in the 1930s. Radcliffe-Brown's (1949) writings offer very similar characterizations of joking-avoidance, as for instance in the following: "The avoidance relationship is in one sense an extreme form of respect, while the joking relationship is a form of familiarity, permitting disrespectful behaviour, and in extreme instances, license" (p. 134). Whether or not Eggan was the first to employ this language of gradience in describing joking-avoidance comportments, it was his description that served as a model for the institutionally powerful figure of George Peter Murdock.

Murdock is known for his massive cross-cultural surveys that sought to understand the causal linkages between different aspects of social organization, settlement pattern, subsistence type, and so forth.[4] In his vulgarization of that work, *Social Structure*, Murdock (1967) addresses kinship avoidances in a chapter entitled "The Regulation of Sex." As might be inferred, Murdock had a Freudian interpretation of avoidance. In the Conclusion, I discuss this interpretation of kinship avoidance as, at base, a supplement to sexual repression. But for the time being I will focus on how Murdock accesses (or, rather, fails to access) the continuum-like properties of joking-avoidance in his cross-cultural study.

As already mentioned, Murdock's (1967) cross-cultural comparisons of avoidance employed the scale that Eggan had proposed in his ethnographically situated description of the Cheyenne and Arapaho. I quote Murdock's characterization:

> Patterns of behavior that prevail between kinsmen ... form a continuum from complete avoidance of speech and physical contact at one pole to extreme license or obligatory joking and horseplay at the other. This continuum may conveniently be divided into five segments, as follows:
>
> 1 From complete avoidance to marked restraint.
> 2 From respect to moderate reserve.
> 3 From informality to intimacy.
> 4 From familiarity to privileged joking.
> 5 From obligatory joking to extreme license. (p. 272)

Incredibly, this is the most detailed account that Murdock gives of his scale. Other than the passing comment on "avoidance of speech and physical contact," he never offers a list of the comportments that might be used to distinguish, for instance, "complete avoidance to marked restraint" from "respect to moderate reserve." He goes on to plot distinct kin relations coded by genealogical products (e.g., wife's mother, daughter's daughter, etc.) onto his scale for a sample of 250 cultures (p. 277, Table 79). This implies that he must have had some working hypothesis for relating actual material practices documented in ethnographies to his "five segments" of the continuum of "patterns of behaviour."

This problem – the lack of any "discovery procedure" for determining how to classify empirically documented relationships in terms of the scale – reveals the fatal flaw in Murdock's model. The "five segments" of Murdock's continuum are etic categories that are never empirically grounded in the working out of distinct emic systems of joking-avoidance. The relations between "patterns of behavior" as would-be distinct segments of a spectrum are simply posited. This is, of course, in violation of the most basic principle of structuralism: the value of each sign is determined by its relationships with the other signs in the system. The structural dimension of avoidances – the ways in which distinct avoidances are culture-internally (or "emically") weighted or contrasted with respect to one another – is wholly occluded from view in Murdock's account. Quite simply, he has posited a scale without a measure or metric.[5]

Faced with the poverty of positivistic accounts like this, one might be tempted to simply deconstruct the categories of "joking" and "avoidance" – to expose them as mere reifications of the anthropological imagination. And yet, if we were to do this, we would close off access to a truth – to be sure, distorted and refracted in Murdock's account – about how kinship is lived and experienced across a wide range of human groups. In this book I set about to "save the phenomenon" of joking-avoidance – and of kinship avoidance, in particular – as a continuum. That is, I offer a framework that suggests why it is that joking and avoidance are so often structurally opposed within different societies, and what the metric of their continuum-like properties is. Considering the avoidance "pole" in particular, the framework explains why it is that kinship avoidance so often manifests as a gradient- or degree-concept, one that has as its peak the "total orientation" toward the other.

Beyond a Metaphysics of Co-presence: Kinship after Schneider

If the "old kinship studies" (after W. Shapiro, 2008) were not able, either methodologically or empirically, to ground the comparative study of joking-avoidance relationships, the "new kinship studies" haven't even tried. Ever since David Schneider (1968, 1984) published his broadsides against kinship studies, anthropologists have been highly sceptical of the possibility of a comparative study of kinship. Schneider's writings on American kinship raised two related issues that challenged the possibility of kinship as a category of cross-cultural analysis.

First, American kinship was seen as a cultural institution that could not be circumscribed to a group of genealogically related individuals and the symbolic codification of their modes of relatedness. Rather, it was essentially informed by other domains of sociocultural life, like religion and nationalism. Accordingly, Schneider argued that kinship does not correspond to a cross-culturally stable and bounded empirical domain of anthropological study. Second, in American kinship, "biogenetic symbols" of blood and sexual intercourse are employed to symbolize and performatively mediate relatedness. But if "biological facts" were a crucial component of American kinship ideology, they could not also serve as etic anchors for the emic realization of kinship systems, generally. Given the boundary problem and the unmooring of relatedness from biology, "kinship" loses its purchase as a category of cross-cultural analysis.

Although I do not think that the premises license the conclusions that he drew from them (cf. Feinberg & Ottenheimer, 2001), it cannot be denied that Schneider's critical interventions participated in a radical paradigm shift. One of the positive advances of the Schneider-inspired school of kinship studies has been its concern to theorize core symbols of relatedness – whether they be connections to land or shared names, blood or milk – which are performatively mobilized to establish, maintain, or rupture kinship relations (see Sahlins, 2013, for exemplification). And yet, despite its pretensions toward a post-foundationalist vision of kinship freed from the biological givens of genealogy, one senses in this "new kinship" literature a nostalgia for an essential or core criterion – a nostalgia for something analogous to, but different from, biology, for an element that might put kinship back on a sure and firm footing. Deprived of the biological bases of genealogy, newer scholarship has tended to locate that core of kinship in a metaphysics of co-presence. As Robert Parkin (2013, p. 7) observes, it is "the notion of relatedness [that] has become almost the key concept in the canon of the new kinship" literature.

The importance of intense, prototypically nurturant, modes of being-together are front and centre in two of the most celebrated recent answers to the question of "what kinship is": Janet Carsten's (1995, 2000) redefinition of kinship as "cultures of relatedness" and Marshall Sahlins's (2013) redefinition of kinship as "mutuality of being." If it is not about relations of biologically based consubstantiality (in nature), kinship must be about relations of experientially based intersubjectivity (in nurture). For Sahlins, "mutuality of being" is intended to go "beyond the notions of common substance, however such consubstantiality is locally defined and established. Neither a universal nor an essential condition of kinship, common substance is better understood as a culturally relative hypostasis of common being" (p. 28). Here Sahlins is intent on negating the importance of genealogical connectedness – whether as putative biological fact or even (in its return-of-the-repressed guise) in folk theories of reproduction. Unfortunately, in Sahlins's treatment, biological essentialization is effectively replaced by a metaphysics of co-presence.

For the present purposes, a presence-centred definition of kinship is doubly problematic (see Agha, 2007, pp. 345, 379; and Stasch, 2009,

p. 8, for critical comments on Carsten, 1995, 2000). First, it recapitulates – though now transposed into the domain of ontogenetic nurture rather than fetal nature – the long-standing opposition between consanguineal and affinal kin as an opposition between natural given and cultural convention (this despite Sahlins's [2013, p. 11] own disclaiming, after Viveiros de Castro, 2009, of just such a distinction.) Second, and more important, it does not address the ways in which important qualities of kinship emerge through the active absencing (rather than presencing) of others, through the attenuation of intersubjective intensities. Rather, and in a way reminiscent of Meyer Fortes's (1969) "axiom of amity," the "mutuality of being" formulation suggests that co-present accessibility to the other is naturally proportional to the thickness of one's kinship with that other (see Bird-David, 2017, for a similar presence-based formulation of kinship).

If the point of departure for understanding what kinship is all about is the idea of a "dual unity" (Sahlins 2013, p. 33), then certainly we have tipped the scales toward one kind of relating before sufficiently taking into account the possibility that "intersubjective participation" (p. 37) accrues its meaning in its opposition to practices of decoupling. This is not simply to re-invoke a primitive polarity between would-be consanguineal unity and affinal separateness. On the contrary, as I will show, qualities of kinship relationship fostered by decoupling may be just as operative for natal kin as they are for relations through marriage.[6]

Kinship Registers

In its incessant return to the question of the bases of kin relatedness – and in particular by substituting co-presence for biology – recent kinship literatures have tended to assimilate questions concerning the dynamics of kinship relationship to an account of categorical relatedness (cf. D. Miller, 2007). In this comparative study of kinship, I have tried to sidestep ultimately unanswerable questions concerning the putatively final bases of categorical relations. Rather than ponder the almost metaphysical question of "what kinship is," I feel it more profitable to put the focus decidedly upon relationship – to attend to the give-and-take of patterned communicative exchanges that differentiate relationships and imbue them with distinct experiential and intersubjective qualities. In what follows I build toward a concept of kinship as a reflexively symbolized, interlocking set of enacted and elicited relationships (after Wagner, 1986a). Here is where a sociolinguistics or social pragmatics of kinship is of vital importance, for it offers a method and means by which to study the specific practices through which kin relationships are summoned into intersubjective being and the ways in which they are reflexively apprehended by cultural actors. Newer work on registers of kin avoidance by linguistic anthropologists guides the way.[7] Exemplary, once again, is Stasch's (2003) approach to kinship avoidances among Korowai:

> Mother-in-law avoidance is a phenomenon of what Goffman (1983) calls "the interaction order," and should be analysed as such. This means providing an account of people's concrete interactional practices of avoidance, an account of culturally distinctive aspects of the interaction order within which these practices are performed, and an account of the distinctive qualities of social relationship that are produced out of these concrete interactional practices. (p. 321)

In my analysis, I follow Stasch's supplication to rematerialize avoidance as signifying practice. Given the comparative nature of this work, I can only access the interactional dynamics of avoidance practice as they are refracted and reflected through ethnography. Nevertheless, and through a close reading of the ethnographic archive, I will try to reveal some of the richness of avoidance as a social semiotic, enactable *as* kin relationship.

The qualities of intersubjective relationship, so imprecisely glossed with terms like "avoidance" and "joking," arise from the pragmatics of interaction. These meanings are not wholly emergent in interaction but rather are sustained by (meta)semiotically complex, collective models of communicative practice that linguistic anthropologists call **semiotic registers**. Semiotic registers have been carefully theorized in the work of Asif Agha (1993, 1998, 2000, 2003, 2007), whose formulation I closely follow here.

Semiotic registers are two-tiered formations. Individuals socialized to a semiotic register associate a particular repertoire of signs with particular frameworks of action, qualities of experience, or attributes of identity and relationship, among other significations. Because the qualities or attributes invoked/evoked by registered signs are understood to be linked to persons who are in spatiotemporal contact with sensible tokens of those sign types (for example, as speakers and addressees of them, or as producers and consumers of them), these signs function as indexes. And because this indexical connection is itself a normative regularity or "rule" of interpretation, they are conventional signs (what C.S. Peirce called "legisigns" [Peirce & Welby, 1977]). Socioculturally salient interpretations (e.g., understanding the affinal index to be a manifestation of shame, or associating it with a particular kin relation) are themselves supported by widely circulating metasemiotic representations that frame occurrences of elements of the register repertoire as summoning forth these meanings. Registers are thus two-tiered: widely circulating meta-signs (register stereotypes) regiment the social significations that a range of object-signs (elements of the register repertoire) have when deployed in actual interactions.

Case Study: Apachean Affinal Avoidance Register

Kinship registers are a specific kind of semiotic register whose use invokes a categorical kinship frame and evokes qualities of relationship prototypic of relations of that type. They involve the various dimensions we have just enumerated; minimally, they are composed of a repertoire of pragmatic signs stereotypically associated with kinship categories and performative of qualities of intersubjective relationship. Further, they are informed by socially circulating metasemiotic models that represent and stabilize those meanings. In order to exemplify these various dimensions, let's return to our opening vignette – the Chiricahua Apache man's story about visiting his wife's cousin soon after getting married. In his narrative the informant alludes to two pragmatic signs of affinal kinship.

First, there is the use of a particular linguistic construction, which he refers to as the "polite form" and which linguists canonically refer to as the grammatical "fourth person." Although used for reference-tracking of non-co-present referents, the fourth person also functions as an indefinite pronoun and can replace first-, second-, or third-person pronominals. It is additionally used as an honorific pronoun in acts of addressing and referring to avoidance relations.[8]

Second, there is the act of not looking at, and not being seen by, the other. Informants simply refer to this as "to avoid." Among the closely related Jicarilla Apache, relations who practice sight-avoidance refer to each other as "one with whom I cannot have contact," or simply as "one whom I cannot see" (Opler, 1947).[9] The visual modality is the sensorial idiom through which Apache avoidance is thematized: To deliberately stare at one's mother-in-law for a sustained period of time was said to result in blindness (if you violate the interdiction on remaining blind to a particular other, you will become blind to all).

Registered signs of kinship avoidance like these involve two dimensions of indexical signification. First, they performatively materialize valued qualities of relationship, like shame and respect. Second, they presuppose (or entail) that the "sender" (origo) and "receiver" (target) of the sign stand in a particular categorical kinship relation to one another.

The first kind of signification, the performative dimension, is continuous with the signification of honorific speech and deferential comportment more generally. So, for instance, the respect function of Chiricahua Apache fourth-person pronominals is wholly in keeping with the respect function of, for instance, the honorific pronouns found in many European languages. Honorific pronouns are performatives in the sense that their use in interaction accomplishes recognizable social acts – they enact respect, social distance, and so on. Registered kinship avoidances are, similarly, consistently conceptualized as enacting mutual, other-oriented restraint and respect.[10]

In Opler's ethnography, the respectful or honorific character of avoidances is revealed in explicit negotiations over the degree of stringency of avoidance to be practiced between affinal dyads – that is, in "ethnometapragmatic" testimony (Silverstein, 1993). Apache avoidances are always reciprocal – whatever signs of avoidance ego employs for alter, alter should also employ for ego. Nevertheless, it is the bride's relations who determine what "setting" or "level" of avoidance will be engaged in between the pair.[11] Upon betrothal, senior kinswomen of the bride would inform the in-marrying and generationally junior man, through his wife, of the avoidance level he was to employ. A stringent avoidance protocol was interpreted as a sign of respect, and its absence as a sign of disapproval (cf. Stasch, 2009, p. 89). When Jicarilla Apache classificatory "sisters" of the mother-in-law choose sight-avoidance, the most extreme kind of avoidance, "when it is not strictly necessary to do so, they are signifying their cordial interest in their kinswoman and their unqualified approval of the step she has taken" in marrying this man (Opler, 1947, p. 456). Similarly, and now from the Chiricahua ethnography, "where the polite form of avoidance is an optional matter but is nevertheless requested, it is an expression of approval of the marriage and of the parties to it. 'I should be very proud, for many of the prominent men of the reservation use polite form to me,' said one Chiricahua" (Opler, 1937, p. 220).

The second kind of signification involves the stereotypical association between particular (ensembles of) signs and particular categories of kin. Elements of kinship registers are stereotypically associated with particular categories of kin. In the Chiricahua Apache example, the use of the "polite form" is the norm in the relationship between an in-marrying man and the grandfathers of his wife as well as the collateral kin of her parents. Meanwhile, sight-avoidance is the norm in relations with his parents-in-law and the grandmothers of his wife. Because of these associations, the use of these signs may reinforce or entail a kin-categorical frame for the relation (Rumsey, 1982). This does not mean that the use of these signs is performatively constitutive of such relations, *per se*. For example, a Chiricahua Apache mother-in-law who does not approve of her son-in-law might refrain from referring to him with the polite fourth-person form and in so doing performatively enact her disdain for him. She does not thereby cease to be his mother-in-law (cf. M. Strathern, 1972, p. 38, on an angry Melpa husband's injurious and ostentatious violation of the taboo on using his wife's parents' names). Conversely, the female cousin of a man's wife may solicit sight-avoidance from him as a sign of her approval of her cousin's marriage. She does not, however, thereby become the man's mother-in-law. These enactable signs are stereotypically associated with particular categories of kin. Usages that constitute deviations from expected practice generate metaphoric or tropic meanings in context (Agha, 2007).

Finally, we should observe a crucial detail concerning the structural organization of the Chiricahua Apache register repertoire. Not all in-law relationships imply the deployment of both signs. Although he engages in sight-avoidance with particular, focal avoidance relations, "there are also affinal relatives from whom a man does not hide but to whom a special form of the verb [i.e., the fourth person] is employed in discourse and in reference" (Opler, 1947, p. 455). The two signs are hierarchically ordered by an implicational relationship; if one avoids looking at a given person, then one must also use the fourth person in referring to that person, but not vice versa. Sight avoidance and the "polite form" are thus constitutive of two distinct **avoidance levels** (a term that I use in allusion to honorific "speech levels").[12] This is shown in Table 0.1.

To summarize, not looking upon the other and the use of the "polite form" are privileged elements of the repertoire of signs whose deployment enacts avoidance. They represent important loci of avoidance, both as it is (pragmatically) enacted and as it is (metapragmatically) modelled by Chiricahua and Jicarilla Apaches. These signs are stereotypically associated with particular categories of kin, where the mother-in-law/son-in-law relation represents the epitome of avoidance. Finally, they performatively enact valued qualities of interpersonal respect and shame.

Let me underscore, though, that Chiricahua Apache in-law avoidance is not reducible to these two register shibboleths. The enactment of affinal relationship also involves a more subtle sensitivity to the possible presence and perception of the other reflected, for instance, in abstaining from conversation that might even remotely touch upon sexual matters, in anticipating the needs of the other, and in indirectly doing what one can to ensure the fulfilment of those needs, or in retiring

Table 0.1. Norms of Chiricahua Apache in-law avoidance

Avoidance signs	Avoidance Level II	Avoidance Level I	No avoidance
not looking	+	–	–
fourth person	+	+	–
	mother-in-law [MIL]	MIL's siblings	brother-in-law
	father-in-law [FIL]	FIL's siblings	sister-in-law
	MIL's mother	MIL's father	
	FIL's mother	FIL's father	

Source: Opler (1937).

from the scene should the avoidance relation be in an embarrassing or awkward position. In its most marked forms, avoidance as a practice must continuously anticipate and respond to the risks and possibilities of the would-be co-presence of the other. In this regard it involves a dynamic "attenuation" of intersubjective relating that goes beyond and operates at a more fluid and interactionally dynamic level than that involved in the performance and recognition of particular, salient, and stereotyped diacritics of relation (after Russell, 2020). Nevertheless, as I hope to show, salient signs of avoidance, their structural organization, and their social associations are essential in scaffolding these modes of intersubjective being, their intensities and attenuations. They are the bedrock of avoidance as a social institution.

Building the Continuum: How Registered Avoidances are Woven Together

With these preliminaries in place, we are now positioned to see how a sociolinguistics of kinship can help us respond to the challenges of a comparative study of joking-avoidance. The empirical phenomenon of avoidance levels, in particular, points in the direction of an answer to the question of why it is that kin-keyed comportments so often present themselves in the form of a graded scale or continuum – for why kinship avoidance "like "incest" and other seriously relational matters ... [is] a degree concept" (Silverstein, 2004, p. 635). Given that the development of a deep understanding of cross-cultural convergences in kinship avoidances is an overarching goal of the book, I cannot in the space of this Introduction fully expand upon my answer to this important problem. Nevertheless, I will here highlight one recurrent structural property of the organization of kinship registers that contributes to the by-degree character of avoidance: implicational relationships between avoidances. Avoidance levels emerge from the ways in which distinct avoidances are networked together by implicational relationships. This structural property plays a vital role in the realization of joking-avoidance as an intensity gradient that "peaks" with the total orientation toward the other.

In the practice of kinship avoidance, what one does *not* do is at least as important as what one does do. Correspondingly, socialization to an avoidance register involves learning two distinct repertoires of signs: a set of taboo signs that should be avoided, and the set of signs that conventionally substitute for them. We will call the set of signs that are taboo in avoidance contexts the **negative repertoire** of the register. In our Apachean example, those taboo signs were (1) looking at someone and (2) referring to someone with a personal pronoun. The set of signs that appropriately stand in place of the taboo signs we will call the **positive repertoire**. In our example these were (1) averting one's eyes and (2) employing impersonal "fourth-person" pronominals. Part 1 develops this distinction between negative and positive repertoires at greater length, but for the time being these placeholder definitions should be sufficient.

Avoidance register repertoires (both positive and negative) can be analyzed as pragmatic structures – ensembles of signs systematically related to one another by virtue of their pragmatic and indexical (rather than their semantic and symbolic) meanings and forces.[13] Fine-grained study of the organization of these pragmatic structures reveals three aspects of their formal organization, each of which contributes a distinct dimension of signification to avoidance practice: (1) chained implicational relationships between avoidances, (2) relations of formal encompassment between avoidances, and (3) the contact-emblematic character of avoidances as "avoidances of" some particular individual. Chapters 3, 5, and 6 offer a treatment of the contact-emblematic character of avoidances. Chapters 4, 7, and 8 are concerned with encompassment relationships between avoidances. Correspondingly, I will leave discussion of those dimensions for later. Although I will focus here only on implicational relationships between avoidances, it is the way in which these three layers are fitted together through the mediation of cultural ideology that accounts for kinship avoidance as a cross-culturally convergent phenomenon. (For a summary statement bringing these three dimensions together, see the closing section of Chapter 8.) Nevertheless, and considering only this parameter, we can get a better grasp on the continuum problem.

To introduce the idea, I return to the Chiricahua Apache case. Recall that the two emblems of Chiricahua Apache avoidance shown in Table 0.1 – sight-avoidance and fourth-person reference – are linked to each other in an implicational relationship. If one is expected to practice sight-avoidance with another, then one also is expected to employ the "polite form" in referring to that person. This is a widely attested property. Close investigation of the set of emically labelled taboos forming the negative repertoires of kinship avoidance registers reveals that avoidances are typically woven together by chained implicational relationships.[14]

To exemplify the phenomenon in greater complexity, I draw on Per Hage's (1969) short essay, "A Guttman Scale Analysis of Tikopia Speech Taboos." I will not contextualize the particular set of debates into which the paper inserts itself. The paper is of value to me for the rigorous way in which Hage pored over Raymond Firth's (1937) classic ethnography, *We, The Tikopia*, looking for all mentions of a set of four registered signs of joking-avoidance and documenting the kin relations with which one is normatively expected to employ them. Table 0.2 adapts Hage's presentation of the data.

Hage's discussion focuses on four signs: (1) the avoidance of singular number and its replacement by the "polite dual" (PD) in reference to a kin alter, (2) the avoidance of the personal name (APN) of a kin alter, (3) the avoidance of the "excremental curse" (AEC) – translated by Firth as, "May your father eat filth!" (though "shit" would probably be the more appropriate transduction), and (4) the avoidance of a range of obscene or bawdy language, metapragmatically characterized as *taraŋa pariki* "bad speech" (NBS).[15] After carefully going through Firth's ethnography for characterizations of norms of practice, Hage plotted these avoidances over primary kin relations.

As the table illustrates, distinct avoidances are stereotypically associated with distinct kin relations. These associations reflect parameters of social difference and identity that often recur in kinship avoidance and joking (for more on this, see the last section of Chapter 3). The honorific dual is stereotypically restricted to in-law relations, the sociological site of most intense interpersonal restraint. The least constraint in interpersonal comportment – and thus the site where *faifakakata* ("jesting") is actively elicited – is associated with same-generation and same-sex relationships, as well the celebrated relationship between a mother's brother and a sister's son (the avunculate). Intermediate levels, meanwhile, are prototypically associated with cross-sex and adjacent generation relations.

Table 0.2. Implicational relationships between joking-avoidance comportments in Tikopia (after Hage, 1969)

kin term	genealogical products	PD	APN	AEC	NBS
taina	//-sex sibling [G^0]	−	−	−	−
tuatina	mMB [//-sex, G^{+1}]	−	−	−	−
iramutu	mZS [//-sex, G^{-1}]	−	−	−	−
taina fakapariki	mMBS, wMBD [//-sex, G^0]	−	−	−	−
taina fakalaui	//-sex, //-cousin [G^0]	−	−	−	−
				AVOIDANCE	LEVEL 0
kave	x-sex sibling [G^0]	−	−	−	+
kave fakapariki	x-sex, x-cousin [G^0]	−	−	−	+
kave fakalaui	x-sex, //-cousin [G^0]	−	−	−	+
tuatina	wMB [x-sex, G^{+1}]	−	−	−	+
iramutu	mZD [x-sex, G^{-1}]	−	−	−	+
				AVOIDANCE	LEVEL I
taina fakapariki		−	−	+	+
kave fakapariki	Father's sister's children [G^0]	−	−	+	+
tama	Child, Sib's Child [G^{-1}]	−	−	+	+
makopuna	Grandchild [G^{-2}]	−	−	?	+
				AVOIDANCE	LEVEL II
mana	F, FB, FZH [G^{+1}]	−	+	+	+
nana	M, MZ, MBW [G^{+1}]	−	+	+	+
masikitanga	FZ [G^{+1}]	−	+	+	+
puna	Grandparent [G^{+2}]	−	+	?	+
				AVOIDANCE	LEVEL III
fongona	SW, DH [in-law]	+	+	+	+
mana fongovai	WF, HF [in-law]	+	+	+	+
nana fongovai	WM, HM [in-law]	+	+	+	+
ma	HZ, WB, mZH, wBW [in-law]	+	+	+	+
taina [in-law]	HB, WZ, mBW, wZH [in-law]	+	+	+	+
matua/nofine	Spouse [in-law]	+	+	+	+
				AVOIDANCE	LEVEL IV

Notes. The table depicts the distribution of four named avoidance signs and the kinship relations (glossed with genealogical products) who are normatively expected to employ them (after Firth, 1937). The signs are the use of the polite dual (= PD), the avoidance of the personal name (= APN), the avoidance of the "excremental curse" (= AEC), and the avoidance of obscene or "bad speech" (= NBS). Genealogical products are listed with the following abbreviations (after Dziebel, 2007): w = woman's, m = man's, Z = Sister, B = Brother, M = Mother, F = Father, S = Son, D = Daughter, W = Wife, H = Husband, x-sex = cross-sex, x-cousin = cross-cousin, //-sex = same-sex, //-cousin = parallel cousin, G = kinship generation of kin alter with respect to ego. Genealogical products are read as possessive noun phrases (e.g., wMBS = woman's mother's brother's son). The question mark represents a norm that Firth failed to characterize.
Source: Adapted from Hage (1969, pp. 101–2).

Table 0.3. Implicational relationships between kinship avoidances in Kobon (Papua New Guinea)

+	+	+	+	+	+	+	+	+	+	+	+	+	IV
-	-	-	+	+	+	+	+	+	+	+	+	+	III
-	-	-	-	-	-	+	+	+	+	+	+	+	II
-	-	-	-	-	-	-	-	-	+	+	+	+	I
-	-	-	-	-	-	-	-	-	-	-	-	-	0
1	2	3	4	5	6	7	8	9	10	11	12	13	

[(1, 2, 3) →   [(4, 5, 6) →   [(7, 8, 9) →   (10, 11, 12, 13)]]]

Notes. Implicational relationships between avoidances are depicted by arrows. See Figure 0.1 for the list of the 13 kinship taboos whose implicational relations are depicted here. Roman numerals in the rightmost column indicate the avoidance levels depicted in Figure 0.1.
Source: Adapted from Jackson (1975, p. 315).

It is not my purpose here to delve too deeply into the Tikopian materials (but for further discussion of the "polite dual," see Chapter 7). Rather, I want to highlight a formal property of Tikopian avoidances that Hage's analysis draws out. Scaling of "more" or "less" restrained degrees of avoidance is not achieved by an unranked summing of the number of avoidances to which an individual adheres in a given relationship. Rather, and just as with the Chiricahua Apache avoidances, the four Tikopian avoidances are related to one another in a chain of implicational ("if p, then q") relationships. Thus, if one "must use polite dual" with a certain alter, one also "must avoid personal name" of that alter, and if one "must avoid personal name" of a given alter, then one "must not curse" in the presence of that alter. Using the column labels from Table 0.2, this can be represented in the form of the following implicational hierarchy: PD → (APN → (AEC → (NBS))).

This structural property is not unique to Tikopian avoidances but reappears in case after case. In some instances we have quite clear evidence that informants are consciously aware of these implicational relationships. So, for instance, one Jicarilla Apache informant told Opler (1947, p. 455), "You can't drink out of the same cup as one who uses polite-form to you and you can't eat out of the same dish." (If polite-form, then no eating or drinking from the same vessel.)

As a second example, I draw on Graham Jackson's (1975) doctoral dissertation on the Kobon of Papua New Guinea. The Kobon neighbour the Kalam (Ralph Bulmer was Jackson's doctoral advisor), and both practice a range of kinship avoidances. Jackson saw taboos as an important structuring principle across a number of domains of Kobon life (see Jackson, 1991), so he was particularly meticulous in documenting them. Table 0.3 and Figure 0.1 present the 13 distinct "kinship taboos"

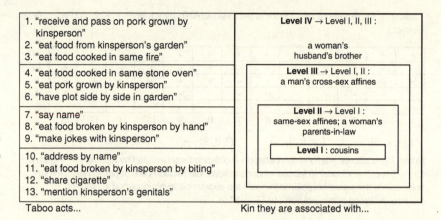

Figure 0.1. Kobon kinship taboos and their organization into avoidance levels
Notes. Taboos are organized into avoidance levels, each of which is either a superset or subset of each other level (graphically represented by the image of the boxes within boxes). Implicational relationships between levels are indicated by arrows.
Source: Adapted from Jackson (1975, p. 315).

that Jackson (1975, p. 315) documents and the kin relations with which they were stereotypically associated.

As with the Tikopia data, Kobon avoidances are chained together by implicational relationships (see Table 0.3) and grouped into avoidance levels each associated with distinct classes of kin (see Figure 0.1). As in the Tikopian example, each "higher" level includes all of the avoidances found in all of the "lower" levels. In these, and other, cases, recursive, implicational relationships between avoidances give rise to the emergent property of avoidance levels – sub-repertoires of avoidances normatively associated with particular categories of kin.

Implicational Hierarchies, Commensurability, and the Continuum

The organization of avoidances into implicational hierarchies gives credence to the intuition of ethnographers that the opposition between "joking" and "avoidance" relationships relies upon a corresponding opposition between the signs through which these distinct kinds of relationship are reciprocally elicited. As Murray Garde (2008b) observes in a wonderful ethnolinguistic study of Bininj Gunwok and Dalabon sociality, "Joking relationship language and behaviour are in most respects the antithesis of the constrained speech and behaviour of avoidance relationships. The range of prohibited linguistic forms and behaviours associated with avoidance relationships is not only allowed in joking relationships; it is mandatory. That which is taboo in one context is exploited in another" (p. 237). The Kobon and Tikopia data illustrate that the poles of "joking" and "avoidance" are instantiated by a normative obligation to avoid the smallest and greatest number of registered signs, respectively.[16] Registered avoidances are the metric of the joking-avoidance scale. They are the discrete substrate that gives the whole its continuum-like feel. And yet, if each kin relation were enacted by an unranked assortment of avoidances, it would be much more difficult to grade relations as being "more" or "less" restrained. The continuum-character of joking-avoidance thus depends upon the **commensurability** of avoidance levels (Carruthers, 2017a, 2017b; Kockelmann, 2016a, 2016b). Where each avoidance level is either a superset or a subset of all other levels, the range of avoidances enacted between a given dyad is more readily legible as an icon of the relative magnitude of the respect (or other relevant quality of relationship) associated with that relationship. Implicational chaining of avoidances creates a robust formal-functional analogy – an analogy between semiotic form (range of signs avoided) and social function (magnitude of the relevant quality of relationship expressed).

Because a full fleshing out of this argument can come only after looking at a wide range of cases, this discussion can serve as little more than a promissory note. A more in-depth synthetic statement must, therefore, be postponed until the end of Chapter 8. Nevertheless, the organization of avoidance repertoires into hierarchically encompassing levels already suggests why it is that joking-avoidance so often expresses itself and is experienced as a continuum. The "total orientation" characteristic of the most focal avoidance relationships is, in an important sense, the phenomenological counterpart to the maximally constrained comportment characteristic of the most stringent levels of kinship avoidance.

Constellating Language in Culture: Structure-Ideology-Practice

As this précis of my argument suggests, in this book I make the claim that the cross-cultural comparability of joking-avoidance as a graded series of kinship relationships is undergirded by convergent properties in the organization of the semiotic registers that mediate these relationships. Correspondingly, throughout the book I will be keen to highlight convergent properties of avoidance registers, properties like the chained implicational relationships observed in the Tikopian, Kobon, and Apachean data.

To account for these cross-cultural convergences, one cannot rely solely upon elicited cultural ideologies of kinship to the exclusion of the sign systems through which they are enacted. Nor can one engage in a blinkered structuralism, documenting only sign structures to the exclusion of their interpretation and implementation. Rather, we must attend to the interplay between semiotic structures, sociocultural ideologies, and practices of relationship. It is the ways in which structure and ideology become dialectically entangled with one another through the real-time practice of relationship that accounts for the cross-cultural comparability of kinship registers. This way of seeing things channels a sensibility concerning languages and linguistic varieties that apprehends them as the provisional and transitional, necessarily unstable sites where structure, ideology and practice gel together:

> The total linguistic fact, the datum for a science of language, is irreducibly dialectic in nature. It is an unstable mutual interaction of meaningful sign forms contextualized to situations of interested human use, mediated by the fact of cultural ideology. And the linguistic fact is irreducibly dialectic, whether we view it as so-called synchronic usage or as so-called diachronic change. It is an indifferently synchronic-diachronic totality, which, however, at least initially – in keeping with traditional autonomous divisions of scholarly perspective – can be considered from the points of view of language structure, contextualized usage, and ideologies of language. (Silverstein, 1985, p. 220)

Generalizing Michael Silverstein's model of "the total linguistic fact," I understand registers to be constellated at the intersection of sign structures, semiotic ideologies, and signing practices. It is to this analytic topography and terrain that I will repeatedly return in seeking to account for cross-cultural convergences in the semiotic media, structural organization, and performative significations of kinship registers.

As linguistic anthropological scholarship has established, ideology and structure have reciprocal effects upon one another (N. Evans, 2003b; Rumsey, 1990; Silverstein, 1979; Whorf, 2000). Regarding kinship registers, ideology informs the valuation of structured pragmatic signs by means of top-down metasemiotic regimentation: Through explicit (metapragmatic) symbolization (e.g., Tikopia labels like "good speech" and "bad speech"), sign users arrive at a coherent construal of socially patterned and internally structured kinship avoidances. Simultaneously, but now in a bottom-up manner, pragmatic structure selects for particular metasemiotic models over others. The implicational hierarchy of avoidances motivates a global interpretation of the system of relationships as one whose end-points are characterized by maximal restraint in signing practice ("avoidance"), at one end, and by maximal licence in signing practice ("joking"), at the other.

The dialectical interplay of structure and ideology through the mediation of usage is already apparent in the data that I have reviewed. The emergence of implicational chaining is almost certainly mediated by metasemiotic acts of commensuration – "a process whereby different entities with shared qualities are characterized and compared along gradations of more-or-less-ness" (Carruthers, 2017b, p. 236; see also Carruthers, 2017a; Kockelmann, 2016a, 2016b). Where one kinship relation is framed as entailing "more" or "less" of a given quality of relationship (e.g., "shame," "respect," "fear," etc.), actors likely realize that "moreness" or "lessness" through the performance of a cumulatively wider or narrower range of avoidance signs.[17] In a circular fashion, ideologically laden metapragmatic judgments of "moreness" and "lessness" of relevant qualities of relationships influence pragmatic structure. This feedback from ideology to structure is mediated by discursive practices that are tropically legible as augmenting or tempering qualities of relationship by either increasing or diminishing the range of avoidance signs deployed in interaction. The distinct avoidance levels thus generated become stereotypically linked to particular kin relations, creating a global system of kinship registers which links an array of interlocking semiotic performances to an array of interlocking human relationships.

An Overview of What Follows

Registered practices of kinship avoidance manifest across a range of distinct semiotic media – from signing and speech, to food sharing and face coverings. And they constellate around a range of distinct social acts – from person reference to propositional discourse, and from ratified address to the mere phatic presencing of the other. And yet, as I will show, avoidance registers consistently share convergent properties at the interrelated levels of sign structure, ideology, and practice. At the most general level, in all cases avoidance involves the elaboration of semiotic repertoires that serve to circumvent – whether by substitution or sublimation – the occurrence of particular signs-in-contexts (e.g., the uttering of a particular name, the act of looking at a particular face, the use of words of the everyday language in the co-presence of a particular individual). And in all cases, cultural ideologies imbue the occurrence of those circumvented signs with an unavoidable, negatively evaluated, causal consequentiality. The registers we will be looking at emerge as conventionalized means for avoiding the occurrence of sign-types whose tokens have, for certain signallers and in certain contexts, an **indefeasible performativity**. That is, they emerge in the surround of taboos.

Semiotic taboos are both the result and the catalyst, the cause and the consequence, of avoidance registers. The different chapters of the book centre on different linguistic loci and semiotic media subject to taboo and avoidance in kinship avoidance. Each showcases a distinct **sociolinguistic kind** attested at these sites and uncovers the convergent diachronic processes of register formation, or enregisterment, which produce these commensurable kinds. The text is divided into four parts.

Part 1, "Proscriptive Regimes of Language and Avoidance Registers," is concerned with registers of linguistic avoidance in general terms. Verbal taboo and avoidance are not, of course, limited to the mediation of kin relationships. Chapter 1 looks at a broad array of speech styles employed to circumvent everyday speech in contexts in which it is tabooed. The most important finding of this chapter is that proscriptive regimes of language invariably pick out words and expressions, as opposed to syntactic constructions, grammatical morphemes, or phonological alternations, as targets for linguistic avoidance and substitution (a confirmation of C.E. Grimes and Maryott, 1994). I show how constraints on explicit (metapragmatic) discourses of linguistic proscription are responsible for this filtering process. Words are the linguistic units that speakers can most easily refer to and predicate about, and thus the most straightforward to censure and interdict.

Chapter 2 treats what are perhaps the best studied and most widely discussed group of in-law avoidance registers – the so-called "mother-in-law languages" of Aboriginal Australia. The chapter accounts for a well-known, convergent structural property of these avoidance vocabularies – the highly abstract semantic meanings of their core vocabulary items. The default assumption in the literature on mother-in-law languages has been that the denotational vagueness, abstractness, and non-specificity of mother-in-law vocabulary items is a reflex of the ideological conceptualization of such avoidance speech as polite, unimposing, socially distanced, and "indirect" (cf. P. Brown & Levinson, 1987). I argue that this formulation conflates layers of analysis by overlooking the role of discursive practices in the diachronic emergence of these language structures. Drawing on a range of other taboo-avoidance registers (e.g., male initiate languages of the Lardil and Gbaya, pandanus languages of the Kalam and the Kewa, fishing argots employed in the British Isles, etc.), I show how the highly general or abstract word meanings of avoidance repertoire items emerge out of a particular tradeoff between social pragmatics and lexical semantics that is associated with verbal taboo.

Part 2, "The Sounds of Reference: Name Taboos," focuses the discussion more squarely on the sociolinguistics of kinship. It is concerned exclusively with avoidance registers that serve to circumvent the use of the names of particular categories of kin and of similar-sounding words – what I call "name registers." Name registers have a highly specific linguistic organization; they are always organized around the avoidance of a set of words which have a similar sound shape to that of a tabooed name. And yet name registers are found all over the world, being anchored to a number of distinct sociological domains. (J.G. Frazer, 1958, surveyed post-mortem, in-law-based, and chiefly- or kingship-based registers of this sort in *The Golden Bough*.) Chapter 3 provides an overview of name registers, issues related to their sociolinguistic patterning, and their global distribution. In addition to its general discussion of the pragmatics of naming, the chapter offers a dedicated discussion of the remarkably similar, femininely gendered "daughter-in-law registers" of Africa and Eurasia.

Chapter 4 treats name registers as a "total linguistic fact" (Silverstein, 1985), showing that this recurrent sociolinguistic kind emerges from a particular conjuncture of language structures, discourse practices, and linguistic ideologies. I identify three distinct language-structural "pegs" that serve as attractors of pragmatic avoidances in name registers: the proper name (i.e., a word type whose tokens refer to a particular individual; e.g., *Mary*, the mother of Jesus), the proper noun (i.e., a word type whose tokens are employed to name multiple individuals; e.g., the name *Mary*), and (near-)homophones (i.e., lexical types phonologically iconic with the proper noun; e.g., "to *marry*," "to be *merry*"). I show how language ideologies that rationalize the performative power of names and naming are guided by the distinctive referential properties of names among noun-phrase types. Finally, I suggest how practices of name and word avoidance drive the diachronic bootstrapping process whereby mere avoidance of name-calling diachronically becomes an elaborate practice of word taboo and avoidance.

Part 3, "The Anti-Phatic Function: Interactional Avoidances," moves beyond strictly linguistic considerations and seeks to understand interpersonal avoidance as a practice of kinship relationship in all its richness. Verbal avoidances are only one part of a broad semiotic range of avoidances registered as appropriate to particular kin relationships. Chapter 5 centres on the strategies – like speech intermediation, the use of shill addressees, and bodily positioning – which avoidance relations employ in order to avoid ratified communicative co-presence.

Avoidance relations are often enjoined not to speak with one another, not to look at one another, and to shield themselves from view in one another's presence. These comportments are all ways of deflecting, forestalling, or rerouting channels of interpersonal communication. Because they operate upon communicative channels, these strategies have what I call an anti-phatic function. (The "phatic function," recall, is the channel-establishing or -verifying function of language; see note 3 above.) I foreground the paradoxical and self-negating character of anti-phatic interaction rituals – communicative acts that deny the very existence of the channels by means of which they are nevertheless accomplished.

Chapter 6 looks in fine-grained detail at visual, haptic, and auditory avoidances. These are shown to mediate intersubjective relationship through idioms of sensorial and corporeal contact. Building upon Rupert Stasch's (2003, p. 321) theorization of a "hierarchy of modes of sensory avoidance" among Korowai, I show how the elaboration of intersensorial avoidances is related to the affordances of the senses for signifying intersubjectivity. I argue that the sense of touch serves as a master metaphor for imagining interpersonal (non)contact; because touch involves an inherent mutuality and reciprocity, it is particularly good for thinking and experiencing intersubjectivity.

Part 4, "The Pattern Which Connects: Avoidance Registers as Scalar Honorific Formations," focuses on the honorific functions of avoidance registers. It returns to the core question posed in this Introduction: How do kinship registers scaffold the differentiated practice and phenomenology of kinship relationship that we call "joking-avoidance"? I argue that the link between register and relationship is mediated by a motivated analogy between semiotic form and social function. The avoidance of signs that point to particular social others is motivated to function as an enactment of deference for those persons. Comportmental restraint geared toward these signs of the other serves as an emblem (or iconic-index) of interpersonal respect, making such semiotic restraint a fecund growth point for the development of honorific registers.

Chapter 7 introduces this idea through the exposition of yet another medium of avoidance – personal pronouns (or "person deixis"). The chapter presents the first broad comparative survey of honorific pronouns linked to kinship relationship (but see Kruspe & Burenhult, 2019). This topic has been largely overlooked in earlier comparative treatments of honorific pronouns, treatments that have tended to be biased toward language communities with a hierarchical social organization (P. Brown & Levinson, 1987; Helmbrecht, 2005). The chapter illustrates how linguistic restraint serves as the organizing principle for the elaboration of honorific registers of person deixis.

Reprising earlier discussions of mother-in-law languages and name registers, Chapter 8 shows how the conversion of semiotic restraint into deference indexicality is recursively mobilized in the formation of avoidance registers. Essentially, the chapter shows that avoidance levels instantiated across a range of semiotic media tend to stand in relations of formal encompassment with respect to one another. Similar to the implicational relationships that I illustrated above for Kobon and Tikopia, these mutually encompassing avoidance levels diagrammatically motivate functional clines or gradients where "more" formal avoidance is apperceived as enacting "more" of the deference function. This finding allows me to be more precise about how the gradient or continuum-like properties of kinship avoidance are scaffolded by the semiotic registers through which they are enacted and apperceived.

Finally, the Conclusion gestures toward the ways in which kinship registers open onto the cultural symbolization and phenomenological experience of intersubjective relationship. I argue that avoidance both experientially actualizes and collectively represents relationship as an intensely felt social ontology and obligation of being-toward-others.

A Note on Kinship and the Comparative Method

There has been a legitimate scepticism concerning comparative, cross-cultural study in the sociocultural and linguistic anthropology of the last half-century. Nowhere has this been more strongly felt than in kinship studies. If kinship once represented the unmoving centre that anchored ethnology, cultural accounts of kinship have cast into doubt the very possibility of establishing the functional, structural, experiential, or symbolic identity of "kinship" across distinct ethnographic contexts. The present volume swims against this current, but in so doing it fills a gaping hole in the current literature – there are no comparative, cross-cultural studies of kinship avoidance. This is what is offered here. As with all comparative research, a comparative linguistic anthropology of kinship has the inevitable effect of abstracting away from rich dimensions of language- and culture-specific signification that would be crucial to a thicker description of any given case study treated in the book. I do not pretend for an instant that the analysis presented here replaces ethnography. On the contrary, this work would not exist without the tireless efforts of the countless ethnographers and field linguists whose work I draw upon and to whom I owe an immense debt of gratitude. Nevertheless, it is my hope that this volume illustrates that it is possible to carry out comparative studies of kinship that are ethnographically sensitive and meaning-rich while at the same time revelatory of dimensions of social signification that are not easily drawn out in the study of a unique social and cultural setting. Drawing upon the tools of linguistic anthropology, this book makes the argument that kinship can be grasped in comparative perspective not by returning to the once solid ground of biology, but by homing in on the structured, sociocultural pragmatics of relationship – that is, by careful study of kinship registers.

PART ONE

Proscriptive Regimes of Language and Avoidance Registers

PART ONE

Proscriptive Regimes of Language and Avoidance Registers

Chapter One

Avoidance Lexicon, Everyday Grammar: Why Words Are Good to Proscribe

The Murui are a Witoto-speaking language group who live in the Amazon rainforest at the border between Colombia and Peru. When Murui men go into the forest to hunt, they refrain from using a number of everyday words and employ a special vocabulary, or avoidance register, in their place (description after Wojtylak, 2015). Most particularly, while searching for prey in the forest, Murui hunters avoid referring to animals by their true names. The rationale for this substitution reflects the power of those everyday terms to make contact with their referents; were the hunters to refer to forest animals by their true names, the animals would be alerted to the hunters' presence and plans. Hunters thus use disguised names, often the names of plants metonymically or metaphorically associated with the animals in question, in order to talk about prey without letting the prey know that they are doing so. For instance, the prized *jɨgadɨma* "tapir" is referred to with the substitute term *zañaraɨ* "decomposed wood" – smoked tapir meat has a similar appearance to decomposing wood. The use of substitute names is called "skilled speech" by Murui. By hiding the hunters' plans from their prey, "skilled speech" helps to ensure a successful hunt.

Speech registers like Murui "skilled speech" link particular words and expressions with particular social identities and activities. They can thus be thought of as bringing together two distinct kinds of socially circulating signs (after Agha, 2007). First, registers are composed of a repertoire of linguistic forms or **object-signs**. In our example, the register repertoire is composed of the set of substitute words and expressions, like *zañaraɨ* "decomposed wood", which are employed in making masked reference to prey. Second, the use of this repertoire is associated with a range of social significations, informed by widely circulating register stereotypes or **meta-signs**. "Skilled speech" is associated with a particular social kind of speaker (adult men) and with particular social spaces (the forest) and activities (the hunt), and it is rationalized in light of culturally specific understandings or ideologies of language (the potential of everyday language to communicate across species boundaries, for instance). Speech registers are fragile achievements. Their meaningfulness in sociocultural life depends upon a historical process of enregisterment through which a network of language users come to recognize a particular linguistic repertoire to be indexically associated with particular kinds of experiences, actions, social identities, beings, and relationships.

The aim of this chapter is to show that there is a non-arbitrary relationship between the meta-sign and object-sign levels in speech registers, like Murui "skilled speech," which are employed to circumvent everyday speech under conditions where its use is taboo – that is, in avoidance registers. Building on the work of others (see, in particular, C.E. Grimes & Maryott, 1994), I show that proscriptive regimes of language that explicitly pick out for prohibition particular sign types (at the meta-sign level) are productive of repertoires (at the object-sign level) that are composed exclusively of words and expressions. Particular syntactic structures (e.g., the order in which a transitive verb, its subject, and its object occur in a sentence), grammatical morphemes (e.g., prefixes or suffixes that mark the tense of a verb or the possessor of a noun, prepositions, and even pronouns), and phonological alternations are not replaced in avoidance speech. Rather, avoidance speech registers are composed exclusively of words and expressions that substitute for everyday words in terms of their denotational functions in socially defined contexts where those everyday words are tabooed. In this chapter I empirically demonstrate that this is the case and provide a causal framework to explain it. The explication of this framework reveals the ways in which linguistic proscription relies upon an explicit, reflexive, and metalinguistic engagement with language that filters, and thus feeds back into, both language structure and discursive practice.

"Avoidance Register": A Note on Nomenclature

There are two overlapping senses of "avoidance register" that should be distinguished in the following discussion. First, kinship avoidance registers are ways of speaking and acting that are understood, within particular cultural worlds, as appropriately respectful and restrained means of relating to others. The social others targeted by these special kinds of speech and action are members of particular kinship categories, like mother-in-law and son-in-law or brother and sister. That is, avoidance registers are normatively employed in relating with individuals who are emically classified as "avoidance relations." Here semiotic ideologies that invest interpersonal and semiotic contact with experiential qualities, on the one hand, and kinship ideologies that distinguish kinship types in terms of modes of social categorical difference, on the other, are coupled to one another and are co-constitutive. In Manus (Austronesian; Melanesia), for instance, the kin term for "avoidance relation" is *kaleal*, which literally means "a person one goes around" (from the verb *kaleani* "to go around") (Mead, 1934, p. 244, note 2). Corporeal avoidance, as a semiotic practice characteristic of these relationships, serves as the metonymic label for the class of in-law relations.

But "avoidance register" can also be given a second, more technical and purely sociolinguistic definition: An avoidance register is a special vocabulary that substitutes for a range of "everyday" (or "neutral" [Laughren, 2001] or "plain" [Smith & Johnson, 2000]) words and expressions in social contexts where those everyday words are socially proscribed or taboo. From chiefly name taboo (e.g., Tahitian: Salmon, 1927) to specialized speech styles used in hunting (e.g., Abkhaz: Khiba, 1980), fishing (e.g., Shetland Norn: Jakobsen, 1897) and gathering (e.g., Malay: Lake & Kelsall, 1894), to the "mother-in-law languages" of Aboriginal Australia (Chapter 2) and the daughter-in-law name registers of Africa and Eurasia (Chapter 3), lexical repertoires that substitute for everyday vocabulary involve diverse sociocultural preoccupations, activities, and relationships. Nevertheless, these diverse linguistic varieties are all members of a common sociolinguistic kind: In all of these cases, special linguistic varieties emerge to circumvent a range of everyday words whose negatively evaluated performative effects, in avoidance contexts, cannot be cancelled out, no matter how they are introduced into discourse. That is, they consist of speech forms employed to circumvent taboo words and expressions.

To be socialized to an avoidance register (in this second sense) is therefore to be able to recognize and distinguish two distinct linguistic repertoires. One of these is composed of the set of everyday vocabulary items registered as targets of avoidance; I will call the set of such proscribed words the negative repertoire of the register. The second repertoire is the set of pragmatically "safe" expressions that substitute for everyday words in avoidance contexts; I will call this the positive repertoire of the register. Verbal taboo and avoidance are productive of paired negative and positive repertoire entries whose pragmatic functions are opposed but whose semantic functions are held, as best as can be managed, constant.

Linguistic avoidance is often integrated into practices of kinship avoidance. In this book I will highlight three kinds of *linguistic* practices employed in the mediation of kinship relations: (1) the use of honorific pronouns in addressing or referring to particular kin (Chapter 7), (2) the avoidance of the name of particular kin, and of words similar in phonological form to those names (Chapters 3 and 4), and (3) the use of substitute vocabularies in speaking about, or in the presence of, particular kin (Chapters 2 and 8). The first two of these sociolinguistic kinds are widespread, being attested all over the world. The third kind, however, is almost exclusively attested among Aboriginal Australian language groups (Fleming, 2014a).[1] Following accepted usage, I will refer to these Australian avoidance vocabularies as "mother-in-law languages" (Dixon, 1972). It is to these registers that I first turn my attention.

The Aboriginal Australian mother-in-law languages represent perhaps the most extensive reworking of linguistic resources and practices as a function of kinship respect and relationship. Mother-in-law languages are composed of sometimes enormous substitute vocabularies – the Dyirbal avoidance register, for instance, has more than 1,000 distinct lexical roots (Dixon, 1990). These vocabulary items replace elements of the everyday lexicon (the negative repertoire) in discursive contexts in which the use of everyday words would be interpreted as disrespectful toward particular categories of kin. Mother-in-law languages may be used in referring to the activities of, in addressing, or merely in the co-presence of, particular categories of kin (e.g., between cross-sex siblings, between members of a cross-sex parent/child dyad, between siblings-in-law, or between children- and parents-in-law). The use of this vocabulary does not just indexically *presuppose* the presence of kin of these kinds; it also indexically *entails* and elicits such a relational footing (Garde, 2008b; Rumsey, 1982). The range of interactional roles that mother-in-law speech can be employed to index and how this variable implementation links up with its honorific functions is discussed in depth in Chapter 8. For the time being, it is sufficient to recognize that in the most constrained avoidance relationships – prototypically the relationship between a son-in-law and a mother-in-law – these speech registers are employed when members of the relevant kin dyads find themselves in one another's co-presence, regardless of who the addressee of the utterance is or what the topic of the conversation is. (This is the case, for instance, in Gooniyandi, Wik, Dyirbal, and Guugu Yimidhirr; see Chapter 8 for more in-depth analysis.) That is, the use of mother-in-law language indexes the presence of a particular kin relation in the interactional context (Silverstein, 1976, 1981).

Mother-in-law languages thus have affinities with context-dependent avoidance registers not linked to kinship. Outside of Australia, context-dependent taboo-avoidance vocabularies are typically linked to particular high-value social activities – for example, planting or reaping crops (Moriguchi, 1995), searching for camphor (I.H.N. Evans, 1970) or pandanus nuts (Pawley, 1992), fishing on the high seas (Knooihuizen, 2008), bear or cassowary hunting (Bulmer, 1967; Knight, 2007). Context-dependent avoidance registers like these are employed in particular places, in the pursuit of certain ends, in the accomplishment of certain activities, or during certain periods of the year. As shown in the Murui example, context-specific registers are often ideologically elaborated by analogy with the discursive logics of speech participant frameworks. Here it is spirits tied to particular localities, animals potentially present in the landscape, or even enemy others, rather than one's flesh-and-blood in-laws, that are figured as potential bystanders or spectral overhearers.[2]

Grammar and Lexicon

Although avoidance registers found in different speech communities serve to articulate a wide range of social concerns and preoccupations – from camphor gathering, to tapir hunting, to in-law avoidance – they exhibit remarkably convergent properties in their structuring as linguistic codes. Specifically, although everyday and avoidance vocabularies (or "lexicons") may be markedly different, avoidance speech almost always employs the same phonology, syntax, and grammatical morphemes as everyday speech.[3] Avoidance repertoires – both negative and positive – are almost always exclusively composed of words and expressions. Numerous linguists with firsthand working knowledge of avoidance registers have made this observation. (With respect to Australian mother-in-law registers, see Alpher, 1993, p. 98; Crowley, 1983, p. 383; Dixon, 1972, p. 314; Harris, 1970, p. 788; McGregor, 1989). R.M.W. Dixon (1972), for instance, writes:

> Dyalŋuy [Dyirbal mother-in-law register] data supports the recognition of a division between grammar and lexicon: all members of open word classes – that is, all nouns, adjectives, verbs, adverbals and time qualifiers – have a different form in Dyalŋuy from that which they have in Guwal [i.e., everyday Dyirbal]. However, all grammatical forms – words such as pronouns, noun and verb markers and particles, and all affixes – have identical form in Guwal and Dyalŋuy. (p. 314)

Charles Grimes and Kenneth Maryott (1994) make a similar observation about *li garan* ("the language of Garan"). Throughout the island of Buru

(Mollucas, Indonesia), indigenous inhabitants practice place-based lexical avoidances. Violations of these linguistic interdictions have a powerful performativity, manifest in meteorological messages sent by the landscape to those passing through it: "Failure to observe the taboos may result in a sudden and violent deterioration in the weather with branches blowing down or roofs blowing off, hurting or killing someone" (p. 279). In one particularly inhospitable area of the island, called Garan, a very large number of everyday words are tabooed and an elaborate avoidance repertoire – Grimes collected more than 400 entries – is employed in its place. The authors note that the "syntax and phonology of Li Garan are the same as those of Buru. Nouns and verbs are usually different ... but functors such as pronouns, prepositions, conjunctions, aspect markers and adverbials are normally the same" (p. 280).

Andrew Pawley (1992) notes the same bifurcation of grammar and lexicon in his writings on the Kalam "pandanus language." Pandanus registers – and analogous varieties like Awiakay "mountain talk" (Hoenigman, 2012) and Huli "bush language" (Lomas, 1989, p. 292) – are widely attested in the New Guinea Highlands (for Kewa, Mendi, and Melpa, see Franklin, 1972; Franklin & Stefaniw, 1992; see Foley, 1986, for an insightful review). The Kalam register was employed during weeks-long sojourns in the forest during the dry season, a period of time during which the collection of wild pandanus nuts was a central subsistence activity (Bulmer, 1967; Pawley, 1992, p. 315, note 6; cf. Franklin, 1972, p. 70). During this time, everyday Kalam vocabulary was not supposed to be uttered lest it cause the pandanus nuts to become waterlogged and spoilt. Instead, *alŋaw mnm* "pandanus speech/talk/language" was employed to avoid these undesirable consequences while still enabling rich linguistic communication: "The phonological and morphological systems of Ordinary Language and Pandanus Language are the same. So, too, are the major details of syntax. However, their lexicons show (with certain principled exceptions) no likenesses in form. The Kalam thus make the same basic distinction between content and form, or meaning and lexification, that linguists conventionally do.... [In the Pandanus Language only the ...] functor morphemes ... correspond ... in form as well as meaning to an Ordinary Language counterpart" (Pawley, 1992, p. 314).

The generalization that avoidance registers consist of exclusively lexical (or word-based) repertoires is remarkably robust. A few examples will make palpable the stark reality of this division between what Whorf (2000) called "primary selective" (lexical or word) classes and "modulus" (morphologically bound) categories in the structurally skewed organization of avoidance repertoires. In the examples below, sentences labelled "a" are examples of the everyday language and those labelled "b" are examples of the avoidance register. I have outlined morphemes that are the same in both everyday and avoidance speech.

1 *li garan* "language of Garan" [Buru vocabulary is avoided in a place on the Island of Buru called Garan.] (Buru, Austronesian) (Abbreviations: PROX = proximal, IRR = irrealis mood, 3s = third-person singular, 1PI = first-person inclusive.)

a.	<u>geba</u>	<u>botit</u>	naa	la-	d	<u>tewa</u>	kita	nani liet	<u>gos-</u>	<u>gosa</u>
	PERSON	WHITE	PROX	IRR	3S	KNOW	1PI	POSS	LANGUAGE	WELL
b.	<u>emkisen</u>	<u>ɲilat</u>	naa	la-	d	<u>salik</u>	kita	<u>wahun</u>	<u>emkaset</u>	<u>pi-pia</u>
	PERSON	LIGHT	PROX	IRR	3S	GET	1PI	POSS	SPEECH	WELL

"This white man wants to learn our language well." (C.E. Grimes & Maryott, 1994, p. 286)

2 *alŋaw mnm* "pandanus language" (Kalam, Papuan) [Kalam vocabulary is avoided during weeks-long forest sojourns at the beginning of the dry season.] (Abbreviations: OPT = optative mood, 2 = second person.)

a.	<u>mnm</u>	<u>tmey</u>	ma-	<u>g-</u>	n-	mn
	LANGUAGE	BAD	NOT-	SAY-	OPT-	2
b.	<u>laj</u>	<u>mayab</u>	ma-	<u>tgom-</u>	n-	mn
	LANGUAGE	BAD	NOT-	SAY-	OPT-	2

"You mustn't use bad language." (Pawley, 1992, p. 314)

3 *damin* second-order initiate (or *warama*) register (Lardil, non-Pama Nyungan) [Lardil vocabulary was avoided in speech with those present at ego's subincision ceremony.] (Abbreviations: WyB = wife's younger brother, GEN = genitive, FUT = future.)

a.	<u>ngithun</u>	<u>dunji-</u>	kan	<u>ngawa</u>	<u>waang-</u>	kur	<u>werneng-</u>	<u>kiyath-</u>	ur
	my	WyB-	GEN	dog	go-	FUT	food-	GO-	FUT
b.	<u>n!aa</u>	<u>n!2a-</u>	kan	<u>nh!2u</u>	<u>tiitith-</u>	kur	<u>m!ii-</u>	<u>ngkiyath-</u>	ur
	my	WyB-	GEN	dog	go-	FUT	food-	GO-	FUT

"My brother-in-law's dog is going to go hunting." (Hale & Nash, 1997, p. 248)

As each of these examples illustrates, word roots have different forms in everyday and avoidance speech. The bound morphology (e.g., prefixes and suffixes) that attaches to the word roots is the same. Even closed class "grammatical words," like the proximal determiner *naa* or the first-person inclusive pronoun *kita* in Buru, typically remain unchanged across register varieties.

The differential enregisterment of lexical as opposed to grammatical morphology is a convergent language-structural property of avoidance registers. Consistently, across a range of speech registers tied to very different social projects but organized around linguistic proscription and substitution, it is exclusively members of open word classes (e.g., noun and verb roots) that are proscribed. Notably, other kinds of speech registers are not typically as convergent cross-linguistically in the structural organization of their repertoires. Honorific register repertoires are, for instance, less constrained in their locus of marking when compared with avoidance registers (Agha, 2007, pp. 179–85). Honorific repertoires may have phonological components (e.g., Samoan and Persian), bound morphological components (e.g., Korean and Japanese), or lexical components (e.g., Tibetan and Ladakhi) (examples after Agha, 2000). "Categorical" gender registers (Silverstein, 1985), to take another example, may have phonological (e.g., Karaja), morphophonological (e.g., Koasati), morphological (e.g., Chiquitano), or lexical (e.g., Island Carib) repertoires (examples after Fleming, 2012).

Case Study: Loci of Sociolinguistic Marking in Yanyuwa

The stark contrast in the formal locus of marking of register distinctions can be seen with an example from Yanyuwa (Northern Territory, Australia; Pama Nyungan). In Yanyuwa there is both an in-law avoidance register and a speaker-focal gender register (Bradley, 1988; Fleming, 2015a, pp. 428–32; Kirton, 1971; Kirton & Timothy, 1982). The avoidance register is employed in speech between brothers-in-law, between a son-in-law and a mother-in-law, and between classificatory cross-sex siblings. The gender register, contrastingly, is employed in all contexts, with men, after passing through rites of initiation, using the male-speaker indexing forms and everyone else employing female-speaker indexing forms (Bradley, 1988).[4] As illustrated in Table 1.1, the loci of marking for the Yanyuwa gender register and the in-law avoidance register are complementary. The avoidance repertoire consists of "a separate set of stems for the general content words. The same syntax and morphology applies as in normal speech" (Kirton, 1971, p. 2). The gender-indexing variants, meanwhile, are bound morphemes, like noun-class prefixes and case markers, and grammatical (or "functor") words, like demonstrative pronouns.

Table 1.1 shows four possible permutations of the noun phrase "the blind man." Observe that the avoidance relationship is indexed by the noun-stem alternation: *gabudjimi* is the everyday term for "blind man," while *ŋamimi* is the avoidance form. Meanwhile, the speaker

Table 1.1. Complementarity in the loci of the social indexing of speaker gender and speaker-addressee kin relationship in Yanyuwa

	Pragmatic Meanings		Semantic Meanings
	Speaker-Addressee = avoidance relations	Speaker-Addressee = not avoidance relations	"the blind man"
Speaker = initiated man	ø-ŋamimi	ø-gabudjimi	ø-/nja-: human masculine noun class prefix ('the')
Speaker = anyone else	nja-ŋamimi	nja-gabudjimi	ŋamimi/gabudjimi: 'blind man'

Note. Four ways to say the noun phrase "the blind man" are depicted.
Source: Kirton (1971, p. 55).

gender-indexing alternation occurs in the noun-class prefix: *nja-* indexes women and children, while *ø-* indexes men. Examples like this one raise the question: Why are avoidance registers, but not other social speech registers, composed exclusively of words and expressions to the exclusion of grammatical morphemes? Why don't we find avoidance registers composed exclusively of bound morphological elements and grammatical words, as in the Yanyuwa gender register?

As I detailed in the Introduction, one of my aims in this book is to understand the sources of the convergent structural properties of avoidance registers. The exclusively word-based or lexical composition of avoidance repertoires is the first property of this kind. I now seek to understand the causal mechanisms that conspire to make the lexicon the locus of marking register repertoire differences in avoidance speech.

Linguistic Proscription as Metapragmatic Discourse

In order to speak in a socially appropriate way in avoidance contexts, language users must draw upon their knowledge not only of the positive repertoire of an avoidance register but also of the negative repertoire – the set of forms proscribed in avoidance contexts. Typically, avoiding the elements of the negative repertoire is of greater social importance than accurately producing the positive repertoire. Individuals who are not competent at producing an avoidance register but who nevertheless seek to avoid employing proscribed words and expressions may use substitute substitute vocabularies, like foreign languages or sign languages. This appears to be especially true of avoidance registers employed in particular locales or in accomplishing particular collective activities. B.D. Grimes (1997, p. 126) observes that "visitors to Garan who do not know Li Garan may speak Malay, English, Chinese or indeed any language other than the Buru language." A similar place-based avoidance register, consisting of around 50 to 100 substitute expressions for "common words," is employed by Yélî Dnye speakers on the small island of Lów:a, found 16 kilometres to the east of Rossel Island (Levinson, 2008, p. 282). Again, what is most important is to avoid the particular subset of Yélî Dnye vocabulary (e.g., *kwadön* "sun," *dwon* "moon," *pchi* "rain," etc.) that constitutes the negative repertoire of Lów:a speech, not to employ "correct" substitute expressions. As Armstrong (1928, p. 150) observes, "apparently pidgin English may be used on Loa and could even be used in place of the Loa word for an object."

To summarize, knowing what not to do is as important – if not more important – than knowing what to do in its place. Avoidance speech does not only rely upon the latent linguistic competence thought to underlie everyday speech production and parsing. It additionally demands an active self-monitoring that ensures that proscribed forms are not employed. And this implies that successful avoidance speech relies upon explicit metalinguistic discourses and consciously accessible metapragmatic models capable of isolating the linguistic units that are to be avoided in speech.

A **metapragmatic model** is one that frames the context-relative or "pragmatic" significations (meanings and effects) of signs (Silverstein, 1993; Slotta, 2020). Such models are given explicit articulation in metapragmatic discourses and through the use of metapragmatic vocabularies. Names for avoidance registers, like Buru *li garan* ("the language of Garan") or Kalam *alŋaw mnm* ("pandanus language"), are metapragmatic descriptors. They denote a repertoire of signs characterized as appropriate for use in particular socially defined contexts. Descriptors like these play a crucial role in metapragmatic discourses that frame particular linguistic forms as capable of circumventing negatively valued pragmatic effects when employed in particular places. Words like *emkisen* "person" that are classified as elements of *li garan* will not cause storms in the region of Garan. Words like *tmey* "bad" that are classified as *alŋaw mnm* will not cause pandanus nuts to rot when in mountainous forests. Enregistered linguistic proscriptions and avoidances like these necessarily rely upon explicit metapragmatic discourses and models. Importantly, as I will now show, it is this metapragmatic modelling that functions as a filter motivating the exclusively lexical composition of avoidance repertoires.

Words are privileged objects of metalinguistic awareness (Silverstein, 1981). As Wittgenstein observes in *Philosophical Investigations*, "we are prone to work with a certain idea of language as consisting of words each correlated with something for which it stands, an object, the meaning of the word. This picture, though philosophically misleading for all words, is better suited to some than to others. When we have it in mind, we are primarily thinking of common nouns like 'chair' and 'bread' and of people's names; even primitive reflection shows that it does not fit, say, logical connectives" (Strawson, 1966, p. 23). The seemingly "direct" referential linkage between free-floating word and worldly referent means that words (where concrete nouns serve as the privileged prototypes) epitomize language for its users (Moore, 1988; Silverstein, 1981).

Edward Sapir defined the word as "one of the smallest, completely satisfying bits of isolated 'meaning' into which the sentence resolves itself" (Sapir, 1921, p. 35, quoted in Dixon & Aikhenvald, 2002, p. 5). The idea that the word is "completely satisfying" invokes an emic perspective on word meaning. And indeed, Sapir's analysis of words parallels his treatment of the phoneme as a sound-shape which has a psychological reality (Sapir, 1985, pp. 46–60). What distinguishes the psychological reality of words from other isolable elements of the speech signal? Even when they occur in isolation, words have seemingly stable and experienceable denotational meanings. While I analytically understand both to be meaning-bearing units, I recognize an isolated token utterance of "apple" as a meaningful unit in a different way than I recognize a token of "-s" – that is, the English plural marker – as a meaningful unit. The first is meaningful "in-and-of itself," while the latter depends upon the co-occurrence of another morphological element for it to be meaningful to me as language.

The difficulty linguists have in giving a set of necessary and sufficient conditions which would define the word as a universal primitive of linguistic theory shows that a purely grammatical analysis is not sufficient (see Dixon & Aikhenvald, 2002, for a review of various attempts). In the final analysis, the word is a convergent object of ethno-theories of language. Rather than having a purely structural ontology, the word is a unit of folk-linguistics which emerges at the limits of speakers' abilities to isolate and characterize elements of the linguistic code – what Jakobson (1971) called the metalinguistic function. The word, as a structural primitive of folk-linguistics, is thus intimately enmeshed with "the natural metapragmatic life of language" (Silverstein, 1993, p. 38). Words are those linguistic units whose semantic or referential meanings can be presenced through their replicas when they are isolated in citational and other metalinguistic discourses. This difference between words and, say, inflectional morphology or case markers, whose meanings cannot easily be separated from the longer linguistic phrases in which they occur, has important implications for proscriptive regimes of language and the kinds of speech registers that they generate.

Because their semantic and referential meanings are experientially presenced by their replicas or tokens, even when stripped of their co-textual, linguistic surround, words are the linguistic units that native speakers can most easily isolate and characterize in explicit metapragmatic discourse. And it is just such metapragmatic discourses that are central to regimes of linguistic proscription. (Linguistic proscription requires discourses of roughly the following kind: "You can't say '[X],'" where X has a sentential, phrasal, or minimally lexical constituency.) Some concrete examples will illustrate this relationship between proscription as it depends upon explicit metapragmatic discourse and the lexical composition of the negative repertoire of avoidance registers.

Linguistic Proscription in Guugu Yimidhirr, Kambaata, and Kwaio

In rich descriptions of avoidance registers, one can sometimes glimpse the ways in which newcomers are socialized to norms and practices of linguistic avoidance. Most frequently it is the anthropologist or linguist who is socialized, and this occurs through explicit metalinguistic elicitation. John Haviland's (1979a, 1979b) descriptions of Guugu Yimidhirr brother-in-law language were based exclusively upon linguistic elicitation. Similarly to Yanyuwa, Guugu Yimidhirr speakers traditionally employed an elaborate lexical repertoire in addressing, or merely when speaking in the co-presence of, a range of in-laws, namely brother-in-law, father-in-law, and mother-in-law. The fieldwork upon which Haviland's descriptions are based was conducted beginning in 1975, but Haviland estimates that the use of brother-in-law vocabulary had largely ceased being employed before World War II (but see Haviland, 1979a, p. 385). Nevertheless, older informants were able to offer quite extensive wordlists and rich metapragmatic representations of avoidance language practices as they had witnessed them in their youth. The following extract of informant testimony illustrates the facility with which speakers can manipulate words as the object-signs of metapragmatic discourses of linguistic proscription: "You can use *mayi banggamu* (potato) to any common person, to *gami* [same moiety grandparent, i.e., prototypical joking partner] or to *dhawuunh* (friend). But not with *ngadhiina* (father-in-law). But *'dhirrguul-dhirr'* – you can use that *guugu* with father-in-law" (Haviland, 1979b, p. 224). Although English is employed as the matrix language, native terms are employed not only for citation forms but also as the metapragmatic term for speech, *guugu*. This term is employed for speech as such, as in the language name "Guugu Yimidhirr" (literally, "word this-way" [Haviland, 1979a, p. 369]). But it is also used for the citational form of words – in this example, *mayi banggamu* and *dhirrguul-dhirr* as everyday and avoidance alternants, respectively, for "potato."

An example of a more "naturally" occurring metapragmatic discourse of linguistic proscription is offered in Yvonne Treis's (2005) description of the Kambaata *ballishsha* avoidance register. As with a number of other groups of central and south Asia, and eastern and southern Africa, Kambaata daughters-in-law are normatively expected to avoid uttering the names of members of their husband's patriline – most importantly, the name of their father-in-law – and of a wide range of words iconic in phonological shape with those names. (For discussion of Afro-Eurasian daughter-in-law registers, see Chapter 3.) A newly married daughter-in-law's husband's sisters painstakingly instruct her, word by word, in the forms she is to avoid. (There is no sanction against these sisters-in-law using the words in question, so they are able to cite them freely.) These words are learned in literally bite-sized morsels:

> On the wedding day the bride empties her stomach and bowels with *xeemú*, a laxative. Until she has learned the *ballishsha* vocabulary, no food is presented to her.... Finally, [on the second day,] the food is presented to her, and spoon by spoon and sip by sip the *ballishsha* words are taught to her. With every spoon and with every sip she swallows one word. If her father-in-law's name starts with #*wo* or #*wa*, the teachers might tell her: "Do not say *waasá*, say *coqqá*; do not say *wo'á*, say *daadaamú*; do not say *wo'ichchú* say *ladiichchú*!" (Treis, 2005, pp. 297–8)

The poetic structure of the ritual instruction equates words, as units of respect, with bites and sips, as units of sustenance and provisioning. As the longer ritual sequence makes clear, the new bride's material dependence upon her husband's family, with whom she will now live, is figured as contingent upon her maintaining a demeanour of deferential respect toward her (especially male and generationally senior) in-laws. But even in this quite onerous regime of linguistic censure, it is only those linguistic units that serve as the object of a verb of speaking – words and expressions – that are targeted by explicit metapragmatic discourses of proscription. Grammatical morphemes – even those iconic with proscribed names – are shared between everyday and avoidance speech. They are not filtered out by explicit metapragmatic discourses of linguistic proscription.

Another example of a naturally occurring explicit metapragmatic discourse of linguistic proscription is provided in Keesing and Fifi'i's (1969) description of Kwaio post-mortem name and homophone avoidance. Linguistic avoidances in Kwaio emerge out of injunctions on the use of the names of *adalo* or "ancestor spirits" and explicitly proscribed homophones of those names. Again, similar-sounding bound morphemes are never targets of avoidance; only similar sounding words are tabooed. For the patrilineal and virilocal Kwaio, name and homophone avoidance is anchored to lineal descendants of *adalo*. It is lineal descendants who most studiously avoid the names of ancestors, but it is also these individuals who typically proscribe others from employing homophones of those names and levy fines on those who utter those homophones in their presence. This transactional logic is undergirded by the performativist ideology that rationalizes linguistic proscription: *adalo* avenge the wrongs done them, but since they are able to affect only their own lineal kin, their punishments are always visited on their descendants, regardless of the culpability of those persons for the offence in any given instance (Keesing & Fifi'i, 1969, pp. 158–9). Non-lineage members who violate taboos within the earshot of descendants may be obliged to pay a fine for having put those descendants in peril. When travelling to other villages, outsiders are explicitly socialized to the linguistic proscriptions of the settlement about to be visited:

> My [= Keesing's] first introduction to word tabooing came when, after five months in Kwaio, I set out to visit a distant settlement: "Don't use *folia* ["buy"], *xu'i*, or *ele* ["fire"] at Maaxona's village" I was warned. "They are taboo for his wife, Fele'i, and if you use them you will have to give a pig right away as compensation." ... [O]ften these warnings are conveyed on the spot. As a party of visitors enters an unfamiliar settlement, they may be warned not to use the particular form." (Keesing & Fifi'i, 1969, pp. 168–9)

Once again, words are the privileged units of linguistic proscription as formulated in explicit metapragmatic discourses. Linguistic proscription is formulated by means of expressions like: "Do not use 'X'!," where X is a word or expression. Importantly, the diachronic incorporation of new elements into the negative repertoire of the avoidance register necessarily depends upon just such explicit metapragmatic discourses. The set of individuals who avoid the homophone of an *adalo* name increases after post-facto divination reveals that it was the use of a token of this or that word iconic with an *adalo* name which was the cause for this or that misfortune. So, for instance, *gwaea* "hold in the arms" was tabooed for a woman named Dedei'a, who had married a man named Seda and moved to his village. When "the wife of one of Seda's kin visited them shortly after the birth of their child," she employed the term: "When the baby got sick several days later, this [linguistic usage] was divined to be the cause of illness; the 'priest' sacrificed a pig in expiation, and members of the local group began to avoid use of the term" (Keesing & Fifi'i, 1969, p. 173). Tabooing as a cultural practice requires being able to pick out and identify the offending sign – to be able to ratify occurrences as tokens of a performative type. It depends upon explicit metapragmatic models.

Reflexivity and Repertoire

In this short chapter I have introduced avoidance registers as a sociolinguistic kind: An avoidance register consists of a vocabulary used in place of everyday words in contexts in which (or by speakers for whom) the use of those words is understood to have indefeasible, negatively evaluated, performative effects. Cross-linguistically, avoidance registers exhibit parallels both at the level of language ideology and at the level of language structure. At the level of language ideology, the distinction between positive and negative repertoire items is conceptualized as a contrast in terms of pragmatic function. Everyday vocabulary has negatively valued performative effects (e.g., warns prey of the hunters' presence, disrespects a co-present classificatory mother-in-law, causes pandanus nuts to go rotten, offends *adalo* ancestor spirits, etc.). The substitute vocabulary serves to circumvent those negative effects. At the level of language structure, both positive and negative repertoires are composed exclusively of words and expressions. My discussion has focused on the ways in which discourses of linguistic proscription – the explicit metapragmatic discourses that frame the pragmatic effects of everyday and avoidance speech – are responsible for this convergent structural property. Words and expressions are the minimal units that explicit discourses of linguistic proscription can readily pick out (see Zuckerman & Enfield, 2023, on the "limits of thematization").

It is the way in which speakers reflexively engage with, and intervene in, language that is productive of avoidance registers as a cross-culturally convergent sociolinguistic kind. Words – rendered into discrete units of linguistic meaning by language structure and metapragmatic discourse – can enter into social exchange and circulation in ways that other elements of linguistic form (e.g., phonological alternations, grammatical morphemes, syntactic constructions, etc.) cannot. Because speakers can explicitly model their meanings and effects with relative ease, words come to objectify the causal consequentiality of language. As I have shown, this hypostatization of words as units of speech-action itself feeds back into the structuring of avoidance registers; it motivates the development of avoidance repertoires composed exclusively of words. I now extend this mode of analysis, one which, following Silverstein (1985), seeks to trace the dialectical relationships between language structure, linguistic ideology, and discursive practice. Turning my attention specifically to Australian mother-in-law languages, I show how word-avoidance, as a discursive practice, becomes dialectically interwoven not only with the structuring, but also with the socioculturally informed ideological interpretation, of avoidance registers.

Chapter Two

Many to One: Lexicon Asymmetries in Avoidance Registers

In 1971, R.M.W. Dixon published a touchstone paper on Dyirbal (Pama-Nyungan; Queensland) mother-in-law language, entitled simply "A Method of Semantic Description." The avoidance register, called Jalnguy by Dyirbal speakers, was traditionally employed when "talking within hearing distance of a parent-in-law of the opposite sex, or a cross-cousin of the opposite sex," but also by newly initiated men "just after their tribal cicatrices had been cut" (Dixon, 1982, pp. 65, 68). These were social settings in which the use of the everyday vocabulary was tabooed. Dixon's paper was not concerned principally with the role of the register in the enactment of social relationship and identity. Rather, it drew attention to the peculiar structural organization of the lexical semantics of the avoidance vocabulary. Dixon showed that each unique term in Jalnguy served to referentially substitute for an often quite large set of items from the everyday vocabulary, called Guwal: "Confronted with a Guwal word a speaker will give a unique Jalnguy 'equivalent.' And for any Jalnguy word he will give one or more corresponding Guwal words. It thus appears that the two vocabularies are in a one-to-many correspondence: each Jalnguy word corresponds to one or more Guwal words (and the words so related are in almost all cases not cognate with each other)" (Dixon, 1982, p. 66). For instance, the Guwal verbs *dyindan* ("gently wave or bash"), *baygun* ("vigorously shake or wave, bash something on something else"), and *banyin* ("split a soft or rotten log by embedding a tomahawk in the log and then bashing the log against a tree") are all translated into Jalnguy by a single term, *bubaman*. There is thus a one-to-many relationship between the avoidance term, *bubaman* "shake, wave or bash," and the semantically more specific everyday terms, *banyin, dyindan,* and *baygun*. One-to-many lexical correspondences like these reveal taxonomically structured semantic relationships between Jalnguy and Guwal vocabulary items. This

Table 2.1. Many-to-one correspondence in verbs of motion between everyday Guugu Yimidhirr and brother-in-law language

Everyday Guugu Yimidhirr (negative repertoire)	Brother-in-law language (positive repertoire)
dhadaa "go" *dhaarmbil* "float, sail, drift" *yaalgal* "limp" *gaynydyarr* "crawl" *biilil* "paddle" *daabal* "wade"	*balil* ("go")

Source: Adapted from Haviland (1979b, p. 218, Table 4.13).

lexicon asymmetry, as I will call the phenomenon, is a characteristic property of Aboriginal Australian in-law avoidance registers. Table 2.1 exemplifies the phenomenon with data from the Guugu Yimiddhir brother-in-law language.

In Table 2.1, six everyday verbs of motion are all translated into the Guugu Yimidhirr in-law avoidance register by one word, *balil*. This word is thus a **hypernym** of the corresponding set of everyday words; its denotation encompasses (and is taxonomically superordinate to) the denotations of the everyday words for which it substitutes; to float or sail, limp or crawl, these are all ways of going from one place to another. Conversely, *yaalgal* "to limp" and *daabal* "to wade" are **hyponyms** of *balil*; their denotations are subsets of (or taxonomically subordinate to) the denotation of the term *balil*; "to wade" and "to limp" describe two, among many possible means, of going from one place to another.

One (hypernym) to many (hyponyms) word correspondences of this kind reveal the implicit taxonomic structure in the semantics of the everyday Dyirbal lexicon. Dixon was able to show this by asking his language consultants to translate mother-in-law terms back into everyday speech. Keeping with the Guugu Yimidhirr example, when consultants are prompted to translate the brother-in-law form *balil* into everyday speech, they will invariably offer *dhadaa* "to go," rather than *dhaarmbil, yaalgal,* or *gaynydyarr* as the translation for *balil*. This ingenious elicitation technique reveals that the everyday word *dhadaa* "to go" is itself a hypernym. Arguing from data of this kind, Dixon hypothesized that the verbal lexicon of languages like Dyirbal and Guugu Yimidhirr (and by implication the lexicons of all natural languages) are divided into two kinds of forms: "nuclear" verbs like *dhadaa* "to go," and "nonnuclear" verbs like *yaalgal* "to limp" and *daabal* "to wade," which are related by definitional equivalences to those nuclear forms. The mother-in-law lexicon, Dixon argued, consists of a purely nuclear vocabulary.

In this chapter, I seek to understand one-to-many lexical correspondences as a convergent structural property of avoidance registers.[1] In the last chapter I showed that avoidance register repertoires are always composed of words and expressions. I offered evidence that this convergent language-structural property derives from constraints on metapragmatic discourses of linguistic proscription (a species of what Zuckerman and Enfield, 2023, call "the limits of thematization"). Pragmatic unmentionability depends upon semantic mentionability. Only words – linguistic units that have a definite and stable meaning for speakers when cited in isolation (i.e., when "mentioned" as opposed to "used") – are susceptible to becoming enregistered as linguistic taboos. Only words can be converted into actionable utterables. Explicit discourses of linguistic proscription function as a filter sieving out words as targets of avoidance and lexical substitution, entraining language users to "appersieve" (after Kockelman, 2013, p. 36) words as targets of verbal taboo.

Having explained this exclusively lexical or word-based organization of avoidance registers, I now seek to describe a second convergent property of the structure of avoidance repertoires: many-to-one lexical correspondences between everyday and avoidance vocabulary or **lexicon asymmetry**. I do so by once again employing the structure-ideology-practice approach (after Silverstein, 1985) outlined in the Introduction. This approach seeks to understand language structures as dialectically related to discursive pratices and the linguistic, and broader sociocultural, ideologies that inform their use. For the specific problem of the diachronic unfolding of lexicon asymmetry as a structural property of avoidance registers, I argue that it is crucial to attend to the tradeoffs between semantic and pragmatic signification involved in successfully "doing avoidance" in discursive practice.

Lexicon Asymmetry in Avoidance Registers

How has lexicon asymmetry been accounted for in the existing literature? A number of scholars working on Aboriginal Australian mother-in-law languages have seen many-to-one correspondences as a form of indirectness-based politeness (after P. Brown & Levinson, 1987; see McGregor, 1989; Rumsey, 1982; cf. Alpher, 1991, p. 99; Dixon, 1971, p. 438; Haviland, 1979b, p. 210). The reasoning is well motivated. In-law avoidance speech almost always occurs alongside strategies that serve to mitigate the force of speech acts. Take, for example, the case of Bunaba (non-Pama Nyungan; the Kimberley).

In Bunaba there is a register distinction between everyday speech (*jada jada* or "straight" Bunaba) and a mother-in-law avoidance style called Gun-gunma, probably a cognate to Gooniyandi *goongoon-* "to speak circumspectly to, to avoid speaking to" (McGregor, 1989, p. 633, note 1). Alan Rumsey (1982) comprehensively documents this register, drawing on linguistic elicitation in the field but also staged conversations by language consultants pretending to be related to one another as avoidance relations, and complemented by myth narration that voices characters who stand in avoidance relationships to one another in the narrative world. He describes a number of features of Gun-gunma that allow for "a wide range of degrees of 'explicitness' or semantic specificity" in the use of the avoidance register (p. 165). These include systematic skewing of number in pronominal paradigms, processes of detransitivization (i.e., the use of a valence-reducing operator specific to the avoidance register and the shifting of the direct object to the status of an indirect object), and one-to-many relationships between avoidance and everyday lexicons. Gun-gunma speech is hedged around with politeness markers of the kind that seek to minimize the imposition made upon an addressee. Transcripts of Gun-gunma talk are peppered with the particle *yungu*, which functions in a way "similar to that of English *kind of, sort of*, etc. It weakens the speaker's commitment to the veracity of what he is saying, or to the intention it expresses, thereby providing the addressee with an easier 'out' if he disagrees with, or is imposed upon by, what is said" (Rumsey, 1982, p. 175; cf. the use of *waya* "bad, no good" in Wik mother-in-law language [Sutton, 1978, p. 220]).

Drawing on P. Brown and Levinson's (1987) universal theory of politeness, Rumsey (1982) reaches the reasonable conclusion that the lack of semantic precision of avoidance speech is a strategy of discursively indirect, "negative politeness" (pp. 174–9; cf. McGregor, 1989, p. 644). By not giving a semantically rich description, speakers give addressees maximal flexibility or leeway to interpret their utterances. Rumsey (1982) argues that Gun-gunma's "formal features are not connected in an entirely arbitrary way with the avoidance relationship which they index, but instead are inherently consonant with that relationship" (p. 160). McGregor (1989) offers a related explanation of the mother-in-law register in the neighbouring language, Gooniyandi, stating that "the ... semantic style [of avoidance speech] ... is clearly an iconic reflection of the relationship of avoidance it encodes" (p. 647). If "negative politeness" is the synchronic pragmatic effect of the more abstract semantics of mother-in-law speech, it seems reasonable to assume that delicacy in denotation could also have been the historical cause of lexicon asymmetry.

But there is a problem with this line of analysis, a problem that is revealed only when one adopts a comparative lens. The comparative study of speech registers reveals that lexicon asymmetry is a widespread property of avoidance vocabularies. Lexicon asymmetry not only appears in avoidance registers related to in-law avoidance. It also appears in avoidance speech employed during the liminal period of male initiation (Lardil: Hale & Nash, 1997; Gbaya: Moñino, 1977), or while harvesting pandanus nuts (Kewa: Franklin, 1972; Kalam: Pawley, 1992), or so as to assure safe passage through untamed lands (Buru: C.E. Grimes & Maryott, 1994), or during a hunting expedition (Abkhaz: Khiba, 1980). It even occurs in signed avoidance registers linked to the maintenance of monastic silence (Barakat, 1975). These registers are similar to mother-in-law languages in that they involve context-dependent word tabooing and replacement. But the sociocultural projects that these registers subtend are radically different from one another. And as I will show, the semantic abstractness of avoidance speech in these cases is not typically conceptualized in terms of politeness or interpersonal respect.

The comparative data that I will introduce thus suggest that the diachronic emergence of lexicon asymmetry should not be reduced to its synchronic conceptualization. Rumsey (1982) and McGregor (1989) are surely right that denotational opacity is apperceived as a "polite" or respectful way to speak by Bunaba and Gooniyandi speakers, respectively. The lack of paraphrase in mother-in-law discourse, which leaves what is said maximally vague, illustrates the discursive manipulation of the avoidance lexicon toward this end (Rumsey, 1982, p. 173). And yet the comparative data suggest that the synchronic realization of semantic-vagueness-as-politeness cannot be postulated as the final, diachronic cause of lexicon asymmetry.

In the rest of this chapter I seek to resolve this contradiction. First, I empirically demonstrate that the abstract lexical semantics of avoidance vocabulary is a convergent property of sociolectal, context-dependent avoidance registers, of which the respectful, kin-relationship-mediating, mother-in-law languages are a special case. Second, I focus on how lexicon asymmetry – in the cases of in-law avoidance registers, but not elsewhere – gets figured as a polite practice through fashions of speaking/signing which suture language ideologies and language structures to one another.

Case Study: The Pandanus Languages of New Guinea

Evidence that something more basic than politeness-based indirection is driving the development of lexicon asymmetry comes from avoidance registers not conceptualized as emblematic of interpersonal respect. Take, as an example, the pandanus languages of the New Guinea Highlands.

Pandanus languages are named speech registers employed during the gathering of pandanus nuts in uninhabited mountainous regions, a space-time in which the use of everyday vocabulary is proscribed. Activity-type avoidance registers of this kind are relatively prevalent cross-culturally, ranging from the camphor-gathering registers of peninsular Malaysia (Skeat & Blagden, 1906) to the Matagi bear-hunting register of Japan (Knight, 2008), from the fishing registers of the British Isles (Flom, 1925) to Apachean raiding registers (Opler & Hoijer 1940; Webster, 1998), to cite only a few examples.

For the Kalam, pandanus nut gathering takes place during the dry season (May/June), during which "people spend up to three weeks camping in the forest collecting, cooking and eating the fruit." During this time, "it is essential that they avoid Ordinary Language ... [and] Pandanus Language must be used throughout such expeditions" (Pawley, 1992, p. 315). The stated ideologies behind the use of pandanus registers differ from region to region and even within particular speech communities. Kalam speakers report that if everyday speech is used, the nuts will become spoiled for human consumption; the supernatural and performative connection between everyday speech and the pandanus nuts is conceptualized as a direct one. Contrastingly, Kewa and Melpa understandings of avoidance speech focus on how its use mediates the gatherers' relationship to mythical spirits and the wild dogs they control, entities that reside in the Mt. Giluwe region where pandanus nuts are harvested. Pandanus language counts as a form of "hidden language" (*sa pi agaa*) used to trick the spirits (Franklin, 1972, p. 69; Franklin & Stefaniw, 1992, p. 4).

Despite distinct ideological framings of the performative consequences of the use of everyday words, all of these registers share the structural property of lexicon asymmetry. That is, just as with Aboriginal Australian mother-in-law languages, pandanus repertoires stand in one-to-many relationships with vernacular varieties.

Table 2.2 illustrates many-to-one relationships for the Kalam verbal lexicon. Observe the marked asymmetries in the elaboration of vocabulary for particular denotational ranges. Note, further, that some of the same semantic domains that were affected in Guugu Yimidhirr, such

Table 2.2. Many-to-one relations between everyday Kalam words and pandanus language vocabulary items

Everyday Kalam (negative repertoire)	Pandanus vocabulary (positive repertoire)
am- "go" ap- "come" saŋd- "depart" sk- "enter" tag- "travel about, return from" taw- "move something back and forth" talk- "break through a fence" tlak- "step or jump over" kom- "encircle, roll up, bury" yok- "displace, get rid of"	tag- "move" [extension of everyday Kalam tag- "travel about, return from"]
ad- "heat stones for earth oven" ag- "(make a) sound" agi- "ignite, heat" ask- "avoid, be in an avoidance relationship" mangi- "warm oneself by fire" pbok- "cook food on separate fires, reheat food" sbk- "scorch, burn surface of something" taw- "make fire by friction" yn- "burn, cook"	tgom- "communicate sound or heat"
ang- "copulate" ñag- "shoot, propel or move something suddenly, spring, flick" pungi- "impinge, press, pierce, force or impose something" su- "bite, sting (insect), nip" tgaw- "draw back a bowstring" pk- "hit, contact"	tgaw- "impinge on, come into forceful contact with" [extension of everyday Kalam tgaw- "drawback a bowstring"]

Source: Pawley (1992, pp. 323–4).

as verbs of motion, are also affected in Kalam avoidance speech. In a number of the examples, an everyday word has become extended in its semantic sense in the avoidance register.[2] For instance, the word *tgaw-* means to "draw back a bowstring" in everyday Kalam. But it has a much wider denotation in the pandanus language, where it covers a diverse range of kinds of impingement on bodies and objects.

As shown in Table 2.3, similar word-formation processes occur in the Kewa pandanus language. The term *yoyo*, for instance, is derived

Table 2.3. One-to-many relations between pandanus register entries and everyday Kewa words

Everyday Kewa (negative repertoire)	Pandanus vocabulary (positive repertoire)
iri "hair" *aane* "ear" *andu* "breast" *nu* "net bag"	*yoyo* "hanging bodily appendage" [extension of everyday Kewa *yo* "leaf"]
ini "eye" *ini kandu* "nose" *repena ini* "seed" *ini agaa* "face" *aalu/asumbaa* "head"	*yandira* [extension of everyday Kewa "nose stick"]
aa "man" *yogane* "skin" *rumu* "knee" *maa* "neck"	*aayagopa*

Sources: Franklin (1972, pp. 70–1); Foley (1986, pp. 43–5).

via reduplication of the everyday term *yo* "leaf." An association is made between leaves, as appendages hanging off of a tree, and hair, ear, breast, and net bag, as appendages of the human, especially female, body.

Case Study: The Language of Garan (Buru; Austronesian)

Another well-documented context-dependent avoidance register exhibiting lexicon asymmetry is *li garan* "the language of Garan" (C.E. Grimes & Maryott, 1994). As mentioned in the previous chapter, this speech style is used by Buru while passing through an uninhabited region, named Garan, on the Moluccan island of Buru, in Indonesia. Rana-Buru believe that the use of everyday Buru in the region of Garan will upset ancestor spirits, who will cause "sudden and violent storms, wind, rain, thunder, lightning, branches breaking and tress falling over, or other disturbing consequences" (C.E. Grimes & Maryott, 1994, p. 281).

Buru avoidance forms are periphrastic constructions using morphological components from everyday speech (see Table 2.4). The meanings of everyday terms may be semantic extended or even reversed – for

Table 2.4. Many-to-one relations between everyday Buru lexicon and Li Garan avoidance terms

Everyday Buru (negative repertoire)	li garan (positive repertoire)	Everyday Buru morphemes used in li garan expressions
kaa "eat, chew" hada "bite" saŋa "bite (as a dog catches a pig)" mama-k "chew (as a healer chews herbs for spitting)"	em-nae	em- STATIVE VERBALIZER -nae "bait"
preŋe "hear, listen" ego "get, take, transfer control"	sali-k	sali "to receive"
junai "world" nete-n "place" rah-isi-n "dirt, soil" mua "forest, jungle"	was-lale-t	was-lale "grove, field (for cash crops)"
em-pei "sick, hurt, pain" em-loo "tired, fatigued"	em-gosa-t	-gosa- "good, beautiful, well"

Source: C.E. Grimes & Maryott (1994, pp. 280–6).

instance, the everyday word -*gosa*-, meaning "good, beautiful, well," is used with the opposite meaning of sickness and fatigue in the avoidance register. And once again, *li garan* illustrates the one-to-many lexical correspondences of the kind described for Australian mother-in-law languages.

As this survey illustrates, context-dependent avoidance registers vary considerably in terms of the local cultural frameworks and language-ideological commitments that rationalize proscriptions of everyday speech. Nevertheless, the structural property of lexicon asymmetry appears time and again. This suggests that the causes of lexicon asymmetry in mother-in-law languages cannot be chalked up solely to politeness-based tropes of semantic "indirectness." The existence of one-to-many lexical correspondences across a range of avoidance registers of different types – some relating to kinship avoidance, some to the harvesting of pandanus nuts, others to safe passage through untamed lands – points to a more general motivation for the one-to-many structure, one relating to linguistic avoidance. In the rest of this chapter, I show how this sociolinguistic convergence emerges at the intersection of "language structure, contextualized usage, and ideologies of language" (Silverstein, 1985, p. 220). Specifically, I highlight the importance of recurring patterns of "contextualized usage" as these negotiate proscriptive regimes and associated performativist ideologies of language in recurrently producing lexicon asymmetry as a "language structure."

Register Cohesion and Large Negative Repertoires

Lexicon asymmetry is correlated with a particular language-structural profile, on the one hand, and with a particular pattern of contextualized usage, on the other. The structural attribute is the existence of large negative repertoires. (At its limit, all word roots of the everyday language are tabooed in avoidance contexts; cases of this kind include, for instance, the Damin register in Lardil and the Jalnguy register in Dyirbal.) The discourse pattern is the tendency toward maximal textual cohesion of avoidance words in avoidance contexts. I treat these two aspects in turn and then show how they conspire to produce lexicon asymmetry.

Large Negative Repertoires

In order to understand lexicon asymmetry, one must consider not only the enregisterment of the positive repertoire (the substitute or avoidance vocabulary) but also the enregisterment of the negative repertoire (the set of words tabooed in avoidance contexts). As illustrated in Chapter 1, in avoidance speech registers it is never the case that all morphemes of the everyday language are tabooed. Only word-forms (technically, "lexemes") are proscribed, not grammatical morphemes like case markers or verbal inflections. Further, it is typically only a subset of the everyday lexicon that will comprise the negative repertoire of the avoidance register. In his description of Guugu Yimidhirr brother-in-law language, Haviland (1979b, p. 220) gives the example of *badhuurr* "zamia-nut fruit" as a lexeme used in both everyday and avoidance speech. The word *badhuurr* is not exclusively registered in either the positive or the negative repertoire of Guugu Yimidhirr in-law avoidance speech; the word is not **differentially enregistered**. It occurs in both everyday and avoidance speech. Importantly, lexicon asymmetry is more pronounced the greater the proportion of the everyday lexicon that is differentially enregistered into the negative repertoire.

This is illustrated dramatically in the mother-in-law languages of northern Queensland and the Cape York Peninsula. In these languages, it is quite typical for all or nearly all everyday words to be part of the negative repertoire of the avoidance register. For instance, for the Dyirbal mother-in-law language Jalnguy, "every open-class item – that is, every noun, verb, adjective, and time qualifier – was different between everyday and Jalnguy styles, with just four exceptions (the grandparent terms *bulu* 'father's father,' *babi* 'father's mother,' *ŋagi* 'mother's father,' and *gumbu* 'mother's mother')" (Dixon, 1990, p. 1). Extremely large negative repertoires like these are correlated with the most pervasive one-to-many correspondences between avoidance and everyday varieties. Although the positive repertoire of Jalnguy contains approximately 1,000 distinct lexical items, four times as many everyday forms are avoided in the co-presence of taboo affines: "Jalnguy contains far fewer words than Guwal – something of the order of a quarter as many" (Dixon, 1982, p. 67). It is avoidance registers of this type, organized around the avoidance of the entire lexicon of the everyday language, that exhibit the most hypertrophied hypernymy (or abstractness) in their lexical semantics.

Maximal Register Cohesion

Competence in an avoidance register demands a heightened awareness about what may *not* be said. Correspondingly, register use often implies a notable suppression, in focal avoidance contexts, of practices of register mixing (whether as intertextual footing, stance taking, voicing, or other represented speech). The relatively abstract semantics of avoidance repertoire items is correlated with a highly monoglossic (as opposed to heteroglossic) discursive performance in focal avoidance contexts (after Bakhtin, 1981). Only words that are part of the positive repertoire of the avoidance register should be used in discursive contexts where the most restrained interpersonal comportment is prescribed (e.g., for Dyirbal, when a man finds himself in the presence of his mother-in-law). Here there is a maximal congruence between words in text-sentences in terms of their register repertoire membership – text-sentences are composed exclusively of words belonging to the avoidance register. As a shorthand, I will refer to this congruence as a function of register-membership of words in text-sentences as **register cohesion** (after Agha, 1998, pp. 161–2).

In some of the mother-in-law registers of north-central Australia and the Kimberley, register mixing is tolerated in less focal avoidance relationships (e.g., Bininj Gunwok: Garde, 2013, p. 179; Bunaba: Rumsey,

1982, p. 166; Djaru: Tsunoda, 1981; Mangarayi: Merlan, 1982a, p. 136; but see also Sutton, 1978, p. 222 for Wik). As I show in Chapter 8, frequency of occurrence of avoidance forms may be an iconic index of interpersonal respect, where a greater density of avoidance words enacts heightened interpersonal respect. However, in descriptions of some mother-in-law languages, and particularly for the registers that exhibit the most pronounced one-to-many relationships, there is a categorical avoidance of register mixing in the most highly ritualized and ideologically valued contexts of avoidance. As Terry Crowley (1983, p. 313) writes, reviewing the use of mother-in-law registers for an array of language groups of the Cape York Peninsula, "The choice of style to be used in conversation had to be absolute. One could not mix the two." That is, avoidance contexts demand not only the use of the avoidance register but its exclusive or monoglossic production.[3]

Maximal register cohesion, on the one hand, and the existence of very large negative repertoires, on the other, are interrelated phenomena that conspire to produce lexicon asymmetry. Maximal register cohesion reflects the heightened negative performativity of everyday language in avoidance contexts. Under local relevant language-ideological framings, the use of everyday words is imbued with a relationship-rupturing performativity. This drives register cohesion, which, in its most radical form, reflects the unmentionability (after Fleming & Lempert, 2011) of everyday word forms in avoidance contexts. Put simply, maximal register cohesion reflects the taboo character of everyday speech forms in avoidance contexts.

Diachronically, I assume that taboos on everyday words are historically prior to their replacement in avoidance speech; lexical taboos pose the problem that avoidance substitutes solve. With this assumption in place, and supported by the data that I will present in the following sections, the following model for the emergence of lexicon asymmetry suggests itself: When the negative repertoire of the avoidance register is small, non-tabooed everyday linguistic resources can be drawn upon to substitute – typically, through descriptive paraphrase – for tabooed words. However, as a wider and wider range of everyday lexical items, approaching the limit of the entire lexicon, is tabooed in avoidance contexts, speakers are faced with the problem of devising avoidance forms without being able to draw upon everyday words in order to fashion descriptive workarounds. In such situations, the pragmatically "safest" option is to use words already registered as members of the positive repertoire of the avoidance register. Through this discursive strategy, words that are enregistered in the positive repertoire early in the diachronic development of the avoidance register get semantically stretched to refer to entities and events for which no ready-made labels yet exist. Discursive practices of this kind serve to progressively extend the (increasingly polysemous) range of semantic meanings associated with avoidance terms. Lexicon asymmetry is thus a usage-driven effect that emerges during the diachronic expansion of the negative repertoire of the avoidance register. In this expansionary phase, speakers tropically extend already enregistered elements of the positive repertoire in referring to entities not stereotypically associated with the term. This tropic repurposing of the pragmatically safe vocabulary has the cumulative effect of washing out the specificity of the lexical semantics of the overtaxed terms, resulting in a lexicon composed of words with abstract or "nuclear" meanings.

Making Do with a Minimal Lexicon

It has long been recognized by philologists that one of the most common means of circumventing verbal taboos is the use of periphrasis. Take, for instance, the Abkhaz "forest language" of the west Caucasus. This was an avoidance register employed to conceal "the presence and intentions of the hunters, to lead the beasts into error and to blunt their sensitive awareness, in order that they should not notice the approach of danger and run away, but that it should be easy to hunt and kill them" (Inal-Ipa, translated and quoted in Khiba, 1980, p. 269). Rather than say *à-bax* "rock," Abkhaz hunters would say *à-cag* "a blunt thing." Rather than *a-xapèc* "tooth," they said *a-tʃà-ga* "that with which one eats" (p. 272). In the hunting register, non-tabooed words from everyday Abkhaz are employed to create descriptive paraphrases. Now compare Abkhaz "forest language" to avoidance registers like Dyirbal's Jalnguy (Dixon, 1990), Lardil's Damin (Hale, 1982), and Gbaya's Lá'bì (Moñino, 1977). In these registers virtually no open-class morphemes are shared between everyday and avoidance repertoires. The entire everyday lexicon is part of the negative repertoire of the avoidance register. Here again, periphrastic expressions may be employed to achieve specific reference, only in these cases descriptive paraphrases are composed exclusively of vocabulary enregistered in the positive repertoire.

Dixon (1990) documents this phenomenon for Dyirbal. As discussed above, elicitation of mother-in-law vocabulary from everyday Dyirbal prompts yielded taxonomically superordinate avoidance words. However, when Dixon pressed informants to give him a more specific gloss

Table 2.5. Descriptive paraphrases used for "non-nuclear" meanings in Dyirbal mother-in-law language (Jalnguy)

Avoidance lexeme	Everyday lexemes	Compositional paraphrase in avoidance register
baɲ-arrmba-l	ŋanba-l "to ask"	baɲarrmba-l "to ask"
	yumba-l "to invite someone"	baɲarrmban yalibili "to ask to come"
	bunma-l "to invite someone to accompany one"	ŋaja baɲarrmban ŋaliji bawalbili "I asked [him] so that we can both go"
	gunji-y "to keep on asking"	baɲarrm-baɲarrmban "ask over and over again" (reduplication is productive in Dyirbal, yielding an iterative reading)

Source: Dixon (1990, p. 12).

in avoidance language, informants invariably did so by creating periphrastic descriptive phrases. Dixon gives the examples of *mabiiRi-y* "to cross a river (or road, railway line) by any means" and the semantically more specific *baaɲa-l* "to cross a river by walking across a log" as an example of two everyday Dyirbal forms that could be glossed by one avoidance repertoire item, *guyabi-l* (pp. 12–13). Although the avoidance term *guyabi-l* can substitute for both terms, the more specific meaning of *baaɲa-l* can be conveyed in avoidance speech through the following paraphrase: *daambiR-a-Ru guyabi-l* TREE-LOCATIVE-ALONG CROSS. This expression employs lexical material sourced exclusively from the avoidance-repertoire (*guyabi-l* "to cross" and *daambiR* "tree") in conjunction with postpositional case markers shared between everyday and avoidance styles (the locative marker *-a*, and the medium morpheme *-Ru*, "along"). (As discussed in the previous chapter, grammatical morphology is shared between everyday and avoidance repertoires.)

Table 2.5 illustrates another example of this kind. It shows that there is a one-to-many relationship between the avoidance term and everyday words for the semantic field of requests. The avoidance term *baɲarrmba-l* can be used to gloss all of the everyday words in the column of Table 2.5 labelled "Everyday lexemes." Nevertheless, more specific, "non-nuclear" meanings like "to invite someone" or "to keep on asking" can be secured by employing grammatical resources shared across the two registers in conjunction with lexical items differentially enregistered in the positive repertoire to create descriptive paraphrases of the actions denoted. (Examples of such descriptive paraphrases are shown on the right side of the table.) Semantically specific denotations are thus achieved in the same way as in the Abkhaz hunting register – through descriptive periphrasis. Only in this case, paraphrases are composed exclusively of words sourced from the avoidance register.

The reliance on core avoidance words to serve as the phrasal heads of complex descriptive phrases is sociopragmatically motivated. This discursive strategy ensures that avoidance speech employs only vocabulary that has been differentially enregistered into the positive repertoire of the register – that is, it ensures register cohesion. It is the way in which core avoidance vocabulary is leveraged in descriptive periphrase that produces the semantic abstractness of avoidance lexemes. Through the consistent use of avoidance vocabulary in descriptive paraphrase, the denotation of core avoidance vocabulary becomes widened or extended.[4]

Semantic Abstraction in Ethnobiological Taxonomies

For another demonstration of the ways in which limited lexical resources are extended to cover taxonomically subordinate denotata, I now showcase the organization of ethnobiological taxonomies in a number of avoidance registers. Table 2.6 contrasts ethnobiological nomenclature across avoidance and everyday registers for four language groups: Gbaya (Central African Republic), Lardil (Queensland, Australia), Uradhi, and Guugu Yimidhirr (both Cape York Peninsula, Australia). The Damin register of the Lardil and the Lá'bì register of the Gbaya are anchored to male initiation, while Uradhi and Guugu Yimidhirr avoidance registers are centred on in-law (or "affinal") avoidance. I will give more sociocultural contextualization of the initiate registers below. For the time being, it is sufficient to underscore that Lá'bì and Damin conform to the functional definition of an avoidance register provided in the last chapter – these registers were employed in contexts where everyday Gbaya and everyday Lardil, respectively, could not be used by male initiates.

Brent Berlin (whose classic early work with Paul Kay concerned cross-cultural convergences in colour classification) has uncovered striking parallels in the organization of ethnobiological nomenclature cross-linguistically. He finds that taxa corresponding roughly to genus or species in the Linnaean framework, and which he calls "folk-generics" and "folk-specifics," respectively, are typically denoted by monomial (one-word) expressions. Meanwhile, higher-order taxa – "life-form" classes like "bird" or "tree" – are often not lexicalized

Table 2.6. Comparison of ethnobiological nomenclature across everyday and avoidance registers of Uradhi, Guugu Yimidhirr, Lardil, and Gbaya

Avoidance register		Gloss	Everyday register	
Mother-in-law language ("cross" speech)			Uradhi ("straight" speech)	
utpumu ("grass")	–	"blady grass"	*iɟan*	*iðamu* "grass"
	–	"spiky grass"	*ukaɟa*	
	–	"spear grass"	*aɲɟara*	
	–	"bandicoot grass"	*iku:namu*	
	–	"tall grass sp."	*ilβi*	
Brother-in-law language			Guugu Yimidhirr	
daarraalngan (macropod)	–	"small wallaby"	*gadaar*	–
	–	"rock wallaby"	*bawuur*	
	–	"small scrub kangaroo"	*bibal*	
	–	"kangaroo rat"	*dyadyu*	
	–	"black kangaroo"	*gangurru*	
	–	"red kangaroo"	*nharrgali*	
Damin (*warama* initiate language)			Lardil	
wuu ("edible shellfish")	*wuu*	"shellfish"	*mala*	–
	jjuu wuu	"small shellfish"	*daangku*	
	kujburrmen wuu	"mangrove shellfish"	*jirkarr*	
	rn!uumen wuu	"freshwater shellfish"	*malmulkarnan*	
	kurrijjuu wuu	"large oyster"	*baakarnan*	
Lá'bì (Gbaya initiate register)			Gbaya-Kara	
bél ("bird")	*bél màn*	"reed cormorant"	*nɔ́ɛ́ yi*	*nɔ́ɛ́* ("bird")
	bél kàpài dátìɔ̀	"cattle egret"	*yòl*	
	bél ndángá	"hammerhead stork"	*dìsà*	
	bél gbòk dátìɔ̀	"marabou stork"	*zìgàwàl*	
	bél gòlìkɛ̀	"spur-winged goose"	*nàsósó*	
	bél kpɛ̀sɛ̀lìkɛ̀	"spotted dikkop"	*kɛ̰́ kɛ̰́*	
life-form taxa	generic taxa		generic taxa	life-form taxa

Sources: Crowley (1983, p. 383); Haviland (1979a, p. 371); McKnight (1999, p.146); Vidal (1976, p. 326).

(Berlin, 1992).[5] Lower-order taxa – "poly-varietals" and "poly-generic specifics" – will be coded for with binomial (two-word) or polynomial (many-word) expressions. Hunn and Brown (2011, p. 328) provide the following heuristic example: *plant* (unique beginner), *tree* (life-form), *oak* (generic), *live oak* (specific), *coast live oak* (varietal). As extensively documented by Berlin (1992), this is a near-universal pattern.

Revealingly, ethnobiological terminology in avoidance repertoires deviates significantly from the expected pattern. Folk-generics, if encoded at all, are either polysemous with a higher-order intermediate or life-form term or they are binomial expressions that employ the higher-order term as the head of the noun phrase. Polynomial expressions are routinely employed to refer to genera that are prototypically denoted by monomial terms in the everyday language. In essence, then, the default pattern of lexical formation is shifted up one taxonomic level – the lowest taxonomic level at which monomial expressions are found in avoidance registers is not the folk-generic level but the life-form level. Interestingly, and as illustrated in Table 2.6, this means that taxa of higher rank, which are often covert in the everyday language, are overtly lexicalized in the avoidance register. In Guugu Yimidhirr, for example, *daarraalngan* is a class designator for a life-form class that I gloss as "macropod" – it encompasses wallabies, wallaroos, and kangaroos – though this folk-biological taxon is not overtly lexicalized in the everyday lexicon. Similarly, Damin *wuu* "edible shellfish," represents an intermediate taxon that is not labelled in everyday Lardil.

Synchronic evidence suggests that the innovation of species labels precedes the elaboration of generic terms in the diachronic development of avoidance vocabularies (*pace* Berlin, 1992; see also McKnight, 1999, p. 154).[6] Take the example of the Damin speech register. As we can see in Table 2.6, there is no generic label for "edible shellfish" in Lardil, so there would be no motivation for the generic meaning to be the originating one within this semantic field in Damin speech. The genus-species polysemy of the term *wuu*, used as a designator both of the generic class ("edible shellfish") and of its archetypal member ("shellfish"), suggests precisely the reverse process: The term was first used as a substitute for "shellfish" and then repurposed in complex noun phrases to refer to similar enough but non-archetypal referents (e.g., large and small shellfish, mangrove shellfish, large oysters). It is precisely through this repurposing – making do with words already present in the avoidance repertoire – that the head noun of all of these noun phrases, *wuu*, comes to denote a generic class (i.e., "edible shellfish").

Syntagmatic, rather than paradigmatic, elaboration of register repertoires is a theme across all of these cases. To take one more example from Damin, *ngajburr wiiwin wujburr* is the Damin equivalent of Lardil *jirrmirn*, a monomial natural-kind term for "button jellyfish." The Damin noun phrase is componentially built up out of the Damin forms *ngajburr* "man" and *wiiwin* "burn" and the Damin genus label *wujburr* – thus Lardil *jirrmirn* ("button jellyfish") is rendered in Damin as "man-burning *wujburr*." This componential use of the avoidance repertoire allows for novel referents to be denoted without either resorting to everyday forms or coining new avoidance words. Speakers use the minimal lexicon of the avoidance register generatively, effectively avoiding lexical taboos by creatively repurposing "safe" substitutes already enregistered in the avoidance repertoire. Even if simplex avoidance lexemes (e.g., *wuu*) were initially employed to refer to the archetypal member of a given class, the cumulative effect of paraphrase has been to make the nominal or verbal head of these complex phrases into a general class-level term. Usage diachronically drives the structural reorganization of the avoidance lexicon, pushing its semantics "up" a taxonomic level.

Lexicon Asymmetries in Signed Avoidance Registers

One-to-many lexical correspondences are also found in signed avoidance registers (for more on manual-visual avoidance registers, see Fleming, 2014b, 2017a; Kendon, 1988, 1990; and the dedicated discussion of Armenian daughter-in-law sign language in Chapter 6). For exemplification, I offer examples drawn from Robert Barakat's (1975) description of the signed language employed within the Cistercian monastery of St. Joseph's Abbey in Massachusetts. Alternate signed languages have emerged in monastic orders that follow the Rule of St. Benedict – most importantly, in the Cistercian order beginning in the eleventh century and then the revivalist Trappist order beginning in the seventeenth century (Bruce, 2007; Delaporte, 2009; Rijnberk, 1954). Monks within these orders must remain silent during particular periods of the day and in particular spaces within the monastery. Alternate sign languages have emerged to enable communication under these circumstances.

Much as in Lá'bì and Damin, folk-generics in signed registers are referred to with complex compound expressions that employ a life-form term as the head of the noun phrase. For instance, the signed register employed at St. Joseph's Abbey relies on a number of "nuclear" nouns to generate a broad range of signs. The signs for WATER, HOUSE, and COURTYARD (as well as other signs like VEGETABLE and ANIMAL) are used extensively in compound constructions. As can be seen in Table 2.7, these nuclear nouns function like nominal classifiers.[7]

Table 2.7. Noun formation in the alternate sign language employed at St. Joseph's Abbey in Massachusetts

WATER "liquid"		HOUSE "built structure"		COURTYARD "place"	
FIRE + WATER	"gasoline"	WASH + HOUSE	"laundry"	HAY + COURTYARD	"field"
BIG + WATER	"ocean"	SICK + HOUSE	"infirmary"	ALL + WOOD + COURTYARD	"forest"
RED + WATER	"blood"	SLEEP + HOUSE	"dormitory"	WATER + COURTYARD	"lake"
CORN + WATER	"beer"	HIDE + HOUSE	"storeroom"	VEGETABLE + COURTYARD	"garden"
HARD + WATER	"ice"	SEW + HOUSE	"wardrobe"	SECULAR + COURTYARD	"city"
APPLE + WATER	"cider"	COW + HOUSE	"barn"	GOD + COURTYARD	"heaven"
FISH + WATER	"pond"	SHAME + HOUSE	"bathroom"	ONE + COURTYARD	"somewhere"

Notes. Taxonomically superordinate nouns (cf. "life-forms") serve as heads of compound phrases that refer to subordinate taxa (cf. "generics"). Signs are written in small capital letters.
Source: Barakat (1975).

Observe that the head of these complex noun phrases is always a term whose semantic meaning has been extended through its consistent use in classifier constructions. For instance, the noun COURTYARD ("hold extended forefingers in front of body with tips down then move them in a semi-circle to sides of body" [Barakat, 1975, p. 105]) has come to be a classifier for all place-denoting terms. The sign WATER serves as the head noun of all expressions referring to liquids. Beyond their classificatory function, monolexemic signs sometimes have polysemic extensions. The sign for GRAIN is also used for "berry," "cereal," and "flour"; HAY is also used for "grass" and "salad." The sign for SECULAR, which functions as a classifier for non-religious persons and places (e.g., SISTER "nun" vs. SECULAR + SISTER "sister"), is also used for "family."

Summary: Lexicon Asymmetry as a Usage-Driven Phenomenon

Through a number of examples, I have shown that lexicon asymmetry is a general feature of context-dependent avoidance registers. I have showcased a range of supporting evidence that backs up the inference that this language-structural property arises from discursive strategies employed by speakers who are concerned to ensure the pragmatic appropriateness of their utterances in avoidance contexts. Essentially, I have posited a stage in the growth of an avoidance register where the negative repertoire (the set of everyday words that are tabooed in avoidance contexts) outstrips the positive repertoire (the set of pragmatically "safe" avoidance words). During this expansionary phase, speakers may have doubts about whether a given everyday word can be appropriately used in avoidance contexts. In such circumstances, they will tend to take the safest option – they will use already enregistered avoidance terms to cover the semantic denotation of the questionable everyday word. Sometimes they will use periphrastic constructions composed of avoidance words in order to achieve more specific or precise semantic characterizations of referents. In these instances, "safe" words are combined to form polynomial noun and verb phrases where the head noun or verb effectively functions as a classifier predicating the taxonomically superordinate class of which the entire noun or verb phrase is a subordinate member. (For instance, WATER "water" comes to refer to all liquids in the Cistercian alternate sign language through its use as the head noun in descriptive expressions like RED + WATER "blood" and APPLE + WATER "cider," used to denote particular liquids.) In summary, lexicon asymmetry is the cumulative effect of the over-burdening of a relatively small set of safe avoidance words. It is most pronounced in languages, like Dyirbal, Lardil, and Gbaya, where the set of everyday words that are tabooed in avoidance contexts is the largest (i.e., it includes all nouns, verbs, and adjectives). Here, monomial avoidance terms are hypernyms of a range of everyday terms – they denote higher-order semantic classes.

Fashions of Speaking, Structure-Ideology Dialectics, and the Cultural Meaningfulness of Hyperpolysemy

On the account presented here, the semantic abstractness of avoidance vocabulary is the cumulative effect of discursive strategies that speakers employ in an attempt to make do with limited lexical resources. Hyperpolysemy (to employ the term that N. Evans, 1992, and Wilkins, 1997, use to characterize these extremely abstract and multipurpose word meanings) is catalyzed by discursive patterns associated with verbal taboo and avoidance. And yet, as discussed at the beginning of the chapter, native speakers of Aboriginal Australian languages often hear the relative lack of denotational precision of mother-in-law speech as figurational of deference for the affinal others whose presence, in interaction or discourse, conditions the shift to avoidance speech in the first place. When attached to kinship avoidance, the semantic abstractness of the avoidance lexicon comes to be interpreted as a respectful and deferential sociolinguistic sign. Why is hyperpolysemy interpreted in this way? Through what mediations do language users come to hear semantic abstraction as a figure of the respectful muting of interpersonal interaction?

The relationship between language structures and language ideologies is mediated by what Benjamin Lee Whorf (2000) called "fashions of speaking." Whorf (2000) argued that cultural conceptualizations

> are not given in substantially the same form by experience to all men but depend upon the nature of the language or languages through the use of which they have been developed. They do not depend so much upon *any one system* (e.g., tense, or nouns) within the grammar as upon the ways of analyzing and reporting experience which have become fixed in the language as integrated "fashions of speaking" and which cut across the typical grammatical classifications, so that such a "fashion" may include lexical, morphological, syntactic, and otherwise systematically diverse means coordinated in a certain frame of consistency. (p. 214)

Fashions of speaking (like the epicene use of "men" in this passage!) are bridges between language-structural and cultural-ideological planes of signification. They point to the non-deterministic relationships between language structures and cultural conceptualizations, not the deterministic language–thought relationship often misattributed to the Whorfian position (e.g., McWhorter, 2014; Pullum, 1991): "It is these 'fashions of speaking' that Whorf attempted to relate to thought and not, as some have supposed, isolated, individual classifications" (Lucy, 1985, p. 78). It is the conceptual cobbling-together of disparate linguistic forms and structures – the grouping together of expression-types that do not constitute a *sui generis* grammatical category – which is the hallmark of a "fashion of speaking." The distributed character of fashions of speaking ("lexical, morphological, syntactic") underscores that language-ideological processes involve a creative and reflexive engagement of speakers with linguistic forms and structures, rather than a passive and unconscious transposition of grammatical categories onto cognitive ones. The disparate is diagnostic because it suggests that it is not language structure, pure and simple, but folk-conceptualization that associatively strings together distinct construction types and grammatical categories, investing them with consistent and continuous social meanings.

Whorf applied his method to the study of semantico-referential categories of language as these condition "worldview": "Fashions of speaking are language particular 'ways of putting things,' combining lexical and grammatical elements in a way that reflects not reality itself, but a linguistically mediated perspective on reality" (Slotta, 2015, p. 531). I follow Silverstein (1979), Rumsey (1990), and Slotta (2012, 2015, 2023) in extending this line and method of analysis to the domain of (meta) pragmatics. I show the central mediating role of fashions of speaking in the dialectical interplay between the semantic abstractness of word meanings *qua* language structure and the linguistic ideologies that interpret the meaningfulness of this structuring of the lexicon in distinct cultural locales.

Fashions of Not Speaking: Hypernymy as Hyperpoliteness in Mother-in-Law Languages

In Aboriginal Australia, there are a number of fashions of (not) speaking to affinal alters which constellate with lexicon asymmetry. The analogical "force" of this association motivates an interpretation of hyperpolysemy as polite "indirectness." Fashions of speaking (and signing) characteristic of affinal avoidance interaction include (a) *non-address of the other* – the use of "shill" addressees (e.g., rocks, trees, dogs, yamsticks, etc.) when covertly addressing taboo in-laws (e.g., Sommer, 2006, p. 109, on Kunjen), the use of undirected or musing speech (e.g., C. Goddard, 1992, p. 101, on Western Desert Language), the use of third-person pronouns to refer to covert addressee (e.g., McConvell, 1982, p. 93, on Gurindji); (b) *absorptive or allusive reference to the other* – the use of plural pronouns (e.g., Tsunoda, 1981, on Djaru), spatial demonstratives (e.g., Dench, 1991, p. 215, on Panyjima), trirelational kin terms (e.g., Garde, 2013, on Bininj Gunwok); and (c) *interactional non-ratification of the other* – the avoidance of eye contact and of body positioning that would suggest mutual coordination toward the ends of consummated discursive interaction, occasional use of head or face coverings (e.g., Thomson, 1935, p. 280, on Umpila) to avoid being a perceptible presence for the other, speaking softly, whispering or even keeping quiet altogether, sometimes complemented by the use of manual-visual signs (e.g., Hale m.s., cited in Kendon, 1988, p. 46, on Winda Winda). (See Chapters 5, 6, and 7 for more comprehensive discussions of these parameters.)

The use of the semantically abstract avoidance vocabulary comes to be seen as continuous with these tropes of interactional negation. A diagrammatic or configurational likeness is established between the core speech-act functions of address and reference; avoidance language describes entities and events in an analogous fashion to the manner in which avoidance relations send and receive messages to and from one another. Just as the actual target of interaction is far from being the explicit addressee, so too is the actual discourse referent at a remove from the semantic meaning that is denoted. The spatial metaphors are apt here; it is the framework of non-congruent, non-proximal and, in the best of all possible worlds, non-co-present bodies in space which has an orienting priority when informants characterize mother-in-law speech as "sideways" or "crosswise" (Guugu Yimidhirr; Haviland, 1979a, p. 369), "curved" or to the "side" (Wik; Thomson, 1935, p. 485), or even "turn tongue" (Wurrung; Dawson, 1881, p. 369). A range of tropes of interactional negation constellate with the taxonomically abstract lexical semantics of the avoidance vocabulary. This association analogically motivates and sets the interpretive conditions for the mother-in-law language to be "locally interpreted as [the] negation of discursive interaction, even though its formally 'indirect' denotational usage looks in principle no different from enregistered usages with very different ethnometapragmatic value" in other languages (Silverstein, 2010, p. 348).

Case Study: Detransitivization in Gun-gunma

Fashions of speaking thus mediate and channel the ideological construal of the language structure of lexicon asymmetry. But through this mediation they may also further feed back into discursive practices and linguistic structures. A case that illustrates this phenomenon is that of the Bunaba avoidance register Gun-gunma (Rumsey, 1982, 2000, personal communication), where the motivated iconicity between interactional and denotational "indirectness" finds further articulation in a morphosyntactic fashion of speaking: detransitivization.

The respectful character of Gun-gunma speech was mediated by features of both denotational and interactional textuality. On the denotational plane, Gun-gunma exhibited one-to-many lexical correspondences with everyday or *jada jada* ("straight") Bunaba. On the interactional plane, honorific non-singular number was used in pronominal reference to avoidance relations. Bunuba speakers offered different stereotypes about the intensity of interactional avoidances between the most focal avoidance relations, the *madjali-langu* "mother-in-law/son-in-law" pair. Some informants reported that they "had been permitted to speak to each other, provided they averted their gaze and spoke slowly and softly to each other" and in the avoidance register (Rumsey, 2000, p. 123). But one informant reported that this pair could not speak directly to one another "and that Gun.gunma was used when they were merely within ear-shot of each other" (p. 124).

A morphosyntactic fashion of speaking in the avoidance register – ubiquitous detransitivization – further reinforced the felt iconicity between interactionally (not fully speaking to) and denotationally (not fully speaking about) mediated, other-oriented restraint and respect. Bunaba verb phrases are composed of a preverb, which carries semantically specific information, followed by a verb root, which takes inflection. There are only 10 of these inflection-taking verb roots – five are transitive and five are intransitive. Although many of the preverbs are also employed in Gun-gunma, all 10 of the everyday inflecting verbs are replaced by one dedicated auxiliary verb (*mal*+NI) (see Tsunoda, 1981, for a similar pattern in Djaru). Crucially, this dedicated auxiliary is intransitive. Remarkably, then, preverbs that co-occur with transitive inflecting verbs in everyday Bunaba receive intransitive conjugation in Gun-gunma. A sentence like *julya ma* [squeeze transitive-verb. past.A = 3rd/O = 3rd] "he squeezed it" is rendered *julya malni* [squeeze instransitive-verb.past.s=3rd] "he squeezed" in avoidance speech (see Rumsey, 1982, p. 167 for this and other examples). The would-be transitive object can be expressed with a verb suffix that in everyday Bunaba is used to mark oblique arguments. The description of an action that would be rendered in everyday speech as involving an agent (A) acting directly upon a patient (O) is rendered as the action of a subject (S) which only obliquely affects a peripheral argument.

Detransitivization (or the reduction of verbal valence) is a fashion of speaking that reinforces the idea that denotational vagueness and the interactional manipulation of participant roles both "count as" the same thing – that is, that both "count as" deferential "indirection." The encoding of propositional roles in the denotational text (what is said) of Gun-gunma utterances presents a diagram of the social relationship that is enacted between affinal speakers and recipients in the interactional text (what is done). The systematic reduction of verbal valence in Gun-gunma is a "fixed ... fashion of speaking" (Whorf, 2000, p. 214) which sketches a semantic portrait of that which the use of the register interactionally achieves; it figurates the "oblique" and non-direct role relationship that interlocutors perform in the very discursive interaction where this style of speaking is employed. Observe that the iconicity between propositional roles and interactional roles operates independent of the actual topic of discourse. It is not just in speaking about avoidance relations, but in speaking about any topic, that a mother-in-law and son-in-law will employ detransitivization. Detransitivization is a non-referential icon (technically, diagram) of the speech producer/ speech recipient relationship.[8]

Gun-gunma detrasitivization is only one among a range of discursive practices that motivate the interpretation of lexicon asymmetry as a respectful withdrawing from interaction. As mentioned above, there are a broad range of fashions, not only of speaking but also of being-in-relation, that sculpt the deferential signification of "hypernymy-as-figurative-indexation-of-non-communication," as Michael Silverstein (2010, p. 348) described it for the case of *rambarr* "mother-in-law" speech in Worora (the Kimberley). Indeed, my analysis here follows quite closely that of Silverstein (2010, p. 347), who argued that "illocutionary acts of 'indirectness' must be studied through their local interpretations to see how very different can be the topologies of identity-in-interaction locally understood by them." Silverstein contrasts the hyperpolysemy of *rambarr* talk in Worora with scientific taxonomies and terminologies of the kind that I used above to gloss avoidance words (e.g., terms like *macropod* and *liquid*). These taxonomic labels enable learned discourses where "the idea of generalization over many specific categorial distinctions ... becomes discursively possible by virtue of deep taxonomies of superordinate hypernyms and their subordinate hyponyms" (p. 348). Whereas the use of scientific taxonomizing distinctions may have "the value of speaking a conceptually powerful, generalizing register" in academic contexts, it is clear that the taxonomically encompassing vocabulary of mother-in-law language is heard very differently in the Kimberley: "*rambarr* register is locally interpreted as negation of discursive interaction, even though its formally "indirect" denotation usage looks in principle no different from enregistered usages with very different ethnometapragmatic value" in scientific discourse (p. 348). The social-indexical meaningfulness of lexicon asymmetry is not transparent or inherent to the structure but is given contour and richness only in conjunction and association with a range of other registered signs, with which it textually coheres in discursive performance.

Hypernymy as Revelation: Lexicon Asymmetry in Male Initiate Registers

Systematic variation in the social meaningfulness of lexicon asymmetry can be seen by comparing mother-in-law languages, whose deployment is saturated with qualities of affinal restraint and respect, with avoidance registers anchored to male initiation. I will highlight two initiate registers: Lá'bì (as employed by Gbaya-Kara speakers) and Damin (as historically employed by Lardil speakers). Although these registers are similarly organized around lexical proscriptions and substitutions, they differ markedly from the mother-in-law languages both in how lexical asymmetries are interpreted and in how they are elaborated.

Among the Lardil there were two levels of male initiation (McKnight, 1999). The first involved the circumcision of all young men by classificatory fathers-in-law and initiated them into the *luruku* social category. The second type of initiation (into the *warama* category) was undergone only when the initiate himself felt a calling, and it involved subincision by classificatory brothers-in-law. Both rites entailed the use of avoidance codes; after both rites, initiates were expected to not use spoken Lardil in a wide range of interactions for up to years at a time. In fact, *luruku* were not to use oral communication of any kind; instead, they employed a sign language, Marlda Kangka ("hand talk"). The *warama* initiates, while similarly proscribed from speaking everyday Lardil, distinguished themselves from *luruku* in being able to employ the spoken register, Damin. In Damin, all word-forms of everyday Lardil are replaced by a vocabulary of no more than 150 words (Hale, 1982; Hale & Nash, 1997; see Fleming, 2017a, for a more in-depth treatment of this register).

The Lá'bì registers employed by Gbaya language groups were used during a year-long period of seclusion of male initiates at bush encampments built at a distance from local villages (Moñino, 1977; Vidal, 1976). During this time the use of the everyday language was tabooed for them; it was thought that using everyday speech would cause death. This symbolic sanction is motivated by the internal logic of the ritual complex: the opening rite of male initiation, making a scar on the belly of the initiand, stands for his death – in a staged murder, a ritual specialist "stabs" with a spear the initiates who are then "buried" under leaves (Vidal, 1976, pp. 121–7). This symbolic death proper to the timespace of initiation – the bush camp where the initiates will live for the next year – may become a real death should the signs of the everyday world, chief among them the Gbaya language, penetrate the world of the initiates.

In both cases, the acquisition of the speech register was figured as a revelatory event that entailed the ontological transformation of its (now competent) speakers. In both cases, the language acquisition process served to figurate the incorporation of a masculine essence that is embodied at levels of both phonic articulation and conceptual organization. In Damin, this is manifest quite literally in the training of the mouth to a phonological system marked in its articulatory alterity to everyday Lardil. The Damin phonological inventory includes ejectives, click consonants, and a number of other sound types (e.g., a bilabial trill and an ingressive voiceless lateral) not attested in any other Australian languages (Hale & Nash, 1997). In Gbaya, too, proper articulation seems to be held in high esteem; initiates are initially drilled in complex polynomial species names, lists of which they must recite without error lest they receive lashes to the back. And acquisition of the register requires learning not only the hyperpolysemous vocabulary but also complexly homonymous expressions.[9] Importantly, lexicon asymmetry means that the lexical semantics of the avoidance repertoire are saliently strange with respect to everyday speech. This allows the acquisition of the conceptual structure of the avoidance lexicon to serve as the self-evidence of the initiates' ontological transformation. This is one reason that the acquisition of these "special languages" (after van Gennep, 1908) is so effectively figurative of *rites de passage* – in both Lá'bì and Damin, the medium is transparently equated with the message, the ends of knowledge transfer with its means. To crack the code is to simultaneously receive the word (see Beidelman, 1997; Bellman, 1984; P. Boyer, 1980).

It is in terms of these cultural frameworks that we should understand some of the notable differences between initiate and mother-in-law languages. As illustrated above, both kinds of avoidance registers evince ethnobiological terminology that is highly divergent from everyday nomenclature, with monomial expressions labelling taxonomically superordinate classes rather than folk-specific or folk-generic categories. Nevertheless, there are also notable differences. In the male initiate registers but not in the mother-in-law registers, there is an elaboration of complex polynomial expressions for folk-generics. (Observe in Table 2.6 the absence of descriptive paraphrases for different species of macropods in Guugu-Yimidhirr brother-in-law language. Compare this to the elaboration of descriptive paraphrases for different species of birds in Lá'bì or for shellfish in Damin.) This difference now comes into focus.

The lack of periphrastic precision characteristic of mother-in-law speech is a denotational icon of the non-consummation of interaction that is the valued ideal of affinal talk. In the Gun-gunma conversations that Rumsey (1982, p. 173) staged between Bunaba speakers, there was "little or no use ... made of paraphrase (or periphrasis) as a way of giving more explicit senses to the [Gun-gunma] words." Utterances were maximally vague – the specific reference of the hyperpolysemous Gungunma words had to be divined by speech recipients. For Bunaba as for Worora speakers, "to speak in mother-in-law register ... is *to speak with suppressed denotational delicacy (differential specificity)*, to speak allusively, 'hintingly,' we might say, about what, precisely, might be the communicative focus and referential and predicational purport of discourse. The local understanding is of minimal, necessary communication that hardly counts, then, as communication at all" (Silverstein, 2010, p. 348). This interpretation is motivated by and harmonizes with tropes of interactional negation negotiated through the manipulation of pronominal reference and the broader signalling of speech participation (for more in-depth discussion, see Chapters 5 and 7). Through these tropes the avoidance relation, "the very target of the communication[, is] rendered the outside 'audience' or overhearer" (p. 348). This ideologically elaborated preference for fostering "denotational delicacy" as a sign of deference feeds back into the structure of the avoidance lexicon, ensuring the relative under-elaboration of polynomial expressions for folk-generics.

For both Gbaya and Lardil speakers, contrastingly, the male initiate register is ritually figured as a depository of exclusive masculine knowledge revealed in and through its acquisition. The elaboration of descriptive paraphrases for taxonomically lower-order semantic concepts, like folk-generic taxa, serves to figurate the initiate languages as a store of just such knowledge. These complex, descriptive paraphrases, often because of the non-transparency of the relationship between the descriptive phrase and its denotation, function as brain teasers – they are linguistic models that produce in miniature the qualitative cognitive and phenomenological experience that male initiation, at a more global scale, is understood to effectuate. They entreat and entrain initiates to search out the connections hidden behind linguistic appearances (P. Boyer, 1980, p. 46).

It is notable that among both the Lardil and the Gbaya, it is precisely these compositional, many-word expressions employed to denote lower-order taxa that have pride of place in the highly ritualized and dramaturgically staged socialization of initiates to Damin and Lá'bì, respectively. In Damin it is a list of animal terms (McKnight, 1999, p. 26) and in Lá'bì the ethnobotanical terminology (Vidal, 1976, pp. 127, 136) that are the first elements of the registers taught to initiates.[10] The use of componentially complex expressions as the initial means of exposing the initiates to the register involves a double hermeneutic challenge. The initiate must realize the relationship between the term and its reference or denotation (i.e., its extension) but in doing this he must also decompose the complex phrase into its minimal and highly abstract sense-bearing units (i.e., its intension). Initiates must make sense out of the act of reference.

Constellating Language in Culture

In this and the previous chapter I have offered an overview of avoidance registers employed in specific social contexts, showing how they constitute a cross-culturally convergent sociolinguistic kind. These context-dependent avoidance registers are comparable to one another at levels of linguistic structure, usage, and ideology. In the various registers that I have showcased – from Kalam's *alŋaw mnm* to Buru's *li garan* to Dyirbal's Jalnguy to Gbaya-Kara's Lá'bì – specialized languages are framed by performativist ideologies of language; avoidance registers serve to contain and circumvent the negatively valued performative consequences of using everyday speech. However, as I showed in the previous chapter, proscriptive metadiscourses that frame everyday language as dangerous, destructive, or disrespectful only filter out words and expressions as targets for censure. This filtering process correspondingly affects the linguistic structuring of avoidance registers; avoidance repertoires are composed exclusively of words and expressions. As shown in this chapter, where the number of everyday words proscribed in avoidance contexts becomes very large, discursive practices of avoidance tend to stretch and extend the semantic meanings of a core vocabulary of already "safe" avoidance words. This once again feeds back into the linguistic structuring of the registers, resulting in the hyperpolysemy of the avoidance lexicon; avoidance words tend to have highly abstract and taxonomically encompassing lexical semantics in comparison to everyday words.

In the last sections of this chapter, I have focused on how hyperpolysemy is interpreted – more accurately, how it constellates – differently in different classes of cases. In mother-in-law languages, many-to-one lexical correspondences are fostered as a sign of interactional negation and restraint. Contrastingly, in the male initiate languages these semantic asymmetries are exploited toward the ends of creating a compositional complexity at the level of the code that makes language the privileged diagram of masculine esoteric knowledge and its mastery. Here, fashions of speaking and other figurations of what is involved in register use play a crucial mediating role in determining the social significance of hyperpolysemy. Through such fashions of speaking, language structures, patterns of discursive usage, and socially standardized understandings of what the register represents and achieves constellate in distinct ways.

The term *constellation* seems a particularly apt appellation. A celestial constellation is a grouping of stars that have no necessary connection to one another besides their proximity in the night sky as seen from Earth. Further, their imputed unity is actualized in their collectively forming a recognizable and named figure – that is, they are unified in and through their symbolization (a whole made up of the stellar parts). The case studies that I showcase throughout this book are analogously constellated; a disparate set of linguistic forms, discursive practices, and sociocultural preoccupations come to be seen (i.e., reflexively apprehended), through processes of enregisterment, as a unified gestalt figure. Here I have focused on how mother-in-law languages constitute a particular sociolinguistic constellation. Abstract lexical semantics – a widely attested end-product of verbal taboo and avoidance – constellates with interactional practices of avoidance in such a way as to be apperceived as the respectful, discursive non-impingement upon particular categories of kin.

PART TWO

The Sounds of Reference: Name Taboos

Chapter Three

Name Registers: A Sociolinguistic Kind

In rural Mongolia, before the collectivization of the 1950s, married women were expected to avoid uttering the names of their *xadamud* or senior male in-laws (i.e., HeB, HF, HFB, HFF) (Humphrey, 1978, pp. 91–2).[1] Mongolian children are often bestowed with names – like "Beauty," "Reason," "Strength," "Flowering," "Light," "Gold," or "Steel" – which it is hoped will imbue them with positive qualities (Hamayon, 1979). Importantly, the everyday words from which names were drawn were also tabooed in the speech of daughters-in-law. In some cases, near-homophones might additionally be proscribed. Caroline Humphrey (1978, p. 94) gives the example of a daughter-in-law who avoided her mother-in-law's name, Tegsh, its homophone *tegsh* "level," and the near-homophone *tevsh* "wooden platter," replacing the latter with *ix tavag* "large bowl." A few examples of name-conditioned lexical avoidances are provided in Table 3.1.

Name registers are built up out of these practices of name and homophone avoidance and substitution. These are named linguistic varieties – in Oirat (Mongolic), for instance, words employed to avoid uttering the names or the homophones of the names of one's husband's senior kin were called *berlsn üg* "words for daughters-in-law" (Birtalan, 2003, p. 227). Mongolic name and homophone avoidance was ideologically framed as an honorific practice, as an enactment of *xündetgel* "respect" (Hamayon, 1979, p. 127). Name-related linguistic avoidances co-occurred with numerous other, similarly respectful, non-linguistic restrictions on the comportment of the daughter-in-law who, after marriage, came to live in the yurt of her husband's parents. For instance, a daughter-in-law was supposed to keep to the southeast quadrant of the yurt – the northern half being consider the "higher" and revered side, and the west the men's side (Humphrey, 1974). And she wasn't supposed to walk around the outside of the yurt along its north side. Keeping

Table 3.1. Some examples of name and homophone taboos in Mongolian

Tabooed name	Homophone	Replacement form
Galzuud	*gal* "fire"	*tsutsal* "spark"
Sandag	*saya* "million"	*toot* "having number"
Shar	*shar* "yellow"	*angir* "a species of yellow duck"
Bayadaa	*bayan* "rich"	*uyen* "ermine"
Xarzuu	*xar* "black"	*bargaan* "darkish, obscure"
Tegsh	*tevsh* "wooden platter"	*ix tavag* "large bowl"
negative repertoire		positive repertoire

Source: Humphrey (1978).

with this spatial code, she was never supposed to be positioned to the north of her parents-in-law and, in parallel, her personal possessions were not supposed to be placed to the north of, or higher than, those of her parents-in-law. She could not eat the first servings of food or drink – called *deéz*, literally "the top" – but was served food last, and she could not eat these leftovers in front of her parents-in-law (Hamayon & Bassanoff, 1973, p. 50). In the presence of her parents-in-law, the daughter-in-law's head and feet were supposed always to be covered, and her hair was coiffed. Careful never to turn her back on her parents-in-law, she would leave the yurt backwards.

Name and homophone avoidance was thus only one component part of a broader semiotic range of registered avoidances indexical of an in-marrying bride's respect for members of her husband's family. Nevertheless, name-based avoidances have a special and emblematic status among the larger suite of deference routines.

> Tous ces interdits n'assombrissent pas également l'horizon journalier de la belle-fille : la coutume a établi une sorte de hiérarchie, attribuant au tabou sur le nom des beaux-parents la place prépondérante. C'est lui qui figure immanquablement en tête des interdits. [All of the these avoidances did not cast the same shadow on the daily horizon of the daughter-in-law: convention established a sort of hierarchy, attributing to the taboo on the name of the parents-in-law a dominant place. It is this taboo which inevitably appears at the head of the prohibitions.] (Hamayon & Bassanoff, 1973, p. 52)

Why is the name taboo primordial? For one thing, the link between personal names and their referents means that discursive reverence enacted in the phonic surround of the name can function as a sign of affinal respect in all contexts, not just when a daughter-in-law is in the presence of her parents-in-law. Indeed, with important caveats, kinship-keyed name registers like this one are normatively expected to be employed in all social contexts. Of course, felt obligation to employ avoidance forms may vary, being particularly heightened in the co-presence of the avoidance target or of their close natal kin or allies. (Paul Michael Taylor, 1990, for instance, observes that Tobelo [Papuan; Halmahera] are less strict about employing *hohono* "substitution words said to avoid saying an in-law name" when "no affected in-laws are present" [pp. 19–20].) In ideological conceptualization, however, the performativity of names is understood to be, like their reference, invariant or "rigid" across discourse contexts – a parallel that I will emphasize in accounting for this sociolinguistic kind in the next chapter. This indexical link between name and person also means that name avoidance serves as a felicitous iconic-indexical or emblem of affinal respect and restraint. Just as a daughter-in-law should not touch possessions that belong to her father-in-law, nor enter his quadrant of the yurt, so too does she respect him by avoiding the sound shapes which make up the name that is attached to him. By showing respect for his name she (iconically) figurates, but also actually (indexically) enacts, respect for his person.

Name registers, like Oirat "words for daughters-in-law," are thus a special kind of honorific register – their use enacts a speaker's deference toward another person. And yet name registers are distinctive among honorific registers in their deference focus properties (after Agha, 1998). Deference focus characterizes the ways in which an honorific specifies the persons whose relationship it marks and mediates as a function of their interactional role inhabitance. (It is a special kind of "indexical focus," a topic discussed in greater depth in Chapter 8.) Honorifics express a relationship between some origo-of-deference (the "giver" of respect) and some target-of-deference (the "recipient" of respect). The origo and target of an honorific are conventionally associated with particular interactional roles. Typically, the origo-of-deference is the person occupying the speaker-role, and the target-of-deference is the person occupying either the addressee- or referent-role (Agha, 1993; Comrie, 1976; Levinson, 1983). Name registers exhibit yet another kind of deference focus, one that Irvine (2009) calls "remote focus": Tokens of avoidance words enact respect toward social alters who need neither be discourse recipients (i.e., addressees, bystanders) nor discourse referents. To see this point, consider the social pragmatics of a homophone like *tevsh* "wooden platter," listed in Table 3.1. Its capacity to performatively disrespect a senior in-law is not based in its lexical semantics or its discourse reference – it is not because one refers, for instance, to a wooden platter owned by an affine that the avoidance term is employed.[2] Rather, pragmatic function is ideologically rationalized in terms of the phonological shape of the avoided lexeme: The word sounds similar to (is an echo of) the name of the person who is deferred to through its avoidance (after Mitchell, 2018, on the "allusive reference" of the homophone to the taboo in-law).

Sociolinguistic Variation in Name Registers: Social Domain, Indexical Orders, and Sociopragmatic Markedness

Name registers like Mongolian daughter-in-law speech are found all over the world. Indeed, J.G. Frazer (1958) catalogued taboos of this kind more than a century ago. Name registers are attested in three distinct sociological domains. First, they are employed in the indexing of kinship relationships, prototypically in-law relationships but sometimes also consanguineal ones (see, for example, Wallace, 1969, p. 71, on Katu; Kintz, 1986, p. 38, on Fulani). Second, they are incorporated into honorific repertoires employed in showing respect to individuals at the top-and-centre of sociocentric hierarchies (see, for example, Sibree, 1892, p. 226, on Malagasy; Oliver, 2002, pp. 40–1, on Tahitian). Third, they are widely attested as a component part of mourning practices, either during a delimited period of time after the death of an individual or as part of a more general reverence toward ancestors (see, for example, Nash & Simpson, 1981, on Central Australia; Keesing and Fifi'i, 1969, on Kwaio).

In each of these arenas there is important variation in the set of persons who are supposed to employ the register – that is, in the **social domain** of the register (after Agha, 2003).[3] Sometimes avoidance repertoires are shared by village settlements or even by all members of larger state-based polities. For instance, in the Society Islands, *pii* "chiefly name taboo" involved avoidance of the chief's name and of near-homophones (Crowley & Bowern, 2010, p. 209). During the reign of Pomare I, a chief in northwest Tahiti, words contained "in" that name were widely tabooed: "In order to avoid common use of the syllables that make up 'Pomare' – which meant 'night' (*po*) and 'cough' (*mare*), *rui* became the common name for 'night' and *hota* for 'cough.' Violations of the avoidance were severely punished. The substitutes prevailed at least during Pomare's chieftainship and at least among his subjects" (Oliver, 2002, pp. 40–1). In the case of Tahitian *pii*, name registers are composed of sociolectal repertoires employed by all members of a speech community. So, for instance, everyone who employed the register used *rui* as a substitute for *po*. In kinship-anchored name registers, however, the names and associated homophones that individuals should avoid are specific to their particular kinship relations. Negative and positive repertoires may be relatively idiolectal, with particular avoidance forms being shared only between co-affines of a specific family.

There is rich and structured variation in the social domain of individuals normatively expected to employ avoidance forms and correspondingly in the degree to which the negative and positive repertoires of name registers are shared across communities of practice. To discuss this variation in as complete a manner as possible would take us too far afield from the core set of arguments and interventions that I seek to make in this book. Rather than intensively explore the attested space of possibilities, here I will showcase a few important dimensions of sociolinguistic variation, with a focus on name registers that mediate kinship relationship. I hope these observations may inform the work of historical linguists or others concerned with the relationship between sociolinguistic alternations and language change. I exemplify the issues concerned by comparing the name registers found in some Austronesian languages of island Melanesia: V'ënen Taut (formerly "Big Nambas"), on the one hand, and Sengseng and Kaulong, on the other.

Case Study: Gendered Respect Registers in Vënen Taut (Malekula)

Speakers of V'ënen Taut (Malekula, Vanuatu; aka "Big Nambas") historically employed a rich ensemble of honorific words and gestures in the mediation of both kinship relationship and chiefly hierarchy. This "extensive catena of avoidance and honorific terms ... had to be employed by women only" (Fox, 1996, p. 375). Drawing upon ethnographies conducted in the 1930s and 1940s, I first discuss practices of affinal avoidance, including name avoidance. I then specifically focus on the analogies between affinal avoidance and chiefly honorific speech and gesture, showing how these intertextual connections influenced the composition of name register repertoires.

V'ënen Taut women were traditionally married at a young age. Though the marriage would be consummated much later, "girls marry when they are very young and long before puberty are sent afar to be brought up by the mother of their future husband" (Guiart, 1953, p. 440). This new residential context was one in which their actions – both linguistic and non-linguistic – were severely constrained. A married woman was normatively expected to avoid the names and associated homophones of a range of her male in-laws: a husband's father (HF), husband's father's brother (HFB), husband's elder brother (HeB), and husband's patrilateral cousins (Fox, 1996, p. 377). These avoidances conditioned the emergence of elaborate idiolectal name registers.

Name registers were only one component of V'ënen Taut in-law avoidance practices. A woman not only avoided affinal names; she also avoided sharing food with, being seen by, or otherwise being in the presence of, her male affines. There were important gestural components to avoidance; women crouched and covered their faces with a "grass-veil" (Cheesman, 1933, p. 201) in front of male in-laws. If a woman encountered her husband's brother or father she would "pull down over her face the part of her hair mat designed for this purpose [baisser sur son visage la partie de sa natte coiffure disposée à cet effet]" (Guiart, 1952, p. 158).[4] The strictures of these interpersonal avoidances even affected settlement organization and house architecture. Because they could not be in the presence of their relatives' spouses, fathers, sons, and brothers typically did not set up residences close by one another, or if they did they made sure that they were "separated by a high fence without any opening" (Guiart, 1953, p. 441). Ubiquitous "wild cane fences" and the miniature, three-foot high openings to dwellings, gave local hamlets a labyrinthine feel: "One could literally get lost in the maze of small enclosures surrounded by plaited wild cane fences, in which the individual houses are" (Guiart, 1953, p. 441).

The kinship-keyed name registers found their complement in a referent-focal honorific register used in reference to (and perhaps only in addressing) the person of the chief.[5] The small vocabulary provided in Guiart (1952, p. 160) suggests parallels to the chiefly vocabularies of Polynesia (Fleming, 2016). As with, for instance, Samoan and Tongan chiefly vocabularies, there are special terms for body-part terms and personal appurtenances (e.g., elbow, head, leg, knife). And substitute expressions sometimes involve allusive or metaphorical reference (e.g., *bwetem* "head" becomes *noteya ram* "for your hair"; *naveyam* "penis sheath [cf. Bislama, *nambas*]" becomes *nil nam* "your decoration"). This vocabulary was employed only by women. Importantly, the chiefly vocabulary as well as the honorific gestures that women enacted in the presence of chiefs were also employed by a mother in addressing her son:

> La mère ne peut se lever tant que son fils adulte est assis, ni marcher auprès de lui. Si la mère et le fils se rencontrent sur un sentier, la mère se courbe et passe en gémissant, lui donnant ainsi les honneurs dus normalement à un chef. [A mother may not rise while her adult son is seated, nor walk beside him. If a mother and her son meet on a footpath, the mother bends over and passes by with a groan, giving him the honors normally due to a chief.] (Guiart, 1952, p. 160)

Table 3.2. Sociopragmatic markedness of avoidance vocabulary in V'ënen Taut

Form is used only in avoidance speech	Form is used in avoidance and non-avoidance speech
-mən- "press down on" -palv- "to trick" nirah "eye" tivrar "fire"	-uln- "let go of" -p'e- "watch" -p'las- "stick together" səvs nai "piece of wood"
sociopragmatically marked	sociopragmatically unmarked

Source: Fox (1996, pp. 379–81).

In summary, both chiefly and kinship respect were highly gendered. The social domain of honorific and avoidance register users was exclusively composed of women. As I now show, this gendering in the social domain of register users – Helen Fox (1996) called it "an honorific sub-dialect used among Big Nambas women" – has important consequences for the patterning and composition of V'ënen Taut avoidance vocabularies.

Table 3.2 provides a sample of avoidance forms employed by at least some women in substituting for the homophone of a tabooed affinal name. Importantly, as Fox (1996) carefully demonstrates, the words and expressions that substitute for the tabooed homophones of the names of male affines are of two kinds. First, there is a sociopragmatically *unmarked* avoidance vocabulary consisting of words and expressions that are also employed in the everyday language, perhaps with slightly changed meanings. For instance, the everyday expression *sevs nai* "piece of wood" substitutes for the everyday word *napel* "seat" in the idiolect of a speaker whose taboo relation's name is *Tunapel*. The use of the lexical form *sevs nai* is not uniquely employed in avoidance speech (although the semantic extension of the term to denote seats is specific to avoidance speech). Second, there is a sociopragmatically *marked* avoidance vocabulary consisting of words that are only ever employed in avoidance speech. For instance, the word *nirah* "eye" is used to replace the everyday word *m'ate-* "eye" by a speaker who has a taboo relation named *M'aten*. Unlike *sevs nai*, the lexical form *nirah* is not employed in everyday speech; it is employed only in avoidance speech. The word *nirah* is sociopragmatically marked in the sense that tokens of it always invoke affinal respect regardless the context of their occurrence.

Table 3.2 illustrates the distinction between marked and unmarked avoidance vocabulary. Although I have included only four examples of each type in the table, the vast majority of homophone substitutes in V'ënen Taut are sociopragmatically marked forms employed exclusively in avoidance speech (see word lists in Fox, 1996).

Why does V'ënen Taut avoidance vocabulary tend to be sociopragmatically marked? It seems almost certain that this is related to the overall gendering of respectful speech and gesture in V'ënen Taut society. Both affinal avoidance and chiefly honorific speech are employed only by women. Women are always the origos-of-deference. And men (whether chiefs, sons, or male affines) are always the targets-of-deference. Women give deference, and men receive it.[6] Respectful speech and gesture thus figurated masculine domination – a theme that was pronounced also in "Big Nambas" sociopolitical organization (Allen, 1984b).

In understanding the sociopragmatic markedness of avoidance terms, I infer a diachronic sequence whereby avoidance vocabulary items have accrued a *second-order*, speaker-focal, feminine-gender indexing value. Indexical orders involve overlapping cultural (metapragmatic) framings of the same pragmatic signal, where "higher"-order framings historically emerge through the, often institutionalized, rationalization of "lower" ones (Silverstein, 2003). In V'ënen Taut, the *first-order* indexical function of name and homophone avoidance is a relational one – it enacts affinal respect. But the rationalization of respect as a gendered practice has led to the emergence of a *second-order* "reading" of respect register use as indexical of women. Because avoidance forms were stereotypically associated with feminine social gender and figurational of social subordination, male speakers – who traditionally strove to achieve higher and higher, exclusively masculine, graded ranks through ever more conspicuous pig-sacrifices (Allen, 1984b) – likely avoided using these shibboleths of avoidance speech. If sexual difference thematized respect, being respectful could also be feminizing. The avoidance of avoidance forms by male speakers resulted in sociopragmatically unmarked words becoming sociopragmatically marked. Whether or not this scenario accurately reflects the actual pathway of development, the link between the markedness of repertoire items and the feminine gendering of avoidance practice is robustly attested elsewhere (see, for instance, the discussion below of Afro-Eurasian daughter-in-law registers). The more general point is the following: Sociopragmatic markedness of avoidance vocabulary is strongly correlated with salient sociological partitioning in the social domain of register users.

Case Study: Marid Tok *in Sengseng and Kaulong (New Britain)*

For a parallel example, I turn to Sengseng and Kaulong, two neighbouring Austronesian languages groups of New Britain which were studied in partnership by Ann Chowning (1985) and Jane Goodale (1980,

1995), respectively. Unlike V'ënen Taut, avoidance practice in these two language groups is not gendered. Both wives and husbands avoid the names and homophones of the names of a wide range of their spouse's cognatic kin or *poididuan* ("all related"). Building upon its first-order indexical value of expressing affinal respect, avoidance speech has acquired a second-order value as an emblem of the married status of the speaker. Using the lingua franca Tok Pisin, Kaulong informants call the register *marid tok*, or "the language of the married" (Goodale, 1995, p. 168). This metapragmatic framing of the name register as a shibboleth of marital status reflects salient local understandings of sex and sexuality. As Goodale (1980) demonstrates, the primary ontological cut that avoidance effects in Kaulong life is a division between the sexually active and the virginal. Sex is understood to cause the wasting away and eventual death of the body, especially for men. A terror of "sexual contamination by women" (Chowning, 1980, p. 14) may lead men to put off getting married until well into their thirties. And newly married couples typically establish a spatially isolated, new residence at a distance from the *bi-* "places" of their cognatic kin, settlements that their new spouse must studiously avoid.

Once again, a culturally salient sociological partitioning of the social domain of users of the name register is associated with the sociopragmatic markedness of avoidance forms: "In consequence of the name tabus, the Sengseng (and Kaulong) languages contain lexical items called 'married talk,' substitutes for many common words. The people actually describe the situation as if there are two distinct languages separating the single from the married, and as if all the married use 'married talk.' In fact, a married person need not use the substitute form unless it appears in the name of a tabu affine, *though many do so as a matter of course*" (Chowning, 1985, p. 184; italics added). Married persons may overproduce avoidance forms, employing not only substitute forms related to the names of their own in-laws but also a wider set of shibboleths of *marid tok*. Chowning (1985, p. 194) suggests that this hypertrophied "use of the 'married' forms [may be] undertaken ... to emphasise the gulf" between "the single and the married." From these data, I infer that the framing of avoidance speech as an index of speaker's marital/sexual status has fed back into the discursive patterning (i.e., the overproduction of *marid tok*) and linguistic structuring (i.e., the markedness of substitute vocabulary) of the avoidance register.[7]

Summary: Name Taboo and Language Change

A number of historical linguists have posited that name and homophone avoidance may lead either to the development of extensive synchronic sets of synonyms or to the diachronic replacement of lexical items (Twana: Elmendorf, 1951; Inuit: Bergsland & Vogt, 1962; Kwaio: Keesing & Fifi'i, 1969; Sengseng: Chowning, 1985; Kewa: Franklin, 1972; Tehuelche: Suárez, 1971; for Polynesian languages, see Dyen, 1963; for Australian languages, see Dixon, 1980; see the review in Michael, 2014). Word taboos may lead to the loss of lexical forms within a language community or stimulate word borrowing from neighbouring languages in order to replace proscribed forms. Historical linguists have suggested that these processes may muddy measures of genealogical relatedness between languages by interfering with cognate counts. Unfortunately, the kind of co-variation that we have just exemplified between the social domain of avoidance and sociopragmatic markedness of replacement vocabulary items has not been sufficiently appreciated in this literature.

Notably, some of the best candidates for detecting the kind of diachronic lexical replacement most of interest to the historical linguist are post-mortem name taboos, and in particular those cases of post-mortem taboos where all members of the speech community are normatively expected to avoid homophones of the names of the deceased (e.g., Tehuelche [Chonan; Argentina]: Suárez, 1971; Greenlandic Inuit: Bergsland & Vogt, 1962; for a particularly poignant case, see I. Goddard, 1979, pp. 359–63, on Tonkawa). Just as with kinship-keyed name registers, there is variation in the social domain of register use in cases of post-mortem name taboos. Sometimes homophone avoidance is limited only to members of the local kin group (e.g., Kiowa Apache: Opler & Bittle, 1961), and affects the speech of others only when they are in the presence of close kin of the deceased.[8] Nevertheless, there are cases of post-mortem name registers where word tabooing affects entire communities of speakers. Crucially, it is in these cases that avoidance vocabulary is sociopragmatically unmarked and becomes fully integrated into the everyday lexicon.

As a last, if highly telegraphed, example, take the case of Kwaio (Malaita; Solomon Islands) post-mortem name taboo, thickly described by Roger Keesing and Jonathan Fifi'i (1969). Name registers in Kwaio mediate speakers' reverential relations with *adalo* "ancestor spirits." Although Kwaio avoid referring to all of their deceased lineal ancestors by name, it is only well-established *adalo* whose names condition homophone avoidance.

Historically, homophone tabooing in Kwaio emerged as a quite explicitly codified practice among the direct descendants of an *adalo*. For instance, word-tabooing may be initiated by divination which retrodictively reveals that a misfortune which has befallen the descendants of an *adalo* has resulted from that *adalo* being angered by the use of a homophone of his or her name. In this first stage of word-tabooing there is a salient sociological partitioning in the social domain of the avoidance form – the avoidance form is used by lineal descendants of the *adalo*, who is respected through its use. However, as the reputation of an *adalo* grows, homophones of his or her name may come to be avoided by all members of a local settlement. Indeed, homophones of the names of the most "sacred" (*abu*, cf. Oceanic *tapu*) ancestor spirits will be avoided by everyone living in a wide swath of geographically contiguous settlements. In this second stage of word-tabooing, the structural opposition between the avoidance form and the everyday form is eroded (cf. Lévi-Strauss, 2021, on Hart, 1930, on Tiwi [Australia] post-mortem name taboos). The avoidance form becomes a victim of its own success – once adopted by all members of a community of practice, the avoidance form becomes sociopragmatically unmarked, for it has effectively become the everyday form.

It is no accident that it is cases of post-mortem name and homophone avoidance that are most strongly correlated with vocabulary replacement. In a subset of these cases, there is little or no partitioning in the social domain of register users, causing avoidance forms to be sociopragmatically unmarked. In-law name taboos, contrastingly, typically exhibit the kind of rich sociopragmatic variation in synchronic practice which is most of interest to sociolinguists and linguistic anthropologists. Historical linguists need to think about the interaction of these parameters in modelling taboo-motivated language change.

Kinship and the Sociopragmatics of Naming

Names and naming are some of the most common loci of sociopragmatic alternations in language (R. Brown & Ford, 1961; Enfield & Stivers, 2007). Kinship relations are no exception to this generalization. Drawing primarily on ethnographic monographs, James Slotta and I surveyed norms of address between consanguineal kin in more than 80 distinct language communities (Fleming & Slotta, 2018). We found that there were remarkable cross-cultural parallels in how the alternation between kin terms and names is mobilized in vocative address to consanguineal kin.

In many societies, names are simply inappropriate in all acts of kin address. This is commonly the pattern in Aboriginal Australia. Indeed, Joe Blythe (2013) has convincingly argued that the avoidance of names is one motivation for the development of pronominal forms that categorize non-singular referents by relative generation or by relative-moiety membership and for the elaboration of elaborate trirelational kin-term sets. A similar default use of kin terms in all address between kin was also attested in most of the Native American language groups in our sample.

Contrastingly, in the vast majority of the sampled language groups from Europe, Asia, and Africa, names are appropriately employed, but only in addressing junior kin. In these cases, names and kin terms enter into an age-stratified sociopragmatic alternation: seniors address juniors with names, or optionally with kin terms, and juniors avoid using names in addressing senior kin, opting for kin terms instead. This asymmetric pattern of address is reminiscent of R. Brown and Gilman's (1960) "power" dynamic, where higher-status individuals employ non-honorific pronouns or omit titles in addressing lower-status individuals, who respond with honorific pronouns or titles. Names are also – probably even more often – avoided in address between in-laws. In these cases, restrictions are more often reciprocal. Among the Huaulu (Seram, Indonesia), for instance, asymmetric rights to use names are conditioned by relative age among natal kin. Meanwhile, kin through marriage reciprocally avoid one another's names (Valeri, 2000).

In summary, the use of a name is not merely a means of efficiently referring to another. Name use is also a socially evaluated speech act reflective and constitutive of the character and content of the social relationship between the speaker and the referent. It is not hard to fathom why this is the case. Silverstein (1979, 1981) argued that speakers' metalinguistic awareness is biased toward the referential functions of language. This biasing of metapragmatic awareness contours the development of honorific language, as well as other socially indexical linguistic formulae (e.g., speech-act verbs). In essence, the nonreferential enactment of deference to an other is conflated with, or assimilated to, the act of referring to that individual. Errington (1985) draws on evidence from the elaborate honorific repertoires of Javanese to show that person-referring expressions have particular "pragmatic salience" as loci of honorific alternations. Agha (2007) provides a large-scale comparative survey of honorific registers which confirms this earlier work: Honorifics that signal the deference entitlements of the referent are much more widespread and common than honorifics that signal deference to any other interactional role. Personal names, as linguistic forms that referentially pick out particular persons, are thus prime candidates for sociopragmatic alternations.

In name registers, however, the sociopragmatics of naming are elaborated or expanded in ways not seen in those cases – like that of American English (Schneider & Homans, 1955, p. 1199) – where it is considered

Table 3.3. True homophone avoidance on the Xingu River (Brazil)

Name	Homophone	Gloss	Language	Source
Tafitse	*tafitse*	"macaw"	Kalapalo	Basso (2007, p. 171)
Tulupi	*tulupi*	"fish species"	Wauja	Ball (2015, p. 339)
Yanumaka	*yanumaka*	"jaguar"	Wauja	Ball (2015, p. 350)
Yapu	*yapu*	"stingray"	Mehinaku	Gregor (1977, p. 284)
Epyu	*epyu*	"turtle"	Mehinaku	Gregor (1977, p. 284)

impolite to address parents by name. In V'ënen Taut or Mongolian, it is not just the use of the name in referring to a particular individual that is viewed as impolite; words that merely evoke the sound shape of the name may similarly cause offence.

There is quite a bit of variation cross-linguistically in what kinds of phonological similarity with a name is sufficient for a word to come to be proscribed in name registers. At the one extreme are cases like Kambaata (Treis, 2005), where mere identity of one syllable between the name of an affine and some given word can be sufficient to condition lexical avoidance. For instance, a woman whose mother-in-law is called *Caa'mmíse* avoids "*cancanáta* 'shouting, noise of human voices, chatter'" (Treis, 2005, p. 295), as well as many other words beginning #ca.

In other languages-in-culture, it is only the true homophones of a personal name that are proscribed. In the languages of the Xingu River area of Brazil, even the most pronounced homophone avoidance affects only the lexical root from which the personal name of an affine is formed (see Table 3.3). The circumscription of lexical avoidance to the true homophone of the personal name is related to naming customs.[9] Wauja bear names that are homonymous with the name of a plant or animal species (Ball, 2015, p. 338). Mehinaku names are homonymous with the names of "animals, household objects, and natural events" (Gregor, 1977, p. 284). Correspondingly, a man whose father-in-law is called Yapu will avoid *yapu* "stingray" but not other similar-sounding but non-identical forms.

Importantly, the set of words that are tabooed in name registers is always a conventionalized one. Sometimes words that might be expected on purely phonetic criteria to be tabooed are not avoided (see, e.g., Florey & Bolton, 1997, p. 47). And, just as we saw in Chapter 1 for context-independent registers, it is only words that are incorporated into the negative repertoire of name registers; bound morphemes that bear a phonological resemblance to affinal names, like the noun-class prefixes in Nguni languages, are not targets of avoidance. In these ways, as Anne Storch (2017) has shown, name registers differ markedly from "ludlings," or play languages, which target surface phonological strings (Laycock, 1972). Name taboos do not automatically filter phonological strings but rather condition the avoidance of a registered set of lexemes. Indeed, lexical substitutes for (near-)homophones of a name generally have the same morphosyntactic properties (e.g., noun-class assignment) of the word forms for which they substitute (Mous, 2001).[10] In summary, the tabooing of phonologically iconic words is an explicit and reflexive process that may be the subject of debate and contestation (e.g., Elmendorf, 1951; Keesing & Fifi'i, 1969), not the automatic effect of phonetic "contagion."

I save for the next chapter further discussion of variability in the range of similar-sounding words that become conventionalized targets of avoidance in name registers. In that context we will see how, culture-internally, variability in the range of (near-)homophone avoidance functions as an analogue sign of interpersonal respect and restraint.

Kinship-Keyed Name Registers: A Global Sample

Name and homophone avoidance registers have a remarkably wide cross-cultural distribution. In this and the following subsection I survey the global distribution of name registers and highlight important differences in the sociological patterning of name registers in the Circum-Pacific (Native Americas and Oceania) as opposed to Afro-Eurasia. (These two regions are reviewed in the top and bottom halves, respectively, of Table 3.4.)

As illustrated in Table 3.4, name and homophone avoidance registers tied to in-law relationships are attested on all continents except for Europe and Australia.[11] Table 3.4 is by no means an exhaustive sample. Cases in Oceania, in particular, are vastly underrepresented. Far and away the most robust loci of name and homophone avoidance of this type are the Austronesian and Papuan languages of Island Southeast Asia and Melanesia (see Simons's [1982] excellent survey). These culture areas are known, of course, for a seemingly endless range of sociocultural taboos both linguistic and non-linguistic (e.g., Valeri, 2000). Affinal name taboos, as well as taboos on uttering the names of ancestors (e.g., Kwaio; Keesing & Fifi'i, 1969) or of chiefs (e.g., Tahiti; Salmon, 1927), are clearly part and parcel of these broader cultural preoccupations and practices.

In the Native Americas there appear to be only two locales where affinal name taboos trigger homophone effects (though my survey

Table 3.4. Global survey of affinal name and homophone avoidance registers

Area		Origo-Target of Avoidance
Americas		
Great Plains		
Hidatsa	(Lowie, 1917)	♂ / ♀ ⇆ WP / HP
Mandan	(Lowie, 1917)	♂ / ♀ ⇆ WP / HP
Xingu River		
Wauja	(Gregor, 1977; Ball, 2015)	♂ → WP
Kalapalo	(Basso, 1975, 2007)	♂ → WP
Kamayurá	(Seki, 2000)	♂ → WP; ♀ → HF
Oceania		
Melanesia		
Sengseng	(Chowning, 1985)	♂/♀ → ∀ of spouse's ascending kin
Kaulong	(Goodale, 1980)	♂/♀ → ∀ of spouse's kin
Mwotlap	(François, 2001)	♂/♀ ⇆ spouse's parents & siblings
Asia		
Inner Asia		
Ordos	(Gáspár, 2003)	♀ → older relatives of husband
Kalmucks	(Gáspár, 2003)	♀ → H's elder relatives
Kazak	(Kim, 2018a)	♀ → husband's elder relatives
Kyrgyz	(Hvoslef, 2001, p. 93)	♀ → older male members of H's clan; ♂ → HM
South Asia		
Tamil	(Pillai, 1972)	♀ → H
Africa		
Ethiopia		
Kambaata	(Treis, 2005)	♀ → HF, HeB, HM
Sidaama	(Teferra, 1987)	♀ → HF, HeB
Hadiyya	(Adane, 2014)	♀ → HF
Oromo	(Mbaya, 2002)	♀ → HF, HeB
Kenya, Rwanda, Tanzania		
Kamba	(Lindblom, 1920)	♀ → H, HF, HeB, HM, HeW; ♂ → WM, WM eldest D
Kerewe	(Komori, 1999)	♀ → HF
Kinyarwanda	(Kimenyi, 1992)	♀ → HF(B), HFBW, HM(B), HMBW
Nyakyusa	(Kolbusa, 2000)	♀ → HF(B), HFBW, HM, HM(B), HZ
Datooga	(Mitchell, 2015)	♀ → HF(B), HFF(B), HFFF(B), HM(Z), HFZS
Southern Africa		
Ndebele	(W.N.G. Davies & Quinche, 1933)	♀ → *not specified*
S. Sotho	(Kunene, 1958)	♀ → HF
Zulu	(Raum, 1973)	♀ → HP, HFF, HFSib; ♂ → WM
Xhosa	(Finlayson, 1995; Herbert, 1990)	♀ → HF, HFB, HM, HFF, HFFF

Notes. Coverage of Asia and Africa is much more thorough than other regions. Abbreviations: ♂ = male; ♀ = female; W = wife; H = husband; P = parent; M = mother; F = father; Z = sister; B = brother; e = elder; Sib. = sibling; D = daughter; S = son; arrows indicate the direction of avoidance (e.g., "♂ → HM" means "A woman avoids the name and homophones of the name of her husband's mother"). The double arrow [⇆] means that avoidance is reciprocal (i.e., the origo and target can be reversed).

of the literature is far from exhaustive). In North America there are the cases reported by Lowie (1917) for the closely related matrilineal Siouan language groups Hidatsa, Crow, and Mandan (see also Barnes, 1980). In South America there is a cluster of cases reported for the upper Xingu River area in central Brazil (Kamayurá, Tupi-Guarani: Seki, 2000; Wauja/Mehinaku, Arawak: Ball, 2015; Gregor, 1977; Kalapalo, Carib: Basso, 1975, 2007). In the Xingu River area, sons-in-law avoid the names of their parents-in-law. Generally, however, the patterning in the Native Americas, as well as in Island Southeast Asia and Melanesia, does not show the same power asymmetry – with simultaneous gender and generational skewing in avoidance practice – that is characteristic of name registers in Afro-Eurasia.

Patrilineal, Patrilocal, and Patriarchal: Afro-Eurasian Daughter-in-Law Registers[12]

Although they are most widespread in Island Southeast Asia and Melanesia, name registers are also attested in a culture-historically connected cluster in Central Asia, on the one hand, and in Eastern and Southern Africa, on the other. These clusters exhibit divergent properties from registers found elsewhere, while showing remarkable parallels to one another. In both Asia and Africa, name registers are found in societies with patrilineal descent, patrilocal post-marital residence, and where seniority often conditions non-reciprocal honorification (for T-V systems, see Kim, 2018b, on Kazak; Vreeland, 1962, on Mongolian). When looked at in terms of the stereotypical social categories of the origo and target of avoidance indexicality, the name registers in these regions are seen to be simultaneously gender- and generationally stratified. (The interested reader should compare the social-categorical properties of the origo and target of kinship indexicality, listed in the rightmost column of Table 3.4, of the Melanesian and Native American name registers to the African and Eurasian ones.) In Africa and Asia, generationally junior women non-reciprocally avoid the names and homophones of the names of elder, prototypically male, in-laws. The most focal avoidance relationship is typically that between an in-marrying daughter-in-law and her father-in-law. Highlighting the social category of the persons expected to employ them, these can be called **daughter-in-law registers** (Fleming et al., 2019).

Daughter-in-law registers are found in almost all major languages of Mongolic. (The discussion here would not be possible without the very helpful survey by Csaba Gáspár, 2003.) This is a relatively young language family, with Proto-Mongolic branching into descendent languages only around 800 years ago, after the dispersal of the Mongols led by Chinggis Khan (Janhunen, 2003, p. 1). It seems likely that it was through contact with Mongolic groups that Turkic groups acquired name registers – a parallel pattern is attested in Kazak and Kyrgyz – but I defer to regional experts for an evaluation of this claim.

The expression of avoidance in all of these languages is markedly asymmetrical: Younger, in-marrying brides are expected to avoid the names and homophones of the names of elder male in-laws, and these extremes of linguistic evasion are almost never reciprocated to the same degree (Birtalan, 2003, p. 227; Gáspár, 2003; Hamayon & Bassanoff, 1973; Humphrey, 1978). Drawing from Humphrey (1978), we have already seen that Mongolian name avoidance practices were anchored to the names of a woman's *xadamud* (male in-laws). A woman avoided the names and homophones of the names of her senior male in-laws (i.e., HeB, HF, HFB, HFF) and of her mother-in-law (pp. 91–2). But these individuals did not practice homophone avoidance with respect to the daughter-in-law. An in-marrying woman was also forbidden from uttering the name of her husband's clan (Hamayon & Bassanoff, 1973, p. 51). Similar patterns are attested in the Turkic languages. Kazak "married women are forbidden to address or mention by name their husband's senior relatives, including the name of his clan, which is usually the same as the name of its apical ancestor," as well as homophones of those names (Kim, 2018a, p. 82).

Because the set of names conditioning homophone avoidances can be so large, the negative repertoire of Turkic daughter-in-law registers is often quite extensive. In a Soviet-era study of Kazak naming customs, Khalel Arghynbaev (1984) offers the following anecdote, "which comes from literary sources," of a woman who

> was not allowed to name a stream ("bulak"), a lake ("kol"), a reed ("kamys"), a sheep ("koi"), a wolf ("kaskyr"), a knife ("pyshak"), or a whetstone ("kairak") as these words were also used as the proper names of her husband's relatives. The young woman, coming to the stream for water, noticed that beyond the stream, on the shore of the lake, in the reeds, a wolf was attacking a sheep. She shouted to her father-in-law 'Master, Master! On the other side of the babbling (stream), on the shore of the shining (lake), in among the rustling (reeds), a ferocious (wolf) is carrying off a bleating (sheep). Quick, bring a sharpened (knife) honed on a sharpener (whetstone)!'" (p. 53; cf. Schuyler, cited in Kim, 2018a, p. 83)

This account of Kazak *at tergew* "name avoidance" (Kim, 2018a, p. 83) underscores how name registers place daughters-in-law in a linguistic straitjacket and how their ability to circumvent those linguistic shackles with grace is an esteemed quality. Similar stories can be found in the literature on Mongolian daughter-in-law word avoidances (Hamayon & Bassanoff, 1973). Indeed, throughout Mongolic and Turkic groups, it appears that successful and inventive circumvention of name taboos was a valued sign of a daughter-in-law's ingenuity: "Such resourceful women were regarded as very wise and were objects of great popular esteem" (Arghynbaev, 1984, p. 53). That is, the ability of brides to successfully negotiate the linguistic prohibitions imposed upon them was a sign of their cognitive quickness and capacity – a demeanor indexical (Kim, 2018a; cf. Berezkin & Duvakin, 2016, on the topos of the "clever daughter-in-law" in Central Asia).

To the west, in the Caucasus, similarly non-reciprocal avoidance of the father-in-law by the daughter-in-law is widely attested in interactional avoidances (for discussion of Armenian daughter-in-law sign language, see Chapter 6). Name taboos were seemingly limited to the use of the name in reference to the target of avoidance and to the use of the name in reference to other individuals (henceforth, "namesakes"); that is, there was a prohibition on the use of all tokens of the proper noun regardless of who the particular token referred to (e.g., Abkhaz [Northwest Caucasian]; Chirikba, 2015). I have not been able to find evidence of homophones being affected, hence its exclusion from Table 3.4 (cf. Tuite & Schulze, 1998, pp. 371, 378, note 18). In South Asia, similarly gender-stratified name avoidance and taboo are common, with the wife often avoiding her husband's name (e.g., Bala & Koul, 1989, pp. 32–3, for Punjabi; Das, 1968, p. 24, for Bengali). In some Tamil-speaking communities, the avoidance of the husband's name by the wife also affects homophones (Pillai, 1972; T. Parasuraman, personal communication).

In Africa, name registers are characterized by a very similar non-reciprocal patterning to that found in Central Asia – women who marry into patrilineages and move into households identified with them are expected to practice linguistic avoidance with respect to the senior agnatic kin of their husbands. Name registers in this region exhibit homophone avoidance of the most dramatic kind, where mere identity of a common syllable between the tabooed name and a lexical item may be sufficient to spur secondary avoidances. There are three loci on the continent where daughter-in-law registers cluster (see Table 3.4 for references). From north to south, the first is found in Ethiopia and northern Kenya: the Afroasiatic languages of Kambaata, Sidaama, Hadiyya, Oromo, Libido, Alaaba, and Xambaaro (Treis, 2005, p. 293). The second, and most disparate group, is found in the African Great Lakes area: the Lacustrine Bantu languages of Kinyarwanda (Rwanda) and Kerewe (spoken on Ukerewe Island, Lake Victoria), the Corridor Bantu language of Nyakyusa (southwestern Tanzania), and the Southern Nilotic language Datooga (north-central Tanzania). The Northeast Bantu language Kamba, the variety spoken in south-central Kenya, represents an outlier in terms of its social patterning and is geographically intermediate between the first two groups – it is the only case where linguistic constraints on husbands are wholly equivalent to the constraints on wives. The third set of cases is found in the Nguni Bantu languages of southern Africa (Ndebele, Southern Sotho, Zulu, and Xhosa).

The first and the third groups clearly constitute cohesive cultural complexes. The second group is more disparate. Heeding the suggestion of Treis (2005), Fleming et al. (2019) sought evidence to demonstrate historical connections between these register complexes but were unable to find any smoking gun. What the survey does demonstrate is the strong correlation between daughter-in-law registers, on the one hand, and patrilineal descent, pastoralism, (often cattle-financed) bridewealth, and patrilocal residence, on the other (Fleming et al., 2019, pp. 184, 187–8). So, for instance, daughter-in-law registers are not attested among any of the matrilineal Bantu groups of central Africa.

As can be seen, even from this cursory description, the affinal name registers in Eurasia and Africa typically involve non-reciprocal, gender-, and generationally stratified patterns of avoidance (but see Kintz, 1986, for the rather divergent case of Fulani). Indeed, throughout a broad geographical area stretching from Ulan Bator to Uttar Pradesh, from Kyrgyzstan to KwaZulu Natal, name registers have second-order speaker-gendering indexical values. And this may even be reflected in local ethnometapragmatic labels for the registers – for instance, the affinal avoidance register employed by Xhosa speakers is referred to as *isihlonipho sabafazi* "women's language of respect" (Dowling, 1988).

Cases like these underscore that the sociolinguistics of kinship cannot be opposed to the sociolinguistics of sociocentric hierarchy (e.g., of caste or class) in any simple and straightforward manner. In Africa and Asia, patriarchal ideologies, patrilineal descent-biasing, and patrilocal post-marital residence – all of which are linked in a feedback loop to greater accumulation and intergenerational transmission of material resources (Holden & Mace, 2003) – remake kinship in a hierarchical mould. A point of conjuncture of particular importance appears to be the way in which gender and seniority are, through diverse semiotic media, figured as analogously complementary in these societies (i.e., male: female :: senior: junior :: wife-receiver: wife-giver :: higher status: lower status). In both Central Asia and eastern and southern Africa, avoidance is simultaneously stratified by gender (women asymmetrically avoid men) and by relative age (younger individuals asymmetrically avoid elder individuals). This set of analogies effectively figurates women as subordinate (i.e., as owing deference) to men in the same way that juniors are subordinate to seniors (compare here to the Afro-Eurasian bias in age-based constraints on the use of names in ascending consanguineal address [Fleming & Slotta, 2018]). Though I do not have data on marriage norms for other regions, I know that in parts of South Asia, marriage norms dictate that a bride be younger than her groom. In these contexts, a married woman is effectively transformed into an iconic-index or emblem of these motivated diagrammatic equivalencies; brides tend actually to be the juniors of their husbands.

Because the semiotics of hierarchy and the semiotics of kinship are complexly entangled, there are important, substantive differences between kinship-based honorification found in hierarchical societies and kinship-based honorification in more egalitarian societies: honorific registers linked to kinship in the Americas and in Oceania are routinely reciprocal in their patterning – in Oceania, in-laws reciprocally avoid one another's names; in Australia, mother-in-law and son-in-law often reciprocally employ mother-in-law languages, and in-laws almost always reciprocally employ honorific pronouns in address and reference (see Chapter 7, Table 7.1). Focusing on name registers in particular, the range of (near-)homophones that are avoided seems to be positively correlated with the degree of stratification of kinship avoidance: The most extensive, syllable-based homophone avoidance is practiced in languages, like Zulu and Kambaata, where deference routines are markedly non-reciprocal, as well as gender- and age-stratified. There are, then, real and substantive differences between sociolinguistic patterns found in Afro-Eurasia and those attested elsewhere. More in-depth research should focus on the relationships between social-organizational profile and the "analogical classifications" (e.g., male: female :: elder : younger) implicit in register patterning (terminology after Needham, 1980). With respect to the specific question of name registers, understanding how complementary "power" relations are historically connected to the range of homophones avoided in name registers remains, for me, an intractable problem.

Symbolizing with Relations: Kin Categories and Register Stereotypes

Attempts to correlate sociolinguistic profiles directly with social-organizational profiles have been justifiably criticized for their overly reductive character (Irvine, 1992). Nevertheless, as this survey of name registers illustrates, there are important correlations between social organization and the kin categories associated with the most elaborate ritual avoidances. Put simply, father-in-law/daughter-in-law avoidance is the focal avoidance relation in the pastoralist and agriculturalist societies of Africa and Eurasia. Mother-in-law/son-in-law avoidance is often the most focal one in the historically foraging societies of the Native Americas and Oceania. How should we understand these correlations? Although I cannot do justice to this question, I will gesture toward the kind of explanatory framework that I think is necessary to approach the problem.

Mid-century comparative studies tended to adopt, by default, a model wherein particular genealogical relations were understood, for a variety of functional reasons rooted in behavioural ecology, to be particularly apt sites for the emergence of avoidance practices. Radcliffe-Brown (1949) emphasizes avoidance as a means of circumventing conflicts that arise between the nuclear families brought together in marriage. Murdock (1967) sees avoidance as a means of safeguarding incest prohibitions that apply to core genealogical relations where these are not sufficiently integrated at an unconscious level. After Schneider (1968, 1984), it is hard not to see these formulations as anything but circular. Within the so-called "new kinship" approach, a "kinship term [is seen as bringing] together a set of relatives and a relationship (Schneider 1968), or a normative code of behaviour, which has a real, symbolic meaning" (Wagner, 1972, p. 603). From this perspective, the would-be universality of the "incest taboo," for instance, is revealed as a "pseudo-problem." "Incest" and "exogamy" are not independent facts about the behaviour of particular genealogically linked individuals that can be treated as causes exogenous to the sociocultural system. Rather, they are meaningful, reflexively integrated dimensions of kin relationship for cultural participants: "The 'remarkable' fact that kinship systems all over the world prohibit mating among close relatives becomes less remarkable when we realize that those very kinship systems (and hence the 'incest taboo' itself) determine who is a 'close' relative, and that the determination and the prohibition are one and the same thing" (Wagner, 1972, p. 610).

In order to appreciated the cross-cultural patterning of avoidance over kinship relations, one must avoid the temptation to read avoidance in a unidirectional manner, as the sign of a pre-existing, biologically or ecologically given relation. In keeping with Wagner's (1972) critical insight, kinship avoidance and kin relation should be understood as co-constitutive. Avoidance can be a sign of a kin relation – when a Chiricahua Apache man studiously avoids looking at a woman, this can be interpreted as an index that she is probably his wife's mother or aunt.

But the reverse semiotic movement is always simultaneously in play; the kin relations that are stereotypically associated with elaborated avoidance routines themselves function as signs of the kinds of ontological difference that avoidance practices are understood to ritually maintain and keep separate. The kinship register approach demands that one attend to this chiastic movement where sign (avoidance comportment) and object (kin relation) are reversed. It is this "backwards" perspective – the figure-ground reversal – that helps to clarify why certain kin categories are so often the loci of avoidance cross-culturally.

With this in mind, we can observe that joking-avoidance relationships are most commonly articulated in terms of three kinds of categorical difference routinely encoded in kinship terminologies. These components of kinship clearly serve to symbolize the kinds of social identity and difference at play in joking and avoidance:

(1) Whether ego and alter are of disharmonic ($G^{[...-3,-1,+1,+3...]}$ or G^{odd}) or harmonic generations ($G^{[...-2,0,+2...]}$ or G^{even}): Harmonic (or alternating generation) kin include grandparents and grandchildren. Disharmonic (or adjacent generation) kin include children and parents. Harmonic kin are prototypical joking relations in most areas of the world, with the exception perhaps of Eurasia (but see R. Parkin, 1988, for the importance of harmonic joking relationships among Austroasiatic groups). Further, the symbolic identification of grandparents with their grandchildren is an important way in which common substance and shared identity are emblematized. Cross-culturally, same-sex grandparents are the most common name-sharing partners (e.g., Ball, 2015; Kintz, 1986, p. 39; Krifka, 2019, p. 71; R. Lee, 1986; D. Parkin, 1988; see also the discussion of homonymous kinship in Chapter 4). In some societies, the harmonic/disharmonic distinction englobes other relevant distinctions, like those related to affinity or gender (e.g., Mijikenda: McGivney, 1993; Ju|'hoan: R. Lee, 1993). This distinction is even integrated into the grammar (or "kin-tax") of many Aboriginal Australian languages, where non-singular pronouns may encode the harmonic versus disharmonic relation between referents (Dench, 1987; Enfield, 2002; Hale, 1966).

(2) Whether ego and alter are of the same or different social genders: Typically, cross-sex avoidance is more pronounced than same-sex avoidance (see Chapter 7 for empirical demonstration). However, reversals sometimes present themselves in ego's generation (G^0), where same-sex siblings-in-law may be more subject to avoidance than cross-sex siblings-in-law (e.g., Eves, 1998; R. Lee, 1993) or marriageable cross-cousins may be prime joking relations (e.g., Landes, 1937). The cross-sex distinction may be englobing of other parameters conditioning

avoidance. This seems to be particularly the case for brother-sister avoidances and their "extensions" in island Melanesia and Polynesia (e.g., Mandak: Clay, 1977, Choiseul Islanders: Scheffler, 1965).

(3) Whether ego and alter are natal kin or kin through marriage: Affinity is the prototype of kinship avoidance. In some cases, avoidance is geared solely toward relatives through marriage. Such is the case, for instance, for the Kaulong and Sengseng (New Britain), who avoid the resting places of spouses' cognatic kin (both living and dead), as well as their names and words that sound similar to them (Chowning, 1985; Goodale, 1980).

Importantly, the union of these three categorical distinctions – that is, relations that are disharmonic, cross-sex, and established through marriage – are the most focal avoidance relationships cross-culturally. (The survey of name-based avoidances presented in Table 3.4 illustrates this in particularly stark terms.) Correspondingly, two relations serve as focal hues of avoidance – the mother-in-law/son-in-law relation and the father-in-law/daughter-in-law relation. In Australia, Melanesia, and North America, avoidance tends to peak in the mother-in-law/son-in-law relation (Hiatt, 1984; Merlan, 1997; Pans, 1998). This relationship is often characterized by reciprocal avoidance, analogically conforming to the more egalitarian profile of local social orders. Contrastingly, as I have shown in this chapter, across a range of cultural groups extending from Mongolia in Central Asia to South Africa, it is the relationship between a woman and her father-in-law that is the most focal avoidance relationship. Among Mongolic, Turkic, Caucasian, Indo-Iranian, Afroasiatic, Nilo-Saharan, and Bantu language groups, generationally subordinate women engage in hypertrophied deference routines that target generationally superordinate men. In these societies, patrilocal post-marital residence and patrilineal descent are overwhelmingly the norm. Avoidance here often has an asymmetrical patterning, with daughters-in-law enjoined to engage in more deferential comportment toward their husband's kin than they do toward her. Corresponding with this often non-reciprocal patterning of avoidance, in many of these societies it is relative age rather than relative generation that is stereotypically keyed to avoidance practice (see, for instance, discussion of Zulu and Sidaama in Chapters 4 and 8). Seniority/juniority is, of course, an asymmetric (non-commuting) relation, while harmonic/disharmonic is a symmetric (commuting) one.

This cross-cultural distribution suggests that categorically encoded relational differences – differences of gender, of age, of generation, of marriage-group membership – are being drawn upon to symbolize the social ontological differences at play in avoidance practice. The "total orientation" of maximally hypertrophied interpersonal avoidance tends to be stereotypically associated with kin categories that epitomize difference. Painting with very broad brushstrokes, the mother-in-law/son-in-law dyad and the father-in-law/daughter-in-law dyads are the focal hues of kinship avoidance in egalitarian and hierarchical societies, respectively. They serve to symbolize the social differences that avoidance, as interaction ritual, keeps separate. Maximally elaborate ways of not interacting are engaged in between maximally different kinds of persons, thereby underscoring that it is a fundamental, ontological difference that the ritual practice of avoidance serves to safeguard. Meanwhile, joking is most elaborated between those who are symbolically identified with one another – like same-sex grandparents and grandchildren. The interpersonal licence of joking is here symbolized as reflecting the identity of the parties themselves – joking behaviours do not violate the other, because the other is not other.

Chapter Four

Rigid Performativity: Cross-Cultural Convergences in Name Registers

In the previous chapter I showed that name registers have a global distribution. In this chapter I seek to account for the recurrent properties of name registers, features that make them a readily recognizable sociolinguistic kind. By focusing on similarities, I do not mean to deny the importance of the divergent cultural understandings and social organizations that inform name avoidance practices cross-culturally. Just as there is variability in the kin categories that condition name tabooing cross-culturally, so too is there variation in beliefs about the consequences of producing a tabooed name from place to place. Some Tamil women believe that if they say their husband's name, "harm will befall him" (Trawick, 1996, p. 95). For a Kambaata-speaking woman in Ethiopia, mistakenly saying the name of her father-in-law would count as an insult and a cause of shame (Treis, 2005). Among the Haruai of Papua New Guinea, the use of a taboo name may make the speaker ill or lead to crop failure (Comrie, 2000, p. 80). For the Sengseng of New Britain, the consequences of failure to follow name-based avoidances are, "in theory at least," catastrophic, including "sickness, possibly the death of the spouse, and failure to have children and to gain wealth in shells" (Chowning, 1985, p. 184).

Nevertheless, and despite distinct local understandings and elaborations of the practice, kinship-keyed name and homophone avoidance is a highly specific and yet global phenomenon. (If one were to include cases of post-mortem and chiefly name taboo, the prevalence of this practice would be even more striking.) In terms of the framework proposed in the Introduction, avoidance registers of this type constitute a sociolinguistic kind; they are recurrent outputs of diachronic pathways in which language ideologies, discourse patterns, and language structures become dialectically entangled with one another – or constellate – in convergent ways. In order to understand the sources of this convergence it helps to pose the following question: Why do names, but not other lexical types, condition the tabooing of phonologically iconic lexical forms? This question points directly toward what makes name registers distinctive; it is not the avoidance of a particular expression type in discourse reference, but the additional avoidance of phonologically identical or similar word forms, that makes name registers distinctive from other sociopragmatically conditioned avoidances of person-referring expressions.[1] Why does the avoidance of names "contaminate ... words of the language with a phonetic resemblance to these names" (Lévi-Strauss, 2021, p. 199)? What is it about names that leads to these excesses of linguistic avoidance? Answering this question will help us to home in on the semiotic affordances and infrastructures that motivate this sociolinguistic kind. It will also shed some light on the special properties of verbal taboos within the broader study of social pragmatics.

Discourse Reference and the Performative Indefeasibility of Verbal Taboos

Verbal taboos are performatives. This is to say, tabooed words do not simply denote things, but rather, in J.L. Austin's (1962) happy idiom, they *do* things. To use the F-word on the nightly news or to use the name of a cross-sex sibling in Arnhem Land is to commit a shocking social act that transforms the context of its occurrence. Such verbal taboos are, however, a special kind of performative. Most performatives require what Austin called "felicity conditions": contextual prerequisites for their success. For a boat-naming ceremony to succeed at naming a boat, the person breaking the bottle over the bow needs to be properly authorized, a conventional procedure needs to be followed, and the proper vessel must be targeted (Austin, 1962, p. 23). Verbal taboos typically require few if any such felicity conditions. On the nightly news, the occurrence of any number of four-letter words will achieve performative effects – of offence, moral consternation, and institutional sanction – regardless of the nature of their introduction into discourse or the intentional state of the speaker. Even in utterance-types, like reported-speech constructions, where the speaker is understood not to be the "author" but merely the "animator" of the utterance (Goffman, 1979), curse words, slurs, and other taboo language may still have performative effects. Such words and expressions are so essentialized with a negatively valued performativity that their indexical entailments are not easily cancelled out. Not only intentionally achieved and felicitous performances but also casual mentions of verbal taboos can count as performative instances (cf. Butler, 1997, pp. 14, 166–7, note 10). Their performative (or "perlocutionary") effects are unavoidable, indefeasible.

I will characterize verbal taboos as performatives whose effects are indefeasible within some specific social context – an F-bomb on live television or the word "bomb" in the security line at the airport. This distinguishes verbal taboos from more run-of-the-mill performatives, like promises and baptisms. Tokens of run-of-the-mill performatives can easily be cancelled out or "defeased," as for instance they are when they occur within reported-speech constructions. By recounting a judge's "Guilty!" verdict one does not risk condemning one's interlocuter to a prison sentence. Not so with taboo speech, where revoicing the sign may also reproduce its perlocutionary effects. Think here, for instance, of the self-righteous media self-censorship in reporting on, or even more self-righteous reprinting of, the infamous *Charlie Hebdo* Muhammad cartoons in the wake of the massacre at the editorial offices of the magazine in January 2015. To reprint was to replicate the offence.[2] Verbal taboos are similarly unmentionable; to merely cite the sign is to trigger its performative effect (Fleming & Lempert, 2011). The **performative indefeasibility** of taboo sign-types is thus a functional characterization of a token-level, or usage-centred, discursive phenomenon.

The concept of defeasibility in pragmatics is associated with Grice's (1975) doctrine of conversational implicatures (cf. Potts, 2005). For Grice, conversational implicatures or inferences are defeasible in the sense that these interpretations are always subject to subsequent revision or cancellation. Contrastingly, logical entailments are indefeasible in the same sense that a logical proposition, "if p then q," may be necessarily true (Lyons, 2002, pp. 169, 286–7). Thus a defeasible implicature is a provisional and context-dependent interpretation whereas logical entailments are context-independent truths that hold across all possible worlds. My framing of performative indefeasibility draws out and plays upon this parallel between logical entailment and performative entailment: indefeasible performatives – like the infamous *Jyllands-Posten* Muhammad cartoons – have perlocutionary effects that cannot be cancelled out, minimally, for certain sign-producers or in certain settings.

Now the key point for this study is the following: Avoidance registers have cross-culturally convergent properties because they are organized around words and expressions whose performative effects are similarly indefeasible. Much as in the relationship between the photographic negative and the print, verbal taboos imprint (with the colours all reversed) their properties onto the avoidance registers that serve to circumvent them. They imprint their indefeasibility onto the avoidance register. In order to see this, I must be more specific about what kinds of linguistic or discursive functions fail to defease the social pragmatics of verbal taboos. The first such **defeasance condition** that I look at is discourse reference.

Social indexicality is often guided by discourse reference. Indeed, as discussed in the previous chapter, honorific language – a cover term that includes both insult and deference – is typically keyed to discourse reference (Agha, 2007, p. 317). Many honorific registers are exclusively referent-targeting. For example, in various Malagasy chiefdoms there were honorific vocabularies used to refer to the actions, belongings, and body parts of chiefs and kings. Verguin (1957) offers an interesting study of an honorific vocabulary used in the 1950s in the Androy region in the south of the island (cf. Sibree's [1892] Betsileo word-lists). At that time, the register had become delinked from the practices of divine kingship but still indexed age-based deference-entitlements of seniors. Here is an example from Verguin (1957, pp. 153–4; orthography follows the source).

1a. <u>Mikana</u> ize hena   "He/She eats meat." [honorific]
    Eat$_{HON}$ 3.sing meat
1b. <u>Huma</u> ize hena   "He/She eats meat." [non-honorific]
    Eat 3.sing meat

The honorific verb *mikana* "to eat" indexes the relative deference-entitlements of the referent of the subject of the verb. The lexeme *mikana* has a Speaker$_{origo}$-Referent$_{target}$ deference focus; the speaker is the origo (or "giver") of deference and the referent is the target (or "recipient") of deference. The sociopragmatic function of the honorific is keyed to discourse reference; we are able to figure out who the target of deference is by determining the identity of the referent of the subject of the verb. But to say that discourse reference guides a sociopragmatic function (here, honorification) is also to say that reference can potentially defease it. In avoidance registers this is precisely where discourse reference comes up short; in avoidance registers, discourse reference fails to defease sociopragmatic function. Let me briefly illustrate this for the two types of kinship avoidance registers – the context-dependent mother-in-law languages and the context-independent name registers – that I have focused on in the previous chapters.

The sociopragmatics of Aboriginal Australian mother-in-law languages sometimes function in a reference-guided manner that parallels Malagasy honorific language. Thus, for instance, Mangarayi mother-in-law language was used in referring to *ganji* or focal avoidance relations (a mother-in-law and her siblings and their kin reciprocals). The word for "foot" in everyday Mangarayi is *jamgaṛ*, while the avoidance term is *madjaṇḍa*. Just as in Malagasy, it is expected that the respectful variant be employed in referring to the feet of a mother-in-law or her siblings. Importantly, however, when speaking to a *ganji* one should always use *madjaṇḍa*, regardless whose foot is spoken of. In speech addressed to *ganji* relations, the discourse reference of a token of everyday speech ceases to be a defeasance condition on its pragmatic function. You can't say *jamgaṛ* to your mother-in-law no matter whose *jamgaṛ* you're talking about!

Similar considerations help to clarify the difference between the more general phenomenon of avoiding calling someone by name, on the one hand, and name taboos, on the other. In the first case, one politely refrains from calling someone by name by not employing tokens of the name *in referring to the individual* in question. The use of Title + Last Name rather than bare First Name when referring to a social superior in American English is an example of such name avoidance (R. Brown & Ford, 1961). Name taboo occurs where the negatively valued sociopragmatic function of tokens of a name are not defeased by their discourse reference. Simply put, one refrains from uttering the name regardless of the identity of the person to whom one refers.

Take the following example from Galela (Papuan; Moluccas). Affinal name registers are particularly elaborated in the Moluccas and well described in writings spanning over a century (Kern, 1893; see also Collins, 1989, on Taliabo). In Galela, words employed in substituting for homophones of the names of in-laws are called *saali* (Taylor, 1990, p. 20). Exemplifying these name-based avoidances, Adeney-Risakotta (2005) provides the following example of a Christian convert's difficulty in reading a Bible passage: "When a man whose father-in-law is named Luke comes to the name 'Luke' while reading the Bible, he is not permitted to speak out the name because it would be disrespectful to his father-in-law" (p. 111). In such examples, the speech act – the man's disrespecting his father-in-law by uttering his name – is not cancelled out by the fact that the referent of the name is here one of the four evangelists and not the speaker's father-in-law. This is a name taboo as opposed to mere name avoidance.

Just as in Galela, in many societies, speakers are enjoined to avoid uttering the names of particular social alters not only in making reference to those individuals but also in referring to others who share the same name, or **namesakes**. Among Indigenous groups of northern California and the Pacific Northwest, where post-mortem name tabooing was particularly prevalent, living namesakes might be paid to give up the use of their names during the period of mourning in which name taboos were in vigour. Kroeber (1925) offers the following account of post-mortem namesake avoidance among the Yurok: "If two men had the same name, the poorer, on the death of the richer, would 'throw his away,' so as to avoid occasion of giving offence. If the wealthy man was the survivor, he would pay his namesake's family, perhaps as much as five strings [i.e., local money], satisfy them, and retain his name" (pp. 38–9). Speaking of the Wik (Cape York Peninsula, Australia) post-mortem name taboo, Sutton (1978, p. 203) observes that namesakes of the deceased will be addressed not by name but by the term *thaapicha* "namesake." Similarly, under conditions of post-mortem name taboo in central Australia, a special form meaning "no name" (Warlpiri *kumunjayi*) is used in reference and address to namesakes of deceased individuals whose names are still proscribed (Nash & Simpson, 1981, p. 172). In many of the societies of the Caucasus where patrilocal post-marital residence was the rule, women were not supposed to use the names of male affines, nor they hers. All of these individuals were given new names that they employed to refer to one another. For example, "a certain Abxaz woman had a brother called Kiasou. Upon marrying, she learned that one of her in-laws bore the same name. The use of the name Kiasou therefore became taboo for her *even when referring to her own brother*, for whom she thereafter used the name Digua" (Tuite & Schulze, 1998, p. 378, note 18, citing Dzavaxadze & Sinkuba).

In all of these cases, the insulting or disrespectful pragmatics of names are not circumscribed by the reference of discourse tokens. Indeed, where name taboos are operative, the social pragmatics of tokens of a name (e.g., a token of Kiasou as uttered by that "certain Abxaz woman") are not defeased by their discourse reference (cf. Irvine's [2009] "remote focus"). But why do names so often have this performative excess that overflows the enclosure of reference? And why is this performative excess unique to names among person-referring expressions?

Avoiding Kin Terms: Uncanny Iconicity, Voicing, and Death-Names

The decoupling of sociopragmatic function from discourse reference is not attested for human noun-phrase types other than proper nouns. Much as with names, kin terms are sometimes avoided in making reference to particular relations – one's cross-sex sibling in Tanga (Melanesia; Bell, 1962), one's daughter-in-law in the Caucasus (Tuite & Schulze, 1998), one's wife in much of South Asia (Subrahmanian, 1978; e.g., Bangla [Bengal; Indo-Aryan]: Basu, 1975, p. 218). Among Karok (northern California) speakers, a substitute set of kin terms was employed to refer to the recently deceased (Bright, 1958, p. 177, note 16; Gifford, 1922, p. 33). Bright (1958) gives the examples of *ko·hímmačko·* "deceased father," *'ihku·s* "deceased mother," and *xaká·nič* "deceased sibling." But again, in all of these cases, the sociopragmatic function of the avoided kin term (e.g., its power to disrespect the close kin of a recently departed Karok kinsman) depended upon its discourse reference.

The famous "death-names" or "necronyms" of Borneo (Lévi-Strauss, 2021; Needham, 1954) offer a case where the pragmatics of kin-term use and avoidance are *partially* decoupled from discourse reference. A parallel case is attested for Kiowa Apache. I will briefly treat these two cases, both of which involve elaborate post-mortem taboos. These case studies underscore how the semantic and referential properties of human nouns guide folk-consciousness in fashioning and conceptualizing their non-referential and socially indexical meanings. The idea that the grammatical properties of noun-phrase types importantly condition the ideologically informed elaboration of their social-interactional effects will be central in the subsequent sections, where I explain why the performativity of names so easily becomes decoupled from discourse reference.

Post-mortem practices among the Kiowa Apache are described in Opler and Bittle (1961) and Sanford (1971), and my analysis is based upon these historical reconstructions. Death coincided with the emergence of a "ghost" or *čí·yé*; "the self decays and dies with the body, while mind and intelligence become the ghost" (Sanford, 1971, p. 83). A ghost, whether harnessed by a shaman or because it "takes a notion" (p. 87), may bring accidents, illness, or even death upon others. The clearest symptoms of ghost attack involve paralysis – a stroke, a twisted neck, a crossed eye; the ghost, by touching the living, "has communicated part of [its] deadness."

Personal possessions of the deceased, cooking implements, foodstuffs that were in the house at the time of death, were all taken out of the house immediately and given away. Sanford's (1971) informants report that in the past some personal possessions were burned or buried with the deceased. Alongside the casting away of these object-signs of the deceased, numerous modes of reference familiar to the deceased were also avoided. Name avoidance begins after the interment of the body. It seeks "to suppress the memory of the dead person and thus to avoid attracting his ghost" (p. 111). These name taboos were practiced "in the presence of his relatives, and words that were similar to or identical with his name could not be uttered"

(Opler & Bittle, 1961, p. 386). As Mooney (1898) noted, "the name of the dead is never spoken in the presence of the relatives, and upon the death of any member of a family, *all the others take new names*" (p. 278; italics added). The use of kin terms was also affected. So, for instance, when a parent has died, his or her "child will avoid the usual term for mother or father when addressing his classificatory parents and will use the secondary [death-related] terms. Should a child accidentally forget and call his deceased father's brother *ace* ('father'), instead of the secondary term *kaan*, the family will be reminded of the dead and will mourn again" (McAllister, 1937, p. 163). Apparently, these substitute terms were employed not only in referring to the deceased individual but also in addressing other of ego's kin of the same social category: "Persons who had used a certain kinship term for the deceased now addressed those of similar relationship with secondary terms" (Opler & Bittle, 1961, p. 386, cited in Webster, 2008, p. 259). Before unpacking the sociopragmatics of these usages, I first introduce the Penan case and then analyze both cases together.

The Kiowa Apache system parallels the use of those special kin terms used in referring to, and especially in addressing, close relatives of the deceased in Borneo, alternatively called "death-names" (Brosius, 1995; Needham, 1954) or "necronyms" (Benjamin, 1968; Lévi-Strauss, 2021; Rousseau, 1978; Whittier, 1981). Here I will draw upon Peter Brosius's (1996) excellent work on death names among the Western Penan. Post-mortem rites and rituals are famously elaborated in central Borneo. Often entire settlements are abandoned upon the death of an individual, or an individual's possessions are destroyed. Among the Western Penan, the deceased individual is quickly buried under the hearth of his or her hut, "the shelter is pulled down or burned, and the entire camp breaks and moves" (Brosius, 1996, p. 200). As among the Kiowa Apache, there is a reciprocal relation of longing between the deceased and their close kin. This is encapsulated by the concept of the *uban*, which I will, with poetic licence, translate as "presence of an absence":

> *Uban* refers to an empty place left by the withdrawal of an object or being. Pig tracks are referred to as *uban mabui*. *Uban* also refers to the empty place left by the death of a relative: for instance, the place in a hut where that person used to sleep.... Penan speak often of the pain caused by seeing the *uban* of someone who has died. It is the desire to avoid this that leads them to move. Upon moving, the entire community enters a period of ritual mourning (*lumu*). During this period ... Penan are concerned that hearing certain sounds or seeing certain activities may make the deceased desire to return or be upset at the thought that people are not mourning

them. Penan also say that the bereaved will be upset if prohibitions are not observed. (Brosius, 1996, p. 201)

Just as residences are shifted, so too are names. And as with the Kiowa Apache, it is not only the name of the deceased that is tabooed among the Penan; the names of their closest living relatives are also changed (Brosius, 1995, p. 126; Needham, 1954, p. 425). The substitute names for the close kin of the deceased are called *ngaran nasu* "moved names." Additionally, during this period of mourning, *ngaram lumu* "mourning names" are used to refer to the bereaved close kin of a newly deceased individual. These are substitute kin terms that indicate that the propositus of the kin term is deceased (Brosius, 1996, p. 198) – think of the English terms "orphan," "widow," and "widower." Remember that kin terms are two-place nouns that express the relationship between a kin-term propositus and a kin-term referent (Agha, 2007, p. 351). The use of a token of the term "wife" presupposes, in addition to the feminine discourse referent, the existence of a spouse (the kin-term propositus); the term "widow" presupposes that that spouse is deceased. Death-names function analogously, but they are much more specific (e.g., *larah* "parent whose third-born child has died") and their use is much more densely entangled with social effects and resonances.

Together, *ngaran nasu* and *ngaram lumu* represent the linguistic repertoire of a Penan post-mortem avoidance register. In both cases, the rationale for linguistic avoidance is the same; it is upsetting for both the living and the dead to hear the same expressions used, whether they be names or kin terms, by which the dead had formerly addressed their close kin. Death terms do not merely acknowledge loss by encoding death in their lexical semantics. Rather, the use of death terms is understood as a strategy for avoiding a certain **voicing structure** imbued with an injurious performativity. Discourse genres give voice to particular characterological figures or personae associated with their use (Agha, 2005; Bakhtin, 1981). If one uses the same kin term to address the kin of the deceased that the deceased had used for that individual while alive, the spectral "discursive figure" or voice of the deceased is summoned. Penan say they use death names because "they find it painful to hear the names by which the deceased addressed themselves and others" (Brosius, 1996, p. 202). The injurious and upsetting usage is one where (a) the participant role of addressee is occupied by a close kin of the deceased, and (b) the kin term employed is the same as the form that the deceased would have employed to refer to that addressee. Death-names, which semantically denote the death of the propositus, also pragmatically insulate both addressees and deceased overhearers from the echo of a usage that death has silenced.

Linguistic avoidances, of names and kin terms, are continuous with other efforts that both symbolically mark death while circumventing, for close kin, the phenomenological experience of the presence of the absence – the *uban* – of the deceased individual (Brosius, 1996, p. 201). The Western Penan seem fully aware of the two levels of performative function that linguistic avoidances mediate. On the one hand, there is a stated supernatural belief in the capacity of the familiar to usher forth the deceased. "The pain of separation following death is felt to be mutual, and it is assumed that the dead wish to return to their living kin. Penan view this frustrated desire to be of the utmost danger: contact with the dead may lead to accidents, illness, or death" (Brosius, 1996, p. 200). But the sentiments aroused by "normal" kin-term usage are equally understood in terms of their affective consequences, as a painful lack of respect for close living kin of the deceased.

The avoidance of default kin terms and the use of substitute kin terms in both Kiowa Apache and Western Penan arise out of performative anxieties provoked by, to borrow Rupert Stasch's (2008) phrase, "uncanny iconic resemblances" (Stasch, 2008, p. 1). In both cases the dead are understood to be dangerously drawn to, and by, what is familiar to them. In both cases, kin terms of address, two-place nouns that symbolically express the relationship between propositus-as-speaker and referent-as-addressee, are focal loci of linguistic avoidance. From the unfortunately very brief description of the Kiowa Apache custom – again, "persons who had used a certain kinship term for the deceased now addressed those of similar relationship with secondary terms" (Opler & Bittle, 1961, p. 386) – it is apparent that it is the usage of kin terms in participant frameworks where the deceased can be construed to stand in an uncanny iconicity with the occupant of the addressee-referent role that is to be avoided. Here interpellation of the deceased is avoided by use of a term that acknowledges that the speaker-propositus has lost a relative who stands in the same kinship relation to himself or herself as does the actual flesh-and-blood addressee-referent of the token. Acknowledging death breaks the symmetry; it undoes the uncanny iconicity. In the Western Penan case, the iconicity pivots to the propositus – here it is the usage of kin terms in participant frameworks where the deceased can be construed to stand in an uncanny iconicity with the occupant of the speaker-propositus role that is to be avoided. Here it is the voice of the deceased that must be silenced. Again, this is achieved by incorporating the death of the addressee-referent's relation into the semantics of the necronym itself, by explicitly mourning the deceased. In both cases a particular configuration of interactional role inhabitance and kin-term use bears an uncanny iconicity with, and indexically invokes, the deceased.

Kiowa Apache and Western Penan post-mortem registers are both systems where mourning is managed by an economy of affect (see O'Connor, 1990, on Northern Pomo post-mortem name avoidance). Names of the dead and the living must be avoided because both palpably invoke the participant frameworks that the recently deceased once occupied. This dangerous voicing structure is crystallized in vocative kin-term address, where the propositus and referent of the kin term are also its speaker and addressee, respectively. But interestingly, the perspectival orientations of the two systems are inverses of each other. In Kiowa Apache, the speaker risks vocatively summoning the dead when addressing someone with the same term that the speaker once used for the deceased. In Western Penan, the speaker risks voicing the dead individual by addressing a particular individual with the same term that the deceased used for that individual when they were still alive.

The takeaway from the present discussion is this: Despite an elaborate, enregistered set of post-mortem kin-term avoidances, in neither Kiowa Apache nor in Western Penan are the unmarked series of kin terms tabooed (in the strict sense of being performatively indefeasible with respect to discourse reference). Indeed, everyday kin terms appear never to be subject to censure independent of their reference. Rather, the sociopragmatic effects of kin terms reflect their relational structure as two-place noun phrases that relate an ego to an alter (see Kockelman, 2010, p. 25, on the "relational function" of pronouns and kin terms). The sociopragmatics of their use and avoidance – even in these mourning registers – minimally require that either the ego or the alter of the kin term refers to the close kin of the deceased individual. Unlike name taboos, the sociopragmatics of kin terms in these cases are only half-way decoupled from their discourse reference.

Nomic Reference and Rigid Performativity

Post-mortem kin-term usage underscores that names, among human nouns, are uniquely prone to becoming taboo. Understanding why this is the case reveals how the semantic and referential structure of linguistic forms "projects" an ideological interpretation of their social pragmatic functions (after Whorf, 2000, p. 263). That is, it suggests that the structural, even semiotic-functional, organization of linguistic categories constrains and motivates particular ideologically informed interpretations of their social consequentiality and meaning (Rumsey, 1990; Silverstein, 1979). Specifically, as I will now argue, the unique properties of names among noun-phrase types can be seen as the template from which name registers – as sociopragmatic formations – arise, again and again, in one language-in-culture after another.

As analytical philosophers Saul Kripke (1980) and Hilary Putnam (1996) have taught us, names have an inherently indexical reference:

> Suppose, let's say, a baby is born; his parents call him by a certain name. They talk about him to their friends. Other people meet him. Through various sorts of talk the name is spread from link to link as if by a chain. A speaker who is on the far end of this chain, who has heard about, say Richard Feynman, in the market place or elsewhere, may be referring to Richard Feynman even though he can't remember from whom he first heard of Feynman or from whom he ever heard of Feynman ... a chain of communication going back to Feynman himself has been established by virtue of his [i.e., the speaker's] membership in a community which passed the name on from link to link.... (Kripke, 1980, pp. 91–2)

Kripke's "causal theory of reference" suggests that names do not refer because of their descriptive backing but because of the way in which they are indexically anchored to their referents. This anchoring cites, and is sited in, an originating baptismal event, where the individual and the name are linked by a more or less explicit (metapragmatic) ritual of naming. Importantly, this anchoring is reproduced every time that someone is initiated into the name-referent connection and thus incorporated into the speech chain "which passed the name on from link to link."

Inherent indexical reference is one important reason that names so often enter into sociopragmatic alternation with other noun-phrase types, like kin terms. Noun-phrase types that specify the indexical reference of their tokens – or inherently referential NPs, for short – routinely develop polite pragmatic alternants (Bean, 1978; Errington, 1985; Silverstein, 2003). Pronouns of address – NPs that specify that their tokens indexically refer to addressee – are perhaps the most elaborated sites of sociopragmatic alternation cross-linguistically. Honorific second-person pronouns appear in languages all over the world (see Head, 1978; Helmbrecht, 2005; and Chapter 7 for surveys). In many languages, third-person anaphors and demonstratives are also loci of honorific alternations. The avoidance of the use of an individual's personal name can be seen in the same light, as a pragmatic phenomenon related to the inherent referentiality of the NP type.

But though inherent indexical reference can be seen to account, in part, for the prevalence with which they are avoided, it cannot account for why proper names – in contradistinction to other inherently referring noun-phrase types – are so often taboo (as opposed to merely avoided). Considerations of inherent referentiality can help account for why pronouns, anaphors, and names are so often sites of contextualized avoidance in honorific address and reference to certain individuals. They cannot, however, account for why names but not these other noun-phrase types so often become unmentionable (Fleming & Lempert, 2011). To understand this crucial difference, it is necessary to attend to differences in how the discourse reference of these inherently referential noun-phrase types (pronouns, anaphors, and names) can or cannot be shifted in actual discursive events.

Pronouns, anaphors, and names are all NP [= noun-phrase] types that incorporate an indexical component. And yet the mapping of the indexical sign onto its referential object is different in all three cases. Each of these three NP types involves a different default **calibration type**. Elaborating on the framework that Roman Jakobson (1971) had formalized in "Shifters, Verbal Categories, and the Russian Verb," Silverstein (1993) fleshed out the different ways in which what is said in discourse (the "denotational text" of a discursive interaction) can be indexically related to what is happening in it (that is, can be related to the "interactional text" of the discursive interaction). He called these distinct modes of indexical mapping "calibration types," and he distinguished three kinds: the reflexive, the reportive, and the nomic.

To say that linguistic signs in context are *reflexively calibrated* is to say that variables of the denotational text are given their values by appeal to features of the co-occurring interactional text. As Jakobson (1971) and Benveniste (1971) recognized long ago, this is precisely how the referential values of first- and second-person pronouns are set. The denotation of such "shifters" can be determined only by knowing the identities of the central participants, the speaker and addressee respectively, of the ongoing discursive interaction.

Importantly, the referential values of reflexively calibrated indexically denotational categories can be reset by their occurrence under a *reportive calibration*, a calibration type in which denotational values are determined with respect to an event of signalling distinct from the ongoing event-of-signalling. Such resetting of the default values occurs when first- and second-person pronouns are used within direct represented speech constructions (see Banfield, 1993; Haviland, 1996; B. Lee, 1997, on the transposition of indexical values; cf. logophoric pronouns). When indexicals that have a default reflexive calibration (i.e., pronouns) occur in reported speech constructions, their sociopragmatic effects do not tend to "leak" (Irvine, 2011) into the signalling event. When an impolite second-person pronoun is "mentioned," its occurrence is not considered to be disrespectful toward the addressee in the here-and-now event-of-signalling. (A tattletale will not risk being impolite to the school principal by reporting that "Johnny said '*tu*' to the French teacher.") Though second-person pronominals may have normatively negatively valued performative effects quite similar in kind to verbal taboos when they occur under a reflexive calibration, they are not unmentionable, in the specific sense of being unreportable or uncitable. Their sociopragmatic effects are defeased by reportive calibration. Metapragmatic models of the non-referential function of pronouns thus appear to be parasitical upon their mode of reference; just as the reference of "shifters" can be transposed out of the event of signalling, so too can their sociopragmatic effects be contained and displaced.

What is true of first- and second-person pronouns is *ipso facto* the case for third-person anaphors and demonstratives. The default calibration of anaphoric indexicals is reportive. Prototypically, and as with other reference-tracking devices, anaphors receive their referential values by appeal to some swatch of denotational text (e.g., a cross-referenced noun phrase) that is distinct from (prototypically, prior to) the anaphor token itself. The reference of third-person anaphors and demonstratives often changes from discourse segment to discourse segment. This means that while, for instance, the impolite third-person masculine singular anaphor in Tamil, *avan*, may be inappropriate at one segment in discourse, it may be expected in the next, as the identity of the individual referred to with it changes. And once again, because anaphors have their values set by reportive calibration, they do not tend to become unmentionable – their sociopragmatics depend upon their discourse reference.

To summarize, the reference of pronouns and anaphors varies depending upon different framed relationships of denotational to interactional text. These considerations help explain why pronouns, anaphors, and demonstratives rarely become taboo or unmentionable. The semiotic-functional organization of these noun-phrase types – specifically, the possibility of their indexical reference being reset by reportive calibration – ensures that their non-referential sociopragmatic functions can be similarly defeased.

Personal names function in a manner quite distinct from these other denotational indexicals. Unlike pronouns and anaphors, in order to identify the referent of a personal name we must be linked through a chain of semiotic events to the performative and baptismal moment wherein referent and name were joined together. Again, as Kripke (1980) illustrated in his 1970 lectures on "Naming and Necessity," it is not that personal names have a semantic intension (some one unique definite description) to which only one thing in the universe (its unique extension) conforms. Rather, the personal name is indexically connected to its referent through a singular (and performative) baptismal event that every use of the name subsequently presupposes. But this also means that, unlike other denotational indexicals, personal names are not given new specification in each speech event, either as a function of which individual occupies the role of speaker or addressee, as with pronouns, or depending on what antecedent noun phrase cross-references them, as with anaphors. Rather, they are **rigid designators** (Kripke, 1980). Their reference is set once and for all.

In this respect, personal names are more like purely symbolic noun-phrase types, like common nouns, than they are like pronouns or anaphors. True (Peircean) symbols have an invariant semantic "content" and denotation across events of speaking. Symbols are characterized by a nomic (that is, "timeless" or immutable) calibration of denotational text onto interactional text (cf. Handman, 2010). Just as the denotation of a common noun is constant across instances of use, so too is the reference of a name constant across instances of its use. Names, invariant in their reference across token instances, share this *nomic calibration* with symbols. This is reflected in the constancy of their reference across token instances, even under reportive calibrations (i.e., even within reported speech constructions). Although the referential values of all other inherently indexical noun-phrase types can be reset, as when they occur within reported speech constructions, personal names have constant reference regardless of their contextualization in discourse.

To summarize, personal names are a special kind of noun-phrase type, uniting the constant denotation of purely symbolic nouns with the indexical denotation of shifters, anaphors, and demonstratives. This unique semiotic-functional "content" of names among all other noun-phrase types (Silverstein, 1987b) accounts for the cross-cultural prevalence of personal name taboos. The "timeless" indexical relation between name and referent motivates a parallel metapragmatic or ideological model that stipulates the context-independent performativity of names vis-à-vis their referents. Just as the relationship between name and referent is immutable, so too does the relationship between the name and its performative function come to be ideologically framed as immutable. Tabooed names are **rigid performatives**.[3] In name taboos, the referential-indexical function of the noun-phrase type serves as a ground, and site of semiotic exaptation, for a non-referential and performative function that, in some cases, all but supplants it.

Referential Telescoping and Linguistic Ideology: Homonymous Kinship

The unique semiotic-functional structure of names among noun-phrase types – the rigid indexicality of names – is a crucial scaffold for the development of the indefeasible performativity of names within sociocultural worlds. The invariable indexical reference of the name undergirds a parallel metapragmatic model of the inviolability of the performative function of the name vis-à-vis its referent. And yet I have also argued that what is unique to name taboos is a pragmatics of use that precisely exceeds reference (e.g., the avoidance of one's brother-in-law's name not just in reference to him but in reference to others who share the same name). This pragmatic leakage beyond the rigid designator is catalyzed by a second ideological process: the referential telescoping of proper nouns into proper names. It is to this latter point of conjuncture that I now turn.

Rare are languages like Chuukese (Oceanic; Micronesia), in which each individual has "a distinctive personal name that he shares with no one else, living or dead" (Goodenough, quoted in Da Matta, 1982, 79). In most human collectivities, the same name is attached to multiple persons. In these situations, a distinction must be made between names that refer to specific persons (i.e., rigid designators) and names as generic types. Following Schlücker and Ackermann (2017), I will distinguish between the lexical category of the name – the **proper noun** – and the name as used in definite reference to a particular person: "Proper nouns (nomina propria, proprial lemmas) constitute the *lexical* category of names.... Proper names, on the other hand, are definite NPs, as they refer (uniquely) to specific individuals in the world" (p. 311). This distinction will be vital to understanding the sociopragmatics of name registers, as linguistic avoidance may be normatively required at the level of both the proper name and the proper noun. Indeed, and as discussed above, in the case of name *taboos* (as opposed to mere *avoidances*), the sociopragmatics of name tokens are not defeased by their discourse reference. Recall the example, discussed above, of the Abkhaz bride who could not utter the name of her brother-in-law, Kiasou, even when she was referring to her own brother, who happened to bear the same name. In this example the proper noun *Kiasou* is taboo. All tokens of the proper noun, regardless of their reference, are insulting when uttered by Kiasou's sister-in-law. Nevertheless, the deference-target of *Kiasou*, the person who is disrespected if the woman utters it, is only one particular referent of the proper noun: the speaker's brother-in-law. At the level of language ideological or folk ethnometapragmatic reflection, speakers model the disrespectful performativity of the proper noun on analogy to the referential structure of the proper name. I call this ideological process **referential telescoping**: The functions (whether semantic or pragmatic) of a word *type* are rationalized by language users in terms of the specific and definite discourse reference of some subset of its *tokens*. Keeping with the example, the disrespectfulness of the proper noun type *Kiasou* is rationalized in light of the differential reference of a subset of its tokens to the speaker's brother-in-law.

The idea of referential telescoping again draws upon Michael Silverstein's work, here his treatment of feminine markedness in English. In that context, Silverstein (1985) argued that speakers conceptualize grammatical categories in terms of their differential reference to existential particulars "out there" in the world. The third-person singular English anaphor *he* is conceptualized as a masculine pronoun because it is differentially employed to refer to men. From the perspective of a structuralist semantics, however, *he* is simply unmarked for the feature [+/− feminine]. For Silverstein, this explains the historically generic value of *he/him/his* (cf. J. Shapiro, 1982). There is much debate on this point, and a feminine markedness approach to English anaphors is not without its problems (see Aikhenvald, 2016). Nevertheless, and leaving aside the question of the correctness of the analysis for the case of semantic gender, the structure of the argument is clear. Native-speaker metalinguistic awareness tends to understand the prototypical or differential real-world reference of linguistic forms – an exclusively discourse- and token-level dimension of their functioning for any (Peircean) symbol – to be an inherent property of the construction-type at the level of the linguistic code. In coordination with non-linguistic cultures of gender, this ideological model then feeds back into how discursive practice is interpreted and judged – the use of *he* as an epicene pronoun is judged as androcentric (e.g., Martyna, 1980), and distinct fashions of speaking (e.g., the use of "he or she" or "they" for generic third-person singular reference) emerge against the backdrop of this rationalization of language structure.

Referential telescoping appears to be a crucial "semiotic process" (Irvine & Gal, 2000, p. 37) by means of which the sociopragmatics of the proper name become grafted onto the proper noun. In reflecting on this process, one might be tempted to frame the emergence of proper-noun taboos as deriving from a sort of ideological "misrecognition" of the proper noun for the proper name. But this would fail to adequately capture the surplus-value of the playful conflation of name and noun, name referent and namesake, within sociocultural life worlds (cf. de Pina-Cabral, 2010). Cultural orders make creative use of the play of difference and identity between the proper name and proper noun.

This creative conflation of proper name and proper noun is seen in the diverse social institutions that imbue name-sharing with culturally specific meanings and effects. For instance, institutions of name transmission often figure persons separated over deep historical time as sharing a covert essential identity in common. In the Pacific Northwest, names are the inalienable property of lineages: "Tsimshian say that people are given to the names rather than the reverse" (J. Miller, 1998, p. 670; Roth, 2008). Here the name is not a unique designator for the person; the person is an avatar for the name. In these cases, language users do not so much fall into the error of mistaking the proper name for the proper noun as they "invent" with that misrecognition (cf. Wagner, 1981) – they exploit the ambiguity between name and noun. What Lévi-Strauss (2021) understands as the "classificatory function of names" (Maybury-Lewis, 1984) emerges out of the possibilities provided by the structural ambiguities and overlaps between proper names and proper nouns.

Another institution that referentially telescopes the proper noun into the proper name is that of **homonymous kinship** (Ball, 2015; Sahlins, 2013). Homonymous kinship is realized through tropes of fictive kin-term use, where two or more namesakes are treated as though they were one and the same person. These tropes are most easily construed (and, correspondingly, most elaborated) in address. This fictive kin-term use involves the transposition of either the origo or the referent of the kin term. (As a reminder, in the noun phrase *Fareed's uncle*, the referent [also called "alter"] of the kin term is the uncle and Fareed is the origo [also called "propositus" or "ego"] of the kin term.) Name-sharers transpose the origo of kin-term reference to a namesake who has kinship with the addressee. Conversely, the kin of name-sharers transpose the referent of the kin term to a namesake of one of their own kin (see Figure 4.1 for illustrations of the transposition of kin-term reference in Ju|'hoan). Homonymous kinship thus figurates a fictive identity between name-sharers.[4] Name-sharers may address the kin of their namesakes with the terms that those namesakes would employ. And the relatives of an individual may address his or her namesakes with the kin terms that they normally employ for that individual. Typically, the interactional modes of being with others associated with the kin categories are also tropically re-enacted in the fictive kin relation.

Case Study: Ju|'hoan Homonymous Kinship

For exemplification of namesake relationships, I draw on Marshall (1957) and R. Lee's (1986, 1993) descriptions of name-sharing among the Ju|'hoan of southern Africa (cf. Barnard, 1978a, on Nharo). Among the Ju|'hoan, the interactional ethoses of joking and avoidance are keyed to kinship categories by the principle of relative generation. Members of disharmonic or odd generations (i.e., $G^{...-3,-1,+1,+3...}$) are stereotypically

Table 4.1. Distinction between joking (or *k"āi* "to joke"/"to play") and avoidance (or *kwa* "to fear"/"to respect") relationships in Jul'hoan, depicted from the perspective of a female ego

Generation	Cognatic kin		Affinal kin	Name receiver	Name giver	
G^{+3}	**great-grandparents**		**great-grand.-in-law**	1st son	FF	G^{+2}
G^{+2}	grandparents		grandparents in-law	1st daughter	FM	
G^{+1}	**parents, uncles, aunts**		**parents-in-law (etc.)**	2nd son	MF	
G^{0}	**brother**	sister	H,HB **HZ**	2nd daughter	MM	
G^{-1}	**children, niblings**		**children-in-law (etc.)**	3rd son	**FB**	G^{+1}
G^{-2}	grandchildren			3rd daughter	**FZ**	
G^{-3}	**great-grandchildren**			4th son	**MB**	
				4th daughter	**MZ**	

Notes. Avoidance relations are depicted in bold, joking relations in regular font. Norms of name transmission from ascending to descending cognatic kin as a function of birth-order appear on the right.
Source: R. Lee (1986).

avoidance relations, while members of harmonic or even generations (i.e., $G^{...-2,0,+2...}$) are joking relations. There is added complexity in G^0 in the relationships among siblings and siblings-in-law. Cross-sex siblings are classed as avoidance relations, while same-sex siblings are classed as joking relations. However, with respect to relations through marriage, this logic gets switched; spouse and same-sex siblings of spouse are classed as joking relations and cross-sex siblings of spouse are classed as avoidance relations. This patterning of joking/avoidance over even/odd generations is depicted on the left side of the display in Table 4.1.

Importantly, this bifurcation of relational kinds by relative generation becomes extended to all members of the social world through name-sharing relationships. In fact, name relationships become the basis for a system of universal kinship whereby all members of the social universe can be called by a kin term (Barnard, 1978b). This "extension" depends upon the structuring of name sets and of name transmission.

There are a remarkably limited number of names among the Ju|'hoan. Lee's 1964 survey of the Dobe area yielded 36 men's names and 32 women's names, with some names shared by as many as 26 individuals (R. Lee, 1986, p. 88). Names are transmitted from senior to junior cognatic kin in a systematic fashion. This is diagrammed on the right side of the display in Table 4.1. Essentially, the first two female children and the first two male children in a family will be named after

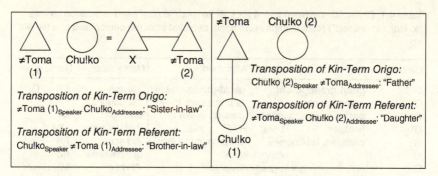

Figure 4.1. Tropes of kin address between namesakes in Ju|'hoan
Source: R. Lee (1986).

grandparents, while subsequent children are named after aunts and uncles, though more distant relations may also be namesakes. Notably, because grandparents tend to be the most frequent name givers, the name transmission relationship is prototypically anchored to alternate generation, joking relationships.

Because there are so many potential name-sharing relationships, homonymous kinship creates conflicting framings of relationship. Richard Lee recounts how he "used to sit in amazement as Sa//gain!a [an older woman] rattled off names, terms, and rationales for dozens of kin pairs" (R. Lee, 1993, p. 76, note 9). Lee (1986, p. 91) gives the example of a woman, Chu!ko, and a man, ≠Toma, who through distinct lines of name-sharing could be related either as "father" and "daughter" (and therefore be unmarriageable avoidance relations) or as "brother-in-law" and "sister-in-law" (and therefore be marriageable joking relations). (Figure 4.1 illustrates in schematic form these two paths for transposing kin-term address through namesakes.) The loosely structured system thus creates a space, and idiom, for expressing agency. But that agency is not absolute – typically, senior kin have the right to specify to juniors which name-sharing relationship will take precedence and thus which kin terms they are to employ for one another (cf. Paulston, 1976, on seniority-based rights of "dispensation" in European T-V systems). The role of seniority is reflected in the only dedicated terms of human reference needed to support these registers of person reference – the terms by which the namesakes call each other. Older namesakes address younger namesakes as *!kuma* "young name," while younger namesakes address older namesakes as *!kun!a* "old name" (cf. the *saunik* "old bone" terminology in the Inuit homonymous kinship system: Alia, 2007; Guemple, 1965).

To summarize, homonymous kinship involves a creative telescoping of the proper name into the proper noun. The fiction of the biographical identity of namesakes is scaffolded by a purposeful misreading of the proper noun as a rigidly designating name. This purposeful misreading, in turn, undergirds an intentional misrecognition of the real-world referent for his or her namesake (e.g., the intentional misrecognition of ≠Toma for his namesake in Figure 4.1). As I have shown, a similar interplay between name and noun is at work in name taboos. In the joking relationships mediated by name-sharing, the referents of a shared proper noun are fictively identified with one another. In the name taboos so common to avoidance relationships, all tokens of a proper name, regardless of their reference, are treated as having the same sociopragmatic effects vis-à-vis one particular referent of the proper noun – the avoidance relation.

Name-sharing, a shibboleth of joking relationships, thus represents the structural inverse of name avoidance, the shibboleth of avoidance relationships. The interaction rituals of kinship avoidance seek to maintain the separation of the categorically different by not impinging upon (signs of) the other and by forestalling various kinds of shared phenomenological experience (see Part 3). Joking involves interpersonal identification, manifest in free licence and access to (signs of) the person of the other. (One can literally borrow one's namesake's personhood.) In name-sharing, the mutual identification of the joking relationship is taken to its limit; the joking relatives are literally identified with one another.

Phonological Iconism and Honorific Grades in Name Registers

To review, I have argued that the unique semiotic structure of proper nouns among noun-phrase types scaffolds convergent ethnometapragmatic models of names and naming. The "rigid" referential relationship between the name and its referent motivates an analogously "rigid" performativity of the name. Further, the ideological ratchet of referential telescoping mediates the extension of rigid performativity from the personal name to the proper noun. And yet, as shown in the last chapter, name-based avoidances often do not stop at the proper noun. They are routinely extended even further into proscriptions on the use of homophones or near-homophones of tabooed proper nouns. Table 4.2 provides examples of this sort of phenomenon from a range of name registers employed in the mediation of in-law relationships.

Table 4.2. Examples of near-homophone avoidance in in-law name registers

Language (source)	Tabooed name	Phonetically similar words also avoided	
Tamil (Pillai, 1972, p. 430)	*maasilaamani*	<u>maa</u>*di* "cattle"	<u>maa</u>ngaay "mango"
Nuaulu (Florey & Bolton, 1997, p. 20)	*tukanesi*	<u>tuka</u> "to make"	<u>nesi</u>e "left"
Sidaama (Teferra, 1987, p. 46)	*dawasso*	<u>daa</u> "to come"	<u>da</u>n*t*ʃa "good"
V'ënen Taut (Fox, 1996, p. 380)	*kalhapat*	na<u>kal</u> "post"	-<u>kal</u>- "to prop up"

In order to understand why name registers so often involve the three levels – avoidance of the personal name, of the proper noun, and of phonologically iconic words of other lexical categories – it is necessary to bring together two facts, one concerning the ideological framing of avoidance speech and the other concerning its discursive implementation. (1) Kinship-keyed name avoidance is ideologically framed and actually enacted as a respectful, honorific practice. In the affinal context, the failure to follow name-based avoidances is disrespectful and read as a sign of a problem in the relationship.[5] (2) In many languages-in-culture, all three of these structural "pegs" (i.e., the name, the noun, and the homophone) are actualized as distinct avoidance levels in the idiolects of particular speakers. The second observation is intimately connected with the first. Close study of these cases reveals that where different "pegs" of avoidance become associated with the enactment of distinct kin relationships, these constitute a series of avoidance levels graded by honorific function.

To understand this phenomenon, it may help to return to the framework presented in the Introduction. In that context I was concerned to think through the continuum-like properties of kinship avoidance. In many societies, kinship avoidance is practiced across a range of relationships, but to varying degrees or intensities. I showed that different gradations of kinship avoidance correspond with distinct avoidance levels: ensembles of avoidance practices that circumvent behaviours tabooed in enacting particular kinship relationships within a given language-in-culture. I illustrated that these avoidance levels are related to one another by implicational relationships such that "higher" avoidance levels incorporate all of the avoidances employed at "lower" levels. (For a review, see the discussion of Tikopia and Kobon avoidances in the Introduction.) Because avoidance levels thus stand in

Rigid Performativity

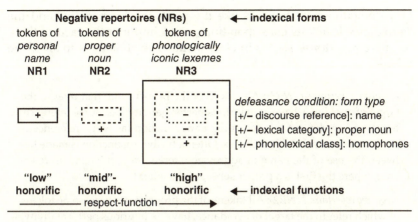

Figure 4.2. Formal-functional diagrammatic structure which produces honorifically graded avoidance levels in name registers
Note. NR = the negative repertoire, an ensemble of signs normatively avoided.

superset-subset relationships to one another, they are readily commensurable – one avoidance level can be judged as "larger" or "smaller" than any other. I argued that this structuring principle is crucial in producing the gradient quality of kinship avoidance, in making some relationships more respectfully restrained than others. This structuring of avoidance levels creates an analogy between formal plenitude and functional intensity; all other factors being equal, "larger" avoidance repertoires enact "greater" respect.

Avoidance levels in name registers involve the same logic of formal encompassment, on the one hand, and functional grading, on the other. Only here, the (minimally) three levels of avoidance practice – avoidance of the personal name, of the proper noun, and of (near-)homophones of the name – *necessarily* stand in class-member relationships to one another. I illustrate this in schematic form in Figure 4.2 and only subsequently offer an empirical example.

Each of the three "rules" of avoidance – avoidance of the name, of the noun, and of homophones – is associated with a distinct, structurally definable negative repertoire. (In Figure 4.2, these are labelled as NR1, NR2, and NR3, respectively.) Recall that a negative repertoire is the set of signs invested with a negatively valued performativity in avoidance contexts. Each negative repertoire corresponds to an avoidance level – the positive repertoire of signs that substitute for the tabooed signs.

(The "negative repertoire" is like the photographic negative and the "avoidance level" its corresponding print.) Importantly, each of these negative repertoires stands in class-member relationships to all of the others:

Negative repertoire 1 (NR1): All tokens of the proper noun that refer to the target of avoidance have an injurious performativity; discourse reference, however, can defease this sociopragmatic function (as when reference is made to a namesake). [Sub-classes: Often a further distinction is made between the use of the name in addressee-reference and the name in reference, where the first is a proper subset of the latter.]

Negative repertoire 2 (NR2): All tokens of the proper noun type, some tokens of which refer to the target of avoidance, have an injurious performativity; but the lexical category of proper noun can defease pragmatic function (as when speakers employ homophones of different lexical categories).

Negative repertoire 3 (NR3): All tokens of any of a registered set of lexemes similar to or identical in phonological form to the proper noun (i.e., members of a phonolexical class), some tokens of which refer to the target of avoidance, have an injurious performativity. [Sub-classes: Sometimes, as in the Zulu example below, a further distinction is made between the lexical roots that are formatives in the proper noun and a wider set of words phonologically iconic with the proper noun.]

In Figure 4.2, each of the three negative repertoires is enclosed by a solid line. Imagine each such box as enclosing the set of possible discourse tokens that would be injurious or disrespectful toward a target-of-avoidance were they used in the speech of some origo-of-avoidance. Looked at in terms of their global organization, these negative repertoires constitute a nested structure of recursive formal encompassment. The referentially bound name (NR1) is but one actualization of a proper noun, so its tokens are a proper subset of the set of tokens of that proper noun (NR2); the proper noun is one of a set of phonologically iconic lexemes, so its tokens are a proper subset of the set of tokens of the class of lexemes phonologically iconic with the name (NR3). Each next "higher" level of name avoidance encompasses all of the avoidances associated with the "lower" levels. If one avoids the proper noun of a particular relative then one avoids the personal name. If one avoids homophones of the name then one avoids the proper noun and the name. Just as with the Tikopia and Kobon avoidances discussed in the Introduction, the negative repertoires that compose name registers stand in chained implicational relationships to one another: [homophone → [proper noun → [personal name]]].

What is the relevance of this seemingly simplistic fact about class-member relationships between linguistic signs? As I will now show with a case study, the important point is the following: This formal structure motivates an analogous functional grading; the avoidance of "larger" sized negative repertoires enacts "more" respect.

Case Study: Nested Name Avoidance in Zulu Daughter-in-law Speech

Zulu (Bantu; South Africa) *isihlonipho* "language of respect through avoidance" offers an example which illustrates how recursive nesting of negative repertoires is functionally realized as a series of honorific grades. I draw on Otto Raum's (1973) ethnography carried out in the 1950s in Zululand.

As illustrated in Figure 4.3, and taking the perspective of a female ego, Zulu name avoidances can be seen to be differentiated into at least four distinct avoidance levels. The least rigorous name avoidance is reserved for elder siblings. Here it is only in addressee-reference that the name must be avoided. (Junior natal kin are freely addressed by name.) A slightly larger range of name avoidances is reserved for parents. Here the name is avoided in all acts where discourse reference is made to the target of avoidance. This only rarely conditions the avoidance of the true homophone of the name (i.e., the lexical root out of which the proper noun is formed), and then only for the father and not for the mother. Name taboos, however, apply to a number of members of the husband's family. A married woman avoids the name, the proper noun, and the lexical root from which that name is composed, of her husband's mother, her husband's father's brother, her daughter's husband, and her own husband, after his father has passed away. (Zulu names, like names in Nguni languages more generally, are often standalone nouns drawn from "everyday objects/events/states, e.g., *Mandala* ('Strength'), *Siqandulo* ('Grindstone')" [Herbert, 1990, p. 460].) Finally, the most enveloping avoidance – avoidance of the name, the proper noun, the true homophone, and of lexemes that share a syllable in common with the proper name – is reserved for a woman's father-in-law.

The greater the range of forms avoided by a speaker, the greater the honorific function enacted in and through the sociolinguistic practice of avoidance. First, within the consanguineal family, the scaling of name avoidance figures seniors as being due respect. Juniors can be called by name, seniors of the same generation cannot be addressed by name, and ascending-generation lineal kin cannot ever be named. But in-laws are owed a

Prototypical target of avoidance	:	Structural "pegs" of negative repertoire
HF	:	proper noun + root + syllable
HM, HFB, DH, H after HF dies	:	proper noun + root
parent	:	name in reference
elder sibling	:	name in address

Figure 4.3. Nested negative repertoires characteristic of the speech of some Zulu married women
Source: Raum (1973).

higher degree of respect than are natal kin. This can be seen by triangulating linguistic avoidances with non-linguistic deference routines. Upon taking up residence in the house of her husband's parents, a woman has to engage in elaborate and marked deference routines. Within her husband's homestead, the daughter-in-law should not "appear improperly dressed (bare head and breasts) before her parents-in-law, establish eye contact with the in-laws, touch their belongings, enter the father-in-law's hut, talk directly to the father-in-law, point at in-laws ... [or] eat food left over from the father-in-law" (Herbert, 1990, p. 458, after Raum, 1973, p. 15). As discussed in the previous chapter, Afro-Eurasian daughter-in-law avoidance is often thematized as respect toward the patrilineage of the husband, where the living father-in-law is the figurehead and focal point of avoidance practice. Homophone avoidance is most pronounced with respect to the name of the father-in-law; even non-morphological phonological sequences in a word which are iconic with those in the name of a father-in-law may condition word avoidance. The mother-in-law occupies an intermediate role; her name and the noun from which it is composed are also respected through avoidance, and by sons-in-law as well. But mothers-in-law also *hlonipha* the names of their daughters' husbands. That is, mother-in-law and son-in-law engage in a reciprocal avoidance; "neither may mention the other's personal name nor the roots upon which the name is based. E.g., if a woman's son-in-law is named *Umanzi* ('Water'), she will avoid the word *amanzi* 'water' ... if the son-in-law's name is *Undlu* ('Home one'), she will not say *indlu* 'house'" (Herbert, 1990, p. 462, after Raum, 1973, p. 61).

Figure 4.3 represents one attested pattern of Zulu name avoidances. There is variation among Raum's informants. For instance, some speakers avoided the lexical root that is a true homophone of their father's name. What remains constant, however, is the relative ranking of kin types over negative repertoires – the name of a living father-in-law always conditions the most extensive avoidances, while the names of junior natal kin do not condition any.

The Zulu name register is arranged into four distinct avoidance levels, each prototypically associated with distinct kinship relations. The formal organization of negative repertoires into recursively encompassing sets projects an analogous grading of the honorific functions associated with the corresponding avoidance levels. The "size" of the negative repertoire is an icon of the "size" of origo's respect for the target of avoidance. Importantly, the relative "sizes" of these sets can be readily judged because they contain or are contained by one another and are thus readily commensurable. Progressively larger negative repertoires, as these emanate "out" from the name of the target of avoidance, are associated with more heightened respect and reserve. To avoid not only the name, but also a range of words similar to the name, is to be more (even maximally) respectful.

As I show in Part 4, this diagrammatic, formal-functional structure recurs across diverse media of avoidance. It is a kind of meta-attractor for kinship avoidance registers. (I use the prefix "meta-" here to indicate that the diagrammatic structure is an abstract "pattern which connects" a set of patterns instantiated across diverse media of avoidance [Bateson, 1980].) The exposition of this recurring fractal pattern – the self-organization of avoidance levels into nested subsets of one another – is the aim of Chapter 8. Correspondingly, I will leave aside further discussion of this theme here.

I have been forced to preview that discussion here because it is relevant for understanding the diachronic development of name registers. Homophone avoidance has as its final (or teleological) cause this nested structure. I infer that, when graded with respect to already registered practices of personal name avoidance (NR1) and proper noun taboo (NR2), homophone avoidance (NR3) serves as a readily legible trope of hypertrophied honorification. The formal-functional analogy that converts the range of forms avoided into an icon of the amount of respect shown for the target of avoidance motivates the diachronic growth and elaboration of the name register. Once name avoidance is established as a sign of respect, the avoidance of a wider and wider range of forms "emanating out" from the name is legible as a trope of heightened respect. Here, structural types that include but are not limited to the personal name become targets of avoidance in tropes of honorification. I suggest that this figurational logic historically pulls sociolinguistic practices of name avoidance "up" from the name to the noun and then to the homophone.[6]

In the most hypertrophic extension of name avoidance, speakers must avoid a large, phonolexical class of near-homophones of a name. In these cases, the very sounds out of which the rigidly referring name of the target of avoidance is built are figured as having a performative "power" decoupled from either their sense or their reference. As illustrated in Figure 4.2, neither discourse reference nor lexical category defeases social pragmatic function. This suggests to folk-consciousness that the "power" of tabooed words and expressions is immanent "in" the sounds making up the name of the target of deference indexicality. Respect toward alter is enacted by not touching any part of their name – by avoiding the very sounds of reference.

PART THREE

The Anti-Phatic Function: Interactional Avoidances

Chapter Five

Not on Speaking Terms: Closing and Rerouting Channels of Communication

Avoidance relationships are often paired with joking relationships (Mauss, 1926; Radcliffe-Brown, 1940). The resulting joking-avoidance "system" is sometimes characterized by ethnographers as a binary opposition (Lévi-Strauss, 1958), but more often it is seen as a behavioural continuum where different comportments along that continuum are stereotypically linked to different kinship relationships (see the Introduction). At one extreme are relationships of free access, where individuals have privileged licence to impose upon the person and property of the other. Robert Parkin (1993) gives the following pithy characterization of joking relationships for Munda groups in India:

> Joking relationships ... normally take place between [certain] kin types ... joking ... may be partly verbal, with much sexual innuendo, or it may be also physical, involving pushing or tripping up the other person, throwing ashes or cowdung or water at him or her, trying to expose the other person's lower body by pulling off their clothing, destroying or stealing his or her property etc. Normally there are limits beyond which joking should not go, but within those limits there is the obligation not only to joke but also not to take offence. (p. 252)

Joking relationships find their counterpoint in avoidance relationships. Here individuals avoid direct physical, sensorial, or discursive contact. In the most extreme cases, avoidance relations seek to never be in one another's co-presence. Concerning the strict avoidance between Nyakyusa daughters-in-law and a range of their male in-laws, Monica Wilson (1951) observes, "difficulties of avoidance are apparent at ceremonies when members of different villages are congregated. Then the women are on the watch all the time, and one or another is constantly taking refuge in a hut, or in the bananas, as her friends warn her of the approach of a [classificatory] 'father-in-law'" (p. 83). All of this interactional evasion is conventionally interpreted as respectful behaviour.

Avoidance and joking relationships are highly stylized, positively valued behavioural routines associated with particular social relationships. As we have seen, they have all the attributes of what linguistic anthropologists call semiotic registers. But they also constitute a deeply ingrained interactional ethic or demeanour. Avoidance relations find it very hard to be any other way in relating to one another (Merlan, 1997). Nyakyusa ethnography again furnishes telling examples. Christian missionaries saw avoidance as "unnecessary and inconvenient, if not unchristian," and tried to get young women converts to treat their fathers-in-law like their own fathers. Wilson (1951) recounts the story of a convert, referred to as S—, who "had come to tea with us, together with another Christian woman" (p. 84). S—'s father-in-law arrived unexpectedly. "Before he was visible S— leapt up, gasped 'father-in-law!' and hid herself in the corner of the room behind the door, facing the wall with her face buried in her hands. She stood there a few seconds gasping, then came back to her place and pushing away her chair, sat down on the floor, whispering determinedly: 'I *won't* avoid him, I *won't* avoid him'" (p. 84). Despite the "iconoclastic gesture" (after Latour) of missionary colonial policy, converts still struggled to overcome their own, highly affectively charged, reactions to presencing avoidance partners. A danger of the semiotic armature of the analysis presented here is that it underemphasizes these important corporeal and affective dimensions of avoidance. Though I approach the problem from the perspective of registered comportment, I want to be sure to also keep this experiential dimension in view.

Comparative treatments of joking-avoidance relationships have tended to focus on functional correlates (e.g., Murdock, 1971; Radcliffe-Brown, 1940, 1949; cf. Bloch & Sperber, 2002; Goody, 1959) or to highlight the structural opposition between licence and constraint (Lévi-Strauss, 1958), but always at the price of abstracting away from the embodied practices through which joking and avoidance are enacted in particular societies. Parkin's disclaimer at the opening of his otherwise excellent article on the articulation between joking-avoidance and harmonic-disharmonic kinship generations among Munda groups is representative: "It should be stressed that although these behaviour stereotypes [of joking and avoidance] will be treated as forming a system of contrasting behaviour patterns affecting these societies as wholes, the form they take – the nature of the joking, etc. – will be covered only in passing" (R. Parkin, 1988, p. 67).

If we do turn our attention to the material signs through which "joking" and "avoidance" are actually enacted, we find that in these often-overlooked interactional details it is the body that serves as the crucial semiotic anchor. The body is central in two ways (framework following Silverstein, 2013). First, the body serves as an emblem of personhood, much as the name of the individual does on the linguistic plane. One respects the other by not touching, not seeing, or not speaking these **rigid signs** of the other.[1] Second, the body is the privileged zero-point of interaction, dialogue, and dynamic other-oriented relating. The body is thus both the semiotic substance and the communicative technology by means of which semiotic registers of joking and avoidance not only conventionally index social relationships but also actually instantiate legitimate and illegitimate interpersonal channels of communication. The body is the pivot of these kinship-based behavioural routines. From a comparative perspective, the body constitutes the "etic" substance out of which "emic" rituals of avoidance are fashioned. The analogy is, of course, to sound patterning in language (Pike, 1954), where the human articulatory apparatus is the phon*etic* ground for phon*emic* inventories – the culture-specific sound types. Much as with articulatory phonology, the anatomical and sensorial affordances of the human body constrain and motivate the elaboration of rigid signs of personhood and interactional signs of interpersonal connection. Following the lead of other scholars, themselves inspired by the work of Erving Goffman, who have considered joking-avoidance relationships from a symbolic interactionalist perspective (Anderson, 1982; Handelman & Kapferer, 1972; Howell, 1973), this chapter and the next focus on the non-linguistic, corporeal and objectual repertoires of avoidance registers and how these are employed to negotiate channels of communication and of intersubjective access.

Kinship Avoidance as Semiotic Register

Up to this point, I have focused on the properly linguistic aspects of avoidance registers. I contrasted two distinct kinds of speech registers: context-dependent mother-in-law languages (Part 1) and context-independent name registers (Part 2). The non-linguistic **semiotic range** (Agha, 2007, pp. 179–85) of avoidance registers can similarly be, at least for heuristic purposes, distinguished into semiotic displays that negotiate the absencing/presencing of the avoidance relation in particular social contexts, on the one hand, and signs of avoidance not dependent upon the presence of the other, on the other. I will call the presence-dependent set of avoidance practices the **anti-phatic repertoire**. These are various comportments contingent upon the (potential) contextual co-presence of avoidance relations, and they form the empirical centre of our discussion. The presence-independent set are context independent in the sense that avoidance is practiced with respect to various rigid signs of personhood (e.g., the footprints of alter, the personal possessions of alter, the sleeping area of alter, etc.) even in the absence of the avoidance relation. I discuss the second set of signs first. It should be underscored, however, that these are overlapping sets and that these dimensions of signification often intersect in particular semiotic media, thus overdetermining them as loci of avoidance. For instance, the human voice and the human face are both rigid signs of personhood – that is, are recognized as indexical of unique individuals – and at the same time both are vitally important interactional resources in face-to-face communication. Further, objects connected to avoidance relations can "presence" them even in their absence, as when a Lelet woman cannot walk on floorboards which, during construction, had been carried on the shoulders of a "brother" because it would be "seen as equivalent to standing on his shoulder" (Eves, 1998, p. 130).

Avoidance relations often attend to and avoid important emblems of taboo kin. As I showed in Part 2, avoidance relations almost always avoid the literal rigid designator or name of the other. But non-linguistic emblems, like symbolically important personal possessions, are also often subject to avoidance. What is avoided are various rigid signs of the other, diverse projections of the social person that all have in common a genuine and direct indexical link (like a saint's relic or a signature) with the avoidance relation. Because of the importance of personal possessions and other appurtenances of avoidance relations, I will call this the *object repertoire*. Haptic avoidances of objects complement, but are also rendered iconic with, interactional ones. In *Ojibwa Sociology*, Ruth Landes (1937) describes the anti-phatic routines in which a daughter-in-law engages to avoid her parents-in-law – the use of speech intermediaries, sitting with her back oriented to the target of avoidance, hiding her feet, and so on. But she also provides evidence of object repertoires: "Once Jim Kavanaugh's father left his axe and gun at Jim's house. Jim's wife could not touch them to return them, or to replace them; in this way she showed her respect for the owner" (Landes, 1937, p. 26).

Bongela (2001) and Hunter (1936) provide in-depth descriptions of Xhosa object repertoires. Much as I distinguished between the avoidance of the name when "used" to refer to a particular individual and avoidance of any "mention" of the name (i.e., proper-noun taboo), so too can an analogous distinction be made for object repertoires. A daughter-in-law is permitted to handle the plate of the patriarch, as when washing it, though she may never "use" it for eating; other personal possessions of the father-in-law, the purse that holds his pipes and tobacco or his walking stick, for example, are untouchable. This last – the walking stick – appears to have particularly emblematic status as a "staff of authority and respect ... always associated with men who are either alive or dead" (Hunter, 1936, p. 41). After initiation, a man should never go anywhere without a walking stick (Bongela, 2001, p. 41). And the daughter-in-law's avoidance of this emblem even "grows" iconic-indexical replicas; a married woman should never step over a stick lying on the ground (Hunter, 1936, p. 117). Not unlike the avoidance of the proper noun from which an in-law's name is drawn, the rule of avoidance is generalized to a wider and wider class of similar instances.

These examples are representative of how avoided signs are those with some direct indexical link to the other. Shareable objects, like food, benches, or beds, are particularly apt loci of avoidance. It is a principle of the "contagious" corporeality of the other that guides the system.[2] This unifying theme of corporeal contagion accounts for much of the similarity in avoidance practices cross-culturally, something that suggests a constraining "etic" space of possibilities for the elaboration of these signs of relationship. To not look at, to not speak to, to not eat with, to not touch – what is circumvented is the constitution of a direct vector between the avoidance relations. Nevertheless, it should be underscored that there are many more degrees of freedom in the cultural elaboration of these non-linguistic avoidances than were attested in name and mother-in-law registers, a theme that I return to at the end of the next chapter.

Corporeal taboos are so often a site of ritual elaboration because of the way in which the body is recruited as a sign of personhood (Gell, 1996; Valeri, 2000): "As far as current anthropological and psychoanalytic theories would have it, the enforcement of taboos is a means of constituting an *embodied subject* – a corporeally whole, self-aware person. By creating a safe distance between a body and symbolically threatening external object or action, taboos protect the integrity of the subject by preventing the disintegration of the body in which it necessarily must be located" (Dowdy, 2015, p. 3). Activities that suggest a porous body – the ingestion of food, sexual relations, defecation, menstruation – are activities that are hedged around with taboos. These taboos define relations of identity and difference.

In-law avoidance produces a strongly paradoxical relationship between the body and personhood. The avoidance relative is respected in precisely not recognizing the signs of their personhood.

Avoidance relations are almost always addressed and referred to by self-reciprocal (i.e., reversible) terms rather than by autonyms (terminology after Dziebel, 2007). The unique and contingent – in other words, diacritic – marks of personhood are precisely the ones that are phenomenologically scrubbed clean – sights of the face, sounds of the voice, indeed, all presencing of the other and its traces. If bodily taboos – taboos on sexual penetration being the most salient – concern the integrity of the subject, in the hypertrophic regress of avoidance practices these taboos paradoxically efface that subject altogether. Here the subject is replaced by a dyad constituted by the irreducible and indefinitely mirrored alterity of its monads.

One scholar who has been concerned to think through the cross-modal aspects of avoidance practices is Rupert Stasch. In his discussion of Korowai mother-in-law avoidance, he shows how different elements of the semiotic range of the avoidance repertoire come to be seen as imbued with common qualities (terminology after Gal & Irvine, 2019). A complex set of analogies are constructed between comportments at once tactile, linguistic, and visual (i.e., not touching : not seeing : not naming :: touching : seeing : naming). Because distinct practices are all registered as indexical of the same qualities of social relationship, they tend to be understood by cultural participants as iconic with one another. And it is the tactile body that serves as the anchoring point and master metaphor for this heterogeneous grouping – to utter the name of an in-law will result in "skin-puncturing ... punishments," which suggests that "the crime of name utterance is understood to be, in a sense, one of touching the affine too sharply, impinging on that person in the manner of bodily injury" (Stasch, 2003, p. 324).

"Metasemiotic typifications" here serves to suture, stick, and stitch together diverse corporeal, objectual, and linguistic repertoires because they

> motivate a type of cross-modal iconism whereby forms of speech ... are likened to object-signs of other kinds ... such as paralanguage, gesture, body comportment or artifactual accompaniment.... The fact that language may be used as a metasemiotic notation for both linguistic and non-linguistic signs [means that often] reflexive activity blurs the boundaries between language and non-language at the level of object-signs, i.e., behavioral displays. (Agha, 2007, p. 22)

In most languages-in-culture where kinship avoidances are registered, a single metapragmatic term covers a broad semiotic range of practices. Among Nguni groups, *hlonipha* means "respect through avoidance" (Raum, 1973) and applies to a wide range of linguistic, proxemic, sartorial, etc., avoidances practiced not only by married women but also by men and children. In order to refer to the specifically linguistic subset of avoidances, the prefix *isi-*, which is used for naming linguistic varieties (e.g. *isi-*Zulu, *i-*Swati, *shi-*Tsonga), is employed, as in *isihlonipho* (Herbert, 1990, p. 458). The Kambaata (Cushitic; Ethiopia) term *ballishsha* "encompasses all aspects of the respectful behavior that a married woman observes in deferences to her in-law: avoidance of their names and words similar to their names as well as physical avoidance" (Treis, 2005, p. 294). Ironically, the privileges of language among semiotic media are part of what makes the frontier between linguistic and non-linguistic indexicals of social relationship so porous and paper-thin.

The Anti-Phatic Function

If bodies are the emblems par excellence of personhood, they are also the anchoring nodes of the interactional order: "The adult human body constitutes what we might term a 'natural' – that is, more precisely, culturally ubiquitous – *origo* or indexical centerpoint … The adult human body is … transparently positioned as the very anchor of the communicative life of micro-contextual experience…" (Silverstein, 2013, pp. 89, 91). It is in terms of this communication-anchoring dimension that bodily avoidances function to foreclose certain channels of communication, but also to reinforce others. If we consider kinship now not so much as a static matrix of relations but as a communicative infrastructure, it is clear that avoidance relationships striate that field, delinking nodes of possible interconnection. Avoidance practices constitute dyads within which a channel of communication cannot be explicitly or legitimately established, nodes in the network between which contact cannot be directly established. Corporeally enacted avoidance defines legitimate and illegitimate channels of communication, possible and impossible pathways of exchange.

The reworking of communicative infrastructures is accomplished via what we might dub the **anti-phatic function** – a species of phaticity "aimed at breaking or avoiding contact, at disattending to or ignoring others, at disrupting connections or making noise" (Zuckerman, 2020; see also Zuckerman, 2016). The phatic function of discourse is, of course, oriented toward the "physical channel" that links speech producer and speech receiver and allows for them to communicate (Jakobson, 1960, p. 353). This "contact phaticity" includes diverse and multimodal interactional signs, from "'back-channel' cues, shifts in gaze, repairs, [to] adjustments in bodily orientation [all of which are employed] to create varieties of physical and psychological contact" (Zuckerman, 2020). And yet the significance of communicative "contact" between humans can never be reduced to the brute facts of the material affordances of communicative channels. "Whenever people talk together they establish and sustain a little world of shared attention and involvement, a 'communion of mutual engagement,' as Goffman (1957) described it" (Sidnell, 2009, p. 125). This "communion phaticity" (Zuckerman, 2020) is a surfeit or supplement of mutually ratified "contact phaticity," a risk or a boon to be mitigated or catalyzed, as the case may be. To communicate (e.g., about the weather) is, unavoidably, to meta-communicate about the relationship between the sender and the receiver (Bateson, 1972).

But though the anti-phatic and phatic functions can be grouped under a common heading – phaticity – there is nevertheless a fundamental asymmetry between the two. Channel-establishing or -verifying phaticity is felicitous where mutually ratified. The symmetry of mutual ratification creates a meta-communicative runaway – *I know that you know that I am addressing you...* (see Bateson, 1980, on "double description"; Sperber & Wilson, 1995, on signalling communicative intent). The fact that the communicative channel is open itself becomes part of the common ground of interaction. The anti-phatic function, meanwhile, denies mutual ratification. Lack of contact cannot be mutually ratified. One cannot check to see that the other is not looking, because that would be to look at the other. One cannot check that the other cannot hear, because that would be to talk to the other.

This asymmetry follows from the unavoidably multifunctional character of positive phatic communication which functions both as a meta-sign *about* the contact and as an object-sign *of* the contact.[3] In this sense, the anti-phatic function is more properly characterized as a channel-denying or channel-withholding function, for it denies and withholds precisely what would reassure the other that the channel is closed – mutual ratification. The paradoxes of the anti-phatic function emerge from this logical impossibility of meta-communicating about the closure of a communicative channel that is not only the object, but also the would-be medium, of that meta-communication. I say "logical impossibility" because, as we will see, anti-phatic communication is, far from being a contradiction in terms, a robustly attested genre of (non)communication between avoidance relations. As with paradoxes of meta-communication more broadly, this only goes to show that "it would be bad natural history to expect the mental processes and communicative habits of mammals to conform to the logician's ideal" (Bateson, 1972, p. 180).

To summarize, if semiotic registers of avoidance are so concerned with phaticity, it is not in order to establish or maintain communicative contacts. On the contrary, in avoidance relationships, channel-establishing contact is precisely what is proscribed. Noise is prescribed, but information is proscribed. Linguistically, this anti-phatic function is enacted through the avoidance of direct address, the use of grammatically third-person forms to refer to "actual" speech recipient, and the use of speech intermediaries. In non-linguistic semiosis it is operative in avoidance of eye contact or even gaze directed at the other regardless of whether it is reciprocal, in fastidious non-alignment of bodies, and in spacing in physical co-presence, often negotiated by the use of technologies like barriers, screens, or head-coverings, or by avoiding physical co-presence altogether. These various practices seek to forestall both channel-initiating contact and various kinds of "feedback" (via sightlines, tactile contact, gestural backchannels) that ratify receipt and confirm contact. It is through the closed or turned-away body of the avoidance partner, but also the available and accessible body of the joking-partner, that joking-avoidance puts in place a communicative infrastructure. That is, scaled up, what anthropologists call "joking-avoidance" constitutes a communicative infrastructure, a phatic institution that differentiates the interactional grid of the social field as mediated by kin categories in a divergent and ego-relative manner.

Phaticity and Communicative Infrastructures of Kinship

Alfred Radcliffe-Brown posited a functionalist explanation for the phenomenon of joking-avoidance relationships. He saw both joking and avoidance as strategies for negotiating the tension between the simultaneously "conjunctive" and "disjunctive" interests inherent in the in-law relationship: "The husband's relation to his wife's family ... can be described as involving both attachment and separation, both social conjunction and social disjunction" (Radcliffe-Brown, 1940, pp. 196–7). The husband is from a different social group (e.g., a different exogamous clan) and in this sense may have different ("disjunctive") interests from those of his wife's social group. But through the marriage union, the couple and the parents of the bride come to have common ("conjunctive") interests. The "permitted disrespect" of joking mediates these competing interests by substituting "sham conflicts" for "real ones" (Radcliffe-Brown, 1940, p. 196; 1949, p. 134). Avoidance accomplishes the same end only by a different means. In closing off the communicative channel between in-marrying spouse and members of the nuclear family, "avoidance ... prevents conflict that might arise through divergence of interest" (Radcliffe-Brown, 1940, p. 197).

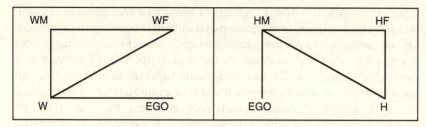

Figure 5.1. Two communicative infrastructures conditioned by affinal avoidance relationships
Notes. On left, in-marrying man's avoidance of parents-in-law (see the example of Tsúùtínà). On right, in-marrying woman's avoidance of husband and father-in-law (see the example of Hindi). Solid lines represent open communicative channels. H = husband; W = wife; M = mother; F = father.

But if the negative phaticity of avoidance closes one communicative channel, it redirects message relay through other channels that must now mediate the relationship between avoidance partners. Here I will sketch out two, in some senses maximally opposed, communicative infrastructures conditioned by avoidance (see Figure 5.1).[4] The first, most often found in small-scale egalitarian societies, closes cross-generational channels of affinal communication and redirects messages – whether discursive, like demands and offers, or more manifestly material, like foodstuffs and personal artefacts – through the linking spousal relation. The other, associated with hierarchical, patrilocal societies, closes cross-gender channels of communication, rerouting communication to and from a wife/daughter-in-law through a gendered circuit – the mother/mother-in-law.

In societies where avoidance is most pronounced between son-in-law and parent-in-law (e.g., Athapaskan groups in North America, Xingu River groups in South America, Vietic and Aslian groups in Southeast Asia), the person who intermediates between the two is prototypically the wife/daughter. By foreclosing other channels of semiotic exchange, avoidance reinforces the relationship between husband and wife, daughter and parent. If avoidance proscribes direct discursive intercourse between a dyad, it prescribes the mediation of that relationship through a third. The resultant speech intermediation is socially organized in just as rich a manner as is the anti-phatic avoidance that gives rise to it.

Some Athapaskan Examples

As a first example I draw upon Scott Rushforth's (1981) article on the sociolinguistics of avoidance among Bear Lake Dene (Northern Athapaskan). Rushforth describes not only the avoidance practices between son-in-law and parents-in-law but also the social organization of speech intermediation; the most appropriate way to speak to "relatives through marriage" is to speak through the partner that constitutes the relation in the first place – the daughter/wife. This **triadic communication** (Ameka 2004; Basso, 2007; Yankah, 1995) is an iconic-index of the mediate or in-between character of the daughter/wife as a structural position. The spouse is a go-between between son-in-law and parent-in-law both in relative-product terms (Keen, 2014) and discursively; the spouse is both the linking relation and the pivotal link in a speech chain.

The Tsúùtínà (formerly "Sarsi"), like the closely related Bear Lake Dene, are a Northern Athapaskan group that practiced son-in-law/mother-in-law avoidance. As is often the case in groups where this pattern is found, the onset of marriage involved a period of bride-service labour "during which the man hunted for his father-in-law and gave the older man gifts of horses" (Honigmann, 1956, p. 25). The most constrained relationship was with the mother-in-law:

> A man would not go near [his mother-in-law's] tipi or even look at her features. She, seeing her son-in-law approach, quickly made off in the opposite direction. A youth who inadvertently saw his mother-in-law's face had to present her with a valuable gift, like a horse. Neither of these affinals ate in the other's presence and necessary communication between them took place through the wife. The latter also conveyed her mother's gifts of moccasins and fancy apparel to her husband. These were gifts designed to reciprocate the steady stream of meat which a man contributed to his father-in-law's household. (Honigmann, 1956, pp. 32–3)

The communicative channel that is closed between the mother-in-law and the son-in-law is transformed into a triadic pathway that passes through the wife. This pathway is a transport system for diverse signs of relationships. It is not just talk, but goods and gifts, meat and moccasins, which are communicated through the mediating third party, the go-between.

Cross-sex sibling and parent-in-law avoidance is common not only to Northern but also to Southern Athapaskan groups. Greville Goodwin's (1942) description of avoidance between Western Apache women and their sons-in-law illustrates a range of methods for entirely closing or, at least, reducing the bandwidth of the communicative channel between the two:

> The avoidance between a man and his mother-in-law in the same family cluster is skillfully managed. The two live in separate dwellings which are usually so placed that ingress or egress is possible without the one being seen by the other. A woman is careful to keep out of sight when she knows her son-in-law is outside, and he does the same for her. At times they may ask another person whether the other is about to make sure that they will not meet. Both usually look before going outside, and if there is danger of their seeing each other a third person may say warningly, "Your son-in-law (or mother-in-law) is here!" Sometimes it is a wife who tells the man that his mother-in-law is about. A woman who accidently meets her son-in-law will immediately put her blanket over her head and turn the other way. The man will also face away and leave at once. Although they supposedly do not see each other, it is not uncommon for one to give a furtive glance over the shoulder at the other going by to make sure he or she will soon be out of sight. .... Nowadays, with the introduction of cars, older people are often dependent on transportation in their son-in-law's car. This is made possible by hanging a blanket between the back and front seats. (pp. 251–2)

Methods employed to close off the communicative channel include advising others of potential run-ins ahead of time; announcing the arrival of an avoidance relation; turning the body away from the avoidance relation; and partitioning interactional space such that a physical barrier stands between avoidance relations (e.g., use of body covering, talking between rooms, dividing spaces with screens). What comes through in Goodwin's account is the work of staging avoidance – it takes a village to manage an avoidance relationship.

The maximal elaboration of avoidance between a son-in-law and his parents-in-law is characteristic of small-scale egalitarian societies, in particular of Oceania and the Americas (refer back to the survey of name registers presented in Table 3.4). Merlan (1997), drawing on Collier and Rosaldo (1981), has argued, quite convincingly, that this pattern should be functionally understood in relation to bride service. In societies where the accumulation of surplus goods is a rarity, like foraging societies, the equivalent of bride price is often "paid" in a constant flow of services and foraged goods (prototypically, game-meat) that pass from the son-in-law to the parents-in-law. This provisioning is typically reciprocated with goods and services flowing in the opposite direction (e.g., handmade clothing, processed or cooked food, etc.). The avoidance relationship displaces or sacrifices discursive exchange for the exchange of material goods and services. Where mutually ratified positive phaticity is foreclosed, it is the exchange of prestige goods – the choicest cuts of meat, the highest-quality moccasins – that must meta-communicate that all is well in the relationship. Objectual repertoires – that is, gifts – are forced to shoulder the weight of meta-communicating relationship. Ritualized exchange relationships in New Guinea and northern Australia that precisely involve interactional avoidance support this line of analysis (Elkin, 1950; Forge, 1970; McDowell, 1976).[5]

From the point of view of communicative infrastructures, what is clear is that in this set-up characteristic of small-scale egalitarian societies, the husband and wife are discursively brought together. The wife is the pivot of interchanges and exchanges between her husband and her parents. From a functionalist perspective, this rechannelling might be seen as contributing to the rapid nucleation of the husband-wife pair.

Some South Asian Examples

The strong correlation between the pattern I have just described and a lack of caste- or class-based social stratification can be seen when contrasted with cases of adjacent generation in-law avoidance in "complex" societies of Africa and Eurasia. As I discussed in the last chapter, in large areas of eastern and southern Africa, Central, Southern, and Western Asia, as well as the circum-Mediterranean region, the most focal avoidance relationship is the one between a daughter-in-law and her father-in-law. This avoidance conforms to standard models of non-reciprocal deference indexicality (the so-called "power dynamic") derived from the study of T-V systems in European languages (R. Brown & Gilman, 1960). The daughter-in-law, as it were, gives "V" (*vos*) to her father-in-law and receives "T" (*tu*) from him. (This is literally the case, for instance, in Sidaama.) With important caveats,[6] avoidance practices in these regions are typically asymmetrical, if not in absolute terms then minimally in the degree and range of signs of respect that the junior female is supposed to demonstrate toward the senior male. These gender- and age-based asymmetries in honorification figurate seniority and masculinity as social predicates that warrant deference-entitlements. Asymmetries of avoidance simultaneously superimpose and create analogies between distinct kinds of status stratification – wife givers : wife takers :: woman : man :: junior : senior :: outsider : insider. The in-marrying woman is consistently marked as an outsider by the elaborated avoidance practices in which she must engage. Fashions of speaking thematically tie these practices of avoidance to the patriarch of her husband's clan. Thus among the Zulu, a bride must *hlonipha* the name of not only her husband's father but also his paternal grandfather and paternal great-grandfather. Here exaggerated deference displays toward the father-in-law metonymically enact respect for the patrilineal descent group of which he is a part. In some cases, deference to the patriclan is quite explicit, as where in-marrying brides avoid the name of the clan or, non-linguistically, its associated totem (Sidaama: Teferra, 1987, p. 44; Teso: Karp, 1978, p. 66).

As compared with the Athapaskan examples that I have just reviewed, the communicative infrastructures that anti-phatic routines foster are quite different in these more hierarchical societies. Take, for instance, the rural Hindu community (621 residents) in Madhya Pradesh where Doranne Jacobson (1982) conducted field research. Married women were supposed to cover their faces before elder, especially male, affines as well as before the husbands of their younger sisters and their husband's sisters' husbands. Later in life, a woman would veil "before the conjugal relatives of her own children" (p. 90). Face covering is achieved by pulling the end of the *sari* over the face (p. 91). Face-covering serves an anti-phatic function, cutting off channels of visual feedback that are crucial in face-to-face communication (for a dedicated discussion, see Chapter 6).

Caste groups (*jat*) were divided into exogamous clans (*got*), and marriages typically occurred between villages. Importantly, this conditioned a strong distinction in the kind of comportment required of a married woman in the village of her *susral* "conjugal home" versus the much more relaxed demeanour appropriate in the village of her *maika* "natal home." At the beginning of a marriage, a woman might spend as much as half of her time in the *maika*, "periods of freedom from purdah" (Jacobson, 1982, p. 89). (All co-residents of a natal village are fictively treated as consanguineal kin, and a "woman observes no purdah in her natal home," p. 89.) Precisely because she could and did return to a context where she was free from the constraints of *purdah* (a term that literally means "curtain" but is metonymically extended to denote the full suite of registered in-law avoidance practices), the demands of avoidance in the village of her *susral* were simultaneously relieved and heightened.

Asymmetrical respect was manifest not only in veiling practices but also in differential rights to address the other. Jacobson (1982) tells us that a senior male has the right to speak to a junior female affine, but the junior can speak to the senior only if she has been interpellated by that senior. Further, a married woman "may speak to the women before whom she veils, but she should not converse with or even speak loudly in front of the men who do not see her face [i.e. elder male relations of her husband]" (p. 91). Importantly, these interdictions include the husband: "A young woman should also veil her face before her husband and avoid speaking to him whenever others are present, most particularly before his or her parents" (p. 91).

In contrast to the Athapaskan examples discussed above, in the socially stratified societies of Central Asia, the Caucasus, and South Asia, the channel-blocking anti-phaticity of prescribed avoidance does not reinforce – at least not overtly – the relationship between husband and wife. On the contrary, wives who take up residence in their husband's parents' compound are enjoined to avoid public interactions with their spouses or any other senior (and therefore "marriageable") male in-laws. Dasgupta (1986), reporting on fieldwork carried out in West Bengal, observes that at the beginning of a marriage the husband and wife perform indifference toward one another when in public: "The husband does not talk to the wife in the presence of a third person, and the wife covers her face using the free end of her sari as a veil (*ghomta*) whenever they are near each other in the presence of other people" (p. 135). After a child is born, avoidance is relaxed, and face covering near the husband is required only when the pair are additionally in the presence of his senior kin.

Here avoidance serves to strongly gender communicative channels, rerouting cross-gender communication into exclusively femininely gendered interactional dyads – messages are rerouted through the channels open between a woman and her mother-in-law, her husband's sister or her co-sisters-in-law. As with these South Asian societies, among many groups in the Caucasus, the husband and wife themselves should avoid overly familiar interaction in the presence of members of the ascending generation (see Luzbetak, 1951, pp. 162–7). The emphasis here is on the woman's subordination to the interactional norms and interpersonal relationships of the members of her husband's house established before her arrival in the household.

Notes on the communicative infrastructures of kinship among rural Kashmiri Pandits (i.e., Brahmins) reveal in a stark manner how "the husband-wife relationship between the junior members of the household ... [is] subordinated to the parent-child and sibling relationships" (Madan, 1989, p. 119). The junior in-marrying woman within a household will be the last to eat. She should not speak or look in the face any adult male and "she should sit with her back turned towards the elders as facing them is regarded as being overbold .... Above all, she should completely avoid her husband in the presence of others" (p. 115). The wife should not do any domestic labour that is specifically directed toward the husband (e.g., prepare him a special meal, wash just his clothes) – "if she wants to wash a single shirt of his, she must collect the dirty clothes of other members of the household as a pretext for the wash" (p. 118). And after he returns from a long journey, the wife should make no public recognition of his return. All of these ways of suppressing public ratification of conjugal intimacy have as their effect the production of precisely what they seek to repress; unable to speak in public, the husband-and-wife pair develops a secret relationship, behind closed doors. She is the *shandagand-tota* "parrot of the pillow" who influences him, but only "when they have both retired to bed" (p. 120). The mother-in-law/daughter-in-law relationship has a "disjunctive" more than a "conjunctive" aspect. Talismans may be obtained to turn a man's loyalties from mother to wife, and the wife's relationship to the brother/son/husband is worried over and seen as potentially pulling his allegiances away from his natal kin.

The anthropology of joking-avoidance has too often treated these anti-phatic routines as mere diacritics of kinship relation (see Valeri's [2000] critique of Lévi-Strauss on taboos generally). And yet, as this brief discussion illustrates, social anthropologists should also be interested in avoidance registers as a crucial component of an institutionalized kinship that functions to (re)configure and engineer culturally diverse communicative infrastructures. Interpersonal avoidances differentiate individuals, keeping subjects separate; but they can accomplish this only by transforming third parties into intermediaries. In these situations, wives/daughters are forced to serve as go-betweens for husbands and mothers, mothers/mothers-in-law for husbands and wives. Note the slash-mark that divides. Interpersonal taboos transform other persons into communicative media – they dividuate (M. Strathern, 1988, p. 13).

Negating Address

The anti-phatic function is genred, being accomplished by stereotyped, socially standardized practices. These avoidance practices thus offer a window onto the cultural ideologies of communicative contact that simultaneously rationalize and inform the active non-presencing of the other (cf. Zuckerman, 2016, on "contact tropes"). The body communicates across multiple modalities, and these modalities are culturally symbolized and affectively activated in different ways. "The intercorporeal experience of visual, acoustic, and haptic materiality in interaction" (Meyer et al., 2017, p. xxix) are all sites for the elaboration of anti-phatic routines and phatic ideologies. In the next chapter, I trace out these different senses and sites of contact and highlight convergences in the technologies and practices of avoidance that target them. There I will be concerned with channel-blocking or channel-diminishing techniques in the broad sense of communicative channel understood as a physical "contact" – that is, as a condition of possibility or affordance for communication as such. Here I want to begin with the avoidance of "on the record" or consummated communication – that is, with communicative channels understood in the narrow sense of mutually ratified participation in focused interaction.

I will use the term **address avoidance** to indicate the avoidance of the illocutionary speech act of discursively constituting an addressee, whether or not this involves an explicit act of addressee-reference. When avoidance partners do "not talking to one another," they meta-communicate the closure of the very communicative channel through which that meta-communication passes. In this sense, address avoidance is instantiated through richly paradoxical tropes of self-negating communication.

Address is a multimodal accomplishment. It may involve explicit referential specification of the addressee, as when a second-person pronoun – a form that literally denotes the speech-act role of addressee – presupposes (or entails) the identity of the addressee. But in face-to-face communication, address also relies upon eye gaze, bodily orientation, and other cues, like the directing of the vocal speech signal. Address avoidance is a classic feature of affinal avoidance registers. Tropes of address avoidance in affinal interaction often involve manipulations not only of pronominal reference but also of the visible and haptic signs that mediate **addressivity** in interaction. A case study will help illustrate how address avoidance is contextualized within a larger field of in-law avoidance practices.

Case Study: Kamayurá (Tupí-Guaraní; Brazil)

As with other indigenous groups of the Xingu River (see Basso, 2007, for Kalapalo; Ball, 2015, and Gregor, 1977, for Waujá/Mehinaku; Seeger, 1981, for the Suyá), Kamayurá engage in a graded set of in-law avoidance practices (Seki, 1983, 2000). The most focal avoidance dyads are composed of lineal, cross-sex, adjacent-generation kin – a man and his mother-in-law, a woman and her father-in-law (Oberg, 1953, p. 49; Seki, 1983). Progressively less stringent avoidance is practiced, first, toward same-sex parents-in-law, and lastly, toward siblings-in-law. Multiple media – the placement of hammocks, interlocking arms, wrestling, the use of personal names and honorific pronouns – index, but also grade, scale, or rank these relationships with respect to one another. Importantly, the channel-closing anti-phatic function of address avoidance instantiates the most focal, limit-cases of interactional avoidance.

The exemplary relationship of interactional liberty is the one between brothers. In adulthood, brothers "wrestle with one another, joke, and play tricks without any show of respect" (Oberg, 1953, p. 48). The relationship between brothers-in-law contrasts markedly. Siblings-in-law employ honorific plural pronouns, both in second-person reference to addressee and third-person reference to non-participants. Brothers-in-law avoid physical contact, they do not wrestle, their hammocks are hung at a distance one from the other, and "they avoid going about arm in arm, which is common between young men" (p. 49). They avoid using the name of the other, and "if one used the name of the other when referring to another man of the same name he would spit, as if to avoid something due to mentioning his name" (p. 49; see also p. 66 on spitting and name taboo violation). Reporting a particular interaction between two brothers-in-law, Oberg observes that, though they do converse with one another, "they would be careful not to speak at the same time and would avoid meeting each other's eyes" (p. 49).

Relations with parents-in-law are even more hedged with respect. The reserved demeanour that a son-in-law must maintain in the presence of his parents-in-law is most intense in the time immediately after marriage and before the birth of his first child. This is a period of time during which a husband lives with his wife's parents and carries out bride service (recall the Tsúùtínà example above). During the "trial marriage" the husband needs to demonstrate his ability to support his wife (Oberg, 1953, p. 44). It is only after the birth of the first child that the new nuclear family goes to live with the husband's parents. During this liminal period, the son-in-law is enjoined to show an asymmetrical deference toward his father-in-law. A son-in-law "would wait to be spoken to by his father-in-law and would answer him with downcast eyes. A son-in-law must carry out all orders given to him by his father-in-law" (p. 49). The son-in-law must exhibit even more dedicated circumspection with respect to his mother-in-law: "A man can never speak directly to his mother-in-law but must speak through his wife or some other person. If he must speak, he looks away from her while speaking" (p. 49). In these most stringent parent-/child-in-law avoidance relationships, individuals reciprocally "avoid being near one another ... can't sit in the hammock of the other, avoid talking directly with one another and avoid passing objects directly back and forth" (Seki, 1983, pp. 78–9; my translation). Indeed, the hammocks of co-resident parents-in-law and children-in-law are hung at opposite ends of communal houses (Oberg, 1953, p. 46).[7]

From hammock placement (neighbouring > at a remove > maximally distant) to pronominal usage (singular address > plural address), to addressivity (direct address > plural address + gaze avoidance > plural reference + speech intermediation), Kamayurá in-law avoidance is rendered a gradient or analogue sign by means of repertoire distinctions that are scaled with respect to one another. (See Chapter 8 for a more rigorous theorizing of grading in kinship avoidance.) Sticking specifically with the theme of discourse address, the following scaling can be observed. Brothers address each other with no circumspection, engaging in open insult and use bare second-person singular pronouns. Brothers-in-law carefully negotiate their conversations, avoiding overlapping turns at talk, addressing each other with plural pronouns, and not looking directly at each other or touching each other. In the son-in-law/father-in-law relation, the elder party has the asymmetrical privilege of opening the channel of communication. Again, eye gaze, honorific pronoun use, and name avoidance all signal deference. Finally, in the most heightened avoidance relationships, those between cross-sex, adjacent-generation in-laws, no direct communicative channel can be legitimately established between the interactants.

Speech Intermediation and Shill Address

The most common strategy by which avoidance relations transmit messages where the legitimate establishment of a direct communicative channel is proscribed is the use of speech intermediaries (Basso, 2007; see Yankah, 1991, and Ameka, 2004, on hierarchically skewed "triadic communication" in West Africa). Typically, as in communication between Bear Lake Dene or Kamayurá sons-in-law and mothers-in-law, it is the linking relative (i.e., the spouse through whom the affinal relation has been constituted) who transmits messages (and non-linguistic objects) between avoidance relations. But this need not be the case. Children often serve as messengers. Even a co-present ethnographer can be recruited to do the job. Marshall Sahlins (1962) reports the following anecdote from his mid-1950s fieldwork on Moala Island (south-central Fiji), concerning cross-sex sibling/cousin avoidance. A young man, Kitione, asked Sahlins to ask the man's parallel cousin to go and purchase benzine for his Coleman lamp: "'You ask her,' he said. I did, and she agreed. All the while, my friend kept his back turned. When she had signified she would go, he reached into his pocket, turned, but without looking at her threw a shilling at her feet. Saying nothing, she picked up the money and went off. As she moved down the path, Kitione whispered in explanation, 'my sister'" (pp. 115–16).

Conventionalized practices of speech intermediation may themselves be troped upon in order to (covertly) address specific social others while (explicitly) not addressing them. This strategy of **shill address** (after Silverstein, 2010, p. 348) is commonly attested in communication between avoidance relations in Aboriginal Australian communities. Here a speaker implicitly "targets" (in the sense of Haviland, 1986) an interactional alter while explicitly invoking a fictive addressee. Crowley (1983, p. 313), for instance, describes the use of invented addressees, like rocks and trees, by Uradhi (Cape York Peninsula) avoidance relations who seek to speak to each other without explicitly acknowledging that they are speaking to each other. (Note that a shift to mother-in-law register in Uradhi has an addressivity function – it is employed only when the actual, intended discourse target is the mother-in-law.) In discourse between son-in-law and mother-in-law in Kugu Nganhcara, "communication is made through the intermediary of a dog, both parties subscribing to the fiction that they are addressing the dog rather than one another" (Smith & Johnson, 1986, p. 454). (Dogs are often treated as classificatory children on the Cape York Peninsula.) An ethnographic case study will offer a richer image of these tropes.

Case Study: Shipibo-Konibo (Panoan; Peru)

Among the matrilineal and matrilocal Shipibo-Konibo, it is the relationship between a son-in-law and his parents-in-law, the *rayos* relationship, that is the most stringent avoidance relationship. There is a normative expectation that *rayos* will communicate with each other only by means of a speech intermediary – prototypically the wife/daughter that connects them. However, should a father-in-law and son-in-law be alone together they may engage in the farce that their daughter/wife is present, and continue to talk as if through her. Valenzuela (2003, p. 17) observes that "this practice is largely followed even by young Shipibo men, regardless of their degree of contact with the Spanish-speaking society."

The oral narrative of a "young [male] Shipibo student" illustrates that the farce of shill address is an established interactional genre:

> Some months ago I went fishing for a few days with my father-in-law. We had to stay together away from the village, prepare our meals and sleep in a small and uncomfortable hut. My wife, my fishing partner's daughter, was not with us. However, my partner and I had to communicate with

each other during the day in order to fish and then light the fire, cook and eat. How could we do this without speaking directly to each other. The way to do it was "as if." We behaved as if my wife were with us, present. I addressed my absent wife: "Ask your father whether I have to start the fire." "Tell your husband yes, because we have to cook the meal." "Ask your father where are the matches." "Tell your husband they are in the backpack." (Tournon, cited in Valenzuela, 2003, p. 17, cited in Fleck, 2013, p. 45)

This is clearly a highly stylized and recognizable trope playing upon the cultural norm that communication between *rayos* should be intermediated. It follows the letter if not the spirit of the "law" of exclusively triadic speech-intermediated communication and its corollary suspension of mutually ratified, direct address. The trope is achieved by means of the ubiquitous use of metapragmatic verbs of speaking (rendered as "ask" and "tell" in the translated narrative), which explicitly sketch the discursive participation of the nevertheless absent wife. Absencing the co-present avoidance relation is achieved by fictively presencing the absent linking relation. Non-address is a practice clearly subject to conscious metapragmatic awareness among the Shipibo (for a similar example, see Young & Morgan, 1980, p. 26, on "polite address" or *'adzoodzą saad* between cross-sex siblings and cross-sex, lineal in-laws in Navajo).

Notably, between the even more focal avoidance pairing of mother-in-law and son-in-law, shill address is not viewed as permissible. Here is the oral narrative of a 40-year-old woman (I provide just Valenzuela's English translation without her Shipibo transcript or the interlinear gloss): "In the past we did not talk to our son-in-law at all, we didn't even pass by his side. Now it is different, now we pass by him, we walk just next to him. It didn't use to be like that. When the mother-in-law saw the son-in-law from far away, she lowered her head, to prevent that her son-in-law saw her face. So it was. Only when her daughter was present, then she could talk to him [in the speech-mediated manner described for *rayos*-relations]" (Valenzuela, 2003, pp. 974–5). Speech intermediation and shill address are scaled with respect to one another. In the more focal, cross-gender avoidance relationship, even shill address is not an acceptable means of establishing communicative contact.

The use of shill addressees symbolically negates the very act of address that it nevertheless thereby accomplishes. That is, co-occurring signs in context point to mutually exclusive or incompatible interpretations. This self-negating metapragmatics ("*I am not addressing you!*") involves a kind of internally contradictory meta-communication about interaction reminiscent of Batesonian "play." Silverstein (2010, p. 348) brings out these productive tensions in his analysis of Worora son-in-law/mother-in-law, or *rambarr*, "non-communication." Worora has an inclusive/exclusive distinction as well as numerous number distinctions (Clendon, 2014) – we need only attend to the distinction between the singular, the dual, and the plural here:

> In order to communicate with figurated non-communication an interactional situation must be set up in which some third party – a child, a dog, the relative linking the two "in-laws," etc. – is drawn structurally into a critical, mediating role-relationship. Each one of the *rambarr* dyad addresses this third party in earshot of – but of course, given taboos, not visible to – the other member of the *rambarr* dyad *using the first person dual inclusive* [along with mother-in-law register lexemes] everywhere that a second person form – the form denoting the would-be "real" addressee in a normal, non-taboo interaction – would be appropriate were the two actually able to communicate and to denote each other. (Silverstein, 2010, p. 348)

By means of this denotational trope, "the very target of the communication [is] rendered the outside 'audience' or overhearer of the mock-dyadic conversation between speaker and shill 'addressee'" (p. 348). For Worora speakers, this reconfiguration of participation by means of denotational indexicals – that is, the exclusion of the "real" target of communication at the level of the denotational text – "counts locally as a trope of *negation*, that is, of non-communication with the intended, though forbidden addressee" (p. 348). (The same use of the first-person dual inclusive "to distract attention from ... [the avoidance relation] ... by focusing attention" on the shill addressee is similarly employed in Gurindji [McConvell, 1982, p. 97].)[8]

Speech intermediation and shill address are multimodal accomplishments. In the Fijian example of speech intermediation between cross-sex classificatory brother and sister, linguistic elements like verbs of speaking ("You *ask* her," Kitione instructs Sahlins regarding his sister) and person deictics (i.e., second-person forms for the go-between, third-person forms for the avoidance relation) explicitly frame the appropriateness of interactional role inhabitance in the ongoing speech event. But body posture ("all the while, my friend kept his back turned") and practices of looking (e.g., not securing the gaze of, or joint attention with, the other) also crucially cancel out the construal of ratified co-participation.

John Haviland has reconstructed some of these kinesic repertoires for pre-missionary Guugu Yimidhirr in-law interaction routines: "If a man was unavoidably in his wife's mother's presence, he would sit silently, *guugu-mul*, with head bowed" (Haviland, 1979a, p. 369). A photograph provided in Haviland (1979b, p. 170) illustrates "proxemic" strategies of interactional negation. The photo shows Fred Jacko, who "uses the avoidance language ... in conversation with another man who married a woman Fred classed as his granddaughter. In such a relationship, both men not only use the respectful vocabulary; they sit far apart, orient their bodies so as not to face one another, and avoid direct eye contact."

Ethnometapragmatic designators for Aboriginal Australian mother-in-law languages treat kinesic non-alignment of bodies as a privileged metonym for conceptualizing affinal (non)interaction. In Wik, mother-in-law language is called *ŋonk wonka tonn* "another side talk" (English-speaking informants often refer to it as "side talk" or "curved talk"), and it is contrasted to *wik koi'um* ("straight talk") (Thomson, 1935, pp. 474, 485). It "may be used only indirectly, that is *at*, and not *to*, the person addressed" (p. 475). Guugu Yimidhirr metapragmatic framing is similar: "a man speaking to his affines *diili yirrgaalga* or *wurriin yirrgaalga*; that is, he speaks 'sideways' or 'crosswise,' neither facing his interlocutor nor, if he can help it, addressing him directly but, rather, communicating through an intermediary" (Haviland, 1979a, p. 369). The early description of Wurrung mother-in-law language in Dawson (1881, p. 29) glosses the metapragmatic designator for the register as "turn tongue." Speakers of Western Desert Language describe the affinal register in that language as "talking to one side" (*kiti-kiti wangkanyi*). If metapragmatic discourse employs a spatial metaphor suggestive of interactional non-alignment to describe speech that is "curved," "turned," or "to one side," this is because it reflects the salience of bodily non-alignment as a kinesic sign of interactional negation.

Paradoxical Meta-communication and Joking-Avoidance

The anti-phatic function involves a species of paradoxical (or self-negating) meta-communication. One avoidance relation says to the other, "*I am not speaking to you.*" Paradoxical meta-communication occurs where co-occurring signs motivate mutually negating interpretive frames. The touchstone for thinking about the phenomenon is Gregory Bateson's essay "A Theory of Play and Fantasy" (in Bateson, 1972, pp. 177–93). (Bateson's famous example is the "playful nip [which] denotes the bite, but [which] does not denote what would be denoted by the bite," p. 180.) But paradoxes generated by conflicts between communicative levels are not only apparent in strategies of address avoidance. Rather, in the sociolinguistics of kinship, such self-negating meta-communication has an almost holographic character, guiding the interpretation of both joking and avoidance comportments. In closing this chapter, I would like to gesture toward those connections.

Joking partners often engage in actions that would, in other contexts, fall under a negatively evaluated cultural description. Gisu (Bantu; Uganda) *bukulo* "joking" partners foster their relationship "by the reciprocal 'snatching'—known by the special term, *xutubuta*—of each other's property" (Heald, 1990, p. 383). The performative potency of "snatching" (which may be of anything ranging in value from a chicken to a cow) relies upon the possibility of the act being taken as a norm violation. It rests upon the possibility that it could count as theft even though, in the instance, it doesn't: "A dig in the ribs, a just-sufficiently uncouth word at the right time, hazards or ventures the possibility of a relationship sufficiently close and trusting that this kind of violation can be accepted. And the other, to whom the venture is made, is given the opportunity either to affirm the 'framing' relationship by taking the joke as a joke, or to deny the relationship by taking the 'violation' seriously" (Wagner, 1986a, p. 53). The ability of the recipient to "take the hit" of the negatively evaluated act – to overcome or bracket the interpretation of conflict – reaffirms the relationship (cf. Bliege Bird & Smith, 2005, on "costly signaling"). Joking thus involves a controlled profanation whose effect is to elicit what the Usen Barok call *malum* "forbearance" (Wagner, 1986a). Joking partners are entrained to take the joke, to be imposed upon, to withstand affronts and violations to their body, person, and possessions.[9] But because frame-ambiguity is a felicity condition on joking-performativity, there is always the possibility of a slippage – is this horse-play or is this an attack?[10]

Avoidance relationships also involve paradoxical meta-communication. Native discourses often characterize avoidance as the expression of "shame" (e.g., Usen Barok, *minenge*). I discuss the symbolism of shame in the Conclusion, but for the time being its ambiguous character should be underscored. Within the context of avoidance relationships, shame is a normatively valued orientation. And yet violations of avoidance protocols are also described as causing intense shame. Further, outside of an avoidance frame, shame is a negative and socially alienating experience. Enacted shame is paradoxical; it projects a framing of the relationship as at once respectful and appropriate but also as out of balance, suggesting the possibility of an unresolved and unaddressed problem that is the cause of intense embarrassment. And yet, because avoidance precisely involves the impossibility of explicit and direct, discursively mediated meta-communication, and because the imagined (often, sexual) causes of this shame are themselves unspeakable, this ambiguity cannot be straightened out, and certainly not by the principals themselves.

A double-voicedness of the act is characteristic of both the avoidance and joking "poles" of the kinship comportment continuum. And in both cases this ambiguity is essential to the iterative (even schismogenetic) elicitation of the other's response. In avoidance, and precisely where the proper protocol is followed, one is also legible as being alienated from the relationship. This ambiguity – fostered by the impossibility of direct phatic feedback across visual and discursive channels – propels the relationship forward. Perhaps it is this infinite debt of the shame associated with avoidance, a shame that can never be expunged, which elicits the incessant flow of exchange goods between avoidance relations, exchanges that constantly affirm the relation through non-linguistic media (see p. 291, note 5). In joking, contrastingly, the act is never completely itself, always cast in quotation marks; it is "just a joke" (cf. Kulick, 2003, on "dual indexicality"; Nakassis, 2013, on "citationality"). Here, too, the ambiguity of the play frame propels the relationship forward – more norm-violating "jokes" are always necessary to test and see if perhaps the last one was taken too seriously, or to show that it wasn't.

Chapter Six

Out of Touch: Sensory Avoidances and the Multimodality of Mutuality

The last chapter looked at the discursive manipulation of channels of discursive communication. Specifically, I showed how avoidance relations symbolically deny and negate the modes of discursive contact through which they nevertheless communicate. I now turn to anti-phatic dynamics linked to sensorial "contacts" more broadly construed. As one moves out of the constraint space of language and discourse, one enters an empirical terrain that is more variegated and proves more intractable to commensuration. In lieu of searching for the kind of constraints that more neatly circumscribed name taboos, mother-in-law languages, and even address avoidance as distinctive sociolinguistic kinds, here one must change footing.

Avoidance relations are almost always proscribed from establishing tactile contact with one another. Often they are enjoined to not visually presence one another. Occasionally, they will not even auditorily presence themselves when they are in the company of the other. Correspondingly, in considering how dyads actively absence one another beyond the realm of (non)ratified discursive (non)interaction, I exploit the ways in which non-verbal avoidance strategies are anchored to the sense organs and to sense perception, theorizing the ways in which the senses serve as a scaffold or affordance assemblage for the elaboration of avoidance routines and technologies. The phrase "anchored to" here should not be read as "reducible to." Because the sense organs and sense perception actually negotiate intersubjective contact, they are attractors for the conventional emblematizing of such contact. But the cultural practices that diachronically drift toward those attractors can also drift away from them (see the end of this chapter for more on this theme). Nevertheless, cross-culturally, norms of appropriate interaction between avoidance relations routinely involve anti-phatic absencing accomplished by forestalling intersubjective mutuality through the suppression of its privileged emblems of touch, eye contact, and voice.

Mutuality and the Phatic Affordances of the Senses

The anti-phatic function is achieved by constraints on both semiotic "output," on "sending signals of deference and respect" (Mandelbaum, 1986, p. 2000), and sensorial "input." I draw on this cybernetic idiom with some trepidation. In discussing the dynamics of human face-to-face interaction, the distinction between "input" and "output" has only limited heuristic value. That which is a constraint on input for ego at one "logical type" or level of abstraction may be output for an interactional alter at a higher logical type (terminology after Bateson, 1972). Think, for instance, of the way in which two strangers negotiate passing each other on the sidewalk. One of them commits to a path by clearly picking a particular direction while at the same time looking away from the second individual, that is, by constraining sensory input. But the act of looking away – that ostentatious positioning of the sense organs – is output for the second. Where felicitous, it is interpreted by the second as an index of the first's inaccessibility to visual feedback, and it thus constrains the second into picking the other available path. Humans in interaction constantly model the mental states of others (Scott-Phillips, 2015), and one of the best sources of evidence for generating such models comes from attending to the sensory information to which the other does or does not conspicuously attend (Baron-Cohen, 1995; Tomasello, 2019). Constraints on input (at logical type "n") are routinely transformed into a privileged kind of output (at logical type "$n + 1$"). In this sense, "input" and "output" mark different moments in, or components of, a semiotic growth. Nevertheless, cultural canons of avoidance do distinguish between input and output as distinct kinds of sensorial contact for which avoidance partners can be held to account (Enfield & Sidnell, 2017).

Take the example of names as material tokens produced by the tongue (output), on the one hand, and as heard by the ear (input), on the other. We have seen examples ad nauseam of output constraints placed on uttering the name of avoidance partners. Interestingly, individuals are sometimes additionally not allowed *to hear* the names of their avoidance relations. Among a number of Highland New Guinea groups, it is customary not only for there to be taboos on uttering the names of affines and phonetically similar words but also for it to be taboo for affines to even hear the names of those affinal relatives (see Franklin, 1967, p. 79, for Kewa; Ryan, 1958, pp. 111, 113, for Mendi; Wagner, 1967, p. 176, for Daribi). Among the Wiru, for instance, a "man must not even hear an in-law's name spoken in his presence," and if he does, "he puts his hand on the top of his head and says *aūwe* [the coverall term for 'taboo affine'], to indicate the shame he is expected to feel in such a circumstance"

(A. Strathern, 1970, p. 71). Correspondingly, among Highlands communities like those of Melpa speakers, "it is polite to avoid the names of other people's *kulpam* [affines] in their presence" (M. Strathern, 1972, p. 38). Just as uttering a taboo name may have a relation-rupturing performativity, the perlocutionary effects of the auditory experience of the name for an avoidance relation may be striking. For Bininj Gunwok (Australia), the experience of hearing the name of a cross-sex sibling is expressed with the terms *kan-begbun* "it causes me concussion" and *kan-bengdulubun* "it stabs my mind" (Garde, 2008a, p. 209).

This double enregisterment of name avoidance, from the complementary perspectives of stimulus production and reception, reflects the ways in which avoidance relations – often with the help of others – cooperatively co-absence one another (cf. Keating, 1998, on the co-construction of social stratification on Pohnpei). As we will see (and hear and feel), input restrictions work in tandem with output-filters in achieving the "effacement work" (Nozawa, 2020) of avoidance relations. But input restrictions, in particular, underscore how cultures of avoidance imbue the phenomenological experience of the other with qualities of impingement (after Stasch, 2003). Norms which frame certain inputs as impermissible foster performativist semiotic ideologies that infuse tokens of rigid signs of the other with a disruptive causal consequentiality.

In the following sections, I focus on the ways in which avoidance relations manage haptic, visual, and auditory contact in (non)interaction. From an output perspective, individuals manage their visibility, audibility and haptic accessibility to others in interaction. Avoidance relations suppress, block, or otherwise interfere with "field[s] of potential stimulation emanating" from their bodies; "reflected illumination" around the face is blocked with a bark-cloth mat or a would-be "field of air vibration" caused by talking is suppressed by silence (Gibson, 1966, pp. 28, 29). As with tropes of negated address, acts that suppress the potential available stimuli sourced from avoiding bodies become conventionalized emblems of deferential interactional negation. From the input perspective, avoidance relations control – where possible and perceivable – their sense organs. Simply put, they refrain from touching or looking at certain persons.

The ways in which avoidance repertoires are elaborated over these distinct sensory modalities suggest that different senses and sense organs offer different kinds of affordances for phatic communication. (My discussion here is indebted to Rupert Stasch's [2003, p. 321] "hierarchy of modes of sensory avoidance.") Considering cases where (parts of) human bodies serve, on the one hand, as sources of output and, on the other, as input receptors, two distinct kinds of input-output scenarios present themselves. These are represented in purest form by the haptic and the auditory modalities, respectively.

Haptic intercorporeality involves a reciprocity absent from hearing. We cannot hear the other hear – at best there is a polar asymmetry between input and output in speech which switches back and forth as the roles of speech animator and speech recipient are exchanged in dyadic discourse; it is only in "next-turn" behaviour that we can know if a first turn at talk has been received. Touch involves a mutuality of sensorial contact not present in audition. When we touch the other, we also stimulate receptors on the skin of the other – our input is also their input. The semiotic fecundity of this mutuality of bodies in physical contact for emblematizing intersubjective relating is reflected in the very idioms we use to describe phaticity – to "stay in touch," to "be in contact" (Gibson, 1966). Vision, I will argue, represents an importantly hybrid and intermediary position between touch and hearing. Just as with hearing, we can see the other without the other seeing that we see them. But just as with touch, we can also see the other seeing us (seeing them...). In eye contact, the visual sense organ not only senses itself being sensed by its double but also infers that the other reconstructs this self-same model of visual input-as-output. There is a mirroring effect of eye contact in the mutuality of reciprocal mind reading that it affords. Both touch and eye contact involve a reciprocal intersensoriality not present in hearing or other kinds of looking. As I will now show, this affordance assemblage of the senses and sense organs for emblematizing phatic communion conditions the topography of avoidance routines cross-culturally.

Touching You, Touching Me: Intercorporeality Emblematizes Intersubjectivity

Phatic sensorial contact as it unites input and output approaches the asymptote of intersubjective mutuality. The apotheosis of this mutuality finds expression in the figure of bodies in contact – touching bodies. To be sure, there is a complementarity to touch – a complementarity between the active, haptic sensing of other and the passive role of being touched (Gibson's [1962] "active touch" and "passive touch"). Nevertheless, there is a symmetry of sensation, a phatic mutuality not present in the case of the other senses; for conscious individuals, to feel the touch of the other is to feel what the other feels. To be touched is not only to be an object of perception for the other, it is to be made into a subject of perception. On "the laying on of hands" in Christian faith healing, Csordas (2008, pp. 111–12) writes that "the interaction and the interpretation [of touch] constitute a dual locus of culture, the objective/behavioral and the subjective/meaningful." He argues that this duality of touch is the emblematic seed/core/pit from which intersubjectivity as the mutuality of the experience of the other is emergent.

Given that, in haptic intercorporeality, one subject's input is always another's output, is it any wonder that physical, bodily contact is the most rigorously proscribed in avoidance relationships cross-culturally? Is it any wonder that haptic "contact" is at the top and centre of a would-be anti-phatic hierarchy of the senses? The affordances of haptic intercorporeality and the differential figurational potential of the skin, among the sense organs, conspire to overdetermine touch as the site and sign of intersubjective encounter. At a basic level, the skin, as sense organ, encompasses the other sense organs that it either surrounds (the eyes and mouth) or covers (the ears and nose). And, of course, the topography of the body – itself, as we have noted, a privileged emblem of personhood – is co-terminous and isomorphic with that of the skin.

Interdictions on bodily contact are so common and so primordial with respect to all of the other avoidances that I discuss in this chapter that I will not enumerate too many examples here. Suffice it to say that descriptions like the following concerning Choiseul Islanders (Solomons) are typical: "Opposite-sex affines are forbidden to touch each other or to hand food or other objects directly to one another; passing of any object must be done through a third party, or the object placed upon the ground or floor before the other can take it" (Scheffler, 1965, p. 82). The centrality of touch is reflected not only in the material practices of the body but also in the importance of touch and the skin as idioms for conceptualizing the performative consequence of violating avoidances. The skin is often conceptually elaborated as the site upon which the negative performative effects of the violation of in-law avoidances surface:

> Korowai understand looking at someone, referring to someone in the singular, touching someone, sharing food with someone, and saying someone's name ... as forms of touch-like contact in which one person impinges intimately on another, or in which two persons impinge intimately on one another.... Korowai routinely say that someone who utters an affine's name will have his or her feet sliced open by sharp sticks on forest paths, be bitten or stung by animals, be scratched by thorns, or be cut and bruised in falls. (Stasch, 2003, p. 324)

Examples could be added from other sources. Relating to proxemic, discursive, visual, and objectual restrictions, the Baganda hold that "any breach of these customs will cause nervous debility with tremors in the hands and other parts of the body.... A man must not touch his wife's uncle's daughters, that is, the man who secured his wife for him; this also will bring on tremor" (Roscoe, 1902, p. 39). "The Moro believe that the penalty for eating with the in-law clan is a short, fatal disease which, after death, causes the skin of the body to peel" (Nadel, 1947, p. 211). A Cagayan Agta "should never throw anything at an in-law, even in jest. If it hits him, a boil is likely to grow on that spot" (Mayfield, 1987, p. 109). Regardless how much stock one puts in these cherry-picked examples, the skin – as sign, site, scene, and sense organ – is multiply positioned at the intersection of the intersubjective encounter.

The privileges of the sense of touch for figuring phatic communion help also to recontextualize the relationship between kinship avoidances and "the incest taboo." Many ethnologists have interpreted kinship avoidances as an ideological superstructure managing "incest taboos" (see Hiatt, 1984, and citations therein). Thus practices as diverse as food sharing and the avoidance of eye contact are seen as signs that point toward a displaced and repressed final referent – sex (Freud, 1918). Arriving at the end of the semiotic chain, ethnologists are able to transduce sex-avoidance into a functionalism that moves back out into the social – according to them, interpersonal avoidances diminish jealousies, channel appropriate marriage pairings, and foster homosocial fraternity. But what if sex isn't the end of the line? We can also understand sex semiotically, as intensely figurational of intersubjectivity in and through the idiom of intercorporeality and thus, correspondingly, of a subject-identity predicated upon the binding and bordering of the body. Valerio Valeri's (2000) discussion in *The Forest of Taboos* serves as a guide for this line of analysis:

> For what are the relations between object and subject that taboo regulates? Principally eating, touching, and penetrating, as in killing and having sex. All these involve the body as desiring, that is, as feeding on its objects, consuming them. Even gazing may be the expression of a desire to consume, and this is why it often enters the province of taboo. Moreover, these relations do not simply imply that the subject exists as a body. They also imply a certain homogenization of subject and object. ... [A] subject conceived as feeding on its objects, as principally endowed with a corporeal existence like theirs, runs the risk of losing itself in them: they invade it and undermine its identity. (p. 101)

The avoidance of the "excessive closeness" of eating (with) the other, or of sex with the other, suggests that "taboo is due ... to a pre-occupation with preserving oppositions (enemy/friend) on which order is based" (p. 372). The "extreme closeness" (p. 373) of bodies in sex is incompatible with their radical subjective-difference, a difference that avoidance at once emblematizes (e.g., through bodily distance) and actually realizes, by creating the conditions of sensorial incommensurability. That is, by denying shared experience. Perhaps the only other intercorporeal relation that approaches the sexual one in its intense haptic mutuality is that of the infant child and caregiver (Gibson, 1966, p. 132; cf. M.H. Goodwin, 2017). Notably, this is a relation which, for the infant, often precedes "subject formation" or full personhood. (For more on the sexual thematic in kinship avoidance, see the Conclusion.)

Invisible In-Laws (Input Restrictions)

After proscriptions on touch, the most common sensorial sanctions are those on sight. In some cases they are perhaps even more salient. For the Chiricahua Apache, Opler (1941, p. 164) writes that "the gravest objection is not to the proximity of the avoided relative or to the sound of his voice but to the sight of him." In-laws negotiate their visible output by use of screening technologies – noise machines, like room dividers and other architectural partitions, or more "portable seclusion" (Papanek, 1973), like polyester or bark-cloth head coverings. But gestures of regarding (input) are also elaborated as salient acts of interpersonal encounter sanctioned in avoidance relationships. Here again both input and output are elaborated as distinct and consequential interactional moments.

Not looking at the other forecloses upon intense and emergent intersubjective dynamics that can be communicated by gaze. This (self-)censorship censorship of affective possibilities is respectful, while inculcating the valued demeanour of embarrassment or shame that ought to be experienced between avoidance dyads. The embodiment of such an affective habitus may be so complete, in fact, that shame and embarrassment appear to be – and indeed actually do become – an important proximate cause of the comportments (e.g., averting the gaze, talking softly) that respectfully index restrained relationality (see the Conclusion for further exploration of this theme).

The ethnographic sources that I and my research assistants consulted often glossed native models of interdictions on visible presencing with rather vague or general statements (e.g., avoidance relations should "not look at each other" [Sahlins, 1962, p. 115] or a man's "affinal relations [are those] upon whom he may not look, and who may not see him" [Opler, 1941, p. 164]). In other instances, particular body parts (the eyes, the head, the hair) or certain actions (ingesting or outgesting substances) are specified as taboo targets of sight.

The face, in particular, is often sited/cited as a taboo visual target. A Lelet informant tells Richard Eves (1998, p. 194) regarding *minmin* "cross-sex sibling" avoidance, "A man must not look at his minmin's eyes or face when he talks to her. Why? because when a man looks at a woman, he notices the way she has combed her hair or that her face is pretty, and he thinks things no good." Here visual presencing stirs desire. Although couched in the idiom of sexual attraction, the face invoked here, speaking in more general terms, is the dynamic face of the other as experienced over the arc of a sustained conversation, a face that adapts itself to ours within and across a historical chain of such interactions. This dynamic face of the other experienced in interaction is both recognizable and mysterious, but most of all it is open-ended, capable of capturing us, of pulling us in.

Parallelling the series of thematic complementarities that I have set up so far – of reference and address, of rigid designation and phatic engagement, of the body as the form-fitting emblem of the subject and as the zero-point of interaction – the face is doubly positioned to serve as an object of visual avoidance. On the one hand, the face is a rigid sign of the other. On the other hand, the face is integrally involved in communication, in initiating and managing encounters; it has addressivity functions. In English, the intersection between these two dimensions is reflected in the polysemy of "recognition." Seeing the face of the other is an overture to interaction – one salutes or hails the other upon recognizing their face. To "recognize" the other is, simultaneously, to identify and call upon (cf. the explicit speech act "I hereby recognize the gentlewoman from California").

The avoidance of the face purely as a rigid sign – an emblem of social personhood which, for this reason, should be revered by not being beheld – and not in its interactional face-to-face function is perhaps most widely known from Aboriginal Australian post-mortem avoidances, maybe because English-language warnings regarding these are widely diffused in Australian televisual, text-artefactual, and online media. Among many Aboriginal Australian groups, the name *qua* proper noun is avoided during a period of mourning (Nash & Simpson, 1981). These avoidances also extended to homophones (Dixon, 1980). In many areas of Aboriginal Australia, photographic images of the deceased were destroyed or placed out of sight either permanently or for a period of mourning, though there is a dynamic refiguring of the performative power of the post-mortem photographic image in contemporary practices (see Deger, 2008, for Yolngu). Token-events of the face-image, like tokens of the name, are avoided.

Work in cognitive science and neuroanatomy suggests that there are dedicated biological bases to facial recognition. Evidence from brain imaging and cognitive disorders apparently offers strong evidence that a part of the brain called the fusiform gyrus, crucially involved in vision, has evolved structures dedicated to face perception and recognition (Kanwisher et al., 1997). Prosopagnosia or "face blindness" is a condition in which individuals have normal visual perception except that they are unable to recognize faces – that is, they are unable to attach faces to biographical individuals, including themselves. These lines of evidence suggest important biological bases for facial recognition, bases that likely stabilize the face as an attractor or target for cultural practices of avoidance (in line with Sperber, 1985).

Avoidance dyads play upon this semiotic-suturing of the face to the biographical individual. Of Nyakyusa daughters-in-law, Wilson (1951) writes that "her father-in-law is pointed out once to the newly betrothed girl, and after that she must never look at him." Note the paradoxical character of the restriction as it is phrased here. Why point out the face of someone you can never legitimately recognize on a subsequent encounter? So that you know, and experience shame/fear, precisely when you have – illegitimately – beheld the face of the other on just such a subsequent occasion. Or, recall again the Daribi saying "to look at one's mother-in-law is like looking at the sun" (Wagner, 1967, p. 173). The experience of visual input – seeing the face of the other – is painful, much as hearing the name of a cross-sex sibling is experienced by Garde's Bininj Gunwok informant as "mind-stabbing." In other cases, the disrespect/profanation visited upon the other by visually presencing their face calls for expiation in the form of a fine. In the 1930s in the village of Kurtatchi (N. Bougainville), a son-in-law was supposed to pay a fine of a string of *imun*, a "ceremonial currency of flying fox or porpoise teeth," if he saw his mother-in-law's face (Blackwood, 1935, pp. 65, 74). As noted above, a Tsúùtínà son-in-law "who inadvertently saw his mother-in-law's face had to present her with a valuable gift, like a horse" (Honigmann, 1956, p. 33). Viewed as an intertextual series, face avoidance serves as a prosthetic prosopagnosia where the non-recognition of the other is actively produced.

If the face is the part of the body most often singled out for avoidance, the eyes are the part of the face upon which even more focused non-attention centres. As noted above, the mutuality of touch is most closely approximated in the visual modality by the mutuality of eye contact.

Eye contact has long been a privileged emblem for theory of mind (cf. Bateson's [1980, 1982] "double description"; Buber, 1970), and, again, there are biological bases for the tight linkage between the eyes and theory of mind as eye-tracking experiments in children (Tomasello, 2019), studies of human eye anatomy (Kobayashi & Kohshima, 2001), and vision in autism spectrum conditions (Baron-Cohen, 1997; Simmons et al., 2009) all indicate. Establishing joint attention between ego and alter with respect to a third object is seen as central to the co-dependent arising of intersubjectivity and consciousness (Fuchs, 2013). And because vision affords mind reading, eye contact is often elaborated as a privileged scene of intersubjective connection. Perhaps because of the reciprocal intersensoriality of eye contact – the way in which one's "input" becomes "output" for the other – vision is often interpreted as impinging upon the target of perception. At the level of cultural ideology, vision is routinely conceptualized as "extromissive" (Dean, 2011) – as a "going forth of the sight towards the object" by analogy with touch (Kramrisch, cited in Gell, 1998, and Eck, 1985). As Melanie Dean (2011) observes concerning the visual ideologies that rationalize evil-eye practices, visual "input" is routinely reconceptualized as causally potent "output." Secondary rationalizations of the performativity of sight and of the eyes seek to capture the profound signifying potency of this modality for intersubjective relating.

Invisible In-Laws (Output Filters)

The complement to input restrictions (where one constrains one's own view of the other) is output filters (where one constrains one's own visibility for the other). Input restrictions are put in place by redirecting the sensory organ. Output filters function by blocking light reflecting off of bodies. These may be divided into two kinds: static and portable technologies. Static technologies include the architectural layout of houses or tents, or the use of hung screens or other partitions to create separate spaces for individuals who should not be co-present/co-visible. Korowai mother-in-law/son-in-law avoidances offer us an example: "For purposes of upholding sight avoidance, most dwellings are divided down their length by a panel of flat sago leaf stem bases. Seated on opposite sides of the middle wall, a mother-in-law and son-in-law can talk to each other and perform routine household activities without risk of glimpsing one another" (Stasch, 2003, p. 322). In undivided houses, a tarpaulin may be hung if a mother-in-law/son-in-law is expected to be visiting (p. 322). There are multiple other examples. Manus (Admiralty Islands) houses were divided by mats hung from the ceiling of the structure to keep a man and his mother-in-law or elder sister-in-law invisible to one another (Mead, 1934, p. 267). Similarly, in northeastern Arnhem Land, a mother-in-law and son-in-law occupy the same standing structure "only when a barrier is placed down the middle of the house or room" (Berndt, cited in W. Shapiro, 1979, p. 108).

Improvised partitions, separate tent entrances, and other static output filters were crucial in keeping Chiricahua Apache mothers-in-law and sons-in-law invisible to one another (Boyer & Gayton, 1992). Narcissus Duffy Gayton's autobiography recounts how her father and her maternal grandmother lived in close quarters while never seeing one another. The family took to fastening a bedspread with safety pins to the ceiling of their car, partitioning the front and back seats, so that the two could ride in it at the same time (Boyer & Gayton, 1992, p. 239). Through a complex choreography, stage-managed by the children, the family could go into town and the ladies could go shopping all without the son-in-law and mother-in-law ever seeing one another. Similar accounts are common in ethnographies of contemporary Aboriginal Australian communities (e.g., Sharp 2004, p. 28, on Nyangumarta).

Portable technologies of visual avoidance are also widely employed. Interestingly, these are employed almost always in cross-sex avoidance relationships and are positioned on the bodies of women rather than of men (cf. Eilberg-Schwartz & Doniger, 1995). Face coverings are, of course, best known, and most elaborated, in the Middle East, the Maghreb, and Central and South Asia (Vogelsang-Eastwood & Vogelsang, 2008). Although veiling is strongly associated with Islam in contemporary imaginaries (e.g., Bowen, 2007; El Guindi, 1999), it is important to recognize that elaborate face- and head-covering practices diachronically emerged in the Levant (inclusive of the eastern Mediterranean) long before Islam and that they are by no means limited to Muslim communities. Indeed, face covering in Muslim communities is not typically linked to in-law avoidance – a husband's relatives may be some of the few men in front of whom a woman may appropriately be unveiled!

The "public sphere" or "stranger social" veiling, of the kind practiced in many contemporary Middle Eastern societies, has a long genealogy in the Levant. More than 3,500 years ago, Assyrian law dictated that "neither wives of lords nor widows nor Assyrian women who go out onto the streets may have their heads uncovered" (quoted in Llewellyn-Jones, 2003, p. 124). Llewellyn-Jones (2003) reconstructs the rich practices of veiling that women in Ancient Greece engaged in when moving about outside of the *domos*. He traces how these practices were seen to instantiate a culturally valued demeanour of *aidōs* "modesty" while still enabling women to move about in public. Echoing Papanek's (1973) felicitous phrase ("symbolic shelter"), in his reconstruction of Ancient Greek stranger sociality Llewellyn-Jones argues that "the veil acts as a portable form of domestic seclusion, an amplification of the privacy of the house" (p. 317; cf. Abu-Lughod, 2015, on the *chador* as a "mobile home"). Indeed, one of the veils employed in Ancient Greece was called the *tegidion* or "little roof."

Veils and face covers do not form a static sartorial background but are dynamically deployed in ways that evidence degrees and intensities of context-contingent visual avoidance. The Turkish *charshaf* or the Uzbek *chashmband* may be worn down over the face or thrown back over the head, as the occasion demands (Vogelsang-Eastwood & Vogelsang, 2008). Turkmen and Gujarati women deploy different named kinds of visual avoidance in the presence of different categories of affinal kin. Further, the enactment of face covering cannot be reduced to the shame or embarrassment of presencing certain social alters (cf. recipient-indexicality); it may also serve to perform a particular stance with respect to the subject of discourse (cf. referent-indexicality). Bedouin women may veil when conversation topics with even oblique sexual undertones are broached:

> When a woman told her husband about a marriage engagement that had been concluded in his absence, she held her veil over her mouth. At a gathering of kinswomen brought together by a wedding, an older woman began teasing her nephew, a patriarch in his own right, about his marital life. At this point in the conversation, the younger women, who had been sitting a bit apart with their backs to the man, suddenly veiled and moved to another room. (Abu-Lughod, 1986, p. 161)

Veiling is a social act, not a static state of being. Like code-switching, it may be performed in a "situational" manner – reflecting the social identity of co-present others – or it may be "metaphorical" – reflecting the tenor, tone, or topic of the conversation (Blom & Gumperz, 1972).

In social patterning, ancient Assyrian and Greek veiling bears similarities to "public sphere" veiling as described in contemporary sources for distinct Islamic societies (e.g., Anderson, 1982, for Afghanistan; Meneley, 2000, for Yemen). Veiling is most pronounced outside of the domestic sphere; women are expected to veil in the presence of men who are not kin. For Ghilzai Pakhtuns, the "basic rule and practice is that persons who could be legitimately married to each other are prevented from direct contact and interaction; so the limit of incest prohibition is the beginning of interactional modification by veiling, seclusion, and other acts" (Anderson, 1982, p. 399). Those who are or who have been *korwala* "home-inhabitants" are either already one's spouse or unmarriageable under the current configuration of role relationships, so they are not avoided: "Thus, the total social field is divided between those who share or have access to the same *kor* ('domestic quarters,' also natal and marital co-residents) and those who veil from each other" (p. 400). Though clearly linked to marriageability, "public sphere" veiling is not co-terminous with the constitution of affinity; it both precedes it and surpasses it.[1] "Children of both sexes interact freely with everyone but are progressively restrained as they mature. As a girl approaches puberty through finely discriminated stages, she is increasingly circumspect until at maidenhood she is the most "shy" and covered of all women. Conversely, child-rearing women are progressively freer in their interaction, the more so as their sons mature" (Anderson, 1982, p. 400; cf. Meneley, 2000, p. 65, for Yemen). Plotted along the timeline of the biographical life-course of the girl/bride/mother/grandmother, the visibility avoidance signal gets stronger and stronger and then starts fading (see Chapter 8 for a dedicated discussion of gradience in face and body covering).

All of these attributes differentiate such "public sphere" or "stranger social" veiling from head and face covering as practiced in the context of in-law avoidance. The use of portable technologies of visual avoidance as a component part of semiotic registers of affinal avoidance has quite different characteristics. Here, covering has a discrete onset at ritual moments marking the constitution, transformation, or dissolution of the affinal relationship. Further, covering as an affinal index has indexical focus properties comparable to those attested for the *linguistic* signs of affinity. That is, the signal is "directed at," and differentially signals respect toward, particular in-laws. This distinct social profile of head, face, and body covering has been recognized for societies in Central and South Asia (e.g., Jacobson, 1982; Sharma, 1978). But it has not, I don't think, been widely appreciated that analogous practices are found outside of Africa and Eurasia. In the following section I exemplify these relational, kinship-keyed dimensions of the deployment of portable technologies of visual avoidance for societies in Melanesia and Aboriginal Australia. I then briefly characterize the difference between affinity-conditioned veiling in Oceania and the better-known Afro-Eurasian cases.

Portable Technologies of Visual Avoidance in Oceania

Three distinct ritual moments commonly mark onset of affinity-keyed covering practices in Oceania (and elsewhere): betrothal, the death of a spouse, and marriage itself. I offer one example of each of the first two kinds and then provide a survey of marriage-linked covering practices in Oceania.

(1) *Betrothal.* In Melanesia and Australia, in-law avoidance practices typically begin with betrothal (see W. Shapiro, 1970, on "mother-in-law bestowal" in Aboriginal Australia; for Melanesia see Weiner, 1988, on Foi; Oliver, 1970, p. 157 on Siuai). In Manus (Admiralty Islands), the use of coverings is most pronounced during this time (Mead, 1934, p. 265). In addition to name and homophone avoidance and the use of honorific pronouns, cross-sex visual presencing is proscribed between prospective and actual affines (for further discussion of the linguistic dimensions of Manus avoidance registers see the next chapter). Mead refers to two portable technologies of visual avoidance – the "peaked rain mat of aboriginal days" (likely similar to the pandanus leaf constructions found in the northern Solomons) and the "modern cloak" which consists of a "piece of unhemmed calico or a blanket which is bunched rudely together at one end to form a pocket for the head" (p. 266). If a child is betrothed at a young age, older kin may negotiate this interdiction for her: "A mother will pull part of her cloak over the face of her two-year-old girl as they pass a canoe in which sits the four-year-old betrothed" (p. 266). Adult women squat and wrap the cloak around themselves in the presence of male affines. "Only women without *kaleals* [avoidance relations, lit. 'those who go around/circumvent'] in their own village go about freely without any head covering" (p. 266). This circumstance was only met for a woman when no senior male affine was a village co-resident and no male in the village was betrothed to her junior female kin. Mead reports the example of the early adolescent girl Piwen, who had come to live in the village of Peri for a couple of weeks. Despite Piwen's younger sister's betrothal to Manawei, a boy from the village, Piwen did not carry a cloak with her. On different occasions, Piwen had to crouch "in the hulls of canoes, with her face flattened against the bottom" when she found herself near Manawei.

(2) *Death of a spouse.* Mourning often involves an exaggeration of auditory and visual avoidances keyed to affinal relationship. Mourning-based kinship avoidance is widespread in Aboriginal Australia and New Guinea. In many parts of Aboriginal Australia, widows are enjoined to not speak during a long mourning period after the death of a husband. It is within this context that some of the most elaborate alternate sign languages have been developed. In some Cape York Peninsula societies (e.g., Winda Winda), such alternate sign languages were used between widows and the kin of the deceased spouse (Fleming, 2014b, pp. 285–90). In Central Australia these sign languages are typically

used in all interactional contexts (Kendon, 1988). Seclusion and silence are sometimes complemented by conspicuous covering of the widow or the widower. The intense dyadic connection between spouses can mean that the survivor is a painful reminder of the deceased. Wik informants say that a widow "shames her late husband's brother 'by reminding them of him' simply by her presence" (Sutton, 1978, p. 201). For this reason, widows covered themselves with sheets of bark or blankets when in the presence of their brothers-in-law. Conspicuous covering of widows and widowers is most elaborated in the Massim. During a months-long period of seclusion (during which "her voice is supposed to remain unheard"), an Orokaiva widow is supposed to occupy herself only with the production of a "mourning jacket" or *baja* made out of Job's tears. When Orokaiva widows come out of their seclusion they "wear a voluminous hood or cowl (pohu) of bark-cloth embroidered with Job's Tears, and they hang their heads so that their faces are invisible" (Williams, 1930, pp. 218, 219).

(3) *Marriage.* Face covering is deployed not just during the liminal periods of betrothal and mourning; it often forms a constitutive part of avoidance practices that are a constant part of married life. I offer a non-exhaustive list of cases from Oceania in Table 6.1.

As can be seen by looking at the cases in Table 6.1, face covering in Oceania is an index of affinal relationship wholly analogous to the linguistic indices of affinity that I discuss in other chapters. Covering is a relational act that expresses deference from some indexical origo (the sign producer) toward a co-present indexical target (the person avoided). Importantly, the indexical origo and target prototypically stand in some categorical kin relation to one another; most typically, a mother-in-law covers her head in the presence of her son-in-law. The social categorical specificity of the kin relation between the origo and the target of the head-covering-index stands in contrast with the more widely known Afro-Eurasian cases, a subtle but important point.

Head or face covering in Eurasia is sometimes keyed to specific social categories. Recall the studies of affinal avoidance from West Bengal and Madhya Pradesh discussed in the previous chapter; married women use the end of their *sari* to cover their face in the presence of particular categories of male affines. Other examples could be cited. In Mongolic head-covering traditions, for instance, married women did not "bare their heads in the presence of ... husband's elder kin" (Krader, 1953, p. 294; see also Vreeland, 1962, p. 72). Nevertheless, in Africa and Eurasia, even where covering is tied to marital status, it is typically a much broader class of individuals whose presence conditions visual avoidance practices – the indexical target is more categorically diffuse.

Table 6.1. Portable technologies of visual avoidance employed between in-laws in Melanesia and Aboriginal Australia

Language	Indexical origo	Indexical target	Negative repertoire	Positive repertoire	Source
Umpila (Australia)	mother-in-law	son-in-law	face	"sheet of tea tree bark"	Thomson (1935, p. 480)
Wurrung (Australia)	mother-in-law	son-in-law	face [?]	"rug"	Dawson (1881, p. 29)
Gurindji (Australia)	mother-in-law	son-in-law	face	*wurruny* "cloth"	McConvell (1982, p. 93)
Daribi (New Guinea)	mother-in-law	son-in-law	face	"bark cloak"	Wagner (1977, p. 629)
Mendi (New Guinea)	mother-in-law	son-in-law	head	*tenk* "woven-string skull-cap"	Ryan (1958, p. 114)
Manus (Manus Island)	mother-in-law; elder sister-in-law	son-in-law; younger brother-in-law	face/body	"calico cloak"	Mead (1934, p. 266)
Buka (North Solomons)	mother-in-law	son-in-law	hair, face in act of eating	pandanus leaf hood	Blackwood (1935)
V'ënen Taut (Vanuatu)	female in-law	male in-law or "strange man"	face/body	"coloured headdress"	Harrisson (1937, p. 397)

Take, for instance, the covering of the hair in some Orthodox Jewish communities. Covering is not limited to contexts where men of a specific and delimited class of kin are present but is generalized to all men who are not the woman's husband (Seigelshifer & Hartman, 2011). Similarly for the mouth covering (*moonch*) worn in the nineteenth century by Armenian brides, the donning of the *moonch* began with marriage but was practiced in all non-intimate social contexts (Samvelian, cited in Panian, 1969, p. 129). Upon marriage, Xhosa women traditionally donned the double peaked *iqhiya* "head cloth" to cover their hair. The *iqhiya* (called *doek* in Afrikaans) is rigidly linked to marital status, but it is worn in all public-sphere contexts rather than exclusively in the presence of affinal relations (Rice, 2015).

In these cases there is an asymmetry in the social specificity of the origo and the target of the index. It is a particular social category of individual – married women – which serves as the origo of the index. Contrastingly, the target of the index is totally unspecific. The head covering provides specific social information about the origo of the index but none concerning the target of the index. Diachronically, this asymmetry appears to motivate a second-order reading of face and head coverings as emblems of the signaller's identity and demeanor.[2] The Orthodox Jewish *tichel* or the Xhosa *iqhiya* becomes a sign of gender and marital status – it indexes a married woman. As one of Rice's (2015, p. 246) informants tells her: "here, the [wedding] ring is the *doek*." Note the parallels to Afro-Eurasian daughter-in-law registers, which, in parallel fashion, develop second-order speaker focal-indexical values as "women's language" (see Chapter 3).

Avoidance as a Cooperative Endeavour

To review, technologies of visual avoidance – a cover-all term for both coverings worn on the body and screens or partitions used to divide interactional space – mediate cross-gender avoidance relationships in a number of distinct culture-historically separated locales. Sometimes static partitions are employed which symmetrically separate those who avoidance each other (as among the Korowai or the Chiricahua Apache). Portable coverings, contrastingly, are affixed to the body of one of the avoidance relations. It is notable that where this is the case, these coverings are almost always placed over or on female bodies (but see Murphy, 1964). That is, cultural emphasis is placed on mediating the visual output of women and the visual input of men. Why this asymmetry recurs remains an open question. It is possible that the pageantry of visual avoidance is most manifest in cross-gender avoidance relationships because heterosexual attraction and modesty are felicitous idioms for – are "good to think" – intersubjective impossibility. But this formulation does not address why avoidance is thematized in terms of female "output" and male "input."

Though female bodies are differentially marked as sights/sites of visual avoidance, it should be underscored that not-seeing/not-being-seen is always a cooperative accomplishment. Jon Anderson's (1982) admirable treatment of veils and veiling in Afghanistan emphasizes the co-constructed and reciprocal nature of cross-gender interactional avoidances among the Pashtun villagers with whom he conducted his ethnographic field research:

> When a man and woman encounter each other outside the *kor* [home], restraint applies equally to both, or more precisely to their interaction, and in parallel fashions. In such encounters, a man will at the very least avert his gaze and "not notice" a woman. He may additionally cover his face and turn away, even face a wall, exactly as she does, with frequently

comical results that are not lost on Pakhtun. He will certainly cover his mouth and avoid eye contact, exactly as she does, if they cannot avoid speaking. (p. 402)

Intentional "not noticing" is again paradoxical meta-communication (Bateson, 1972) of the kind theorized in the previous chapter. One signals respect to another by conspicuous non-recognition of that other. Meanwhile, the mouth-covering gesture is a self-negating emblem of speaking/not-speaking.

In the Middle East and South Asia, men who encroach upon femininely coded social spaces may conspicuously announce their arrival. In north Yemen, when a man enters his house while there is a gathering of women taking place there, "he is required to say 'Allah! Allah!' loudly a number of times while climbing the stairs of his house, so that the women, hearing him, are able to change their comportment and cover their faces before he sees them" (Makhlouf, 1979, p. 29). Yemeni men "co-operate in gender segregation by lowering their eyes from women, avoiding their spaces, and avoiding conversations with non-related women, especially young women" (Meneley, 2000, p. 66). Jacobson (1982, p. 92) offers a similar observation for the Madhya Pradesh village where she worked and in which Hindu women were expected to cover their faces in front of certain senior affines: "When a man enters a courtyard or house, he makes coughing or throat-clearing noises to warn the women within of his approach. The women can identify individual men by these noises and act accordingly."

Felicitous avoidance relationships require interactional work on both sides. As we all know from our own experiences of successful non-interaction with those with whom we do not wish to interact and who do not wish to interact with us, non-recognition is a cooperative achievement. In a related manner, avoidance comportments are neither automatic nor inviolable, a fact recognized by cultural participants themselves. The Foi (New Guinea; neighbours to the Daribi) characterize the avoidance relationship between son-in-law and mother-in-law in the following terms: "The name of this relationship is *yumu* and the Foi say that *yumu* is 'built' or 'woven' (both described by the verb *tege-*) as a house is built or a bilum [string bag] woven. In other words, people in this relationship do not practice avoidance as such but rather positively enact a characteristic protocol that entails such behavior" (Weiner, 1988, p. 94). And where in-laws do not feel that their partners are living up to their side of the bargain, they may ostentatiously omit engaging in avoidance practice. A Mendi (Highlands, New Guinea) mother-in-law covers her head in the presence of her sons-in-law. Toward this end she should always wear her small, woven-string skull-cap (*tenk*). If [the bridegroom fails to offer a gift to his future parents-in-law], or [if it is] deemed unsatisfactory, she shames her ungenerous son-in-law by bearing her head in front of him in public and continues this embarrassment until the proper gift has been made. Hence the name of the gift, *shumba tenk mowä* ("that which is laid down to cover the mother-in-law's head"). (Ryan, 1958, p. 114)

Part of what makes avoidance a valued sign of social relationship is that it is cooperative and coordinated. Because of the ways in which convention resignifies avoidance, the act of disregarding the other comes to be read as a sign of one's regard for the other. And under this frame, acting "normally" toward the other becomes recast as an insult and a sign of problems in the relationship.

Inaudible In-laws

I have argued that the mutuality of the senses and of the sense organs differentially motivates their recruitment as signs of intersubjective relationship. The sense of touch involves an inherent mutuality; to touch the other is to cause the other to touch oneself. The sense of sight need not, but can, imply such mutuality; when you see another seeing you, the other sees you seeing them. It is this inherent mutuality, I have suggested, that explains why the tactile and visual presencing of others are so often elaborated as loci for interactional avoidance routines. By breaking tactile or visual contacts, avoidance relations semiotically sketch the negation of their intersubjective mutuality. Hearing does not involve this inherent mutuality. In and by hearing, we cannot hear the other hearing. We cannot listen to the other listen. Unlike the other sense organs, the human ear does not betray the fact of its sensory perception. Perhaps this is one reason that the suppression of audible "output" for the other and the screening of audible "input" from the other are not commonly elaborated cross-culturally in avoidance registers.

Where silence is enjoined of avoidance partners, this most often seems to be related to the linguistic and discursive implications of sound. Proscriptions linked to audition are not typically related to the sounding body, as such, but to the implicit addressivity of vocal production – vocalization, in particular, as an entreaty to discourse. In this vein, enjoined silence involves the hypertrophic extension of the strategies of negated address discussed in the last chapter. Thus, in addition to non-address and triadic communication, avoidance relations may dampen the audible speech signal when in co-presence.[3] But inaudibility as a sign of interpersonal respect may extend beyond ratified or "focused interaction," conditioning comportment even in "unfocused interaction," that is, in interaction involving "the management of sheer and mere copresence" (Goffman, 1963, p. 24, cited in Rampton, 2018, p. 3). On Gau Island in Fiji, there is a strict avoidance relationship between a woman and her husband's brother (*veidakuni*). The two do not speak to each other, and typically the woman will "slip out" when a husband's brother enters a social setting where she is present. But if the woman remains in her brother-in-law's co-presence, she does "not utter a word unless absolutely necessary—and then only as softly as possible" (Nayacakalou, 1971, p. 151).

Whispering often, of course, has an addressivity function apparent in its use in off-the-record, hushed asides or Goffmanian "side-play" between bystanders to a discursive event. Even if the signal is audible to all present, muted speech figures only proximal others as intended addressees. For avoidance relations for whom non-interaction is the stipulated norm, whispering may work as yet another trope of self-negating meta-communication. Avoidance relations communicate while, through their manipulation of "aural range" (Goffman, 1981, p. 136), figuring non-interaction. As an illustration of how oral-aural avoidances are linked to addressivity and languaging, more broadly, I provide the case study of Armenian daughter-in-law alternate sign language.

Case Study: Armenian Daughter-in-Law Sign Language

As I have shown for multiple media of avoidance, avoidance relationships in Afro-Eurasian societies often have a markedly hierarchical, gender-stratified, and non-reciprocal character. In keeping with this pattern, in the ethnography of South Asia and the Caucasus it is not uncommon to find descriptions which state that a married woman is normatively expected to not speak to male members of her husband's family. In some cases, married women are expected to modulate the volume of their voices, or to be completely silent, in the co-presence of, especially, ascending generation male affines. The injunction to silence as an emblem of affinal respect and reserve is particularly widespread in the Caucasus (see Luzbetak, 1951, for a review). A young bride's silence served as a particularly salient sign of respect toward the family into whose house she moved after marriage. Among the Abkhaz the restriction was, once again, strongest between the bride and her father-in-law: "A woman may not speak to her father-in-law, nor may he hear the sound of her voice" (Benet, 1974, p. 62). But there is also a shorter period of speech-avoidance practiced with respect to the mother-in-law (p. 62).[4] In various Caucasus societies, affinal avoidance was most intense right after marriage, with some avoidance practices being liable to dispensation over time, though never at the initiation of the daughter-in-law. In some Udi (Nak-Daghestani; Azerbaijan) communities, daughters-in-law could not speak to their fathers-in-law for years after marriage. This ban on addressing the father-in-law was lifted only when he presented the daughter-in-law with a gift (Volkova, 1994, p. 377, cited in Tuite & Schulze, 1998).

Descriptions of Armenian post-marital avoidances are, however, the most remarkable. Historically, the period of post-marital silence could last as long as 15 years, being always and only subject to dispensation by the mother-in-law (van Lennep, cited in Villa & Matossian, 1982, p. 185). Haxthausen's nineteenth-century report from Armenia suggests the most generalized avoidance of speech. The new bride could speak only to her husband, and then only in private. With everyone else, including her own consanguineal kin, "she can only communicate by gestures, and by talking on her fingers" (Haxthausen, 1854, p. 227).

The vocal restraint expected of the new bride in some Armenian communities was sartorially underscored by face and mouth coverings:

> Her face was usually veiled in public for at least one year (and sometimes it was tightly bound, a practice known as *mounj*), and during a ritual period of silence she was allowed to speak to no one except children and her husband (should they find themselves completely alone). After the birth of her first child, she was sometimes permitted to speak to the women of her household. Some women maintained a period of ritual silence for ten years or for life. (Platz, 1996, p. 30)

While Platz (1996) refers to the mouth covering and veiling of the bride as *mounj*, Villa and Matossian (1982) suggest that the period of silence itself was called *moonch* (perhaps "muteness").[5] The length of this period of time was variable, as its cessation was subject to the will of the bride's mother-in-law. Dispensation was again achieved through the offering of a gift, and in at least one account the mother-in-law uttering the command: "Speak my daughter" (Villa & Matossian, 1982, p. 92). Still, even after this dispensation of the speech ban, the daughter-in-law could speak only when spoken to (Berberian, 2004, p. 11).

The period of *moonch* was described by informants as a time during which "the bride swallowed her tongue" (Villa & Matosian, 1982, p. 92). Not only was the bride not to speak in the presence of her affines, but she was also supposed to abstain from eating in their presence

(Berberian, 2004, p. 11). The mouth, the locus of speech production, should never be seen, even when at work for other motives than for talking. Among some Armenian women in nineteenth-century Persia, a newly married woman would speak through children. But if they were not present then she "would speak with her hands or facing a wall" (Berberian, 2008). The technique of facing a wall is a practice of negated address of the kind that we looked at in the last chapter (recall also Anderson's [1982, p. 402] description of cross-sex interaction between Pashtun strangers cited above).

As these descriptions make clear, it is not all sound, but the sound of the voice in particular, which is proscribed. Here the linguistic modality of speech itself constitutes the negative repertoire of the avoidance register, and an emergent manual-visual sign language serves as the positive repertoire that substitutes for it. The existence of an alternate signed language employed by newly married Armenian brides and employed in place of speech is reported as early as the mid-nineteenth century (Haxthausen, 1854, p. 227; see also Samvelian, cited in Panian, 1969). But Armenian brides' sign language is thoroughly documented only in a rare, Russian-language volume, written by Karbelashvili (1935).[6] New brides were expected to employ the sign language in the co-presence of a "wide range" of affines (Kendon, 1988, p. 409). That is, they used it precisely in those contexts where the use of the oral-aural modality was proscribed.

The silence of Armenian brides was variable across time and space, sometimes being conditioned by the mere fact of interactional co-presence with an in-law (northern Armenian; Karbelashvili, 1935) and in others by the kin categorical relation between the signer and the addressee (e.g., daughter-in-law → father-in-law) (Persia; Berberian, 2008). As this survey of the literature illustrates, Armenian brides' sign language emerges from the backdrop of these speech bans. It is not a coincidence that the only grammatical description of Armenian brides' sign language comes from a region – northern Armenia – where normative injunctions on speech were the most generalized. Where speech is not permitted in the presence of the widest range of taboo affines, whatever their interactional role (i.e., whether addressee or mere bystander), alternate sign language is most robustly attested. This suggests that the signed avoidance register – though it replaces a spoken linguistic code – emerges out of dynamics of interactional avoidance (e.g., restrictions on turn-taking behaviour, address avoidance) rather than directly from taboos on vocalization as such (see Fleming, 2014b, for a fuller exposition of this argument). The silence of the daughter-in-law – thematized as the period of *moonch* "muteness" or "mouth covering" in Armenian – appears as the endpoint of a progressive extension and generalization of more limited and interactionally specific practices of avoidance. (Note, for instance, that where sign language is found in Armenian speech communities it does not fill in for direct spoken discourse between a woman and her in-laws. Rather, it stands in for speech relayed through speech intermediaries, typically a woman's children [Berberian, 2008].)

In this case, the voice becomes a metonym for dialogic discourse and the mutuality that it implies. To avoid the voice is to perform not speaking, even if rich denotational content is still communicated by the hands. Just as the use of shill addressees counts as a trope of "negated address," the use of an alternate signed language serves as a trope of "negated speech." By exploiting the affordances of the manual-visual modality, Armenian brides engaged in languaging while meta-communicating their silence.

Constraint and the Design Space Problem in Non-linguistic Semiosis

In concluding this discussion of non-verbal, sensorial signs of avoidance, I want to highlight some of the differences between the study of the non-linguistic semiotic range of avoidance registers presented in Part 3 and the treatment of linguistic avoidances elsewhere in the book. In particular, I want to reflect on what the implications of these differences are for a would-be comparative linguistic anthropology of the kind attempted in this volume.

The flourishing of language typology as a comparative study of language structures is predicated upon the constrained character of its empirical object. Languages are highly structured at multiple interconnected levels. Though the challenge of "characterizing the full dimensions of the design space" of language is a formidable one (N. Evans, 2013, p. 233), promising proposals for how to go about it for certain domains have been put forward (e.g., Bull, 1960; Cysouw, 2003). Formal-functional relationships that manifest in language – even if they are not oriented around what Jakobson called the "referential function" – are importantly constrained by the *sui generis* properties of languages as systems of Peircean symbols (Deacon, 1998).

The highly structured character of language also constrains the patterning of its non-referential, iconic, and indexical significations. This has already been seen in the treatments of mother-in-law languages in Part 1 and of name registers in Part 2. To exemplify the point, take the case of name registers. As I have illustrated, there are a limited number of language-structure-defined "pegs" around which, time after time, the sociopragmatics of name avoidance become organized (i.e., avoidance of the name *qua rigid designator*, avoidance of the *proper noun*, and avoidance of *[near-]homophones of the name*). Although there is cross-cultural variability in which structural pegs are actualized and distinguished in the sociopragmatics of any given culture of naming, there is nevertheless a highly constrained space of variation. The cross-cultural comparison of non-linguistic avoidance media does not appear to be so constrained, certainly not in the same manner.

In theorizing the comparability of non-linguistic signs of avoidance, I have not invoked structural constraints of the kind central to language description. Rather, and following the lead of others (e.g., Keane, 2003; Kockelman, 2006; Manning, 2012; Meneley, 2008), I have suggested that cross-culturally recurrent norms of non-linguistic avoidance exploit "ecological affordances" (Gibson, 1966) of the signalling media through which they are expressed and experienced. I have argued that the human body – and in particular its perceptual possibilities – conditions (as affordance assemblage rather than as sign structure) which non-linguistic signs get taken up as emblems of interpersonal avoidance. Granting, for the moment, that the body constrains the space of possibilities for signifying social relationship, it is clear that the character of these constraints is quite different from those that condition the sociolinguistic patterns that I highlighted in Parts 1 and 2.

To illustrate the implications of the difference, compare the linguistic repertoires that crop up around the names of in-laws to the non-linguistic repertoires that cluster around the visual presencing of in-laws. Although there is a great deal of variability in naming traditions, in the grammatical and lexical properties of names and proper nouns and in the modes of their social transmission and sharing, names are anchored to their referential function within an etic space of possible noun phrase types (Silverstein, 1987b). It is against the backdrop of this highly constrained space of possibilities that linguistic avoidances become "pinned" to the name, the rigid designator of the avoidance relation. The distinct pegs of name avoidance, like homophone avoidance or proper-noun avoidance, all have the indexically referential name as their anchoring centre point.

No such anchoring is assured in practices of visual avoidance. There are no necessary pegs of visual avoidance analogous to those attested in name registers. I have hypothesized that ritual (in)attention to the face – a rigid sign of personhood – or to the eyes – an intersubjectively knowable mode of perception – is particularly apt to emblematize interactional avoidance. And, indeed, there are numerous cases where either the entire head is rendered invisible, or the eyes are covered, as a sign of interpersonal respect. And yet other cultural preoccupations anchored to different parts of the head or body are also elaborated in avoidance registers (see Landes, 1937, p. 26, on foot covering among Anishinaabe in-laws; Roscoe, 1965, p. 129, on breast covering among Baganda in-laws). Even remaining with instances of head covering, specifically, in some societies women are enjoined not to cover their faces or eyes but rather to cover their hair. Hair covering, for instance, was the principal preoccupation for women in the northern Solomons (Buka and Bougainville Islands): "The hair of a woman is close-cropped ... The women wear a hood made from pandanus leaves sewn horizontally together, with every other leaf dyed red with the root of a bush. This custom is to prevent certain of their male relatives from seeing their hair, which is taboo" (Thomas, 1931, p. 222). And head coverings, as opposed to face coverings, are themselves found all over the world, from the practice of Orthodox Jewish women wearing *tichel*, to those of Xhosa wives who wear the *iqhiya*, to Hutterite women's headscarves. Of course, scenarios centring on the symbolism of hair as a function of its affordances could also be proffered – hair, for instance, is "good to think with" because it continues to grow throughout the life-course of the individual (A. Strathern, 1989, p. 86). But the more our explanations multiply, the more we worry that our comparative anchor may no longer really be touching the seabed. So again, the eyes may be *one* cause of the elaboration of veiling, head covering, and the like. But they are not a necessary point of reference, and historical process can readily push a cultural form out of this "attractor" or cause a distinctly emergent form to drift into it.

In summary, the semiotic kinds attested in the realm of non-linguistic semiosis seem not to have the same kind of fixity and discreteness as the sociolinguistic kinds that I have documented in the linguistic range of avoidance registers. Correspondingly, the character of the semiotic typology presented in Part 3 is quite different than that of the sociolinguistic typologies provided in the other parts. The best comparative argument that I was able to formulate for these non-linguistic media was to characterize the sensory organs and sense perception as an **affordance assemblage** and attend to the sign systems that crop up on that scaffold. Within the sign systems that grow on and around the sensory organs, perhaps the closest thing to a semiotic kind that I have identified is a species of paradoxical meta-communication that is *virtually* self-regimenting in the ways in which it iconically figures non-interaction. But this is more of a semiotic "operation" than a "kind," and one long ago identified by Gregory Bateson as having deep routes in mammalian interaction and as manifesting in diverse dimensions of human interaction and personality (see the diverse examples which Bateson, 1972, provides of paradoxical meta-communication in "A Theory of Play and Fantasy"). As I have shown, in each sensory modality, closure of an input or output function iconically-indexes non-interaction – not looking (visual modality, input function) figures the "negation of interaction" just as not speaking (auditory modality, output function) does. In the non-linguistic domain, such paradoxical meta-communication – the emblematic negation of the interaction that such emblems nevertheless instantiate – is the closest thing we get to a meta-sign/object-sign structure of the kind that provides the constraints on linguistic forms and functions and which, ultimately, grounds the commensurability of (socio)linguistic kinds (see Silverstein, 1976, pp. 16, 48, on "metasemantics" and "metapragmatics").

None of this should be read as foreclosing upon the possibility of commensurable structures in non-linguistic semiosis. It is an open question whether non-linguistic semiosis can be characterized in terms of cross-culturally commensurable *sui generis* structures and how these might – should they have a reality – differ from those attested in linguistic and language-adjacent structure. If Part 4 isn't completely off base, perhaps we needn't be wholly sceptical about the possibility of discovering the kinds of structural constraints necessary for a comparative semiotic anthropology that could cut across linguistic and non-linguistic semiotic media.

PART FOUR

The Pattern Which Connects: Avoidance Registers as Scalar Honorific Formations

Chapter Seven

The Pragmatic Suspension of Semantic Distinctions: Honorific Pronouns in Kinship Avoidance

The indefatigable mid-twentieth-century anthropological field researcher Raymond Firth makes the following observation in his classic ethnography, *We, the Tikopia*: "In many languages (French and German for instance, and formerly English also) a courtesy differentiation is made between the singular and plural forms of the personal pronouns. In Tikopia there is also a dual form, commonly used for situations involving two people, but employed by affinal relatives in addressing each other singly. This may be termed the 'polite dual'" (Firth, 1937, p. 311). In Tikopian, the "polite dual" is a component part of a broader semiotic register of affinal avoidance. Father-in-law and son-in-law, for instance, not only are proscribed from addressing one another with singular pronouns, but they should also not directly take objects from each other, not discuss sensitive matters, and not laugh, and they should sit with their legs crossed in each other's company.

In this chapter I look at the role of honorific pronouns, like the Tikopian dual, in kinship avoidance registers (see Kruspe & Burenhult, 2019, for a path-breaking study of this phenomenon in Aslian languages). The topic merits attention in its own right; honorific pronouns, like mother-in-law languages and name registers, are important sociolinguistic signs of avoidance relationship. Beyond the substantive importance of the topic for a sociolinguistics of kinship, a focus on honorific pronouns helps to put into relief how and why avoidance comes to count as respectful practice, more generally. Why does avoidance – of someone's name, of their person and possessions, or even of singular number in referring to them – so consistently enact interpersonal respect? Answering this question will enable me to paint a more detailed and expansive portrait of how and why registered avoidances mediate kinship relationship. And this, in turn, will better position me to respond to the questions posed in the Introduction concerning the gradient expression of avoidance – from muted formality to the maximal avoidance of the "total orientation" (Merlan, 1997) – across kinship relationship types.

Formal-Functional Analogy in Honorific Pronouns

In a text, "Shifters, Linguistic Categories, and Cultural Description," widely seen as foundational for the reimagining of linguistic anthropology (Nakassis, 2016b), Michael Silverstein (1976) uses honorific pronouns to exemplify the semiotic multifunctionality of language. In honorific pronouns, referential and nonreferential indexical functions – person deixis and social indexicality – overlap in the same linguistic signals: "On the one hand, the pronominals have discourse-referential values that contribute to description, and on the other hand, they have nonreferential values that structure the factors of the speech situation. The first indexical aspect contributes to the propositional mode of speech, while the second constitutes part of the social mode of marking equality or inequality" (Silverstein, 1976, pp. 36–7). Just like other person deictics, honorific pronouns pick out speech participants as discourse referents and thus contribute directly to the "denotational text" of what-is-said in discourse (Silverstein, 1993). However, they simultaneously nonreferentially index the social relationship between the speaker and the addressee-referent and thus contribute directly to the "interactional text" of what-is-done in interaction (Silverstein, 1993). In languages that employ honorific pronouns, "patterns of participant deixis (i.e., forms that indexically denote speaker or addressee) [are re-analyzed as] stereotypic social indexicals, whether indexical of speaker's own attributes or relationship to interlocutor, thus yielding sociocultural registers of person deixis" (Agha, 2007, p. 278).

Following R. Brown and Gilman (1960, p. 254), who employ "T" and "V" – after Latin *tu* and *vos* – as "generic designators for a familiar and a polite pronoun in any language," honorific registers of person deixis are often referred to as T-V systems. In his discussion of honorific pronouns, Silverstein is at pains to underscore the cross-culturally convergent, formal-functional analogy that grounds T-V systems. T-V systems manifest a motivated and non-arbitrary relationship between linguistic form and honorific function. What makes the canonical T-V distinction (e.g., French *tu/vous*, Russian *ty/vy*, German *du/Sie*) particularly intriguing from a formal perspective is that "instead of distinct forms indexing the quality of speaker-hearer relations, the 'second person' pronouns incorporate *skewing of otherwise semantic categories*" (Silverstein, 1976, p. 37; italics added). By far the most common way for pronominal honorifics to be fashioned cross-linguistically is through systematic distortion or misapplication (when evaluated with respect to the "objective" properties of the referent) of semantic feature values, in particular, of number and person (Head, 1978). Here there is a dynamic tension between semantic and pragmatic functional modalities. Does a token of *vous* denote more than one individual (the semantic/referential reading of number) or non-referentially index the relationship between the speaker and a unique addressee (the pragmatic/nonreferential reading of number)? These semantic and pragmatic functional modalities could easily be disambiguated, as they are when they receive distinctive morphological marking. This is what happens, for instance, in those dialects of Spanish where politeness (*Usted* [honorific singular] vs. *tú* [nonhonorific singular]) and plurality (*Ustedes* [plural]) are formally distinguished. And yet V forms seem most often to accomplish the social function of enacting respect by means of the suspension of semantic features, by parasitically inhabiting the "otherwise semantic." In the honorific skewing of a semantic feature value, "politeness is ... expressed by *conditions* on the use of other morphosyntactic features" rather than being a feature in its own right (Corbett, 2012, p. 12).

To review, T and V pronouns as attested in a diverse range of languages-in-culture are "formally analogous indexicals" in that "there is formal comparability in the expression of deference through pronominal categories themselves, which can be isolated in the referential mode" (Silverstein, 1976, p. 40). Honorific (V) pronouns are given formal expression by analogous means: the skewing of a semantic feature value. But they are also "functionally analogous ... indexes" in that the pronominal form employing the non-singular number value (e.g., French *vous*) or the third-person feature value (e.g., German *Sie*) consistently accomplishes the sociocultural function of enacting respect.

There is a deep connection between "the parallel formal-functional analogy" of T-V systems (Silverstein, 1976, p. 41) and other of the linguistic and non-linguistic signs of interpersonal respect that I have investigated in this volume. As I have shown, time and again, respect (social function) is enacted in similar ways (semiotic form) in kinship avoidance relationships. In-laws are honoured through the avoidance of their names, their person, their property, their presence. Registered semiotic avoidance (form) enacts interpersonal respect (function).[1] Formalizing this insight for a range of semiotic media of avoidance is the goal of the next chapter. In this chapter, I illustrate this dynamic for the special case of honorific pronouns. I show how the avoidance of, for example, singular number (form) comes to enact, in language after language, interpersonal respect (function). I then show how, from this seed, avoidance registers "grow" in what might be thought of as a runaway process of cumulative cultural evolution wherein progressively more and more onerous avoidance routines are enregistered as enacting ever more heightened interpersonal restraint. To begin, I consider the distinctive articulation of honorific pronouns with social relationship in kinship registers.

In-Law Avoidance Registers of Person Deixis

Honorific registers of person deixis (Agha, 2007, pp. 278–300) have been most thoroughly studied in European language communities (Fleming, 2023). In contemporary German or French, the choice between V and T typically reflects specificities of the developing intersubjective relationship between speaker and addressee (frequency and intensity of prior contacts between interlocutors) rather than being a simple and direct reflex of their social identities, statuses, and role-relationships (Clyne et al., 2009). Contrastingly, in societies where kinship provides an enveloping institutional framework for reckoning social roles and relationships, usage of T or V is typically associated with particular kin relations. That is, the use of T or V indexically presupposes or entails a kin-categorical framing of the relationship between the person employing the pronoun (the origo-of-deference) and the addressee or referent of the pronoun (the target-of-deference). I illustrate this, in Table 7.1, with a sample of T-V systems stereotypically linked to kinship relationships characterized by interactional restraint. Adapting terminology from Choksi (2010), I label these **kinship-restricted honorifics**. The epithet "restricted" is meant to indicate that metapragmatic stereotypes exclusively associate the use of honorifics with specific social categories of person or role relationships.

Table 7.1 is not an exhaustive survey of honorific pronouns keyed to avoidance relationships, nor is it composed of a balanced sample. The sample reflects my own incomplete and uneven reading of ethnographic and sociolinguistic literatures. In particular, the table should be viewed while keeping in mind the ways in which colonial language contact has contoured the typology of social indexicality.

As alluded to in the Introduction, social speech registers are often some of the first to be lost in the processes of language shift and obsolescence connected with European colonialism, environmental destruction, and globalization. Instances where rich descriptions of affinal avoidance registers are available often correspond to a particular conjuncture: field work that was conducted by ethnographers or linguists with sufficiently advanced methods and the anthropological curiosity necessary to attend to sociolinguistic variation, on the one hand, and

Table 7.1. Examples of kinship-restricted T-V systems

Language (location)	Number feature skewed	Honorific restricted to social relationship of ...
Oceania		
1. Gooniyandi (Kimberley, Australia)	PL	*maddiyali* son-in-law/ mother-in-law
2. Djaru (Kimberley, Australia)	PL	*maliji* son-in-law/ mother-in-law
3. Mangarayi (Arnhem L., Australia)	PL	*gaṇji* son-in-law/ wife's mother('s B/Z)
4. Kobon (Papua New Guinea [PNG])	D I PL	same-sex in-law I cross-sex in-law
5. Usan (PNG)	PL	sibling-in-law/ parent-in-law
6. Boazi (PNG)	PL	father-in-law/son-in-law
7. Daakie (Vanuatu)	D	parents-in-law [// sib.] + their G^{-2} lineal kin
8. Korowai (New Guinea)	PL	*lalum-bandaxol* son-in-law/ mo.-in-law
9. Lelet (New Ireland)	PL	cross-gender consang. $=G^{-2,0,+2}$; cross-gender affines $=G^{-3,-1,+3}$
10. Rotokas (Solomons)	PL	brother-sister
11. Birao (Solomons)	D	parent/child; mB/zS; child-in-law/parent-in-law
12. Wuvulu (Admiralty)	D	in-laws
13. Mwotlap (Vanuatu)	D	*qe:/ge-* adjacent generation, lineal in-law
14. Tikopia (Polynesia)	D	in-laws
South East Asia		
15. Toba Batak (Sumatra) [1800s]	PL	members of a distinct clan
16. Temiar (Malaysia)	D I PL	spouse's ySib./eSib.'s spouse; parent-/child-in-law
17. Kri (Laos)	D	son-in-law [=referent] / father-in-law [=speaker or addressee]
18. Jahai (Malaysia)	D I PL	G^0 or G^{-1} affine I G^{+1} affine
South Asia		
19. Raji (Nepal)	D I PL	sibling-in-law I parent-in-law [inferred]
20. Santali (India)	D I PL	adjacent generation, lineal in-law I co-parents-in-law
Africa		
21. Mijikenda (Kenya)	PL	disharmonic kin
22. Jul'hoan (Botswana)	PL	disharmonic kin; cross-sex sibling
23. Gǀui (Botswana)	PL	in-laws; cross-sex sibling; cross-sex parent/child

(continued)

Table 7.1. Continued

Language (location)	Number feature skewed	Honorific restricted to social relationship of ...
NATIVE AMERICAS		
24. Achumawi (California)	PL	DH(B)/WM(Z); HF(B)
25. Yana (California)	PL	cross-sex sibling
26. Central Pomo (California)	PL	parent-in-law
27. Kamayurá	PL	G^0 and G^{+1} in-laws

Sources: 1. McGregor (1989); 2. Tsunoda (1981); 3. Merlan (1982a, 1982b); 4. J. Davies (1991); 5. Reesink (1987); 6. Busse (2005, p.86); 7. Krifka (2019, p. 71); 8. Stasch (2003, p. 322); 9. Eves (1998, p. 127); 10. Robinson (2011, p. 176); 11. Hogbin (1969, p. 18); but see Hogbin (1937, p. 69, for conflicting description); 12. Hafford (2015, p. 59); 13. François (2001, p. 458); see also Codrington (1957, p. 45); 14. Hage (1969, p. 98); 15. van der Tuuk (1971); 16. Benjamin (1999); 17. Enfield (2022); 18. Kruspe & Burenhult (2019); 19. Sah (2010, pp. 199–200); 20. MacPhail (1983, p. 21). McGivney (1993); 22. R. Lee (1993); 23. Ōno (2016); 24. Gifford (1922, p. 261); 25. Sapir (1910, p. 95); 26. Mithun (1988, p. 532); see also Loeb (1926, p. 208); 27. Seki (1983).

linguistic informants who still could reconstruct such patterns of usage, on the other. The greater representation of west coast over east coast Native North American languages, for instance, needs to be understood in this light. Descriptions of the use of pronominal honorifics in native languages of California are almost all derived from the "salvage" work of anthropologists associated with the University of California, Berkeley, in the early twentieth century (Golla, 2011). Correspondingly, the quality of descriptions varies considerably across cases. Most gravely, I cannot determine from extant sources how closely the norms stated in ethnographic or linguistic descriptions corresponded to actual practices of honorific usage. With these caveats in mind, let's look through the sample.

As Table 7.1 illustrates, the skewing of pronouns in reference to taboo in-laws is widespread in Oceania. Further references than those listed in the table could be supplied. For Aboriginal Australia, for instance, Tsunoda (1981, p. 215) cites personal communications with Patrick McConvell and Joyce Hudson to inform us that non-singular pronouns are employed in honorific reference to taboo in-laws in Mudbura, Gurindji, Malngin, and Wandjira (see also Garde, 1996, p. 73, on Dalabon and Bininj Gunwok; Sutton, 1978, p. 220, on Wik). Papuan and Oceanic languages exhibit some of the most elaborate kinship-restricted T-V systems (see in-depth discussion below of Manus [Oceanic] and Kobon [Papuan]; see also Krifka, 2019, for an important study of Vanuatu). Honorific pronouns keyed to avoidance relationships appear to be less widespread in the Native Americas. In North America there is a clustering of cases in the Athabaskan language family. Affinal avoidance is pronounced in both northern Athabaskan (e.g., Bear Lake Athabaskan [Rushforth, 1981]) and among Apachean groups (e.g., Navajo), as well as among the Pacific Athabaskan language groups of California (e.g., Wailiki [Gifford, 1922, p. 261, citing unpublished field notes of P.E. Goddard]). As elsewhere, honorific pronouns comprise only one component of a much broader semiotic range of avoidance repertoires. In South America, the Xingu River area yet again furnishes examples (recall our discussion of the Kamayurá honorific plural in Chapter 5). But again, this is only a subset of the South American cases.

In Eurasia, honorific pronouns are less often uniquely tied to kinship, being typically also linked to caste- or class-based reckoning of social difference. Nevertheless, there are some languages with honorific pronouns linked exclusively to kin-based avoidance relationships. The "affinal kin register" in the Nepalese language Dhimal (Tibeto-Burman) is a particularly clear case of this kind (King, 2001). Intriguingly, Austroasiatic languages across multiple, disparate regions are robustly attested with this feature. Members of the Aslian branch – languages of the indigenous, traditionally foraging peoples of peninsular mainland Southeast Asia – have rich in-law pronominal sets (Kruspe & Burenhult, 2019; see the discussion of Jahai and Temiar, below). But so do members of the Mundic branch (Santali, Mundari, Ho), languages spoken in India. In the dialect of Santali documented by Ghosh (2008), dual number is employed reciprocally in both speaker- and addressee-reference between lineal adjacent generation in-laws. Remarkably, Enfield's (2022) description of person reference in Kri, a member of the Vietic branch of Austroasiatic spoken in Laos, also documents the use of the dual for son-in-law. The dual is used in addressing a son-in-law and in self-reference by that individual when addressing his father-in-law, and it complements dedicated affinal forms.

In Africa, honorific pronominals linked to kinship are most robustly attested in Khoesan languages (see the detailed treatment of G|ui in Ōno, 2016). However, the Bantu language Mijikenda represents a particularly interesting case, as T and V presuppose, respectively, the harmonic and disharmonic generational relatedness of the origo- and target-of-deference (McGivney, 1993).[2]

The Structural Underdetermination of Language Ideology: Duelling Duels

As Table 7.1 exemplifies, kinship-restricted honorific pronouns are almost always formally instantiated by the skewing of number feature values (for discussion of person skewing, see the Aslian case studies, below). The widespread use of non-singular number to achieve the social function of honorification begs an explanation. There have, of course, been several attempts at ascertaining "the exact psychological basis of why it is considered more polite to address a single individual as if he were two or more" (Firth, 1937, p. 312). Most proposals understand the honorific signification of the skewed semantic feature value to be based – as Firth's formulation already assumes – in a "pragmatic metaphor" (Silverstein, 1976, p. 39) or icon related to its normal semantic value (Bean, 1970; P. Brown & Levinson, 1987, p. 199; Malsch, 1987). Silverstein (1976), for instance, argued that the use of non-singular number in singular honorific address "makes the addressee count for more than one social individual; to his persona accrues the social weight of many, as compared with the speaker" (p. 39).

The problem with proposals like these is that they presume an invariant iconic meaning (e.g., of plural grandeur) for non-singular number across languages and cultures.[3] In actuality, the figurational potential of non-singular number for honorific function is configured differently in different languages-in-culture. Close inspection on a case-by-case basis reveals that the precise signification given to the honorific skewing of a semantic feature value is mediated by fashions of speaking – "ways of analyzing and reporting experience which have become fixed in ... language" (Whorf, 2000, p. 214; see Chapter 2 for further discussion of this concept). Here I will briefly treat two examples that illustrate the mediating role of fashions of speaking, one from Tikopian (Oceanic; island Melanesia) and one from Yokuts (Hokan; California), both involving dual number. The comparison of these cases illustrates that the language-structural organization of honorific registers of person deixis are relatively underdetermining of the "secondary reasoning and ... re-interpretations" (Boas, 1911, p. 67) that ideologically rationalize why this or that linguistic structure is imbued with this or that social meaning. Though dual number has an honorific function linked to affinal relationship in both languages, it emblematizes or epitomizes valued norms of in-law relationship in divergent manners.

Case Studies: The Honorific Dual in Tikopian and Yokuts

As mentioned above, Firth (1937) describes the use of a "polite dual" employed in addressing in-laws on the Polynesian outlier island Tikopia. His examples almost all involve acts of address between father-in-law and son-in-law. The use of the dual in affinal address is ideologically elaborated by a fashion of speaking whereby in-laws employ dyadic kin terms to refer to each other. An informant, Pa Tekaumata, offers the following (explicit metapragmatic) testimony:

> One calls out to the father-in-law, "*Tau puna E*" [= grandfather + grandchild]. He hears and calls, "What?" The speech "*Tau puna E*" is based upon the children, though they may be anywhere at all, or absent ... One does not call out thus, "Where didst thou go?" but calls "Where did you (two) go?" The single man, the *tautau pariki* [avoidance relation]. This is the base of the speech indeed to the father-in-law ... The father-in-law calls out to the son-in-law, "Come hither and enter here, son-in-law. Take up and eat something for you two, *tau ma E*" [= brother-in-law + brother-in-law]. When he speaks to that person does he mean two? O! it is a single man; he makes it weighty for the *tautau pariki*. Because he calls upon their own children; he makes a brother-in-law for him. I here am one alone, but am two; am provided with a brother-in-law from their sons. (Pa Tekaumata, quoted and translated in Firth, 1937, pp. 311–12)

The term *tau puna* and *tau ma* are dyadic kin terms. (The clitic *E* is an honorific particle.) Dyadic kin terms are formed by preposing *tau* to a kin term, which then is interpreted as referring to the dyad corresponding to the alter and propositus of the kin term (see N. Evans, 2006, on dyadic kinship constructions). The use of these dyadic kin terms resonates with the use of dual number in pronominal address. But this trope of kin address goes beyond that, since it symbolically highlights the link between the affinal alter and ego's consanguineal kin (Firth, 1937, p. 312). Thus "dual"-ing an in-law is a way of signifying his bond to ego's family unit, metonymically signified through the other monad in the dyadic kin term. A father-in-law is also grandfather to one's child; a son-in-law is also one's son's brother-in-law. The dual links the outsider with the inside, kin through marriage with natal kin.

The second case study comes from Stanley Newman's (1944) grammatical description of Yawelmani Yokuts. In Yokuts, the dual was used as an honorific in second- and third-person reference between a son-in-law and a mother-in-law. In his description of the durative aspect, Newman provides the following example and gloss: "*bɔnɔ[.]y-'ɔn 'amin 'ɔnitpa*, '(he) dualizes his mother-in-law' (i.e., reference here is to the polite form of address practiced by a man toward his mother-in-law; he must address her as *ma'ak'*, 'you (dual),' and refer to her as *'amak'*, 'they (dual)'): <*bɔnɔy*, 'dualize, make two'" (p. 101; italics added). The metapragmatic designator for "use an honorific pronoun" in Yokuts is notably different from analogous metapragmatic terms employed in other languages to denote the speech act of uttering an honorific pronoun. In

European languages, delocutive verbs – French *tutoyer/vouvoyer*, German *duzen/siezen*, Spanish *tutear/ustedear* – are employed to denote the act of employing a (non-)honorific pronoun (Benveniste, 1971). That is, the honorific signal (indexical type: e.g., *vous*) is "rank-shifted" into a metapragmatic lexeme (symbolic type: e.g., *vouvoyer*) employed to denote the act of employing the honorific signal (Silverstein, 1987a). In Yokuts, contrastingly, the metapragmatic term employed to describe the use of an honorific pronoun is not lexicalized through the reproduction of a replica of the honorific signal itself (i.e., *ma'ak'*) but by means of one of a small class of "numeral verbs" (Newman, 1944, p. 54). These are a set of special verbs that have a distinct form for each of the counting numbers up to ten. The numeral verbs have a causative reading implying that a homogeneous entity is divided into the number of parts denoted by the numeral root (e.g., *hɔdbɔnɔy* "four" > *hɔdɔb* "make four"). The use of the numeral verb doubles here as the metapragmatic term for denoting the act of addressing/referring to a mother-in-law with respectful dual number. It focuses attention on numerosity-as-division and associates that reading with the skewing of dual number in honorific reference to in-laws. Since numeral verbs denote division (e.g., of a food stuff), I infer that "dual"-ing in Yokuts had the connotation of ritually separating or dividing mother-in-law and son-in-law from each other.

In both Yokuts and Tikopian, dual number comes to be seen as a non-arbitrary sign of social relationship. The semantics of duality come to be seen as reflective of, appropriate to, or inherent in affinal relationality. To employ the polite dual in Yokuts is to engage in a respectful splitting or separating that cuts off mother-in-law from son-in-law. This is conceptually objectified in the metapragmatic term employed to denote the speech act of employing the polite dual, *bɔnɔy* "to halve." This splitting is not merely linguistic but interactional – all throughout Native California, mother-in-law and son-in-law were separated in interpersonal space by the kinds of anti-phatic interaction rituals discussed in Part 3 (Gifford, 1922). In Tikopian, contrastingly, to employ the polite dual is to signal a bonding or linking of affinal and consanguineal kin – not "halving" but "coupling." This is made explicit in the dyadic kin terms used to refer to single affinal alters, terms that pair affinal alters with a member of ego's consanguineal group. Tikopian dyad constructions "agree" – both grammatically and conceptually – with the dual number of the pronominals that are appropriate to affinal relationality.

Employing a more technical semiotic metalanguage, the ideological elaboration of number as a sign of kinship relationality involves a *rhematization* of the honorific pronominal index: The number category that is skewed in honorific reference not only indexes a kinship relationship but is also interpreted as an icon of that relationship.[4] I call these culture-specific figurations of dual number **semantic echoes**, because they involve a refracted or "as if" parsing of a semantic content that is nevertheless not incorporated into the propositional content of the utterance.[5] In the examples I have just treated, the iconic or figurational potential of the skewed dual is realized when it constellates with other linguistic idioms (e.g., dyadic kin terms, numeral verbs) and with the broader sociocultural context and conceptualization of kinship. Language structure affords particular ideological construals, but it does not determine them.

Deference and the Pragmatic Suspension of Semantic Distinctions

So where does this leave us in seeking an explanation for why semantic skewing – rather than, say, the use of dedicated forms – is the most common way in which honorific pronouns are fashioned cross-linguistically? As I mentioned, earlier treatments of this problem have focused on how the skewed semantic feature *figures* the social meaningfulness of the honorific. (Semantics regiments pragmatic function.) Here I offer an alternative, if complementary, account. My approach, contrastingly, highlights the way in which feature skewing *disfigures* semantics, how honorification is achieved by creating cybernetic noise over the semantic signal. (Pragmatics suspends semantic function.)

Feature "skewing" is a two-sided coin; while semantic echoes sketch socioculturally rich meanings, the pragmatic signal also suppresses the workability of a semantic distinction. Feature skewing achieves honorification by the re-signification of a semantic distinction (singular vs. plural) along the pragmatic functional modality ("impolite" vs. "polite"). The effect of this re-signification is to suspend a semantic value distinction in participant frameworks where honorific address or reference is the norm.

In French conversation between multiple interlocutors who *tutoyer* one another, participants can switch back and forth between *vous* and *tu* to signal shifts from group address to, for instance, one-on-one sidebar exchanges. Such shifts are not possible where *vous* is the default form of address. In this latter case, the semantic distinction between the singular and the plural is not neutralized; the singular can still be used and parsed, just not without risking a supplementary perlocutionary effect of disrespect. Where plurals are employed in honorific addressee-reference there is a suspension of the dynamic nuance that can be achieved between distinct kinds of addressivity in switching between second singular and second plural forms.

More generally, the suppression of the default referential option, the singular, has the effect of reducing the capacity of the speaker to richly semantically characterize the referent. Importantly, and this is a subtle point, this line of analysis applies both to cases where referent-focal honorification is achieved in number skewing in third-person anaphors or demonstratives (as in Mangarayi and Yokuts) and to cases where addressee-focal honorification is achieved in number skewing in first-person pronouns (as in Boazi and Santali).[6] The linguistic agency of the speaker – exercised in the choice between singular and plural number – is quite concretely constrained or curtailed. In this sense, semantic skewing is highly motivated to serve as an iconic-indexical of respect, since in showing deference – but not in not showing deference – the speaker's semantico-referential resources are constrained by the other. One shows deference by reducing one's capacity to refer and predicate, by a performed reduction of referential agency that is causally coupled to the deference-target.

By calling semantic skewing an iconic-index, I mean that it is a sign which embodies what it portrays. The form used to signal deference (the use only of the plural as opposed to unencumbered switches back and forth between the singular and the plural) reflects a constraint on the agency of the speaking subject which is socially imposed upon them by the deference-target. The form provides an iconic portrayal of the restraint that it simultaneously actually (i.e., indexically) realizes.

Viewed in this light, there is a profound continuity between the pragmatic suspension of semantic distinctions in honorific pronouns and other of the convergent kinds of deference indexicality that we have looked at in this volume. A diminution in the space of *semantico-referential* manoeuvre may be peculiar to language-based deference indexicals. Nevertheless, comportmental constraint is prototypic of registered signs of respect in kinship-keyed avoidance relationships. As the previous chapters have documented, avoidance relations are routinely proscribed from making eye contact or even looking at one another, from touching or even directly transferring objects to one another, from talking to or even speaking near one another. The "univocal" and monoglossic quality of registered kinship avoidance (after Merlan, 1997) – the felt necessity to be one and only one way in the presence of an avoidance relation – is fostered by exaggerated and registered restrictions on other ways of being with, or acting in relation to, the other. Putting things in their most general terms, the sociopragmatically conditioned suspension of degrees of freedom of action serves as an emblem of the relational "power" of alter over ego, and thus as a fecund sign of respect.

I contend that it is because skewing of semantic features serves as an emblem of other-imposed restraint that this formal mechanism is such a fertile resource for fashioning honorific pronouns cross-linguistically. Although they work in tandem in any given language-in-culture, the *iconic-figurational* potential of the "otherwise semantic" is, in this sense, secondary to the *indexical-disfigurational* suspension of semantic distinctions. It is the cybernetic "noise" (i.e., the collapse of the singular/plural distinction), rather than the figurational "information," that anchors the formal-functional analogy and makes it so robust cross-linguistically. The possibility of an alternation between the singular and the plural is suspended in favour of the plural. The possibility of a dynamic alternation is suspended in favour of the more encompassing alternative (thus flagging the fact of the suspension by means of the conflict between expected referential number and attested number). A degree of freedom is eliminated. And this suspension of variation serves as a sign of respect. Semiotic-avoidance-as-honorification conventionalizes the intuition that I am constrained by the other.

Some of the best evidence in favour of this admittedly abstract and reductive line of analysis comes from the phenomenon of avoidance levels – distinct repertoires of avoidance signs stereotypically associated with the enactment of distinct kinship relationships. As I illustrated in the Introduction and then again at the end of Chapter 4, avoidance levels that more stringently constrain signalling possibilities consistently enact heightened interpersonal respect. Kinship-restricted T-V systems that involve more than a binary honorific distinction illustrate this grading of honorific function by progressively heightened constraints on signalling possibilities. These avoidance registers employ multiple distinct levels of pronominal honorification. In these cases, the principle of the enactment of respect through the sociopragmatic suspension of formal variation has been employed as a ratchet for elaborating and complexifying the register. It is to these examples – which illustrate the generative building out of this principle of constraint-as-honorification – that I now turn.

Scalar Kinship-Restricted T-V Systems

In kinship-restricted registers of person deixis, norms of honorific usage are structured by indexical stereotypes that associate honorific forms with particular kin relations. So, for instance, the Gooniyandi plural/augment is used as an honorific, but only for a *maddiyali* ("son-in-law/mother-in-law"). The Yokuts dual has an honorific function, but again it is "restricted" to the son-in-law/mother-in-law dyad. In languages with more than a binary singular–plural distinction in the category of number, the structural opposition between distinct non-singular values can be leveraged to create a scalar honorific system associated with a differentiated set of avoidance relationships (terminology after Hickey, 2003). As I now show, these **scalar kinship-restricted T-V systems** recursively suspend number categories in creating a graded set of honorific distinctions.

Case Study: Scalar Honorific Pronouns in Kobon

To exemplify the phenomenon, we can look at the example of Kobon, a Papuan language spoken in the Schrader Range of the highlands of Papua New Guinea and closely related to Kalam. (I draw here upon J. Davies, 1991; see the Introduction for a discussion of non-linguistic avoidances in Kobon, after Jackson, 1975.) Kobon has a three-way contrast of grammatical number, distinguishing between singular, dual, and plural. Crucially, both the dual and the plural are employed in pronominal honorification. Their use is normatively restricted to distinct affinal and related cross-cousin relationships: The dual is employed in referring to affines of the same sex as speaker and the plural in referring to affines of the opposite sex from speaker (see Figure 7.1).

Importantly, number values do not appear to be arbitrarily assigned to distinct relationship types but rather appear to be motivated, with feature values that denote higher numbers being employed for avoidance relations with whom more reserve should be expressed. This claim is supported by evidence drawn from the non-linguistic semiotic range of avoidance repertoires (see also Table 0.3 from the Introduction). Taking the perspective of a male ego, Davies (1991) writes,

> Ego cannot utter the name of any affine nor can he use the house entrance or other part of the house which his WM [wife's mother] or cross-cousin's wife (CW) uses, and cannot share their fire, cooking or eating utensil, food or water, or eat any part of an animal raised by them. He cannot make any physical contact either directly or indirectly, e.g. by eye contact, by leaning against the same wall, sitting on the same log, being in a river or on a bridge at the same time, or by playing a game which might involve physical contact either directly or by the passing of a ball from one to the other. In the case of direct or indirect physical contact, but not the other situations mentioned above, the prohibition extends to WZ [wife's sister]. All of these restrictions on behaviour are reciprocal. (p. 401)

Certain avoidance practices – like name avoidance – are employed reciprocally between all affinal relations (as well as cross-cousins),

	Grammatical numbers avoided/employed in reference to ...		
	SINGULAR	DUAL	PLURAL
cross-sex affine	*	*	+
same-sex affine	*	+	−
others	+	−	−
... social category of the deference target	non-honorific	"mid"-honorific	"high" honorific
	←——————— respect-function ———————→		

Figure 7.1. Kobon pronominal honorifics
Note. * indicates normative sanction on the use of the linguistic category where the social category (listed in the left column) is the deference target.
Source: Davies (1991).

while the most heightened anti-phatic routines – avoidance of eye contact, avoidance of coordinated activity, avoidance of commensality – are limited to the relationships between cross-sex affines and the cross-sex spouse of a cross-cousin. Importantly, the skewing of dual and plural number reflects and participates in this grading of avoidance practices. The singular is the unmarked form employed in referring to non-avoidance relations. The dual is employed in honorific address and reference to same-sex affines, the relations with whom name taboo is required. Finally, the plural is employed in honorific address and reference to the most focal avoidance relations – cross-sex affines and cross-cousins' spouses, those with whom, not only name taboo but also various taboos on coordinated activity are required. The singular, dual, and plural numbers thus constitute a scalar honorific series where *higher* numbers index *greater* respect.

Forms	:	Functions
singular	:	non-honorific
dual	:	"low" honorific
plural	:	"high" honorific

Here the relationship between indexical forms and indexical functions is diagrammatic – the relations between the singular, dual, and plural number categories are iconic with the relations between the honorific functions that they enact.

Numerosity as Indexical Gradience: Mead's Manus (Austronesian)

For an even more reticulated system where multiple numbers are sutured to multiple kin relations, I turn to Manus (Austronesian). Here I draw on Margaret Mead's (1934, pp. 242–73) rich description of joking and avoidance relationships in the community of Peri on Manus Island.

SINGULAR	DUAL		TRIAL		PLURAL
	HyB(S)	←→	m(F)oBW		
	WyZ(D)	←→	w(M)oZH		
mZH ←→	WB		w(D/Z)DH	←→	WM(M/Z)
wBW ←→	HZ		m(S/B)SW	←→	HF(F/B)
	myBW	←→	HoB		
	wyZH	←→	WoZ		DEFERENCE FOCUS:
	w(Z/D)SW	←→	HM(M/Z)		Speaker$_{Origo}$-
	m(B/S)DH	←→	WF(F/B)		Referent$_{Target}$

Figure 7.2. Manus in-law relationships by the numbers
Notes. Grammatical numbers stereotypically employed in pronominal reference to particular in-laws (each is listed along with its reciprocal). Abbreviations: W = wife; H = husband; Z = sister; B = brother; M = mother; F = father; w = woman's; m = man's; o = older; y = younger. Parentheticals should be read as possible alternatives (i.e., "non-exclusive or"), a slash mark should be read as "exclusive or." Genealogical products are listed under the semantic number feature stereotypically skewed in reference to relations of that category by the reciprocal encased within the same box. So, for instance the box [w(D/Z)DH ←→WM(M/Z)], which straddles the TRIAL and PLURAL columns, should be read as follows: a man employs the plural in reference to his wife's mother, his wife's mother's mother, and his wife's mother's sister. These individuals employ the trial in return; that is, in referring to daughter's husband, daughter's daughter's husband, or sister's daughter's husband. Mead's data appear to come from direct elicitation combined with some observations of usage. On pp. 256 and 269 she gives contradictory information on pronouns used for a man's sister's husband (mZH). A definitive passage on p. 269 leaves little doubt that the use of the singular was the norm.
Source: Mead (1934).

Once again, Manus evinces a complex diagrammatic relationship between the grammatical category of number and the grading of interpersonal avoidances. The global set of honorific number distinctions forms a diagram of the differentiated set of *kaleal* "avoidance relations" (lit. "to go around") which, in referential practice, the use of these grammatical numbers contributes to realizing.

Like many other Austronesian languages, Manus has a quite elaborate set of number categories. In addition to the dual and the plural, there is also what Mead labels a "trial," though it is possible that "paucal" would be a more accurate label (Corbett, 2000, pp. 21–6). Remarkably, all three of these non-singular number values are honorifically skewed in reference to different categories of affinal kin.

Figure 7.2 lists the different number values that are skewed in reference to the kin relations listed in each corresponding column. Each box encloses a kin dyad, showing the number values that the members of that dyad are normatively expected to employ when making reference to one another. So, for instance, a mZH ("man's sister's husband") is addressed by his WB ("wife's brother") in the singular and addresses him in the dual.[7]

How to understand the sociocultural logics that produce this array of kinship-keyed pronominal practices? Observe that there are no kin dyads where there is a gap of more than one number value. This reflects the largely mutual and only minimally non-reciprocal nature of kin avoidances in Manus. This minimal non-reciprocity of usage is explicable by considerations of relative age (seniors are owed more respect than they owe their junior reciprocals) and by the vector of affinal linkage (siblings of spouse are owed more respect than spouses of siblings). Additionally, a reciprocal monadic rise of pronominal avoidance level is correlated with relative generation (if the origo and target are members of different generations) and relative gender (if the origo and target are of different sex). Recall from our discussion at the end of Chapter 3 that different gender and different generation are often associated with heightened avoidance cross-culturally. This "analogical classification" (after Needham, 1980) of avoidance through the idioms of sexual and generational difference implicitly frames interpersonal avoidance as a ritual mediation of social-categorical difference.

A componential analysis that correlates kinship components, like relative generation or gender, with distinct honorific levels effectively predicts honorific number. Nevertheless, this should not be taken to imply that this model corresponds to an underlying cognitive model. On the contrary, this patterning emerges only at the level of the collective. Indeed, if there is a relevant psycholinguistic model of honorific number at work here, it is one that interprets the set of honorific numbers as an analogue gradient or intensity slope. The Manus register of person deixis is a scalar system where each higher number value is (figurated as) more respectful than the preceding one.

Confirmation of this claim comes from the observation that the intensity of non-linguistic avoidances precisely parallels these graded number-based avoidance levels. The most unmarked affinal relationships are those between same-sex, same-generation in-laws (i.e., between sisters-in-law or brothers-in-law, respectively). A man who has been married for a long period of time is "on terms of near equality" with his wife's brothers, "the slight shade of purely technical superiority of woman's brother over woman's husband only showing with difference of the pronoun of reference: *i* [third singular] for sister's husband, *iaru* [third dual] for wife's brother" (Mead, 1934, p. 269). The younger cross-sex siblings of one's spouse are treated with a bit more restraint – as with all other avoidance relations, their names and near-homophones of their names should not be mentioned. But additionally, this pair should also not eat in each other's presence. Between this pair, the dual is used for the junior cross-sex sibling-in-law and the trial is used for the senior cross-sex sibling-in-law. Relations with the elder cross-sex siblings-in-law are often fictively upgraded to a parent-/child-in-law relationship, in which case the use of the plural replaces the trial (see note 7, above, for more on this). It is the cross-generational avoidances that are the most pronounced. In the case of the relationship between father-in-law and daughter-in-law, mats are hung up as partitions in the house so that the two will not even accidentally lay eyes upon one another (cf. Stasch's [2003, p. 322] description of an "orange plastic tarpaulin" used to shield a Korowai son-in-law from his mother-in-law). In the case of the mother-in-law's relationship with the son-in-law, avoidances are the most stringent; the pair cannot be in each other's co-presence, and should she find herself in his presence, the mother-in-law quickly covers herself with her "calico cloak ... which is bunched rudely together at one end to form a pocket for the head.... In a canoe gathering at which her *kaleals* [affines] are present she sits huddled up on the canoe platform, her head bowed between her knees, her knees hunched, and her whole form wrapped in the cloak" (Mead, 1934, p. 266). It is in reference to these cross-sex parents-in-law that the highest grammatical number – the plural – is employed. The ethnographic description is dispositive; it shows that there is a diagrammatic relationship between the formal system of honorific number and the functional scaling of in-law avoidance relationships in Manus.

Numbers are not apprehended as merely arbitrary or conventional markers, diacritic of distinct relationships. Rather, they are conceptualized as graded emblems of progressively heightened respectful avoidance. This can be seen in the special status of the plural as the "most" honorific number value. After betrothal but before marriage, and for a man up until the moment that the bride price has been paid, the plural is employed for all senior affines (Mead, 1934, p. 257). After this time, the plural continues to be employed only in the most focal of avoidance relationships – for a man, with his mothers-in-law (which may include genealogical WeZ). After keying various pronominal forms to kinship relationship types, Mead (1934) writes, "This usage is not absolute and many deviations occur. *The young and the timid are likely to speak of all their affinal relations in the plural*" (p. 257; italics added). The form that maximally suspends the grammatical category of number – the plural – is also the pragmatically "safest" form.

"A cline of interactional distance between affines": Some Aslian Examples

To my knowledge, Geoffrey Benjamin (1967, 1999) was the first scholar to point out the global organization of scalar honorific kinship-restricted T-V systems (with an additional tip of the hat to one I. Carey cited in Benjamin, 1967, p. 11, note 7). It is an observation he makes in the course of his treatment of Temiar kinship. The Temiar language, spoken on the Malaysian peninsula, is a member of the Aslian branch of the Austroasiatic language family. For Temiar, the most focal avoidance relationship is the one between cross-sex, adjacent-generation in-laws (i.e., mother-in-law/son-in-law or father-in-law/daughter-in-law). These are dyads that mutually maintain "complete verbal and physical avoidance ... though they may live in the same house and communicate through intermediaries" (Benjamin, 1967, p. 10). Same-sex parents-in-law/children-in-law can address one another, but "there is a relationship of respect" and the elder party has "considerable authority to demand service" of the younger (p. 10). With elder siblings of spouse who are of the same sex as the speaker, there is an "unequal relationship having much the same content as the same-sex relationship between spouse's parent and child's spouse" (p. 11). With younger siblings of spouse who are of the same sex as the speaker, there is "a cooperative, non-joking, non-avoidance relationship." Finally, in the cross-sex sibling-in-law relationship, there is a joking relationship that "often has a strongly sexual content"; these are preferred partners for a second marriage (p. 11). Importantly, each of these four relational kinds are associated with a distinct kind of pronominal address: cross-sex, cross-generation, total avoidance = address avoidance; same-sex, seniority-based respect = honorific plural; same-sex, same-generation cooperation = honorific dual; and cross-sex same-generation joking = non-honorific singular (see Figure 7.3).

Reflecting on this pattern, Benjamin (1999, p. 13) observes that "the gradation between Singular, Dual and Plural is thus used as a trope, marking a cline of interactional distance between affines."

As the Temiar paradigm illustrates, pronominal honorification may interact with prohibitions on explicitly ratifying particular social alters as addressees (see the discussion of "negated address" in Chapter 5). This is visible in the systematic gaps in the honorific paradigm – specifically, the notable absence of any second-person pronoun that can be appropriately employed in addressing adjacent-generation, cross-sex in-laws. Of course, where avoidance relations are proscribed from speaking directly to one another there will be no honorific pronouns employed in addressee-reference. Recall that absolute address avoidance

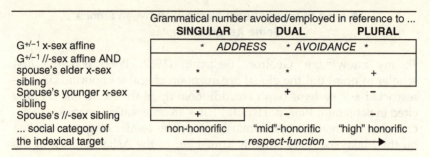

Figure 7.3. Temiar honorific number in addressee-reference
Note. For abbreviations, see p. 22.
Sources: Benjamin (1999); Kruspe & Burenhult (2019).

(which requires the use of speech intermediaries) often contrasts with tropes of negated address, where a range of signs – linguistic, gestural, and even objectual (e.g., the use of yamsticks as shill addressees [Sommer, 2006, p. 109]) – may figurate non-address of the avoidance relation while actually accomplishing dyadic discourse. In such cases, grammatically third-person forms are employed to refer to the intended "target" of communication (in the sense of Haviland, 1986). Because third-person forms are linguistic symbols that explicitly characterize the referent as *not* the addressee, they are a privileged means of (metapragmatically) negating the act of address that is nevertheless (pragmatically) accomplished through their use. The interaction between the cline of address avoidance and the cline of pronominal number can be seen in the case of Jahai, another Aslian language (see Figure 7.4).

Gradations of number avoidance reflect relations of affinity and then of seniority between affinal relations, while gradations of address avoidance reflect relative-gender and relative-generation relations among affines. Number values are keyed to particular kinship relationships across acts of both addressee- and non-addressee reference. Reflecting the importance of seniority, the plural is employed for ascending generation in-laws. The dual is employed in reference to all other in-laws. Overlapping with this grading of affines by grammatical number, however, there is a differentiation of avoidance dyads in terms of their normatively sanctioned modes of interpersonal and, more specifically, discursive contact. Cross-sex, adjacent-generation in-laws – once again, the most focal avoidance pairing – avoid interpersonal and discursive contact of any kind: They may "not touch each other, look each other in the eyes, or give things to each other ... they may not talk to each

	SINGULAR	**DUAL**	**PLURAL**
G^{+1} x-sex affine	*	ADDRESS * AVOIDANCE	*
G^{+1} //-sex affine	*	*	+ *gin* (= 2nd/3rd)
G^{-1} //-sex affine	*	+ *wih* (= 3rd)	
G^0 sibling-in-law	*	+ *jih* (= 2nd)	
Children, strangers	+ *paj* (= 2nd)		

Norms of ADDRESSEE-reference (above)

Norms of NON-PARTICIPANT-reference (below)

G^{+1} affine	*	*	+ *gin* (= 2nd/3rd)
G^0 or G^{-1} affine	*	+ *wih* (= 3rd)	–
Children, strangers	+ *'o'* (= 3rd)	–	–
	non-honorific	"mid"-honorific	"high" honorific

⟵————— respect-function —————⟶

Figure 7.4. Jahai number skewing in pronouns employed in addressee-reference (above) and non-participant-reference (below)
Notes. Grammatical person of pronominal forms is provided in parentheses. (Observe that the distinction between second and third persons is collapsed in the plural.)
Sources: Burenhult (2005); Kruspe & Burenhult (2019).

other or in other ways take part in the same conversation, nor point to, mention by name or otherwise make explicit reference to each other if they are within earshot of each other" (Kruspe & Berenhult, 2019, p. 295). Same-sex, adjacent-generation in-laws can interact, only here they employ some of the strategies of negated address that were discussed in Chapter 5: "Communication between them is respectful and discreet, and vocatives and loud address are avoided" (p. 295). Members of this dyad differ in terms of the grammatical numbers that they use to refer to one another – the junior uses plural number in referring to the senior while the senior uses dual number for the junior. Importantly, neither participant uses a form that deictically categorizes the referent as addressee. Neither the dual form *wih* (used in reference to the child-in-law) nor the plural *gin* (used in reference to the parent-in-law) classifies the co-present referent as addressee.[8] Both forms thus serve to mitigate the act of address that they nevertheless covertly negotiate. The only avoidance relations who can appropriately employ pronouns that deictically categorize the referent as the discourse addressee are siblings-in-law.

A Note on the Skewing of Grammatical Person

The survey of kinship-restricted T-V systems presented in Table 7.1 focuses almost exclusively on skewing of grammatical number in honorific address or reference. But the skewing of grammatical person is also often a source of honorific pronouns (Head, 1978). The Europeanist tradition – think here of German *Sie* or Italian *Lei* – tends to present person and number as two equally available grammatical categories for indexing social relationship (Head, 1978; Malsch, 1987). Certain implicational relationships have been suggested. For instance, skewing of person is typically viewed as being more honorific than skewing of number: "Variation of person in pronominal reference indicates greater differences in degree of respect or social distance than does variation of number" (Head, 1978, p. 191). But this line of analysis misses an important distinction between the skewing of person and number values, a distinction that cases like that of Jahai underscore.

Consider the difference between skewing of number and skewing of person in terms of figure-ground relationships. Referential number has an "objectivity" independent of our description of it. Tropic deviations of number (the figure) are legible against the actual properties of the real-world referent (the ground). Contrast this with tropes of referring to addressee with grammatically third-person expressions. The speech act that we purport to accomplish (the figure) may play off against the speech act that we "actually" accomplish (the ground), but it also actively participates in its final determination – second-person pronouns do not only "presuppose" the identity of the addressee; they also "entail" it. Correspondingly, grammatically third-person forms cannot be unreflectively categorized as addressee honorifics (as in Head's [1978] survey) without attending to accompanying – often non-linguistic – signs of addressivity.

The use of third-person forms in reference to a co-present avoidance relation is often accompanied by non-linguistic signs (lack of consummated eye gaze, lack of reciprocally coordinated bodily orientation) which serve to cancel out the act of address. As Bickel et al. (1999) point out in their discussion of Maithili speech levels, third-person honorifics in European languages like German, Italian, and Polish "are synchronically reanalyzed as honorific second-person forms" (p. 499). In Maithili, however, "this does not seem to be true", as "using high-honorific second-person forms [i.e., grammatically third-person forms for addressee-reference] usually entails the speaker's avoidance of any glance at the highly respected hearer while using these forms, thus physically enacting a third-person situation. Typical situations of this are the taboo relations that prevail in traditional society between various 'in-laws' of opposite sex and differing generation" (p. 499). The suspension of a distinction between addressee- and non-participant-reference is often part and parcel of a multimodal suite of interactional displays that serve to symbolically negate the discursive act of which they nevertheless form an integral part (see Chapter 5). As the cases like Jahai and Maithili make clear, linguists must carefully control for practices of address avoidance when analyzing grammatically third-person forms employed in would-be addressee-reference. In summary, skewing of person categories often interacts with the pragmatics surrounding the speech act of address as distinct from the sociopragmatics of honorific reference. That is, second-person forms may be avoided because they presuppose the social authority of speaker to ratify an interactional other as addressee. Setting aside the European cases, which involve distinct pathways in the grammaticalization of third-person addressee-referent–targeting honorifics (i.e., via the cross-referencing of grammatically third-person titles, abstract nominalizations, etc.), the interaction of the grammatical category of person with the speech act of address helps to explain why Head (1978) found honorification by skewing of person categories to be ranked "higher" than honorification by number skewing.

Suspended Numbers

Honorific registers employing multiple number categories are attested in quite a few languages beyond those that I have already surveyed.[9] Where the necessary social anthropological data are available, it appears that progressively higher numerical values are associated with progressively heightened honorific functions. That is, number values do not have a purely diacritic value but rather form an ensemble with a global coherence. In the cases that I have showcased here, pronominal forms that semantically encode higher numerical values are employed to pragmatically index more constrained and restrained social relationships. Returning to the Manus data, although each number value is associated with a particular relationship type, in ideological conceptualization and global paradigmatic patterning, number values (i.e., SINGULAR, DUAL, TRIAL, and PLURAL) are graded with respect to each other in such a way that their notional cardinal values on the denotational plane (i.e., 1, 2, 3, and more than 3) are converted into ordinally valued, or ranked, signs of respect on the interactional plane (i.e., least respectful, more respectful, still more respectful, and most respectful).

Clearly there is a "figurational" logic at work here: Number, uniquely among grammatical categories, allows for this transduction of the cardinally graded semantic series into an ordinally scaled pragmatic ranking. But the "disfigurational" dynamic is also present, for the

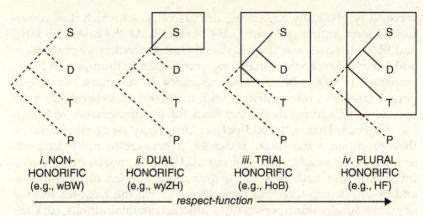

Figure 7.5. Inferred recursive suspension of number values in Manus avoidance register

Notes. Abbreviations: S = SINGULAR; D = DUAL; T = TRIAL; P = PLURAL. Solid boxes enclose the negative repertoire – the set of number values that should be avoided in the speech of an individual making discourse reference to a relation of the associated kin category. Note that for each step-wise increase of honorific function, the corresponding negative repertoire encompasses the prior one, creating a formally nested structure.

numerical series once again exhibits the logic of deference as formally enacted through the performed suspension of semantic distinctions. Restrained social relationships are indexed through the imposition of linguistic restraints. Only here, those restraints are applied recursively, yielding a scalar set of honorific distinctions rather than just a binary one.[10] This is illustrated in Figure 7.5, which infers the progressive, recursive suspension of number values for each step "up" in avoidance level for the Manus affinal avoidance register.

Reading from left to right in the display: (*i.*) In non-honorific speech there are no constraints on the use of the grammatical category of number. In reference to an individual who is not in an avoidance relationship to speaker, any number value may be employed (e.g., if that individual is accompanied by another person, the DUAL would be used to refer to the set). Speakers have maximal semantico-referential agency. (*ii.*) In making reference to a same-sex sibling-in-law, the use of SINGULAR number is suspended. Although the DUAL is employed in making reference to this relation, other number values may be employed if the sibling-in-law is, for instance, part of a group larger than two individuals. (*iii.*) In making reference to an older cross-sex sibling-in-law, the use of the SINGULAR and the DUAL are suspended. Although the TRIAL is employed in unique reference, the PLURAL can be used for larger groups. (*iv*.) Finally, in making reference to cross-sex parents-in-law, there is a maximal suspension of number values – only the PLURAL can be employed.

Unfortunately, Mead's (1934) data are not fine-grained enough to enable us to know whether the scaling of honorific number in Manus involved only a hierarchy of honorific functions fashioned on analogy to notional number values (1 < 2 < 3 < 4+) or an actual series of pragmatic suspensions (SINGULAR ⊃ DUAL ⊃ TRIAL ⊃ PLURAL), as posited in Figure 7.5. Closer study of patterns of suspension in scalar restricted systems is needed. However, in languages possessing both more than one non-singular number value and where the higher number value is employed as an honorific, honorific plurals do appear to suspend lower non-singular feature values. In Mangarayi, reference that includes *ganji* (spouse's mother and her siblings and their reciprocals for a male ego), whether notionally singular or dual, should be "raised" to plural number (Merlan, 1982b, p. 237). Similarly, in Wik (as spoken at Cape Keerweer), reference to *wiinhtha* ("taboo") kin, whether that person is alone or part of a dyad, should employ plural number (McConvell, 1982, p. 189). In Warlpiri, honorific plurals are a respectful resource recruited for reference between mother-in-law and son-in-law, between men initiated in the same ceremony, or between cross-sex siblings (actual or classificatory). The plural is used in place of both singular and dual number (Laughren, 2001, p. 209). The same pattern of suspensions – not just of the singular but also of the dual – is also attested for the Yir-Yoront honorific plural (Alpher, 1991, p. 103, cited in Laughren, 2001, p. 209) and again for the Gooniyandi honorific plural (or would-be "augment") with respect to the dual (or would-be "unit augmented") (McGregor, 1989, p. 643). Further confirming the model of progressive suspensions, where relevant data are available it does *not* appear that suspensions occur in the opposite direction. So, for instance, in Boumaa Fijian the dual is employed for parents-in-law and the paucal for cross-sex siblings. But if speaker addresses "a group of seven of his cross-children, he will use the paucal pronoun form ... rather than the dual" (Schmidt, 1988, p. 71, note 7).

Deference Diagrams

In this chapter I have added another linguistic item – pronouns – to the inventory of registered avoidances. As the survey has illustrated, honorific pronouns are widely employed in the mediation of avoidance relationships. My interest in this topic does not derive simply from a desire to endlessly catalogue and classify. Rather, and following

Silverstein (1976, p. 41), I was concerned to highlight the "parallel formal-functional analogy" that recurs in honorific pronouns cross-linguistically: Time and again, the skewing of an "otherwise semantic" distinction in pronominal address or reference (form) affords the pragmatic enactment of respect (function). Demurring from earlier explanations, I argued that the sociopragmatically conditioned suspension of semantic distinctions comes to index deference because performed constraint on signalling flexibility is readily interpreted as an emblem of the relational "power" of the other over the speaker's linguistic agency. This same explanatory framework helps us to understand why semiotic avoidance – not just avoidance of singular number in person reference, but avoidance more generally – is so often registered as respectful interpersonal practice.

Strong evidence in favour of this interpretation comes from scalar honorific T-V systems. In these systems, the range of signs that speakers can appropriately employ becomes progressively more and more constrained in the sociolinguistic mediation of social relationships that are, correspondingly, more and more restrained. For example, in Kobon, the honorific dual suspends the use of the singular, but not the use of the plural, and it is associated with less focal, same-sex avoidance relationships. Meanwhile, the honorific plural suspends both the singular and the dual, and it is associated with the most heightened cross-sex avoidance relationships. This recursive suspension of semantic distinctions – registered as mutually encompassing avoidance levels (e.g., plural encompasses dual, dual encompasses singular) – enables scalar honorification.

I will call these internally complex formal-functional structures **deference diagrams**. The rationale for the terminology is the following. A diagram is a special kind of icon where the indexical relationships between the parts of the sign are iconic with the indexical relationships between the parts of its object (e.g., the lines on a map [taken as the sign] and the roads covering a territory [taken as the object]) (Parmentier, 1994). In scalar restricted T-V systems there is a diagrammatic relationship between the set of honorific forms and the set of deference functions that they accomplish. Differences between the forms (singular vs. dual vs. plural) that enact avoidance are iconic with the differences between the social functions (non-honorific vs. "mid"-honorific vs. "high" honorific) that their deployment enacts. And further, this formal-functional structure, taken as a whole, itself stands in a diagrammatic relationship to the analogical classification of relational kinds – natal kin versus in-laws, same-sex in-laws versus cross-sex in-laws, senior kin versus junior kin – onto which it is grafted in avoidance practice and at the level of kinship ideology.

The identification of deference diagrams helps us to move beyond some of the aporias that have characterized the characterization of joking-avoidance in the anthropological literature. For one thing, they demonstrate that the gradient or continuum-like quality that anthropologists often impute to avoidance relationality is, at least in part, an effect of the structured commensurability of the object-signs through which avoidance is enacted. Anthropological talk of "mild" or "extreme" avoidance – where no indication is given of how graded respect is accomplished – simply reifies what is in actuality an effect projected from implicationally structured relationships between semiotic avoidances both across semiotic media (e.g., kinesic, objectual, onomastic, pronominal, etc.) and within them (e.g., plural, dual, singular). Deference diagrams help us to move beyond some of the impasses of structuralism by articulating the purely pragmatic structuring of "collective representations." As I will now demonstrate, deference diagrams are attested across a wide array of linguistic and non-linguistic media of avoidance. This formal-functional structure is thus a "pattern which connects" (after Bateson, 1980, p. 8) both different avoidance media and different cultures of kin relationship.

Chapter Eight

Degrees of Unfreedom: From Pragmatic Structures to Intensities of Experience

The last chapter homed in on the relationship between semiotic avoidance and the enactment of respect. I showed how the identification of comportmental restraint with interpersonal respect serves as a structuring principle in honorific registers of person deixis. Where this principle is recursively applied, scalar honorific systems – like those of Manus and Kobon – may emerge. These internally complex avoidance registers distinguish multiple grades of honorific function. Further, they exhibit a diagrammatic relationship between indexical forms and functions. Their register repertoires are organized into a series of avoidance levels, each of which is encompassed by, or encompassing of, each other avoidance level. Globally, the ensemble of avoidance levels thus constitutes a nested series of classes of registered avoidances such that each level is either a subset or a superset of each other level. If there were not a social coherence or a cultural logic that attached to the subset–superset relations between avoidance levels, their relevance for anthropological study would be far from evident. And yet what one consistently finds is that, where different avoidance levels are associated with different social relationships, they are invariably interpreted as analogue measures of the relational qualities (e.g., "respect", "shame") that avoidance practices are understood to manifest. More encompassing avoidance levels enact more interpersonal respect and restraint.

In this chapter I show that internally complex pragmatic structures of this kind – I called them "deference diagrams" at the end of the last chapter – recur in name registers, mother-in-law languages, and even in non-linguistic avoidance media, like head coverings. This chapter begins with further empirical exemplification of deference diagrams in name registers. (At the end of Chapter 4, I discussed the nesting of avoidance levels within one another in name registers; I exemplified the phenomenon by drawing on Otto Raum's [1973] treatment of Zulu in-law name registers.) I then turn to the considerably more complex question of how scalar honorification is achieved in Aboriginal Australian mother-in-law languages. As a last empirical exposition of deference diagrams, I illustrate a similar nested patterning in non-linguistic visual avoidances. Finally, I theorize ways in which these deference diagrams, in conjunction with the chained implicational relations between avoidance media discussed in the Introduction and the phatic (contact) rituals discussed in Part 3, nourish the experience of avoidance as an intensity gradient in the living out of kinship relationship.

Name Registers Revisited: Nested Avoidance Levels in Sidaama and Siuai

The Cushitic language Sidaama is closely related to Kambaata, and their *ballishsha* registers form a cluster of Ethiopian daughter-in-law registers of the kind discussed in Chapter 3 (Teferra, 1987; Treis, 2005). Figure 8.1 presents distinct avoidance levels distinguished in the speech of a married woman of the higher ranked, land-holding Yemereero caste. Members of this caste are ideal speakers of *ballishsha*. Similar to *purdah* practices in South Asia, higher-caste women engaged in more hypertrophic avoidance displays than did lower-caste women (Mandelbaum, 1988). This phenomenon appears to be continuous with the robust finding that mastery over, and elaborate usage of, honorific registers often becomes a second-order status indexical of speaker refinement, finesse, or modesty (Agha, 1998, p. 164; see further discussion below).

Figure 8.1 illustrates four distinct avoidance levels that can be distinguished in the Sidaama name register: (*i.*) avoidance of the name in reference, (*ii.*) avoidance of the proper noun, (*iii.*) avoidance of words sharing the first syllable as the name, and (*iv.*) avoidance of words sharing either the first or the second syllable of the name. Observe that the negative repertoire of each progressively "higher" avoidance level is a proper superset of the negative repertoires associated with all "lower" levels (see Chapter 4, Figure 4.2, for in-depth discussion of this point). The table links these four avoidance levels to the kin types with which the corresponding avoidance practice is normatively associated. I have drawn on textual evidence from Teferra (1987) and have additionally inferred name avoidance for senior consanguineal kin.

Fleming and Slotta (2018) studied patterns of name avoidance in consanguineal address – in no society surveyed in Africa was the use of names of senior consanguines in address normatively acceptable, and typically names were avoided also in reference. Konso (East Cushitic), a

Target of the avoidance index	PROPER NAME	PROPER NOUN	SIMILAR-SOUNDING WORDS 1st syllable	1st or 2nd syllable	
Father-in-law (= HF)	*	*	*	*	LEVEL *iv*
Husband's FF(F)	*	*	*	–	LEVEL *iii*
Other elder in-laws	*	*	–	–	LEVEL *ii*
Elder consanguines	*	–	–	–	LEVEL *i*
Juniors	–	–	–	–	

Figure 8.1. Avoidance levels in Sidaama name register
Notes. Origo = married woman of Yemereero caste. * indicates normative sanction on the use of the linguistic category where the social category (listed in the left column) is the indexical target. A minus sign indicates no constraint on usage.
Source: Teferra (1987).

language like Sidaama that is spoken in southwestern Ethiopia, evinces this pattern (Hallpike, 1972, p. 106). I assume that calling elder consanguineal kin by name is similarly proscribed in Sidaama. Contrastingly, it appears to be the case that speakers are unconstrained in the use of the names of younger individuals – "a woman treats her husband's younger siblings as her own siblings and hence she doesn't pay much respect to them" (Teferra, 1987, p. 54). Proper-noun taboo (i.e., namesake avoidance) applies to the name of the husband, to elder siblings-in-law, and to elder in-laws who are not male members of the husband's patriline, like the mother-in-law (pp. 53–5). Finally, homophone avoidances are conditioned by the names of the lineal male ancestors of a woman's husband. As in Kambaata (Treis, 2005) and Hadiyya (Adane, 2014), similarity between the first syllable of the name of a lineal male affine and the first syllable of a word is the privileged principle of phonolexical recruitment to the negative repertoire of a woman's idiolect: "If a woman's father-in-law is named 'Bakura' and his father was named 'Samago' and his grandfather was 'Kayammo' then the woman observing this stricter form of the taboo [i.e., a woman of the Yemereero caste] does not use words which have initial ba-, sa- or ka- as their initial syllables" (Teferra, 1987, pp. 51–2). For some Yemereero women "of the older generation," the father-in-law is even further distinguished: "some of these women also avoid words, especially proper names, which have an identical second syllable as that of their father-in-law" (p. 52). (The example of a father-in-law named "Barasa" conditioning the avoidance of the proper name "Worasa" is given.)

Importantly, scaling of name avoidance maps onto the degree of focality of the avoidance relationship as attested in other semiotic media. (That is, it is confirmed by implicational relationships across avoidance media.) Lineal male ancestors of a woman's husband are owed the highest respect. The thematization of respect as centred on the husband's patriline is emblematized in married women's normative avoidance of the name of the sub-clan of the husband and the replacement of this name with a *ballishsha* term (Teferra, 1987, p. 55). The living father-in-law, however, is the most focal avoidance relation for a daughter-in-law: "a woman must show the greatest respect for her father-in-law" (p. 45). After betrothal and until the birth of the first child, the daughter-in-law "hides at the sight of [the father-in-law] or at the sound of his voice.... If she is at a meal, she must stop eating at the mention of his name. The Sidamas believe that a woman will go mad if she does not observe this taboo" (p. 45). With all senior affines, married women are supposed to employ honorific pronouns in both second-person address and third-person reference. With juniors, T-form pronouns are employed. Once again, there is a non-arbitrary (motivated) relationship between the avoidance level that is employed and the focality of the avoidance relationship that it indexes. Much as with scalar honorification in pronouns, graded honorification in name registers is achieved by the suspension of a progressively broader and broader range of formal resources. Again, the crucial point is that *greater* suspension of formal resources (sociolinguistic form) enacts *greater* respect (sociolinguistic function).

As a last example of this phenomenon for name registers, I draw on Douglas Oliver's (1970) detailed ethnography *A Solomon Island Society*. In 1938 and 1939, Oliver conducted field research with the Siuai of Bougainville (speakers of the non-Austronesian language Motuna). I will focus here on how three recursively encompassing name avoidances distinguish between three distinct cross-sex, adjacent-generation kin relations: (1) a man and his mother's brother's wife [mMBW/HZS], (2) a man and his father's sister [mFZ/wBS], and (3) a man and his wife's mother [WM/wDH]. Note that Siuai value cross-cousin marriage, so ideally it is one of these two aunts (the mother's brother's wife or the father's sister) who will become a man's mother-in-law. Kin-term usages foreground this possibility – all three are called *apu* (Oliver, 1970, p. 256).

The relation with a mother's brother's wife, though "clearly defined," is least tinged by avoidance – the pair do not refer to each other by personal name and avoid sexual relations or any imputation of them, "but otherwise they might even treat each other with affectionate informality" (Oliver, 1970, p. 265). This contrasts with the much more stringent avoidance relationship that obtains between a man and his father's sister. The pair should not "touch each other nor handle items

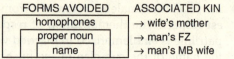

Figure 8.2. Encompassment relations between name avoidances in Motuna
Note. Although avoidances are reciprocal, the table lists associated kin from the perspective of a male ego.
Source: Oliver (1970).

just touched by the other" (p. 263). Between this pair, "the name taboo is [so] strictly observed that neither may so much as utter the name of the other. If, for example, an eldest son addresses or refers to some female whose name is the same as his father's eldest sister's, he calls her "Old Apu" or 'Name-like-that-of-Apu'" (p. 263).

The final, and most focal, avoidance relationship is the one between a son-in-law and a mother-in-law. The same haptic avoidances are in effect. But now taboos on particular kinds of commensality are additionally innovated: "Food for this pair may be harvested from the same plot and cooked in the same pot, but if they happen to eat parts of the same taro corm or banana, etc., it is believed that the teeth of both will drop out. To avoid this accident, identifying marks are cut on the corms or tubers or bananas intended for the woman when their food is cooked in the same pot" (Oliver, 1970, p. 264). It is in the case of this pair that the most expansive name avoidance is practiced, for in this relationship name avoidance extends not only to the proper noun but additionally "to syllables contained in each other's name: for instance, the wife's mother of a man named Tomo cannot use the word *mo*, the common name for coconut; when she speaks of coconuts she uses a circumlocution, of which there are many in the language" (p. 264).

As illustrated in Figure 8.2, the relation between a man and his mother's brother's wife, his father's sister, and his mother-in-law are distinguished by three iteratively encompassing levels of name avoidance. He avoids using his mother's brother's wife's name when referring to her. Here the proper name is taboo. He avoids using his father's sister's name, not only when he refers to her but also when referring to other individuals who bear the same name. Here the proper noun is taboo. With his mother-in-law, he avoids not only the proper name and the proper noun but also a range of homophones or partial homophones of the name. Each next "higher" level of name avoidance encompasses all of the avoidances associated with the "lower" levels. As expected, the "vertically" more encompassing name avoidances are consistently associated with a wider "horizontal" range of avoidances (e.g., haptic and commensality avoidances), and they are metapragmatically framed as performatively enacting "greater" respect.

As these examples and the examples already presented in Chapter 4 illustrate, deference is indexed through a reduction in the range of semiotic resources (here, names, proper nouns, and homphones) that the speaker has at his or her disposal. The more resources that the speaker is proscribed from employing, the greater the respect that ego enacts toward alter through avoidance practice. Again, these avoidance levels are rendered commensurable with respect to one another because they stand in superset–subset relationships to one another.

Scalar Honorification in Mother-in-Law Languages

I have demonstrated that nested avoidance levels, or deference diagrams, emerge in both pronominal- and name-based honorification. I now illustrate that this same pattern can also be discerned in the sociopragmatics of Aboriginal Australian mother-in-law languages. Here I return to some of the same empirical materials that were treated in Chapter 2, only now I will focus on the ways in which the discursive implementation of mother-in-law language involves graded degrees of restraint and respect. There are two kinds of formal-functional analogy productive of scalar honorific effects that I will underline: (1) variable degrees of honorific register cohesion of text-sentences as an iconic-indexical of respect (but also of other social qualities), where the use of a higher ratio of honorific alternants to everyday alternants is construed as more respectful, and (2) nested avoidance levels as a function of interactional role inhabitancy, where the use of honorific speech to index more encompassing interactional roles is again associated with heightened respect. (What I mean by "encompassing interactional roles" here will be made clear in the discussion below.) In both cases I am concerned to show the ways in which locally discrete or "digital" honorific distinctions (e.g., the distinction between honorific and non-honorific lexical alternants or the distinction between referent-targeting and addressee-targeting deference focus) are converted through their global, diagrammatic patterning into continuous or "analog" honorific gradients. I discuss these two kinds of formal-functional analogy separately.

Speech Levels and the Textual Cohesion of Honorific Alternants

The first kind of indexical gradience – where use of more honorific lexemes is construed as more respectful – will, I think, be intuitive for most readers. Indeed, there has even been some discussion of this topic in literatures on formal morphosyntax and pragmatics. Greville Corbett (2012), who always marshals a range of fascinating empirical materials in his analyses (see, e.g., Corbett, 2000, on Kobon and Fijian pronominal registers), has worried over the problem of the morphosyntactic status of honorification. Drawing on the treatment of Korean honorifics in Kim and Sells (2007), he observes that, "simplifying somewhat, we may say that the more honorifics [there are], the more polite [the utterance]." Within the formal pragmatics tradition, it is this quantity-linked interpretation that was one of the motivations for Potts (2005) to treat honorification as a dimension of "expressive meaning" as opposed to "propositional meaning" (Corbett, 2012, p. 14).

Within linguistic anthropology, there is an ample literature that treats textual cohesion of honorific variants and/or hypertrophic plenitude of honorifics as incorporating a nonreferential and iconic-indexical mode of signification. Think here of Steve Caton's (1986) classic study of Yemeni greeting formulae, of Penelope Brown's (1980) quantitative analyses showing gendering in the use of politeness markers in Maya, or of Paul Friedrich's (1986) studies of tropic aggression through hyperpoliteness in the Russian novel. Asif Agha's (1998, 2007) work on speech levels in Tibetan honorific speech has been particularly important for illuminating the issues at play. Following Agha, in the rest of this discussion I will refer to the text-level cohesion of honorific alternants as register cohesion.

Honorific register cohesion in socially stratified human aggregates is typically interpreted differently than it is in more egalitarian ones where kinship offers an idiom for reckoning relationship with all members of the social universe. In Tibetan, for instance, "pure" honorific utterances – that is, utterances employing the maximal number of honorific alternants – are construed not only as "more" respectful but also as second-order indexicals of "speaker refinement," while mixed honorific/non-honorific utterances may be associated with subordinate social categories of speaker. Agha (1998) makes the strong claim that "in every community where the sociolectal distribution of speech styles is grasped by natives in terms of stratifying ideologies of value reckoning (style X is 'higher' than style Y, which is 'higher' than style Z, etc.), the stereotypic construct yields a higher-order system of [speaker-focal] demeanor indexicals derived from the lower-order system of deference indexicals" (p. 166). This transposition of speaker-addressee or speaker-referent deference indexicality into a second-order emblem of speaker demeanour depends in part upon the ways in which social hierarchies condition segregated infrastructures of communication. Social segregation limits opportunities for individuals to be socialized to register varieties with the effect that the social domain of individuals competent to employ honorific speech is conditioned by proximity to elites and their semiotic productions. That is, performed mastery over honorific speech (e.g., employing register-cohesive, "pure" honorific utterances) is an "honest signal" of phatic access to social elites (Bourdieu, 1979; A. Zahavi & Zahavi, 1997). The relationship between social structure (sociocentric hierarchies) and indexical value (demeanour indexicality) is mediated by communicative infrastructures.

Agha (1998, p. 155) makes the further fundamental point about the semiotic organization of "stratified systems of pragmatic value": Any interpretation of the degree of register cohesion of an utterance presupposes a metapragmatic classification, as either honorific or non-honorific, of the morphemes, words, or other expressions, types of which its constituent units are tokens. For Tibetan speakers, the "'respect'-fulness of WORDS is conceptualized in terms of a discrete, binary type of distinction: Native speakers say that words of their language are of two kinds, those that are *šesa* ['respectful'], and those that are not *šesa*" (p. 163). Explicit metapragmatic testimony evinces just such a type-level classification of words and expression. This is what is going on, for instance, when Haviland's (1979a, pp. 366–7) Guugu Yimidhirr language consultant tells him: "*Balin.ga* is 'porcupine'; that's my word. I got another word, too, *nhalngarr*; you can use that word to Brother-in-law and Father-in-law."

Honorific discourse, however, does not consist of isolated, single-morpheme vocables. It comes in utterances and turns at talk. Contrasting with the word-level perspective, in these larger syntagmatic sequences the "'respect'-fulness of sentences is typified in gradient terms" (Agha, 1998, p. 163). That is, "native speakers ... readily point out that some *šesa* sentences are more potent in their effects than others. Such sentence gradations correlate highly with degrees of lexeme cohesion" (p. 163). In other words, a discrete digital and binary distinction (honorific/non-honorific) becomes the basis for enacting respect in an analogue or indexically gradient manner. A binary, type-level distinction – honorific or non-honorific – can be leveraged to project degrees of respectfulness (or respectability) as a function of register cohesion at the level of text tokens (cf. Michael Lempert's [2018] work on "poetic performativity").[1]

Returning to the Australian materials, honorific gradience as a function of register cohesion is attested in a few languages. (Note that we are controlling for indexical focus type; see discussion below.) In some instances, register cohesion is interpreted as an emblem of speaker attributes. In Wik, the use of "big language" [= the affinal, respect style] is associated with the attribute of full adulthood, and a plenitude of avoidance vocabulary may be a sign of the weighty importance of the discourse topic (see also Smith & Johnson, 2000, p. 454, for Kugu Nganhcara): "Younger people in general are not expected to have a strong command of [respect] style, because 'big language is more difficult; if they can't understand big words we have to use small words'" (Sutton, 1978, p. 196). Reminiscent of the lexical parallelisms of eastern Indonesian oral traditions (J.J. Fox, 1988), "older people, especially men, make elaborate use of [respect] style, frequently interlarding their speech with equivalent [respect] and non-[respect] terms. This is one of the salient characteristics of being /wuut manthal-tharrana/, a 'big man'" (Sutton, 1978, p. 196). The association of "big language" with speaker-maturity is fleshed out with figures of flora and fauna: "People have independently told me more than once that the difference between "big language" and "small language" *is the same as* that between mature forms of a species and its juvenile forms" (p. 196). In adjacent-generation relationships where respect language is the expectation (e.g., father-daughter), it is "especially incumbent upon the older generation to use [respect] speech with the younger" (p. 195). The second-order indexing of speaker-maturity, as with the second-order indexing of speaker-refinement in Tibetan, is mediated by asymmetries of register acquisition and associated competency to perform the register. However, in Wik, unlike Tibetan, differential competency is not stratified by social class or caste but is rather age dependent.[2]

Elsewhere in Australia, greater and greater register cohesion is associated either with more and more constrained and restrained social relationship types or with the sensitivity of the discourse topic. In Mangarayi, "use of the avoidance style is the only correct way to breach the barriers to speech which exist between those in the *ganji* [spouse's mother and her siblings and their reciprocals for a male ego] relationship" (Merlan, 1982a, p. 132). This was the relationship involving "the greatest degree of constraint" (p. 131). Members of these dyads limit their interactions with one another, avoid eye contact when talking, and do not "walk or stand too close together; when they must give each other things they should do so with both hands (especially junior to senior), instead of disrespectfully passing things with one hand" (p. 133). The relationship between a son-in-law and his father-in-law is also a respectful one, but it is less constrained: "The use of avoidance style with reference to *barangali* [father-in-law] and in speaking to *barangali* is not required, though people say one may use some avoidance vocabulary to signal respect."

It appears that a similar grading of social relationship by differing degrees of register cohesion occurred in the Panyjima (Pilbara) avoidance language, *Paathupathu*. Alan Dench (1991) writes that "the more elaborated, full Paathupathu, is used between in-laws" (p. 211). However, there are some non-affinal relationships – like those between a brother and a sister, a child and his or her father, or between a son and his mother – that also require a degree of reserve: "Words of the Paathupathu style may be used to emphasise the affectionate respect due to such 'dear' kin, a usage occasionally described as speaking kurnta-ka ('shame-LOC')" (p. 211).

More dense usage of mother-in-law vocabulary is not always a reflex of the social relationship between interlocutors or between the speaker and the referent. It may also reflect the topic of discourse. For instance, Bruce Sommer (2006) underscores that in some Kunjen consanguineal cross-gender relationships (e.g., the father-daughter relationship), the avoidance register might be used in reference to alter when certain topics, like body parts or bodily functions, are being discussed. In Kugu Nganhcara, the respect register is "mandatory" when engaged in shill address of a mother-/son-in-law, but it may also be used "in important situations, talking about customs and giving instruction on ceremonial matters" (Smith & Johnson, 1986, p. 454). In Wik, "big language" is used not only in speaking to or about avoidance relations but also in speaking about important matters or making reference to "a major totem" (Sutton, 1978, p. 220). Further, the use of respect vocabulary may function as a politeness strategy. In the Gooniyandi respect language transcripts provided by McGregor (1989, p. 644), use of mother-in-law vocabulary is most pronounced in initiating a request, with subsequent discursive turns evincing a smaller ratio of respect to everyday vocabulary. And again, Sommer (2006) offers an example of Kunjen avoidance register being used with a classificatory grandparent (not an avoidance category) as a politeness strategy in making a somewhat delicate request.

As underscored in Chapter 2, in languages like Dyirbal and Umpila which possess the most extensive avoidance vocabularies, avoidance speech is typically characterized by very high levels of register cohesion. In Kunjen, "all of the content words in a proper respect register sentence belong to the respect vocabulary rather than the ordinary vocabulary" (Alpher, 1993, p. 98). In Dyirbal, "the avoidance style entails complete lexical replacement so that no vocabulary items are common to 'ordinary' and avoidance styles" (Merlan, 1982a, p. 132). In the languages where nearly all open-class lexemes have substitute forms, high-register cohesion of utterances appears to be the norm.[3] This seems particularly to have been the case for Cape York and northern Queensland avoidance registers: "The choice of style to be used in conversation had to be absolute. One could not mix the two" (Crowley, 1983, p. 313). Nevertheless, even where there was not variability in register cohesion, there was another way in which scalar honorification could be achieved in mother-in-law languages: progressive pragmatic suspensions over indexical focus types.

Mother-in-Law Languages as Fluid Focus Systems

Cross-linguistically, the use of honorific morphemes and vocabularies is construed as signalling deference entitlements emanating from, and directed toward, the occupants of particular interactional roles (Agha, 1993; Comrie, 1976; Silverstein, 1976).[4] Honorific repertoires are typically keyed to interactional role inhabitancy – that is, they are keyed to roles like "speaker of," "addressee of," "referent of," or "bystander to" text-sentences. Typically, but not always (see Fleming, 2016, p. 296, note 3), the origo-of-deference indexicality is the occupant of the "speaker of" or the "animator of" role. And in the majority of languages with lexical honorific repertoires, honorific alternations are interpreted as indexing deference entitlements toward the occupant of the "referent of" role (Agha, 2007, pp. 315–22).[5]

Exclusively referent-targeting honorifics are found in languages scattered all over the world (e.g., Nahuatl: Hill & Hill, 1978; Tibetan: Agha, 1993; Sinhala: Chandralal, 2010; Tongan: Haugen & Philips, 2010). In these languages, honorific repertoires may be quite large and yet consistently the default construal attendant on the use of honorific alternants is that respect is shown to the discourse referent. Ladakhi (Sino-Tibetan), for instance, possesses a large number of verbs and nouns that have distinct honorific and non-honorific lexemes (e.g., non-honorific/honorific body-part term doublets like "eye" *mik/rtsan*, "nose" *sna/shang*, "hand" *lakpa/chak*, "tongue" *lce/ljaks*), as well as a range of semantically vacuous affixes that convert "neutral" nouns that lack honorific stem alternations into honorifics (Koshal, 1987). But tokens of all these honorific expressions always express deference to the individual associated with the reference of the term itself (whether the person literally referred to by an honorific noun phrase, the referent of the subject of the honorific verb, of even the notional possessor or recipient of the referent of an honorific inanimate noun).

To summarize, the use of honorifics involves the enactment of respect by some person toward some social other. Importantly, the honorific index specifies (i.e., metapragmatically regiments) who these persons are by associating the origo and target of the honorific with particular interactional roles. After Agha (1993, 1998), this aspect of the type-level pragmatics of the honorific is called its indexical or deference focus. Employing the standard notation for representing indexical focus, Ladakhi honorific/non-honorific lexical alternants have an exclusively Speaker$_{origo}$-Referent$_{target}$ deference focus.

Though referent-targeting honorifics are the most prevalent type cross-linguistically, other deference focus types are attested, most robustly in East and Southeast Asian languages. In a number of languages of Island Southeast Asia, formally distinct lexical honorific repertoires are functionally differentiated – one set signals deference toward addressee, another set toward discourse referent. In Javanese (Austronesian), for instance, the ethnometapragmatic distinction between *krama inggil* honorific vocabulary, on the one hand, and *krama* (vs. *madya* and *ngoko*) vocabulary, on the other, alludes to sets of forms that are functionally differentiated by indexical focus type. That is, *krama inggil* forms are prototypically referent-targeting honorifics and *krama* forms are prototypically addressee-targeting honorifics: "The oppositions between krama inggil/non-krama inggil on one hand, and krama/ngoko on the other, are skewed pragmatically: the former keys to connections created by referring to someone, the latter to existential links presupposed in addressing someone" (Errington, 1985, p. 293). For instance, *tindak* and *késah* are both honorific words that can be glossed as "to go out" (Errington, 1988, p. 101). The first, however, expresses deference toward the referent of the subject of the verb (whether or not that referent is additionally the addressee of the utterance). The second expresses deference toward the addressee of the utterance (whether or not the addressee is additionally the referent of the utterance).

In the typology of honorific registers, the mother-in-law languages of Aboriginal Australia present unique indexical focus properties. Unlike Ladakhi, honorific alternants often index respect toward either the discourse referent (who need not be a speech recipient of the utterance) or to a speech recipient (who need not be the discourse referent). But unlike Javanese, there is no formal differentiation of vocabulary sets that makes clear which interactional role is indexed in a given instance. In many Australian languages, switching to the affinal register can index either the speaker's relationship to a person associated with the topic of discourse or the speaker's relationship directly to a speech recipient. Because the honorific target may be identified with the occupant of more than one interactional role, I have called these **fluid indexical focus systems** (Fleming, 2016). (See Rijkhoff, 1998, for an important treatment of bystander-indexicality which anticipates some of the issues of scaling over interactional roles that appear in the following discussion.)

The use of Australian in-law, mourning, and initiate registers is stereotypically associated with particular social categories (of speaker, of referent, of addressee, or of bystander). They are "restricted honorifics" (see Chapter 7). The high specificity of the social-categorical stereotypes guiding the use and interpretation of honorific vocabularies may be one factor that allows for greater flexibility and fluidity in their indexical focus characteristics. If the target of the index can be determined by virtue of social stereotypes concerning who uses the form and for whom, indexical focus doesn't need to bear such a high functional load in specifying the target of the social index.[6] Where Australian avoidance registers do have distinct honorific *sub*-repertoires, these are functionally differentiated not in terms of deference focus properties (as in Japanese or Javanese) but in terms of the social category of relationship that is stereotypically indexed by their use (as in Tongan or Samoan). This occurs in the Kokatha and Pintupi varieties of Western Desert Language and in Warlpiri (Elkin, 1940, p. 348; Hansen & Hansen, 1974, p. v; Laughren, 2001).[7]

To give a clearer idea of the fluid focus properties of Australian in-law avoidance registers, Box 8.1 provides quotations from researchers who have directly elicited or – more rarely – observed the use of mother-in-law languages. Given that my analysis relies exclusively on the field research of others, I feel it important to provide the exact wording of the source-text descriptions. The reader should remember that many of these descriptions are drawn exclusively from reconstructed practice.

BOX 8.1. ACCOUNTS OF FLUID REFERENT/RECIPIENT TARGETING IN USE OF ABORIGINAL AUSTRALIAN AFFINAL AVOIDANCE REGISTERS

Nyangumarta (Pilbara): "The style is used whenever someone is near to or referring to another community member who is in [an] avoidance relationship with him/her" (Sharp, 2004, p. 30).

Djaru (Kimberley): Son-in-law to mother-in-law: "when he talks in her presence or refers to her (while talking to someone else) he must use the avoidance language and she must use it back..." (Tsunoda, 1981, p. 14).

> **Gooniyandi (Kimberley):** The avoidance "style was reportedly used in four main contexts: (1) when <u>speaking to</u> a classificatory *maddiyali* [classificatory "mother-in-law"]; (2) when <u>speaking to</u> the actual (or a close) WMB; (3) <u>in making reference</u> to any *maddiyali*; and (4) <u>in the presence of</u> (<u>within earshot of</u>) a close *maddiyali*" (McGregor, 1989, p. 641).
>
> **Gurindji (Northern Territory):** *pirnti-ka* "on the side" speech is employed <u>in referring to</u> a *mali* [wife's mother, her siblings, and their reciprocals]. Where "direct conversation does take place ... *pirnti-ka* should be used and the speakers should maintain the fiction that an intermediary is present by using the third person pronoun to the *mali* and by not talking to his/her face" (McConvell, 1982, p. 94).
>
> **Mangarayi (Northern Territory):** "people who call each other *ganji* [mother-in-law, her siblings, and their reciprocals] should <u>speak of each other</u> in avoidance style; in addition, use of the avoidance style is the only appropriate way for them to <u>speak to each other</u>" (Merlan, 1982a, p. 132).
>
> **Warlpiri (Central Australia):** "Avoidance subregisters ... [are] ... used by men <u>to address</u> and <u>refer to</u> other men in their father's matrimoiety" (Laughren, 2001, p. 204).
>
> **Kunjen (Cape York):** "<u>Before his WM</u> [wife's mother], a man must always use the respect vocabulary (even when he speaks, to her dog or yamstick, as he ought) ... [with] ... a D [daughter] or M [mother] or Z [sister] ... [he uses the respect register in] <u>referring to</u> them, especially with respect to body parts or functions" (Sommer, 2006, p. 109).
>
> **Yir-Yoront (Cape York):** "respect register ... used <u>with</u> or in <u>speaking about</u> or <u>in the presence</u> of certain relatives" (Alpher, 1991, p. 103).
>
> **Wik (Cape York):** "[Respectful] speech is used not only <u>between</u> these pairs but also in <u>reference to</u> one member of such a pair by the other or by a third party (e.g. 'my/your wife's brother')" (Sutton, 1978, p. 194).
>
> *Note.* Underlining is added.

Although fluid focus appears to be the most commonly attested indexical focus pattern, there are some mother-in-law languages where only recipient-targeting honorification is described. Examples of these are provided in Box 8.2.

BOX 8.2. ACCOUNTS WHERE ONLY RECIPIENT-TARGETING USE OF AVOIDANCE REGISTERS IS DISCUSSED

Panyjima (Pilbara): "Full Paathupathu [respect register], is used <u>between</u> in-laws" (Dench, 1991, p. 211); in final events of male initiation, "jiny-janungu [ritual workers; $G^{-2,0,+2}$ with respect to initiate] are expected to use Paathupathu <u>within earshot of</u> members of the karnku [ritual bosses; $G^{-1,+1}$]" and "karnku ... use Paathupathu amongst themselves" [i.e., in the manner of mourning sign languages] (p. 212).

Bininj Gunwok (Northern Territory): "use of a special polite register [*Kun-kurrng*] ... involving near-complete lexical replacement, <u>between</u> or <u>in the presence</u> of certain categories of relative" (Evans, 2003a, p. 59; see also Harris, 1970, p. 783). Additionally, the *kun-kurrng* avoidance register is used by widows "during their period of mourning" after the death of their husband (Evans, 2003a, p. 59).

Yanyuwa (Queensland): "avoidance speech ... is <u>used between</u> speakers who are in avoidance kinship relationship" (Kirton, 1971, p. 54). "If speech is permitted in the specific relationship, then avoidance speech must be used" (Kirton & Timothy, 1982, p. 2).

Uradhi (Cape York): avoidance speech was used in negated address of taboo in-laws: "Should one wish to communicate with one's spouse's family, one would speak to someone else within hearing distance of them, signalling the fact that one is not addressing that person but is in fact addressing an in-law by switching to the special style" (Crowley, 1983, p. 313).

Guugu Yimidhirr (Queensland): "A man, <u>in the presence</u> of certain affines, was obliged to speak with special words in place of certain ordinary words" (Haviland, 1979a, p. 368).

Dyirbal (Queensland): "The avoidance style was used <u>in the presence</u> of a relative (typically a mother-in-law or son-in-law) ... the everyday style was used in all other circumstances" (Dixon, 1990, p. 1).

Woiwurrung (Victoria): "there is a hybrid tongue or jargon in use, comprising a short code of words, by means of which a mother-in-law can carry on a limited conversation <u>in the presence</u> of her son-in-law..." (Mathews, 1905, p. 103)

Note. Underlining is added.

Note that the importance of Dixon's (1971) early treatment of Dyirbal mother-in-law language meant that secondary literatures often characterized mother-in-law language exclusively as a recipient-targeting honorific formation (e.g., Comrie, 1976; Levinson, 1983). Finally, there is at least one case where mother-in-law vocabulary has only referent-targeting values. In passing, Nicholas Evans (2003a) characterizes mother-in-law vocabulary in Dalabon as well as in the Manyallaluk Mayali dialect of Bininj Gunwok as exclusively referent-targeting:

> In Manyallaluk Mayali [a dialect of Bininj Gunwok], the sociolinguistic conditions on the use of Kun-kurrng ["in-law language"] are different [from the other dialects], even though the vocabulary is essentially identical; as in Dalabon, it is used when referring to, rather than in the presence of, relatives who are *nakurrng* [son-in-law; mother-in-law's brother] or *ngalkurrng* [mother-in-law]. (p. 61)

It is notable that where mother-in-law language has either referent-targeting or recipient-targeting functions, but not both, that recipient-targeting is more common. This goes against the typological finding, discussed above, that referent-targeting honorification is the most commonly attested indexical focus type cross-linguistically. Lacking a clear understanding of how these systems have diachronically come into being, we are clearly missing an important part of the big picture of how these sociolinguistic formations hang together (but see Blythe, 2018, on the historical pragmatics of trirelational kin terms).

Recursive Encompassment by Interactional Role: Avoidance Levels in Mother-in-law Language

If register cohesion affords one kind of scalar honorification in mother-in-law languages, fluid focus of the sort exemplified in Box 8.1 enables a second kind of grading of honorific function. In fluid-focus systems, the dependencies between referent-targeting and recipient-targeting honorification are quite different than those in languages like Javanese where distinct honorific words are employed to achieve these distinct indexical functions. In Javanese, deference to referent and deference to addressee can be accomplished in the same utterance (even where the occupants of these two roles are not the same individual) by using lexical items keyed to both of these indexical focus types (i.e., by the blended use of both *krama inggil* and *krama* lexemes). With important caveats, Speaker$_{origo}$-Addressee$_{target}$ and Speaker$_{origo}$-Referent$_{target}$ honorification run along two independent tracks. In many mother-in-law languages, however, avoidance vocabulary may index respect toward either a speech recipient or a discourse referent. How is this functional ambiguity resolved?

In Wik, Mangarayi, Gooniyandi, Kunjen, and the other languages depicted in Box 8.1, addressee-targeting and referent-targeting implementations of mother-in-law count as distinct avoidance levels. Those levels are distinguished by the variable performative indefeasibility of everyday speech vis-à-vis the discourse addressee. In the "highest" avoidance levels, the performativity of everyday speech vis-à-vis the addressee is not defeased by discourse reference. Setting aside uses linked to initiation (e.g., Dyirbal, Panyjima, Kokatha) and mourning (e.g., Bininj Gunwok, Yanyuwa, Kugu Nganhcara), these higher avoidance levels are prototypically employed in contexts where speech animators and recipients are focal avoidance kin to one another (e.g., are related as son-in-law and mother-in-law). In contexts where core avoidance relations are co-present, mother-in-law language is used in an addressee-targeting manner that suspends referent-targeting alternations between everyday and avoidance speech. Much as with higher plurals in scalar restricted T-V systems or homophone avoidance in name registers, addressee$_{target}$ indexicality *encompasses* referent$_{target}$ indexicality.

I will draw on the Mangarayi data to exemplify this point. In discursive contexts where no avoidance relations are co-present, shifts between mother-in-law register and the everyday register enact different relational footings of greater or lesser restraint between speakers and the persons about whom they are conversing. Register switches reflect the shifting identity of the reference-keyed indexical target in the sequential unfolding of discourse. Alternatively, through a voicing effect, they may figure the shifting identity of the speaker *qua* indexical origo. For in these non-avoidance contexts, the avoidance register may be used in reported-speech constructions, as when Mangarayi speakers used it in "narrating texts that tell of interactions between *gaɲji* [taboo in-laws]" (Merlan, 1982a, p. 132). Dynamic shifts in the identity of the indexical origo and indexical target are situation-specific affordances of the mother-in-law register: When speech animators are not in the presence of any avoidance relations, avoidance speech may be used by speech animators to indexically target particular discourse referents or even to represent talk between speaker/addressee dyads portrayed as standing in an avoidance relationship in a narrated event.[8]

Notably, the functional flexibility of mother-in-law language becomes much more constrained when avoidance relations *are* in one another's presence. In talk between *gaɲji*, the mother-in-law vocabulary will be employed regardless of the identity of the discourse referent: "use of the avoidance style is the only appropriate way for them to speak to each other" (Merlan, 1982a, p. 132). Therefore, when speaking to a *gaṇji*, even if one refers to someone – like a same-sex grandparent – who is a prototypical joking relation, the use of the avoidance vocabulary is required. In avoidance contexts, the use of everyday vocabulary is taboo in the technical sense that discourse reference fails to cancel out or defease the socially disruptive performativity of everyday words vis-à-vis the flesh-and-blood speech Recipient$_{target}$ (see Chapter 4 on performative indefeasibility).

And similarly, shifts between everyday and avoidance registers in reported-speech constructions are suspended (cf. Rumsey, 1990). Here, the reportive calibration of speakerhood fails to defease the taboo-performativity of everyday speech vis-à-vis speech Animator$_{origo}$. Use of the Animator$_{origo}$-Recipient$_{target}$ avoidance level of the mother-in-law language radically constrains the speaker – the nuances of register shifts, so useful in indicating social relationships between narrated characters or between speaker and discourse referents, are completely washed out. Heteroglossic speech, where everyday and avoidance varieties play off one another in stance taking and voicing of various kinds, occurs most freely in discursive contexts where avoidance relations are not in co-presence. Monoglossic speech, where everyday speech is categorically avoided, is a sign that the speech participants are themselves avoidance relations to one another.

To review, indexical focus-defined avoidance levels are structurally articulated by pragmatic suspensions associated with both the indexical origo and the indexical target: (1) *Target*: The use of Addressee-targeting mother-in-law language functionally suspends the possibility of Referent-targeting alternations between everyday and avoidance speech; (2) *Origo*: In a parallel fashion, the use of mother-in-law speech where the Animator is the indexical origo suspends the possibility of shifts between everyday and avoidance speech to signal distinct relational footings between Speakers and other characters in narrated events. In this most hypertrophic use of avoidance language, context collapses into the here-and-now interaction – the only possible contextualization of pragmatic signs is with respect to the here-and-now phatic infrastructure of discourse. This falling into, and immersion within, the scene of the encounter reflects and contributes to the intense quality of the phenomenological experience of avoidance relationship as a "total orientation" toward the other (after Merlan, 1997, p. 106).

These functional suspensions are not a glitch in the sociopragmatic system. Rather, they involve precisely the principle of deference indexicality that is our central theme in Part 4: The sociopragmatic suspension of formal resources is once again emblematic of (heightened) respect. I now illustrate this dynamic with a couple of case studies.

Case Study: Of Recipients and Referents in Kunjen Mother-in-Law Language

Avoidance levels keyed to indexical target types can be seen with examples drawn from Bruce Sommer's detailed ethnography of Kunjen communication. Sommer (2006) is at pains to underscore that the use of mother-in-law language (*Uw Ilbmbandiy*) cannot be reduced to static social categories – the following should thus be understood to be a selective presentation of norms of use linked to social categories, certainly not an exhaustive treatment of the discursive instantiation of respect language in Kunjen.

Taking the perspective of a male ego, and as shown in Figure 8.3, the relationship in which the respect register is most categorically employed is again the one between a man and his (either actual or classificatory) mother-in-law. Sommer (2006) writes that a "man would almost totally avoid both [classificatory and actual mother-in-law], being permitted conversation with them only by use of the avoidance vocabulary when no alternative avenue of communication – such as an intermediary (perhaps his wife) – was available" (p. 106). Later in the monograph he writes that "before his WM [wife's mother], a man must always use the respect vocabulary (even when he speaks, to her dog or yamstick, as he ought)" (p. 109). From this wording it appears that the use of the register has a covert addressivity, indicating that the avoidance relation (who is conspicuously not the addressee at the level of denotational text) is the actual intended recipient. In Uradhi, another language of Cape York Peninsula, mother-in-law language had a covert addressivity of this kind (Crowley, 1983, p. 314; see note 8 in Chapter 5).

The avoidance register can be employed in addressing categories of kin other than mother-in-law. For instance, the respect vocabulary may be used in non-avoidance contexts to make polite requests. Sommer (2006) gives the example of a woman who employed the respect vocabulary in directing a classificatory daughter's son (not an avoidance relationship category) to not throw grass cuttings onto the path near the Sommers' pig-pen. And it is clear that requests made of a mother, daughter, or sister will be more likely to use the respect vocabulary. Nevertheless, for these other cross-gender relations, the use of the respect vocabulary is not obligatory in address. Rather, it is used in "referring to them, especially with respect to body parts or functions, in which cases it is mandatory" (p. 109).

Target of the avoidance index	REFERENT	ADDRESSEE	INTENDED RECIPIENT	
Wife's mother	*	ADDRESS AVOIDANCE	*	LEVEL *ii*
Daughter	*	–	–	
Mother	*	–	–	LEVEL *i*
Sister	*	–	–	
Wife	–	–	–	LEVEL *o*

Figure 8.3. Stereotypical cross-gender uses of kinship respect vocabulary (*Uw Ilbmbandiy/Olkel-Ilmbanhthi*) among Kunjen speakers; male origo, female target
Notes. * indicates the normative obligation to avoid everyday speech and its corollary replacement by mother-in-law language. Note that a man cannot directly address his wife's mother but uses the avoidance register with a shill addressee (e.g., a yamstick or a dog) to communicate with her.
Source: Sommer (2006).

Observe that the relationship between recipient-targeting and referent-targeting uses of mother-in-law language, as these are keyed to distinct kinship relationships, yet again instantiates the formal-functional structure that I have been concerned to expose. When a man communicates – by means of a shill addressee – with his mother-in-law, there is no longer any possibility of shifting between everyday and avoidance speech to signal his kinship relationship with the discourse referent. Use of mother-in-law language to target discourse-recipient encompasses the use of the register to target discourse-referents. And once again, it is between more focal avoidance relations – that is, the mother-in-law/son-in-law dyad – that this most encompassing usage is attested.

Case-Study: Of Bystanders and Addressees in Gooniyandi Mother-in-law Language

Addressee-targeting, which suspends referent-targeting, may itself be suspended by bystander-targeting uses of mother-in-law language. This is exemplified by William McGregor's study of Gooniyandi mother-in-law language. For a Gooniyandi man, all women who are classified as MMBD, but also those who conform to that structural position with respect to subsection (*gooroo*) reckoning, may be classed as a *maddiyali* "mother-in-law" (McGregor, 2012, p. 164). As noted in Chapter 7, non-restricted (plural or "augment") number is employed in referring to *maddiyali*. This usage is most categorical for a man's wife's mother and her siblings, although it is also the norm in referring to

Target of the avoidance index	REFERENT	ADDRESSEE	RECIPIENT	
Wife's mother	*	*	*	LEVEL *iii*
MMBD	*	*	–	LEVEL *ii*
Female member of MMBD's subsection	*	–	–	LEVEL *i*
Others	–	–	–	

Figure 8.4. Three levels of *maddiyali* "mother-in-law" avoidance in Gooniyandi
Note. * indicates the normative obligation to avoid everyday speech; these are the contexts in which mother-in-law language would be used. The table is represented from the perspective of a male origo.
Source: McGregor (1989).

classificatory *maddiyali* (i.e., MMBD). Use of the plural is felt to be less obligatory in referring to those *maddiyali* reckoned exclusively through their subsection membership and with whom ego is in only infrequent contact. A similar "sliding scale of obligatoriness" (Keenan, 1973) can be divined in the use of the mother-in-law register. The mother-in-law language was used in referring to "any *maddiyali*," in addressing "classificatory *maddiyali*," and "in the presence of (within earshot of) a close *maddiyali*" (McGregor, 1989, p. 641; see Figure 8.4).

Although this description is derived from elicited and remembered practices, comparative ethnography suggests that avoidance language was often used not only in address but merely within "earshot" of the most focal avoidance relations. Where avoidance vocabulary must be employed in all speech that takes place in the presence of a given alter, switches between everyday and avoidance speech cannot be drawn upon to differentially pick out distinct co-present others as addressees. In Gooniyandi, there is thus a recursive set of suspensions constitutive of three distinct avoidance levels: $Referent_{target} \supset Addressee_{target} \supset Recipient_{target}$.

It is no accident that the most focal avoidance relationship in Aboriginal Australia, the relationship between a wife's mother and a woman's daughter's husband, is consistently associated with the most encompassing kind of deference indexicality – $Animator_{origo}$-$Recipient_{target}$ deference focus. This is a ritual centre of the sociolinguistic system, where a maximally monoglossic and register-cohesive honorific discourse is produced. (Mourning and initiation were two other ritual centres for the production of avoidance registers; see Fleming, 2014b, 2017a.)

Note that recipient-targeting usages are not limited to address or even tropes of negated address. Though mother-in-law language has a covert

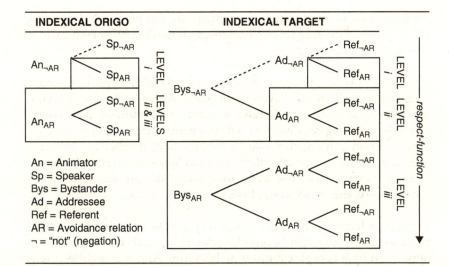

Figure 8.5. Avoidance levels determined by indexical focus type in mother-in-law languages

Notes. Each box, moving "down" in the display, represents a progressively more encompassing indexical focus type conditioning the avoidance of everyday speech and its replacement by mother-in-law language. A dotted line denotes contexts in which there is no normative constraint on the linguistic forms employed by speaker/animator. A solid line denotes contexts where speaker/animator is normatively expected to employ avoidance speech. The subscript "¬AR" indicates that the occupant of the interactional role is *not* an Avoidance Relation [AR] of the speaker/animator, while subscript "AR" indicates that the occupant of the interactional role is an avoidance relation. For the origo of the honorific index (top left of the display), Animator-indexing encompasses Speaker-indexing (i.e. [Speaker$_{origo}$ ⊃ Animator$_{origo}$]). That is, when a speech Animator is co-present with a taboo in-law, he or she should not employ register shifts between avoidance and everyday register to indicate represented Speakers who are not in affinal contexts. For indexical target, there is a sequence of three-nested levels: [Referent$_{target}$ ⊃ Addressee$_{target}$ ⊃ Bystander$_{target}$]; see main text for exemplification.

addressivity in Kunjen and Uradhi, in Dyirbal, the code was to be employed whenever the son-in-law and mother-in-law were in co-presence, even when no covert communication was involved: "There was never any choice involved, [Dixon's chief consultant on mother-in-law language or Jalnguy,] Chloe [Grant] said. A man would talk with his wife in Guwal, the everyday language style, but if a mother-in-law was within hearing, he had immediately to switch to Jalnguy" (Dixon, 1984, p. 91). Similarly, in Guugu Yimidhirr, a "man would use [brother-in-law] words if his mother-in-law was within earshot, even if she was on the other side of an obstruction or otherwise out of view" (Haviland, 1979a, p. 370). I must again cite Francesca Merlan's (1997) perspicacious observation concerning

> the mother-in-law avoidance taboo, in which the highly prescribed and institutionalised forms – aversion of gaze, relative taciturnity, special proxemics, and so on – tend to give *one* aspect of the relationship between people overriding determination of their conduct in each other's presence. Thus, a man in his mother-in-law's presence finds it difficult to behave towards her in any way other than as her son-in-law; and further, his conduct towards everyone else on the scene is very strongly shaped by their co-presence, and the social emphasis placed on it. (p. 108)

Though perhaps overly formalistic in its presentation, what I have tried to show here is how this "overriding determination" of conduct is underwritten by a complex register architecture. And this architecture is based, as with scalar T-V systems and name registers, on the principle of the recursive pragmatic suspension of formal resources as a sign of progressively heightened respect. For those interested in the formalism, Figure 8.5 offers a schematized representation of the structure of mother-in-law avoidance levels as a function of the suspension of indexical origo and target types.

Deference Diagrams in Visual Avoidance Repertoires

Linguistic anthropologists have increasingly turned to the investigation of the quanta as well as the qualia of social semiosis (Harkness, 2013, 2015). One line of investigation has focused on metadiscourses that compare and contrast – or commensurate – semiotic intensities (Carruthers 2017a, 2017b; Kockelman, 2016a, 2016b). The empirical particulars that I have worried over in this chapter and the last one provide a complementary perspective on this important problem. In addition to the role of metadiscourses of commensuration, I have shown how the structure of avoidance register repertoires underwrites the analogue (or by-degrees) effects of indexical signs. The architecture of this "pragmatic structure" (Silverstein, 1976, p. 52) is quite different from the Saussurean structures studied in descriptive grammar. These are structures of iconic and indexical signs organized in such a way as to maximize the "comparative grounds" (Kockelman, 2016a) that enable deference displays to be graded with respect to one another. Here I will summarize, in highly programmatic fashion, four important features of these pragmatic structures.

1 Globally, diagrammatic structure of avoidance repertoires: A diagram is a complex sign where the (indexical) relations between the parts of the sign are iconic with the (indexical) relations between the parts of the object that the sign represents. (The classic example is of a map as a sign of a territory.) In the examples that I have showcased, a graded series of formal-functional analogies is established wherein lesser/greater semiotic avoidance is iconic of lesser/greater interpersonal respect. Against the backdrop of this *globally* diagrammatic (or indexically-iconic) structure, particular registered signs of avoidance have *locally* emblematic (or iconic-indexical) values (e.g., the Manus plural is an iconically intensified index of respect).
2 Diagrammatic structure as "breakthrough" semiosis: These sociolinguistic structures involve a "'breakthrough' mode of semiosis" of the kind identified by Silverstein (1994, p. 42) for Chinookan "denotational and indexical sound-symbolism."[9] The key point here is the following: Through the mediation of these diagrammatic structures, linguistic categories and discursive parameters that subtend symbol-rich reference and predication are "rank-shifted" into non-referential iconic and indexical functions. Whether in the variable range of phonolexical avoidances in the Siuai name register, in variable numerosity in the Manus pronominal register, or in referent- versus recipient-targeting indexicality in Australian mother-in-law languages, the raw materials out of which these structures are constructed are themselves discursive/linguistic categories: the lexical category of proper nouns in Siuai, the grammatical category of number in Manus, the participant role-structure of discursive interaction for Gooniyandi. In these diagrammatic structures, analogue meanings are emergent out of digital distinctions, not vice versa. Breakthrough semiosis thus demonstrates the reductive fallacy of seeing "motivated" (or "natural") signs as more "primitive" (both in the sense of more simple and as antedating) than "arbitrary" (or "conventional") ones, a longstanding background assumption in the Western philosophical tradition (Kockelman, 2003, pp. 467–8; Silverstein, 1994, p. 40).
3 Diagrammatic structure as an attractor of cumulative cultural "evolution": As I have shown, graded formal-functional analogies constitute a structuring principle of avoidance repertoires across diverse signalling media. Further, this patterning is attested across a diverse range of culture-historical settings. Diagrammatic structure thus appears to be a common end-point or "attractor" in the diachronic development of social semiotic systems.

4 Diagrammatic structure as a cultural, rather than specifically linguistic, semiotic: Although the pragmatic structures that I have analyzed are built out of linguistic and discursive distinctions (interactional roles, lexical classes, grammatical categories), there is no in principal reason to believe that they are circumscribed to linguistic media. After all, diagrammatic structure subtends iconic and indexical significations, the default semiotic modes of "other cultural media" (Silverstein, 1976, p. 54). Some empirical examples suggest themselves. For instance, spatial codes expressed through intercorporeal proximity or relative inclination of the body in honorific gesture are often organized into graded series of these kinds (see, e.g., Firth, 1969, for Tikopia; Gregory, 2011, for Halbi [east-central India]).

As a final empirical exemplification, I focus on this last point: Diagrammatic structures that grade intensities of avoidance also occur in nonlinguistic media. I offer a few examples drawn from the study of technologies of visual avoidance (see Chapter 6 for the comparative survey). Interactional technologies of visual avoidance are frequently wedded (thinly veiled pun intended) to the forging and enactment of kinship "alliance" and to the consummation and upkeep of affinal relations and relationships. In these social settings, different degrees of bodily covering can come to count as graded deference-indexicals. And here, too, the signs that form the graded series of visual avoidance displays may stand in relations of recursive encompassment to one another.

Case Study: Gujarati Body Covering

As an example, I draw upon Emma Tarlo's (1996) description of clothing customs in a village in the Saurashtra region of Gujarat. Much as in the case of rural Madhya Pradesh discussed in Chapter 6 (after Jacobson, 1982), veiling among Hindu women in Saurashtra is keyed to affinity. In their natal village, women are not expected to veil, although at about 10 years of age girls begin to wear a half-*sari* (or *sadlo*) and "learn to keep their heads covered with the cloth" (Tarlo, 1996, p. 154). It is, however, only upon marriage that head and body covering is practiced in earnest, and then only in the husband's village. Veiling is conceptualized as "a form of deference and respect" directed at, especially, husband's elder male relatives, but extended "to senior males in the village through the belief that all men of the village are relatives"

(p. 160). Women refer to veiling with the term *laj kadvu*, which literally means "doing shame." Tarlo (1996) describes three "different degrees" of veiling:

> Simple *laj* consists of taking the veil by the hand and pulling it rapidly sideways across the face; this is the type of *laj* typically performed when women are out of doors in an apparently secluded spot, and a man unexpectedly walks past.... The term *ardhi laj* (lit. "half shame") refers to the custom of drawing the veil over the face down to waist level, which is often performed in the presence of a senior relative within the home.... The strictest form of *laj* observed in [the village of] Jalia is referred to as *akhi laj* ("complete shame"). It involves pulling the veil forward at an angle so that it obscures even the arms, and its aim is to leave no part of the woman's body visible. Many informed me that all brides of the village used to maintain *akhi laj* throughout the marriage ceremony.... [Y]oung women who live in seclusion [i.e., high caste women] are expected to be fully veiled on the rare occasions when they enter the public space of the village. At the Diwali festival, for example, young *Brahman* wives could be seen being led by other family members to visit their relations. They were totally veiled and resembled large bundles of expensive cloth, with only their toes and the tips of their fingers visible from beneath their saris. (pp. 160–2)

Focusing solely on the question of deference diagrams, the three veiling styles appear to form a set of recursively encompassing levels such that the more covered the woman is the more modest and/or respectful she is construed to be (see Table 8.1).

A fuller analysis would ideally attend to the ways in which visual avoidances link up with other avoidance media, on the one hand, and how they operate across multiple orders of indexicality, on the other. With respect to the first point, Tarlo (1996) observes that "most refined women will never speak" when they employ "half shame" (*ardhi laj*) (p. 161). This suggests that for women of higher-caste groups there is an implicational relationship between visual and oral avoidances. With respect to the second point, the description suggests that registered visual avoidances operate across multiple indexical orders. The most intense forms of veiling are associated with the highest-caste group, and thus function as second-order indexical of the veiler's status.[10] The important point for our purposes is that these three veiling styles form a nested series, where greater modesty is enacted through more encompassing invisibility (see also Jacobson, 1982, p. 92, for similar degrees of veiling in Madhya Pradesh).

Table 8.1. Different veiling styles among Hindu women in rural Saurashtra, Gujarat, India

Veil type	Social category and context	Kind of visibility avoidance
no veil	girls under 10 years of age	head and hair visible
sadlo "half-sari"	girls over 10 in natal village	hair covered, face and arms visible
laj "shame"	classificatory relations of husband in conjugal village	face hooded, arms visible
ardhi laj "half shame"	senior relatives of husband in conjugal village	face covered, arms visible
akhi laj "complete shame"	marriage ceremony OR being in public for highest-caste young brides	face and arms covered, only fingers and toes visible

Source: Tarlo (1996).

Case Study: Turkmen Body Covering

Another example of graded levels of visual avoidance is found William Irons's (1975) ethnography of Turkmen nomads (see also Vogelsang-Eastwood & Vogelsang, 2008). In the Turkmen context, veiling again forms a component part of a daughter-in-law avoidance register. Veiling is most hypertrophied in the co-presence of a woman's father-in-law, and this in the period right after marriage, when the bride is only a periodic inhabitant in her husband's parents' yurt: "During her earliest contacts with her father-in-law she throws a cloth over her head completely covering her face. Ordinary female Turkmen garb leaves only the face, neck, hands, and feet visible. Thus, a single large cloth added to the usual female garb leaves nothing visible except her hands and feet" (Irons, 1975, p. 150). This most extreme veiling not only occludes the head completely; it blocks off the visual channel, rendering the signalling subject literally dependent upon a member of the conjugal household to move her through domestic space. It is thus a powerful emblem of the bride's newfound dependence upon her husband's household in a society where patrilocal post-marital residence is the norm. In the prototypical situation described by Irons, it is a husband's younger sister (HyZ) who serves as the blinded bride's guide. During this time, the bride's head is uncovered within the residence only when she is positioned behind "a gaily decorated curtain," or *tuti:*, hung in such a manner so as to sequester her in the northwestern quadrant of the yurt.

For the first few years of marriage, the bride alternates between residing with her parents and residing with her husband's parents.

After the fourth year she typically establishes permanent residency in the patrilocal household, at which time the *tuti:* is used only at night, or "when the bride changes clothing or combs her hair" (Irons, 1975, p. 106). Her head covering is also diminished, with the bride taking up a style of covering called *bürünmek,*

> which consists of covering the face below the eyes with a cloth, and then pulling one's head cloth down over one's forehead in such a way that only a slit is left open for the eyes. A new bride who is practicing bürünmek also tries not to let anyone senior to her husband see her eyes. She does this by sitting close to and facing the wall of the yurt while sitting indoors and by holding her head cloth with her hand in such a way as to block the view of individuals she is avoiding while she is moving about. (p. 106)

After the birth of the first child, a third style of veiling, called *yaşmaq,* where only the mouth is covered, becomes the norm:

> The degree of avoidance associated with yaşmaq entails concealing one's mouth and not speaking to, or eating from the same dish, as the person avoided. The sort of avoidance associated with yaşmaq is not reciprocal. A father-in-law and a mother-in-law can speak to their daughter-in-law in order to direct labors and frequently do so. If necessary for her work a daughter-in-law can respond with hand motions, nods of her head, or by whispering to a junior individual who can relay her communications. (p. 106)

Beginning with marriage, then permanent residence in her parents-in-law's residence, and finally with the birth of her first child, the bride's progressive incorporation into her husband's family is sketched out by a scaled reduction in avoidance practice – by a progressive "lowering" of visual avoidance levels. Names of veiling styles are employed metonymically to refer to a suite of practices that includes the veiling practice itself but also discursive, gestural, and other non-linguistic practices like food sharing. The three veiling styles are graded with respect to one another. The cloth over the head hides the eyes and the mouth from others and makes seeing impossible. The *bürünmek* liberates the eyes for seeing while carefully protecting them and the mouth from being seen. Finally, with *yaşmaq* only the mouth remains covered. This grading figurates degrees of phatic accessibility. In total covering, the bride is forestalled from co-presencing, in any way, the members of her husband's household. In the *bürünmek* style, she hides her eyes and studiously forestalls eye contact with senior men, closing off a crucial means by which interactional co-presence is mutually ratified and face-to-face communication secured. Lastly, the covered mouth of *yaşmaq* represents the asymmetric closure of the speech channel (cf. the Armenian mouth-covering or *moonch*). Although she can now be presenced and even interpellated, the bride cannot initiate communication with her parents-in-law or channel communication directly to them but must indirectly – through non-verbal gesture or whispered use of speech intermediaries – respond to their entreaties.

In kinship-keyed head covering, limits on non-verbal communication – limits of vision (input) and visibility (output) – are recruited to serve as signs of respect. Within this signalling medium, however, constraints are self-organized into a graded series. A bride sequentially progresses through the three styles of head covering: first with the cloth fully draped over her head; second with the *bürünmek* covering the nose, mouth, and forehead; and third with the *yaşmaq*, which covers just the mouth. She is, after each step, discretely less constrained in her signalling possibilities than she was at the last stage. The distinct conventionalized head-covering styles of the Turkmen constitute a set of mutually encompassing visual avoidance levels (i.e., full head-covering > nose, mouth, forehead covering > mouth covering). And because this is a sequence that unfolds sequentially in biographical time, it figurates the bride's – never fully complete but nevertheless progressive – incorporation into her husband's family.

From Pragmatic Structures to Intensities of Experience

Comparative ethnography suggests that the most focal kinship avoidance relationships are lived as an intense "total orientation" toward the other, with members of these dyads experiencing an "overriding determination of their conduct in each other's presence" (Merlan, 1997, p. 108). In this book I have sought to understand the linguistic, and more broadly sociocultural, structures that scaffold this quality of the phenomenological experience of being-toward-others. But how, precisely, are the pragmatic structures that I have analyzed related to the lived experience of relationship? In this section I sketch an answer to the question of how the structure of avoidance registers scaffolds the phenomenological experience of kinship avoidance. Answering this question requires understanding how the distinct dimensions of kinship registers that I have showcased are conceptually and experientially joined together in the practical living out of kinship relationship.

I have focused on three layers of pragmatic structure which recur in the organization of avoidance as a semiotic practice: (*i.*) implicational relationships between avoidances, (*ii.*) relations of formal

Degrees of Unfreedom

(META) PRAGMATIC SYMBOLIZATION OF AVOIDANCE
named ethoses: e.g., *kwa* "joke," *kxa* "avoid" [Juǀ'hoan]   *named speech varieties*:   e.g., *taraŋa laui* "good speech," *taraŋa pariki* "bad speech" [Tikopia]   *(iv.)*

EMBLEMATIC (ICONIC-INDEXICAL) CHARACTER OF AVOIDANCES
e.g., NAME = rigid designator of a person → avoiding the name...   is ICONIC of the avoidance of its referent   & an actual INDEXICAL instantiation of such avoidance...   *(iii.)*

ENCOMPASSMENT RELATIONS BETWEEN AVOIDANCES (e.g., Siuai name avoidances)

forms avoided	functions	associated kin
homophone	→ highest respect	→ wife's mother
proper noun	→ higher respect	→ man's FZ
name	→ respectful	→ man's MB wife

    (ii.)

IMPLICATIONAL RELATIONSHIPS BETWEEN AVOIDANCES (ex. Kobon avoidances)

*	*	*	*	*	*	*	*	*	*	*	*	*	IV
✓	✓	✓	*	*	*	*	*	*	*	*	*	*	III
✓	✓	✓	✓	✓	✓	*	*	*	*	*	*	*	II
✓	✓	✓	✓	✓	✓	✓	✓	✓	*	*	*	*	I
✓	✓	✓	✓	✓	✓	✓	✓	✓	✓	✓	✓	✓	0
1	2	3	4	5	6	7	8	9	10	11	12	13	

[(1, 2, 3) → [(4, 5, 6) → [(7, 8, 9) → [10, 11, 12, 13]]]]   *(i.)*

Figure 8.6. Layers in the (meta)pragmatic structuring of avoidance repertoires

encompassment between avoidances, and (*iii.*) emblems of interpersonal contact as privileged semiotic media of avoidance. Finally, I have noted the ways in which these distinct "layers" of pragmatic structure are imbued with meaning (*iv.*) by ethnometapragmatic discourses and vocabularies that name and characterize interpersonal styles of relating and the registered signs that enact them. Figure 8.6 offers a summarizing picture of these distinct layers of (meta)pragmatic structure. Here I briefly review those structural properties, suggesting how they are conceptually and practically brought together in experience.

Layer i (chained implicational relationships between avoidances): This layer was discussed in the Introduction. Distinct avoidance comportments – sharing food, name calling, pronominal honorification, for example – tend to become chained together through **implicational relationships**. Let me quickly review the idea by recalling the implicational relationships between Chiricahua Apache avoidances shown in Table 0.1 of the Introduction: If ego cannot look at a particular social alter, then ego cannot refer to alter with a personal pronoun but should instead employ the "polite form." However, the reverse is not true: There are relationships in which ego is expected to employ the "polite form" without avoiding face-to-face interaction. At the bottom of Figure 8.6, I exemplify implicational relationships by once again reproducing Graham Jackson's (1975) data on thirteen distinct Kobon kinship taboos (see Table 0.3 from the Introduction). Roman numerals denote avoidance levels ("level 0" denotes no avoidance); the Arabic numerals denote distinct avoidances (see Figure 0.1 in the Introduction for the key). This structural layer consists of an ensemble of distinct, named avoidances (e.g., don't eat from same bowl as the other, don't employ singular number in reference to the other, etc.). These avoidances are related to one another by iterative implicational relationships: if P then Q, if Q then R, if R then S. In the Kobon example, *if* ego engages in the commensality avoidances labelled 1 (i.e., not touch pork raised by alter), 2 (i.e., not eat food grown in alter's garden), and 3 (i.e., not eat food cooked in a fire where food for alter has been cooked) vis-à-vis a particular alter, these being the avoidances distinctive of avoidance level IV, *then* ego necessarily employs all the other avoidances for that alter as well. Chained implicational relationships ensure that progressively "higher" avoidance levels entail all of the avoidances of "lower" levels. This make avoidance levels commensurable – they can readily be interpreted as enacting relatively muted or heightened respect.

Layer ii (relations of encompassment between avoidances): The second to the bottom layer depicts relations of **notional** or **logical encompassment** between distinct avoidances. I have shown in Part 4 that this pattern recurs in name registers, mother-in-law registers, pronominal honorification, and visual avoidances. The crucial observation is that within particular avoidance media, registered avoidances stand in proper superset-subset relationships to one another, not by virtue of conventionalized implicational relationships (as with the first layer), but because avoidances *necessarily* stand in actual class-member relationships to one another. These relations of formal encompassment between avoidances instantiate a diagrammatic (or indexically-iconic) relationship between registered indexical form and function. More encompassing avoidances figurate greater respect. Note further that because these relations of encompassment involve formal class-member relationships, they make relatively more explicit the subset-superset relationships already implicit at the first layer.

Layer iii (contact emblems): The first two layers of pragmatic structure – "horizontal" implicational relationships across avoidance media and "vertical" relations of formal encompassment between avoidances within a given medium – undergird the analogue- and continuum-like character of joking-avoidance as a system of relationships. They are built upon the formal-functional analogy between semiotic constraint and interpersonal restraint theorized in Chapter 7: Greater constraint on signalling possibilities (form) enacts greater interpersonal respect (function). But there is nothing about these structural principles, in themselves, which indicate who is avoided or what avoidances are understood to accomplish. This aspect of indexical signification – the specification of the indexical focus or target (Agha, 1993; Fleming, 2016) – is dynamically figured by the emblematic character of avoidance signs themselves.

As I showed in Chapters 3–6, avoidance indicates its focus or target – the "who" of kinship indexicality – by tabooing rigid signs of the other. Rigid signs are signs that are indexical of particular persons – their possessions, their names, their faces (after Nakassis). Importantly, these avoidances have a ritual performativity, in the sense of Tambiah (2017) and Silverstein (2004). In ritual performativity, iconic and indexical relations are established between concrete signs and more ineffable orders (Keane, 2007). Once established, operations upon the manipulable and material signs, where felicitous, effect changes within the more ineffable orders – the communion bread that is sanctified makes manifest "the body of Christ"; blowing upon the dice summons forth "luck." Such ritual gestures are iconic-indexicals: They iconically sketch or portray the very act that they actually (read, indexically) accomplish.

Take the example of the Siuai woman's avoidance of *Tomo*, the name of her son-in-law, and of the similar sounding word *mo* "coconut." Avoidance of the phonetic string [tomo] (the manipulable, material sign) enacts respect for Tomo, the person (an ineffable concept, if ever there was one). This ritual work is achieved by exploiting the indexical connection between the proper name and its referent, a connection initially established in an act of name-bestowal (after Kripke). By virtue of this indexical name-referent link, the speaker's treatment of the name can function as an icon of her treatment of the referent. She enacts restraint toward the person of her son-in-law by refraining from using the phonological string out of which his name is composed. Because avoiding the name "counts" as enacting respect by local custom, her reverential treatment of his name is an iconic-indexical of her respect for him.

The Phatic Supplement of Avoidance

The various interaction rituals most characteristic of kinship avoidance cross-culturally – not making contact with the other's name (orally/aurally), with the other's face (visually), with the other's body and possessions (haptically) – serve to identify the target of avoidance. And yet there is a crucial supplementary kind of signification that rides along with this specification of the indexical target; rigid signs of the other are also the channels and sites of contact through which communication with and about that other is actually accomplished. Felicitous indexing of the other by the avoidance of their semiotic emanations simultaneously entails an abrogation or attenuation (after Russell) of intersubjective relating with that other.

The avoidance of rigid signs of the other thus occupies two overlapping but distinct fields of signification. First, as we have just seen, it picks out the focus/target of the honorific index. For instance, one person dynamically figurates respect for another person by studiously avoiding touching the skin that covers the body that indissociably "stands for" that person. But the avoidance of rigid signs of the other also opens onto a second kind of signification, one involving the communicative-channel establishing, or phatic, connection (Jakobson, 1960; Nozawa, 2015; Zuckermann, 2020).

As semiotic avoidance is put into practice in real-time interaction, it is realized as the phenomenological experience of dynamic other-oriented relating, of presenting oneself to, or withholding oneself from, the other. In this way, interpersonal avoidance emerges as the supplement of semiotic avoidance – the conventional indexing of the other through the avoidance of their rigid signs. And yet, from the perspective of the subjective experience of relationship, this supplement is the centre, since it provides the clearing and the opening for the intense phenomenological experience of the other, for the "total orientation." Indeed, avoidance practices and the cultural ideologies that inform them thematize kinship avoidance as a problem of intersubjective accessibility, of permissible and impermissible modalities of sensorial mutuality – in short, as a problem of impossible kinds of being-together and being-in-contact. Here contact – with tactile intercorporeality being the most richly emblematic form of contact – is cast with a negatively valued performativity capable of rupturing relationship and even relation. Touch transforms. (As I will show in the Conclusion, the symbolism of sex, in all its polysemic plenitude, is central to thematizing this transformative potential.) At this vanishing point, ontological categories of personhood and ontological categories of experience fuse.

These observations suggest that structured semiotic constraint, ideologically construed as interpersonal restraint, is not translated in some simple or deterministic way into the experience of intersubjective relationship. Although the practice and experience of relationship are grounded in (social) ideology and (semiotic) structure, they are not reducible to them. The total orientation toward the other emerges from registered signs of kinship but it is not itself registered.

Putting the matter slightly differently, the enchained relations between registered avoidances, rationalized in terms of logics of intersubjective contact, scaffold the experience of socially differentiated intensities of presencing the other. But again, I must underscore that by "scaffold" I do not mean to suggest a direct conversion of graded avoidance levels, at the level of pragmatic structure, directly into an intensity gradient of lived experience. Rather, it appears that the purely pragmatic structure offers itself to subjective experience as intensity – that intensity is a parsimonious interpretation, or actualization of structure at the level of subjective experience. Through the mediation of linguistic and cultural ideologies – ideologies that imbue avoidance with affective, moral, and symbolic values – discrete and digital diacritics of relationship can be experienced as analogue gradients; structure can be experienced as sensitivity. But these quanta and qualia of experience emerge only in the living out of actual human relationships.

Two implications derive from this scaffolding relation. First, the cultural structure of implicationally chained and formally encompassing avoidances is not a structure from nowhere (as in Lévi-Strauss's analyses of myth or cuisine, for instance). Rather, these pragmatic structures are anchored to the first-person experience of being-toward-others.[11] Second, intensities of intersubjective experience themselves interpretively "subsume" structure. To use Roy Wagner's (1986b) argot, intensity "obviates" structure.[12] This second point in some sense follows from the first, for inasmuch as cultural structure is indexically anchored to experience, we must consider this anchoring zero-point to be also the hinge between structural value and phenomenological intensity, a site where relationship is invented over and over and over again in experience.

Conclusion

The Mutuality of Being Apart

Why is human kinship so often instantiated through a system of relationships arrayed along a continuum of codes of conduct ranging from ribald insult and licence ("joking") to the impossibility of intersensorial mutuality ("avoidance")? In this book I have argued that we can gain traction in answering this question by paying close attention to the material practices through which kinship avoidance, as a socially recognized activity, is accomplished. Kinship avoidances always have a conventional, symbolized, and standardized character, rendering them recognizable as signs of relation and enactments of relationship for the persons who participate in these meanings. Kinship avoidance is registered semiotic practice. I have illuminated cross-cultural convergences in kinship avoidances by looking closely at how registered signs of avoidance and the ideologies that render them significant are brought into dialectical tension in the actual enactment of kinship relationships. Each part of the book offered dedicated descriptions of dialectical dynamics of this kind.

Part 1 highlighted the salience of words as units uniquely available to proscriptive regimes of language. Part 2 showed how names, as rigid referential signs of persons, are privileged loci for the linguistic enactment of avoidance. Part 3 considered how communication with the other is managed beyond language and showed that the kinds of contact which are most often circumscribed involve intercorporeal and intersensorial modes of co-presencing. Part 4 theorized convergences in the structuring of avoidances across a range of semiotic media, illustrating how avoidance levels become recursively encompassed one within the other and how this is productive of grades and gradations of avoidance.

In this Conclusion, I return to the set of questions that animated the Introduction concerning the phenomenological experience of relationship that is fostered through the institution of kinship avoidance. In that context, I sought to home in on the "total orientation" (Merlan, 1997, p. 106) which the most focal of avoidance relatives feel toward one another in interaction. In the Introduction, and then again in the last section of the last chapter, I argued that the pragmatic structuring of kinship avoidances fosters or scaffolds that feeling. Here I look at collective representations of the qualities of experience – in particular, shame – which animate this intense experience of the other and seek to understand how these qualities of experience are mutually elicited in the interactional back-and-forth of relationship.

The Existentialist Turn in Kinship Studies

The seeming naturalness of kinship has long impeded us from grasping its nature. For too long, kinship was seen as the cultural and categorical codification and building out of biological relations of sexual reproduction. David Schneider's (1968, 1984) "cultural account" effectively banished this genealogical reduction from the sociocultural anthropology of kinship (Bamford & Leach, 2009). And yet it did not provide a satisfying answer to "what kinship is," as Marshall Sahlins (2013) would later come to formulate the question. On the contrary, in Schneider's rendering, "kinship" is a Euro-American institution projected onto the ethnographic other. Kinship, as a cross-cultural category of analysis, has no referent "out there" in the world.

Only the most blinkered of nominalists could be content with this Buddha-like pronouncement – kinship is an illusion. Ethnographers, first and foremost, are constantly confronted with the central importance of socially structured and interactionally patterned networks of differentiated human relationships, culturally symbolized as categorically interrelated to, and generative of, one another. Everywhere the ethnographer goes, kinship is central to people's lived experience. It was perhaps inevitable, therefore, that the "new kinship" studies would begin to coalesce around a novel understanding of the essence of kinship after biology (after M. Strathern, 1992).

That coalescence is encapsulated by the important work of Carsten (1995, 2000), Sahlins (2013), and Bird-David (2017). All three understand the essence of kinship as arising from and reflective of modes of being together. For Carsten, Bird-David, and Sahlins, intimate intersubjectivities of childhood in the domestic sphere seem to be prototypic of "cultures of relatedness," "pluripresence," and "mutuality of being," their respective short-hand definitions of kinship. Carsten's (2000, p. 18) formulation is motivated by her ethnographic materials, where

"Malay relatedness is created both by ties of procreation and through everyday acts of feeding and living together in the house." For Bird-David, the essence of kinship among the Nayaka (Dravidian; S. India) is intensive co-presence in a shared camp. Sahlins (2013) goes the furthest in identifying co-presence with the essence of kinship. "Mutuality of being" is invested with a presence-based positivity – it is a rich and dynamic, face-open, body-touching, nourishment-sharing experience of and with the other.

As with all post-Schneiderian scholarship, the challenge here is to define kinship without appeal to biological relatedness. And the solution that all three authors offer is a definition in terms of modes of "being-with" (Bird-David, 2017, pp. 15–16, after Jean-Luc Nancy). Correspondingly, I will label this the "existentialist turn" in kinship studies, for it seeks to locate the essence of relatedness in the phenomenological experience of the other. I applaud this turn toward experience (see "From Pragmatic Structures to Intensities of Experience" in the last chapter) and feel that it could set kinship studies on a productive path forward. However, we must be vigilant if we are not to fall back into a background understanding of "being-with" as spatiotemporal co-presence. That is, we must avoid the reduction of "being-with" to the mutual and multimodal accessibility and responsiveness of the here-and-now, face-to-face encounter.

Empirically, a presence-based definition of kinship cannot capture the "social quality of engaged separation" (Stasch, 2003, p. 325) which characterizes avoidance relations' experience of one another. It fails to capture the ways in which "deferral" (Wagner, 1986a) and "attenuation" (Russell, 2020) are equally essential and non-derivative modes of "being-with." Again, I approve of the desire to restore and safeguard – to undeconstruct – kinship. But to save a concept like "mutuality of being," one would have to think it not only in harmony with but also in opposition to (co-)presence. That is, one must conceive of a mutual being of constant closure and vanishing access, of turning away and aside. Inspired by Rupert Stasch's (2009) theorization of qualities of experience keyed to asynchronous and spatially removed modes of relating, as well as by Roy Wagner's (1986a) theorization of kinship as the elicitation of relationship, in the following, I suggest some ways to save an existentialist understanding of kinship from the reduction to presence.[1] My reflections are intended less as a closure on what has been said in this book than as an overture for further reflection.

To invest "mutuality of being" with a wider, but also richer, meaning requires attending to the registered character of kinship comportments – that is, to the cultural mediation of (signs of) presence/absence. But it also demands a perspective that complements the register approach, one that understands relationship rather than presence as the ground of being-with. I have not sufficiently addressed the question of how the dynamic back-and-forth of relationship articulates with kinship registers. Nevertheless, I am convinced of the importance of this connection for a fuller and more filled out account of kinship-as-lived-experience. Correspondingly, I briefly turn to human, interpersonal relationship as a process through which we learn ways of feeling and being. Although these phenomenological modes are emergent in experience, they articulate with rich collective representations of social sentiments and ontologies, representations that symbolically saturate relationship and give the experience of the other its multidimensionality.

Binocular Signification: Kinship as the Elicitation of Relationship

In his last published writings, Gregory Bateson (1980, 1982) compares human (as well as animal) relationships to binocular vision. Why (he asks) has evolution selected for two eyes only to place them so close to one another that the visual fields largely overlap? The reason is that the difference in the perception of the same stimuli offers information of a "higher logical type." Each visual field in isolation can offer only two-dimensional information about length and width. But the perceptual differences between the two eyes projects a third dimension, that of depth. A "double description" of the same "thing" offers information that is not present in either description in isolation (see Hui et al., 2008).

Human relationships are similarly more than the sum of their parts. They are "always a product of ... double description. That is, the relationship as seen by B and the relationship as seen by A" (Bateson, 1982, p. 4). The higher-order level, analogous to depth perception, that emerges from the "double description" implicit in human relationships is what Bateson calls "characterological learning" (p. 5). By this he means habitual ways of understanding, being and acting, like "moods" or "personality traits." We have a tendency to reify characterological traits as inherent attributes of individuals. But this erases the interpersonal and interactional contexts in which these habitual modes of being and responding are inculcated and reinforced.[2] It erases the learning process through which persons have acquired these habits (a process that Bateson calls "learning to learn," or "deutero-learning"). Far from being inherent attributes of isolated individuals, habitual ways of being are intimately linked to interpersonal interaction: "the unit of characterological learning – that is, the unit of that learning which changes you characterologically, the unit of deutero-learning – is the same as the unit of interaction" (Bateson, 1982, p. 4). Relationships, from this bottom-up perspective, emerge out of interactional ("contingency") patterns which, through abductive learning, produce relatively inflexible habits (of responding and feeling), or "characterological attributes."[3]

Roy Wagner (1972, 1977, 1986a) drew explicitly upon the work of Bateson to flesh out a novel understanding of kinship as the elicitation of relationship. Wagner, like his doctoral advisor David Schneider, takes a radically culturalist approach to kinship: "There are no kin relationships that are not 'made' or 'fictive' in the sense that they must be learned, and their motivations renegotiated, by purely cultural means" (Wagner, 1986a, p. 69). Central to kinship, on his account, is the differentiation of human relationship. Functionalist, structuralist, and cognitive anthropological approaches have all tended to see "joking, avoidance, and respect ... as conventional strategies for converting a naturally differentiated kin universe into a functioning society, and a comprehensive account of a people's relationship protocols yields their social homologue of genealogy" (Wagner, 1977, pp. 625–6). Rather than begin with a "set of "given" genealogical relatives," Wagner's (1977) "analogical analysis" invokes, as initial condition, "a situation in which all kin relations and all kinds of relatives are basically alike, and it is a human responsibility to differentiate them" (p. 623).

Kinship avoidance is the central and originating gesture in this work of differentiating kin. For the Daribi, the "initial differentiation, or interdiction ... [which is] (as the Daribi themselves consider it), the 'maker' or 'creator' of kin relationship" (Wagner, 1977, p. 627) is not the biological act of reproduction, but the social act of betrothal (*orowaie* "to betroth"). Upon betrothal, "the force of the interdict is to commute all or most interaction ('relating') between two sets of persons, focused on the dyad involved in the exchange of wealth and meat" (p. 627), the substances of matrimonial exchange. Betrothal is marked by a "total, formal abrogation of intercourse and even recognition between the prospective groom on one side and his prospective bride and her mother on the other" (p. 629). They do not speak to one another or utter one another's names, and they must avoid setting eyes on one other. Already, here, one can see the importance of modes of relating not based in pure presence to the operation of kinship as a social institution. Less (co-present interaction) is sometimes more (relationship).

In his ethnography of the Usen Barok, Wagner (1986a) more fully develops this picture of the "differentiating elicitation of kin relationship." He draws on Bateson's concepts of "ethos" and "schismogenesis" (see note 3 for definitions): "The core of Usen Barok *kastam* ['custom'] ... [is the] conceptual as well as behavioral elicitation of ethos ... And the elicitation [between matrilineal moieties], rather as in Bateson's concept of 'schismogenesis,' is a matter of challenge and response, of how the actor or actors rise to the situation posed by an alter.... The behavioral core is a matter of the differentiating elicitation of kin relationship (respect, joking, and avoidance)" (pp. 49–50). Without delving too deep into the Usen Barok materials, let me draw on Wagner's Bateson-inspired account as a springboard for considering the "characterological attributes" that emerge out of the interactional sequences characteristic of joking and avoidance relationships.

Among the Usen Barok, pulling pranks or "snatching" the possessions of the other, among other ambiguously aggressive behaviours, is characteristic of certain inter-moiety relationships. In particular, the relationship between *naluwinin* (sing., *lawuke*) is the "epitome of joking relationships" (Wagner, 1986a, p. 66). *Naluwinin* relationships are necessarily reciprocal same-sex relationships (i.e., mFMB, mZSS, mMBS, mFZS, wFM, wSD, wMBD, wFZD). From the perspective of a junior male, *naluwinin* are senior men in a position of authority over ego's father. Most important here is father's mother's brother (or *orong*) – that is, the man most crucially involved in provisioning the bride price for ego's mother. The *naluwinin* relationship is characterized by "elicitative provocation." *Naluwinin* do "not merely appropriate an ax or a tin of fish; rather, he or she will come and take all of one's clothes, or *mis* [native money], or even a car or radio" (p. 67). Because "revenge is considered perfectly legitimate, and is in fact the appropriate response" (p. 67), joking sequences (like an arms race or a feud) may form symmetrically schismogenetic sequences.[4] These reciprocal interactional sequences "elicit" the "characterological attribute" of *malum* "forbearance." One puts up with the provocation of the other; one is unflappable in the face of the other's instigations: "*Malum* is the ethic of forbearance, of self-restraint ... it is the 'appropriate response' to any inter-moiety joking, or humiliating or potentially shaming solicitation, however harsh (and the harsher it is, the more poignant the realization of *malum*)" (p. 75).

Contrasting with Barok joking relationships are the cross-sex sibling and affinal avoidance relationships. For the Barok, the affinal relationship is "a reciprocal, encompassing condition" (Wagner, 1986a, p. 59), and it is mediated by the classic anti-phatic rituals discussed in Part 3. The most focal in-law avoidance relationships are those centred around the parents of one's spouse and their siblings – these relationships "are elicited by an almost total avoidance" (p. 58). If *malum* is the characterological attribute elicited by joking, what is the mood or attitude associated with avoidance? For the Usen Barok, it is *minenge* "shame." The force of "the interdict" on communication between in-laws is not simply that it withholds co-presence and suspends pre-existing ways of relating. Equally important is the learning that avoidance fosters; through the conventionalized deferral of interaction, interpersonal avoidance entrains those who participate in it to abductively acquire the moods and dispositions that make them averse to interacting with the other. For the Daribi, much as for the Barok, through constant avoidance any and all "contact" between a parent- and child-in-law comes to be experienced as *hare* "shame" (Wagner, 1967, p. 176). Shame is the "characterological attribute" elicited by avoidance.

The Etiology of Shame in Kinship Avoidance

In 1916, Elsie Clews Parsons published a seductively simple theory of "Avoidance in Melanesia" in the *Journal of American Folklore*. Her analysis echoes that of E.B. Tylor – both employ a strategy of frontal (us/them) comparison (after Candea, 2019) to render avoidance natural for their readers.[5] She explains in-law avoidances by recourse to the psychological attitude that anyone (the author and reader included) might have to the arrival of "new-comers into the family" (Parsons, 1916, p. 288). Her argument proceeds by reducing institutional rule to instinctive reaction: "It is indeed only necessary to glance at the particulars of avoidance to appreciate the instinctive character of the 'rules,' – to turn your back on a man, to go around him, not to go into a house where he is, not to look him in the eye, can behavior be more instinctive?" (p. 288). Here the naturalization of avoidance as an autonomic, affective response is so complete that even the anthropologist herself becomes blind to its sociocultural mediation, ceding all explanatory power to personal psychology.[6]

There is something that rings true in Parsons's argument. "Shame" is far and away the most common English translation given by ethnographers for native terms employed in both characterizing the experience of avoidance relationship and in rationalizing the cause of avoidance practices (e.g., Tokelau: Huntsman, 1971; Apinayé: Da Matta, 1982; Trumai: Murphy & Quain, 1955; Futuna: Burrows, 1936; Mardudjara: Tonkinson, 1978; Gooniyandi: McGregor, 1989; Bininj Gunwok: Garde, 2008b; Melpa: M. Strathern, 1972; etc.). So, for instance, a newly married Mehinaku (Xingu River; Brazil) man, living in his wife's parents' residence and under obligations of bride service to them, is "chronically ashamed" in their presence (Gregor, 1977, p. 283). And the interpersonal avoidances prototypic of the relationship have all the hallmarks of shame displays: A son-in-law fastidiously avoids the area where his parents-in-law's hammocks are hung and where they do their cooking. He moves away from the door when they enter the house, and he schedules "his day to reduce the chances of meeting" them. He never makes physical contact with them and if he wishes to pass them an object he will place it on the ground rather than directly hand it to them. He "looks down and to the side in their presence so that their eyes seldom meet." A "sense of shame" (*iaipiripyai*) suffuses the son-in-law/parent-in-law relationship, and "the respect and avoidance associated with the role must be kept permanently in mind" (p. 283).

The Mehinaku are not alone. Shame is consistently the mood (sign) elicited by the discursive or interactional presencing of avoidance relations cross-culturally. And "shame" is the reason that informants most often give for their avoidance practices.[7] Although the enactment of avoidance is read as relational respect, the emotional quality of experience most often described as accompanying avoidance practice is that of shame, embarrassment, or even fear. Shame is an essential experiential quality of the "total orientation."

And yet even if shame is often talked about by cultural participants as the cause of avoidance, Parsons's argument can be only partly right. For one thing, the sequencing of cause and effect – the presentation of shame as the cause of actions like turning away or hiding the face – fails to account for the conventionalized and standardized character of avoidance. It fails to capture the idea that to employ plural pronouns, to step off a path, or to avert one's eyes at the approach of an avoidance relation – these are registered as respectful acts appropriate to particular kin relations. Shame is the expected and elicited experiential quality of being in avoidance relationship, not its quasi-natural psychological source, and certainly not one emerging from a lack of familiarity with the other. In certain places, like northern India, an in-marrying bride may indeed be a "newcomer into the family." But in Melanesia and Australia, where avoidance is often the most sustained over the lifecourse, the establishment of affinal relations typically involves a reclassification of prior patterns of relating, not the integration of "strangers" into the family. The discrete establishment of an avoidance relationship, with, for instance, the rite of betrothal, involves the active and valued estrangement of relationship (Shapiro, 1970; Wagner, 1977). Far from pre-given strangers, affines are made through the suspension of prior modes of relating.

Why, then, are avoidance relations ashamed in one another's, if only sensorially spectral, presence? Why is kinship avoidance so often symbolized through the sentiment of shame? Shame is entangled with kinship avoidance in at least three ways:

1. Shame is the characterological abduction (or learning) generated out of the practice of registered avoidance. Shame is easily read off of the semiotic of avoidance-as-honorification detailed in Part 4. The social disengagement and withdrawal characteristic of shame-displays have formal similarities to the anti-phatic repertoires of kinship avoidance registers. Characteristic of shame is an aversion to interpersonal interaction – the ashamed individual withdraws from the social scene, looks away from the reproving gaze of the other, and shies away from participating in collective activities.[8] But of course these are all signs also enregistered as emblems of respect in kinship registers. Cultural participants appear to rationalize avoidance in terms of shame – to apperceive avoidance as a manifestation of shame – because of the formal overlap and similarity between the anti-phatic rituals that are associated with both. Through this pathway, the sentiment of shame emerges as a widely shared, interpretive framework that renders intelligible what I have referred to as "the phatic supplement of avoidance" (see the last section of Chapter 8).
2. The lived experience of avoidance relationship as shame hypertrophies the anti-phatic repertoire of the avoidance register. Registered signs of avoidance, under a cultural framing, elicit "shame" as the appropriate experiential mode of being in avoidance relationship. But inasmuch as qualities of shame are actual dimensions of the lived experience of relationship, there should also be a reciprocal effect. Just as avoidance elicits shame (as its *interpretation*), so too does shame elicit avoidance (as its *representation*). Heightened feelings of shame may (schismogenetically) condition exaggerated shame displays, providing source materials for the further enregisterment of signs of avoidance. Diachronically, the anti-phatic repertoires of kinship avoidance registers are likely hypertrophied through this feedback relationship. Shame is read off of registered avoidance, but it also feeds into it.
3. The sentiment of shame emblematizes avoidance as a mode of being for the other. Because shame necessarily involves the other's evaluation and perception of oneself, it powerfully elicits other-oriented regard and reciprocity, the life force of affinal relationships (particularly in bride-service societies [Merlan, 1997]). Symbolized through the sentiment of shame, the practice of avoidance comes to speak

not only to *this* or *that* relationship but to "relationalism" (after Robbins, 1994) as a supervening cultural value, as such.

It is to these resonances of the sentiment of "shame" as a symbol of difference-respecting, other-oriented relating to which I now turn.

The Sentiment of Shame

In analyzing the "shame" of kin avoidance, one must be careful not to assimilate ritualized avoidance to the shyness, pathologized as "social anxiety," felt by some in stranger social interaction in "our" sociocultural worlds. (One should also avoid Tylor's [1889] mistake of assimilating it to shunning, giving the cold shoulder, or "cutting" someone off.) Side-stepping psychosocial reductionism, I will approach shame as a sentiment, in the sense in which Lila Abu-Lughod (1986) uses the term: "I use the term *sentiment* rather than *emotion* or *affect* specifically to signal the literary or conventional nature of these responses.... I intend to show that sentiments can actually symbolize values and that expression of these sentiments by individuals contributes to representations of the self, representations that are tied to morality, which in turn is ultimately tied to politics in its broadest sense" (p. 34). The "shame" so often attached to avoidance relationships is a sentiment in just this sense. It is a crucial component of the collective representation of avoidance as "otherness-focused" (Stasch, 2009, p. 12) relationship. And as such, it does have moral and even political resonances (see Heald, 1990, on Gisu kinship morality). But what is it about the structure of shame as sentiment that makes it so fecund for symbolizing values of intersubjective relationship and kinship morality?

The shame of avoidance stands in an interdiscursive relationship with "everyday" shame – with shame as an experience that has as its object a discrete series of biographical events and their wider social evaluation. Brenda Johnson Clay (1977) draws this connection in her discussion of the most focal Mandak (New Ireland) avoidance relationship, the one between cross-sex siblings (or *minmin*). In speaking about this relationship, Mandak invariably invoke *emangai* "shame" (Tok Pisin *sem*):

> The word may refer to a person's sensitivity to and embarrassment about immoral actions in a role, relationship, or situation. A person can "have shame" because of a violation of normative prescriptions in a role. The concept may also be involved in descriptions of the "quality" of normative interactions in a category or situation. For example, a common expression about the minmin relationship was: "I have shame toward my minmin."

In this expression, a person is not confessing to an immoral act, but is indicating a sensitivity to restrictions on minmin interaction. (p. 94)

Although "avoidance" shame is parasitic upon "everyday" shame, there are important differences between the two. In the context of kinship avoidance, the enactment of signs of avoidance, like turning away from the other or not eating in the presence of the other, are apperceived as materializations of shame (they are "qualia" of shame, in the sense of Harkness, 2015). Here shame is a positively valued quality of experience. Conversely, the shame that arises from the contingent violation of social mores is negatively valued. Catherine Thompson (1981) underscores this double valence of shame in her penetrating analysis of Hindi *sharm* "shame/shyness" in a rural Hindu village in 1970s Madhya Pradesh, India. Her informants tell her that "there is good and bad *sharm*." In the context of gendered affinal relations, *sharm* is a positively valued quality exuded by the "good daughter-in-law": "A young married woman who leaves the house only for work, and who goes about her work silently, refraining from answering back to members of the household will be praised. 'She has so much *sharm*.' ... In contrast, the young married woman who quarrels with her mother-in-law and talks freely with men, will be criticised as *besharm* (without *sharm*), thus with respect to the daughter-in-law *sharm* is evaluated positively" (p. 43). Contrastingly, should a woman run away with a man, "the matter becomes 'a thing of *sharm*'" (p. 43). Here, where *sharm* is linked to a particular event of norm violation, it has a negative valuation.

Negatively valued, "everyday" shame has some particular event (e.g., of theft, adultery, etc.) as its object. In avoidance relationships, contrastingly, positively valued shame saturates the experience of mutual accessibility to the other. Here the precipitating cause of shame is blurred, for that cause is, in some sense, the relationship itself, so it is impossible to remedy or remove. Among the multiple topics that should not be discussed in the presence of Kalapalo in-laws is the topic of in-law relationships (Basso, 2007) – the relationship itself is shameful/shame-filled. Similarly, Usen Barok spouses conceal their marriages by not widely publicizing them and delaying cohabitation: "Avoidance, in other words, extends to the admission of the fact of marriage itself; it is a 'taboo' subject" (Wagner, 1986a, p. 58).

Importantly, as shame comes to saturate the avoidance relationship, it becomes detached from a specific precipitating event or incident and becomes a diffuse and general condition of the relationship as such. Thus abstracted away from local, precipitating causes, the schematic structure of shame is foregrounded. It is that schematic structure which makes shame such a uniquely apt sentiment for symbolizing "otherness-focused" relating. To explicate that schematic structure, let me draw on another ethnographic description of everyday shame, once again from New Ireland ethnography:

> For the Lelet, shame lies not in the commission of forbidden acts but in their disclosure or revelation. To disclose, *asu*, signifies the movement from the inside which is hidden, to the outside which is not. People who commit adultery, for instance, feel no sense of embarrassment or shame so long as it remains hidden. But should an adulterer's or a thief's deeds be revealed, he or she will experience great shame, and will embody the typical disposition of bowed head and avoidance of other people. (Eves, 1998, p. 132)

The structure of "everyday" shame thus presupposes three events: (1) a narrated event [E^n] of norm violation, (2) a narrated speech (or cognitive) event [E^{ns}] of disclosure (or realization) whereby the other comes to epistemic awareness of the precipitating event, and (3) the here-and-now experience [E^s] of shame of the wrongdoer who knows that the other knows about their norm violation: "I know [E^s] that he/she has come to know [E^{ns}] of the wrong I committed [E^n]." For the ashamed, co-presence with the other is unbearable, because the other has become a sign of my wrongdoing. It is only with the ritual removal of the shame that social intercourse with the other can be re-established.

Jean-Paul Sartre (2003) argues that "shame" is particularly potent for thinking our being with respect to others. Shame, "rather than merely being a self-reflective emotion, an emotion involving negative self-evaluation, is an emotion that reveals our relationality, our being-for-others" (D. Zahavi, 2012, p. 306). This quality of shame is exploited in the symbolization of kinship relationship. In avoidance relationships, the schematic structure of the sentiment of shame, now imbued with a positive valuation, serves to symbolize the being-toward-others that avoidance, as an interaction ritual, is supposed to foster and enact. There is a symbolic surplus value of shame; avoidance relatives live the emotion in order to symbolize the relationship through the sentiment.

In Euro-American philosophical and social-scientific discourse, social alienation, marginalization, and exclusion are often framed as inherent attributes of shame (e.g., Goffman, 1986; Nussbaum, 2006). Shame is localized in the individual – as, for instance, "stigma" – rather than in relationship. The positive valuation of the shame in avoidance relationships suggests the cultural relativity of this interpretation. For communities that hold relations to have primacy over persons (after Robbins,

1994), the sentiment of shame is often understood and actualized not just as exclusion but as a valued connection.

"Our skins are joined": Sex and Its Opposite

"Avoidance" shame as opposed to "everyday" shame is relatively diffuse; lacking a clear precipitating cause, it saturates the relationship. Nevertheless, in the collective representation of avoidance, sex is a recurring theme (see Pans, 1998, pp. 80–2 for a number of examples). This is not universal; there are cases where a sexual dimension to shame is not foregrounded. Among Kalapalo and Mehinaku (Xingu River; Brazil), it is the investment of resources which the wife's parents have put into her upbringing that are invoked as the cause of the son-in-law's shame before his parents-in-law (Basso, 2007; Gregor, 1977). Nevertheless, the sexual thematic is a remarkably recurrent one (Hiatt, 1984; Pans, 1998).

In order to understand the figure of sex within the larger social semiotic of avoidance, the temptation to reduce kinship avoidance to sexual regulation and repression must be resisted. That is, one must resist simply seeing sex as the cause of avoidance. This was precisely the functionalist reduction that guided Freud's (1918) analysis in *Totem and Taboo*. There he wrote of avoidance "'customs'" (the scare quotes were his) that "are maintained with almost religious severity and of whose object there can hardly be any doubt" (p. 26). That "object" was the "protection against possible incest" (p. 35). The son-in-law's avoidance of the mother-in-law was to be understood as rooted in the displacement of a repressed sexual desire for his mother "and perhaps of his sister" (p. 34). As a consequence, the mother-in-law "represents an incest temptation for the son-in-law" (p. 35).[9]

Even if one grants the existence of unconscious "internalized sanctions" against incest, "customs" cannot be mere algorithmic transforms of them. This is because customs always have a reflexive and meta-semiotic dimension. And, as such, they symbolize with and through unconscious dispositions or innate biases, but toward multiple and potentially contradictory ends.

Brother–sister avoidance poses particular difficulties for the sexual repression thesis. There is now a large and convincing body of empirical evidence in support of the so-called Westermarck effect – the idea that "early association inhibits sexual attraction" and that this bias is biologically based (Wolf, 2004, p. 5). Confusingly, ethnologists have rejected the Westermarck effect on the grounds that it would be redundant given the existence of registered sexual avoidances (i.e., the "incest taboo"). (Wolf rightly calls this a "functionalist fundamentalism" [p. 5].) To my perspective, the acceptance of the existence of a biological basis for incest avoidance strengthens the culturalist, rather than the psychologistic, interpretation of avoidance. If there is a biologically based bias against brother–sister incest, one must take even more seriously the symbolic dimensions of the elaborate pageantry of cross-sex sibling avoidance relationships. Where its would-be functional utility is absent, one must seek out its symbolic surplus value.[10]

Functionalist theories of the supposed sexual causes of kinship avoidance do not hold up under scrutiny. If anything, culture (through avoidance) amplifies the sexual question precisely where nature (through evolved aversion) mutes it. Staying with the analysis of avoidance as a social semiotic, how then should one understand the salience of sex for cultural participants? Why is sex so often invoked as the final and phantasmagoric object of shame as it is experienced in avoidance relationship?

To answer this question, I will channel the sensibility concerning corporeal contact which informed my discussion of sensorial and corporeal mutuality in Chapter 6. Heterosexual intercourse blurs the boundaries between bodies at the very site of their sexed difference. Heterosexual intercourse is a rite of joining differentiated bodies and, through them, groups. Viewed through this lens, the incest taboo – understood as a moral code rather than a natural fact – is about making sexual difference symbolize social difference (Wagner, 1972). Conversely, the spousal relation gathers together that which is at once both social and sexual difference. It obviates (overcomes, sublates, transcends) that difference through sexual reproduction (Wagner, 1986b, p. 138). For these reasons, sex serves as an epitomizing emblem of intersensorial and intercorporeal mutuality across ontological difference. Avoidance, as a ritual practice of keeping separate in sensory experience that which is socially differentiated, stands as the counterpoint to sexual intercourse and parturition.

Sex represents an exception to our claim that avoidance signs are constitutive of relationships, not of relations (see Introduction). In fact, heterosexual intercourse *is* often understood to be performatively transformative of social ontologies. The Kaulong (New Britain), for instance, have only one word, *nangin*, for "sex" and "marriage." Sex does not just consummate marriage; it is the transformative rite. Is it any wonder that it is in the surround of the spousal relation that avoidance – the maintenance of separation and difference – is most fully emphasized? Avoidance is most pronounced in the surround of those "linking" relations where persons go into and come out of one another. For in sex and childbirth, two become one and one becomes two.

The Lelet (New Ireland) are quite explicit on this point. As with the neighbouring Mandak, the cross-sex sibling (or *minmin*) relation is the focal hue of kinship avoidance. Upon marriage, avoidance is extended to the spouse of the cross-sex sibling, the *laramasik* "same-sex sibling in-law." Importantly, the enactment of avoidance between *laramasik* draws upon the same symbolic idioms that govern the cross-sex *minmin* relation. In the *minmin* relationship, the clothes or body of the female may not be positioned above the male, for "this means figuratively that her genitals are above his eyes and within his gaze," involuntarily causing desire (Eves, 1998, p. 130). In the *laramasik* relation, the man who is having sex with a man's sister occupies this female role within the frame of the relationship. An informant explains to Richard Eves that the sexual relation causes this gender switch, saying, "'the skin of myself and my wife is one, it is joined' and 'our skins are joined' ... To have married and slept together, means that the body of the spouses has become consubstantial, and their personhood merged" (p. 130). As concerns a woman's husband, from the perspective of her brother, "he is ... she" (p. 131).

Why is sex so crucial to the collective representation of kinship avoidance? The sexual thematic simultaneously objectifies the two kinds of ontological difference – the categorical and the phenomenological – which, in kinship avoidance, are brought together through their being kept separate. Sex emblematizes the overcoming of categorical difference through reproduction. And phenomenologically, it intimately involves the mutuality of touch, which, as argued in Chapter 6, sits at the apex of the "hierarchy of modes of sensory avoidance" (Stasch, 2003).[11] If avoidance keeps separate that which is different, sex achieves the opposite. Correspondingly, the mutuality of intercorporeal touch represents the inverse of the mental impingement and preoccupation characteristic of the "total orientation." Compare the flow of intercorporeality perhaps most characteristic of intense nurturant relations between caregivers and infants with the avoidance relation – unseen, untouched, but spectrally present: the mutual being of the senses versus the mutual sense that the other being is near.

A Shared Experience: Of Kinship Categorical and Phenomenological

Two kinds of ontology – one categorical and the other phenomenological – are brought together in kinship avoidance. Put differently, a difference of being in one mode is alchemically realized as a difference of being in the other. For instance, a difference by virtue of social categorization is realized as – and revealed to be – a difference of being by

Table C.1. Joking and avoidance symbolized through their association with dimensions of social categorical identity and difference

Avoidance	Joking
• relations through marriage • adjacent-generation kin (G$^{-5,-3,-1,+1,+3,+5}$) • different-sex kin PROTOTYPE: different-sex, parent-in-law / child-in-law (e.g., Merlan, 1997; Mitchell, 2018)	• natal relations • alternating-generation kin (G$^{-4,-2,0,+2,+4}$) • same-sex kin PROTOTYPE: same-sex, grandparent / grandchild (e.g., Garde, 2008b; R. Parkin, 1988)

virtue of embodied experience. It is kinship register and lived relationship that mediate this alchemy, whereby categorical and phenomenological ontology are titrated in just such quantities and combinations that the one appears as the holographic projection of the other.

Categorical Ontology: Joking-avoidance is stereotypically associated with kin categories and the semantic features underlying those categories (see Table C.1; see also the last section of Chapter 3). Cross-culturally, avoidance is associated with relations of categorical difference – difference of social gender, clan group membership, or relative generation – and joking is associated with categorical identity. As we saw with the honorific pronoun data from Manus and Kobon (see Chapter 7), increased markedness for "features" of categorical difference is correlated with a progressive raising of avoidance levels.

Through the suturing of avoidance levels to kinship categories, avoidance is symbolized as a practice of keeping separate and guarding the integrity of categorical difference – as a ritual practice that concerns the incommensurability of the essential identities of the members of the dyad.

Phenomenological Ontology: At the same time, avoidance is an end in itself, a means of forestalling a shared existential being. At the level of (interaction) ritual practice, avoidance realizes the incommensurability of the phenomenological experience of the members of the dyad. The "mutuality of being" (Sahlins, 2013) characteristic of the avoidance relationship relies upon the denial of being mutually present to one another. Avoidance relatives don't talk to or touch one another, they don't "make contact" or "connect with" one another. But at another level their experience is incommensurable with respect to particular objects and subjects. Avoidance relatives do not share a joke, share a laugh, share a meal, share a smoke – they avoid the shared experience of the same qualities and percepts. Interpersonal taboos create "a "hole" in

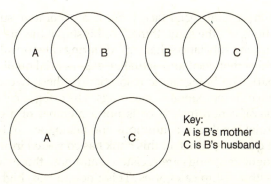

Figure C.1. Spheres of (un)shareable experience

the texture of shareable intersubjective reality," which, in its negativity, is constitutive of the dyad's mutual being (Gell, 1996, p. 118).

Importantly, intense modes of co-presence figure in the surround (and in the often sexually thematized imaginary) of avoidance relatives. In the most focal avoidance relationships, it is often the irreducible difference in how avoidance relatives "presence" a particular third person – the linking relation – that is at issue. Take the mother-in-law/son-in-law relation that is so often the most focal avoidance relationship in Australia and Melanesia. The relation that links these two persons is a woman who is at once a daughter born from her mother's womb and nursed at her breast and a wife joined to her husband's skin. These are relations (wife–husband and mother–daughter) in which the categorically different (woman–man, adult–infant) is involved in intense modes of kinship-performative intercorporeal and intersensorial presencing. It is in the relationship between those linked to one another through this woman – that is, in the relationship between her husband and her mother – that conjoined experience must be forestalled through ritual avoidances. These two do not look at each other, do not eat together, do not touch each other. These two cannot (fully) be together. (As represented visually in Figure C.1, their spheres of experience do not overlap.) It is as if, in order to conserve their differently intense modes of sensual and corporeal mutuality with one and the same person, these two must themselves never fully be present to one another (cf. Héritier, 1994). Paradoxically, this other-abnegation is a shared experience. It is an experience made mutual not by what is jointly beheld (presence) but by what is similarly withheld.

In kinship as a total social fact, there is a generative subsuming of two descriptions of "the same thing," of kinship either as (1) relations between or among substance-sharing/-differing categorical kinds, or as (2) relationships that elicit and actualize experiential qualities of being together/apart. The holographic resolution of these two descriptions combines two different kinds of meanings. The categorical is a discrete system of classification (one is or is not a member of a given class). The experiential involves a continuous and analogue – or by-degrees – activation of qualities. Much of this book has consisted in an exposition of how analogue meanings are registered and how those meanings are associated with kinship categories. This fine-grained, high-magnification, and technical analysis was necessary; it enables us to see how the socioculturally structured experience of relationship breathes life into kin categories and, reciprocally, how the experience of being together/apart is given its deep significance because of the way in which it invokes, as its "cosmic context" (after Silverstein, 2004), a cultural framework of social kinds and their modes of transformation into and out of one another.

The kinship register approach, augmented by the Bateson-Wagner theory of elicitative relationship, suggests an alchemical understanding of kinship where it is the transformation of categorical-being into phenomenological-being, and vice versa, that is emphasized. This understanding is motivated by the particular empirical materials that I have worried over. There are certainly many aspects of, and perspectives on, kinship that it will not sufficiently capture (for instance, the political economy of kinship). It is intended as another description of the phenomenon, by no means a final or definitive one (even if it is offered in the form of a definition):

Kinship (institution of): an interlocking set of reflexively symbolized, enacted, and elicited relationships which realize categorical identity and difference *as* phenomenological experience, as modes, moods, and meanings of being together/apart.

The "old kinship studies" (Shapiro, 2008) located the essence of kinship in frameworks of categorical relatedness ultimately grounded in filiation. The "new kinship studies" has turned away from category and toward shared experiences of being-with. The kinship register approach suggests a dialectical relationship between the (pragmatic) experiential living out of relationship, on the one hand, and the reflexive (metapragmatic) symbolization of kinds of categorical relatedness and of the signs that are indexical or iconic of them, on the other.

This is, to be sure, an analytical purification. Nevertheless, distinguishing the categorical and the phenomenological is heuristic. First, it stops us from falling back into thinking of relationship as a function of degrees of co-presencing. There is no pure presence (e.g., of the skin-to-skin) that precedes "inscription" in a register. Practices of being-with are registered signs that materialize experiential qualities as a function of the categorical relatedness of the persons involved. They are motivated signs because they dialectically emerge out of the modes of contact – visual, haptic, auditory – by which humans interact with one another. But this "natural" basis does not mean that their experiential realization is culturally unmediated. Second, it stops us from falling back into a conception of kinship as essentially a social-categorical grid and grammar – just the facts, with no values – upon which social norms of comportment are laminated. Again, the miracle of kinship is its differentiation of the human universe. And this can be achieved only by the alchemical operation that invests category with experiential meanings.

Notes

Introduction: The Total Orientation

1 The same interaction rituals were practiced – though on an optional basis, typically where they felt a strong connection – between cross-sex cousins. A fuller analysis would have to include these mirror image avoidances, associated with the natal family of a man. See Opler (1937, pp. 193–8) for the relevant discussion.
2 Interestingly, the question of what causes avoidances to be present in one society but not in another has been answered. Driver (1966) conducted a rigorous comparative survey of kinship avoidances. He found, as had Lowie (1920) before him, that the best explanation for the presence of avoidance in a given culture is phylogenetic descent from or diffusionary contact with a culture that practiced avoidance. That is, most people practice avoidance because they have been exposed to practices of avoidance. But of course this isn't the kind of final cause that grand theorists were looking for. Above all, Freud-influenced mid-century comparativists were almost certain that avoidance could, in the end, be reduced to sexual repression.
3 Jakobson (1960) defined the phatic function as the "function of language" concerned with the communicative or psychological channel or "contact" that links interlocutors (see Zuckerman, 2020, for an overview). The phatic function is manifest in "messages primarily serving to establish, to prolong, or to discontinue communication, to check whether the channel works, ('Hello, do you hear me?'), to attract the attention of the interlocutor or to confirm his continued attention" (Zuckerman, 2020, p. 355). My thanks to Courtney Handman and James Slotta for discussions of "phatic infrastructures." Phaticity is discussed in more depth in Chapters 5 and 6.
4 Murdock's lasting disciplinary heritage has been the Human Relations Area Files, which were a great asset in conducting this study because of the way in which they have enabled searches of the ethnographic archive.

5 Stephens (1962; quoted in Driver, 1966, p. 134), building upon Murdock's (1967) sample (as well as his Freudian interpretation of avoidance), revised his scale by listing actual behaviours:

1. No avoidance rules.
2. Can't talk about sex.
3. Can't talk directly.
4. Can't eat together; can't look eye-to-eye: 1 of these avoidance rules present.
5. Can't eat together; can't look eye-to-eye: both of these avoidance rules present.

The inclusion of a set of actual practices is an advance over Murdock. The method is still fundamentally confused; particular signs (e.g., not talking, not eating together, etc.) are still understood as having intrinsic (transcultural) values (e.g., of formality, shame, respect, etc.), rather than being structurally related to one another culture-internally.

6 For instance, the making of a heterosexual marital pair may involve a corresponding unmaking of a cross-sex sibling pairing (Clay, 1977, on Mandak; R. Lee, 1993, on Ju|'hoan; Aberle, 1961, on Navajo). As an example, take Navajo brother-sister avoidance, a practice that literally involves un-dual-ing: "Once a brother and sister have passed puberty, they may not use the dual form of the verb to one another, or refer to joint activities they have carried out.... At least traditionally a brother and sister were not to hand objects to one another. This prohibition was stringent when both were married, weaker if only one was married, and inoperative if both were single" (Aberle, 1961, p. 151). For similar cases, see the discussion of "semantic echoes" in Chapter 7.

7 See, *inter alios*, Ball, 2015; Basso, 1975, 2007; Choksi, 2021; N. Evans, 2003a, 2003b; Garde, 2013; Haviland, 1979a, 1979b; Herbert, 1990; Kim, 2018a, 2018b; King, 2001; Laughren, 2001; McConvell, 1982; McGregor, 1989; Merlan, 1982a, 1997; Mitchell, 2015; 2018; Rumsey, 1982, 1990; Rushforth, 1981; Storch, 2011; Sutton, 1978; Treis, 2005.

8 On the fourth person as honorific in Navajo, see Willie (1991, p. 112) and Witherspoon (1977, p. 84).

9 Opler worked with Chiricahua Apache at the Mescalero Apache Reservation, New Mexico. A group of Chiricahua Apache took up residence there, at the consent of local Mescalero Apache, after being finally released from imprisonment; the US Government had held the Chiricahua Apache at Ft. Sill, Oklahoma, as prisoners of war for 27 years (Webster, 2021, p. 469). Opler also worked with Jicarilla Apache in northern New Mexico, on Jicarilla Apache Reservation lands.

10 Kinship avoidance registers are a special class of honorific registers. Their honorific character can be attested both at the level of metapragmatic characterization and at the level of pragmatic function. So, for instance, the Zulu term employed for in-law avoidances, *hlonipha*, is translated as

"respect-thru-avoidance" (cf. the ethnometapragmatic designator for the Zulu daughter-in-law register, *isi-hlonipha sabafazi*, "women's language of respect-through-avoidance") (Herbert, 1990). At the level of pragmatic function, kinship avoidances, like honorific vocabularies, have a **relational indexical focus** relating some **origo of deference** (the person who defers) to some **target of deference** (the person who is deferred to) (Agha, 1993; Fleming, 2014a, 2022; Irvine, 2009). (Contrast here to the non-relational, or "absolute," indexical focus of sociolects as markers of speaker identity [terminology adapted from Levinson, 1983].) The continuities between avoidance speech and honorific speech, as well as the framework of indexical focus, are discussed in detail in Part 4.

11 After marriage, a man would move into the *gò·tàh* or "encampment" of his wife's family – a group of residences sheltering a set of sisters and their families as well as their parents and unmarried brothers. This was a crucial moment of transition, for it was with betrothal and the taking up of co-residence in his wife's encampment that the tenor and tone of the in-marrying man's relationships with his wife's kin were cast. As in many other historically foraging societies (Collier & Rosaldo, 1981; Merlan, 1997; M. Strathern, 1985), beginning with betrothal to a woman, a man was obliged to provide "bride service" to her parents for the rest of their lives – even if his wife should pass away before them. This is reflected in the kin terms that are employed for relatives through marriage – a man calls them "one for whom I carry burdens" and they call him "one who carries burdens for me" (Opler, 1937, p. 214). "Ask any Chiricahua for whom a man should work," Opler (1937, p. 213) writes, "and his immediate answer is, 'For his mother-in-law and his father-in-law.'"

12 Avoidance levels are the distinct ensembles of signs (e.g., impersonal pronoun) that substitute for signs normatively avoided (e.g., personal pronouns) in enacting distinct kinship relationships within a given language-in-culture. Part 4 of the book seeks to articulate an understanding of convergent patterning in the global, structural organization of avoidance levels. The discussion of "implicational relationships between avoidances," below, begins that work. The term *avoidance levels* is intended to resonate with *speech levels*, a term used in the sociolinguistic literature to describe linguistic registers that instantiate a minimally three-way honorific contrast. Speech-level systems are thus a set of empirical materials that help us to think about analogue or gradient indexical functions. As we will see, this is crucial in developing our understanding of kinship avoidance. The best-studied speech-level systems are the lexical honorific registers of a group of Austronesian languages spoken in Indonesia (specifically, Balinese, Sundanese, Madurese, Javanese, and Sasak). See Fleming (2016) for a survey and overview. Joseph Errington's (1985, 1988)

work on Javanese has been foundational for understanding speech-level systems from a semiotic-functional perspective.

13 Because these "purely pragmatic," or "cultural," structures are oriented toward nonreferentially indexical and iconic modes of signalling, they pattern in quite different ways than do the language structures that undergird symbolic reference and predication (Silverstein, 1976). And given that "icons and indexes in themselves 'assert nothing'" (Peirce, as cited in Keane, 2003, p. 419, as cited in Manning, 2012, p. 11), their significations are particularly dependent upon shared interpretive frameworks – that is, upon social and semiotic ideologies. These ideologies rationalize what occurrences of signs accomplish and locate such accomplishments within a social context. Because of the way in which they inform events of sign production and interpretation, these ideological frameworks feed back into the structuring of pragmatic signs (Silverstein, 1979, 1985). As shown throughout the book, it is the dance between structure and ideology, played out through the mediations of practice, that gives kinship avoidance registers their cross-culturally convergent properties.

14 Of the three layers of pragmatic structure to which I have alluded, this is the layer that I have studied least. More research is needed on the topic of interrelationships between avoidances. There is at least one documented case where joking-like and avoidance-like comportments are mixed, though here there is clearly a reflexively appreciated, interdiscursive relationship with more canonical in-law avoidance (see Stasch, 2002, on ritualized name-sharing friendships among Korowai; see also Elkin, 1950, for a similar institution in northern Australia).

15 To get a flavour for *taraŋa pariki*, the following two episodes can be cited. In one, Firth was in the midst of writing down a bawdy tale "containing some rather frank anatomical details," when the narrator's father entered the house. "'My father has come; we will finish it another time,' he murmured, adding in parentheses, 'In this land father and son do not talk thus'" (Firth, 1937, p. 172). In another, Firth is walking with Ariki Kafika (i.e., the chief) when they come upon a group of men all related to each other and to Kafika as classificatory brothers. "With one accord they fell upon each other with obscene chaff. Epithets of 'Big testicles!' 'You are the enormous testicles!' flew back and forth to the accompaniment of hilarious laughter" (pp. 189–90).

16 For examples of implicational chaining of specifically joking comportments, see D. Thomson (1935) and Drucker-Brown (1982).

17 For an example of naturally occurring metadiscourses of commensuration, take the Kalapalo (Carib; Brazil) concept of *ifútisu* "respect." Through the "enactment of ... norms" like the sharing of personal possessions, labour, and food, and through the reputational defence of the other, natal kin

index their respect "for one another" (Basso, 1975, p. 210). Such respect is upgraded in the affinal context: Kin through marriage must enact "intense behavioral constraint," which they characterize as *ifútisu ékugu* "strong respect" (p. 208). This "*ifútisu ékugu* is a special marked relationship that affines should have with each other, one that goes far beyond the relatively diffuse *ifútisu* ('respect') that should prevail among all Kalapalo and especially among kinsmen" (p. 226). I do not have smoking-gun proof for feedback from meta-semiotic modelling like this into the pragmatic structuring of object-signs. Nevertheless, such a link appears highly probable. Metadiscourses of commensuration presuppose the "qualic transitivity" (after Harkness, 2013) of pragmatic signs. That is, such metadiscourses frame diverse semiotic media as manifestations of the same qualities – here, the relational quality of respect. For more on this theme, see the discussion of the cross-modal experience of the "quale" of tactility in Korowai avoidances in Chapter 5.

1. Avoidance Lexicon, Everyday Grammar: Why Words Are Good to Proscribe

1 One of the only candidates for a kinship-keyed, avoidance speech register of this kind outside of Australia is the kinship register described for Yélî Dnye (non-Austronesian; Rossel Island, Papua New Guinea): "There is a taboo vocabulary to be used in the presence of in-laws, tabooed or *choko* kinsmen ... this involves substituting special words for numerous words denoting body parts, clothing and personal possessions" (Levinson, 2006, p. 231). Although this description suggests a context-dependent rule of use, the lexical classes affected (inalienable nouns) and the ubiquity of possessive marking referring to taboo in-laws in the examples provided by Levinson all suggest that the use of the vocabulary also depends upon discourse reference – that is, it appears that the substitute terms are used only when reference is made to the possessions, body parts, etc., of a taboo in-law (see also Armstrong, 1928, p. 54; Fleming 2014a, pp. 141–2; Simons, 1982, p. 214 for supporting evidence). Note that in many Australian languages (e.g., Dyirbal and Guugu Yimidhirr), the mother-in-law language is used in the co-presence of certain taboo in-laws regardless of the identity of the person to whom discourse reference is being made.

2 A few telegraphed examples must suffice to show that activity-based avoidance registers are rationalized through logics of discursive participation. Faroese *sjómál* "sea-language" was an avoidance style employed by fishermen based out of the Faroe Islands while at sea: "The use of secret words when handling hooks and lines would help to *confuse* unfriendly spirits intent on ruining the fishermen's chances. If the fish heard their names mentioned, they would be *warned* and swim away. On the other

hand, to speak openly of creatures known to be evilly disposed towards fishermen, such as whales, ravens and crows, was like *tempting* them to come along and cause trouble" (Lockwood, 1955, p. 2; italics added). Within local understandings, the use of everyday words while out at sea had undesirable perlocutionary effects; it "warned" the fish, "tempted" the whales. Activity-based avoidance registers often tropically reconfigure everyday reference as interpellative address. Among the Semai, the names of animals are tabooed while hunting, but also during both food preparation and the consuming and digesting of the animal (Diffloth, 1980). During these times, special substitute words should be used. At the level of language ideology, such avoidance is conceptualized as masking or concealing speech from a spectral overhearer, a vengeful animal spirit who will bring thunderstorms upon the hunters should it recognize their designs or desires to hunt or eat animals. Abkhaz (Caucasus) "forest language" (*àbna bèzsa*) was employed during hunting expeditions. It was understood to prevent "the prey [from having] any possibility of recognising the presence and intentions of the hunters" (Inal-Ipa, quoted in Khiba, 1980, p. 269). Matagi (Japan) "mountain vocabulary" (*yama kotoba*) was used while on long hunting expeditions, and again the special vocabulary was thought to "avoid disclosing to the animals ... hunted what [the hunters] planned to do" (Knight, 2007, p. 123). Among Puyuma (Taiwan), everyday terms of reference for animals of prey should not be used: "Animals possess ... sharp hearing. [Their] names are not pronounced, as otherwise 'they would flee'" (Cauquelin, 2004, p. 206). Sangir (Sangir Islands) "limit speech" (*sasahara*) was employed while fishing, but also during maritime warfare (Adriani, 1893). The register repertoire consisted of "hidden words" used "at sea so that the spirits of the sea will not be able to overhear and interfere with [the] plans or intentions" of the fishermen (Steller & Aebersold, translated in C.E. Grimes & Maryott, 1994, p. 286). Among the Kodi (Sumba Island), there is a belief that wild (but not domestic) animals can understand human language: "Hunters, knowing they can be overheard, use a special code of alternative words [*paneghe kalola* "hunting language"] ... to confuse their prey" (Hoskins, 1993). In these and other examples, the relationship between human predator and animal prey is consistently framed as one of potential discursive participation. A human–animal boundary may be ritually maintained by masking reference and thereby confounding the comprehension of animal alters. Alternatively, it may be bridged by supplicating animal others and tropically elevating them to human status (e.g., Matagi hunters use of *oyaji* "boss/old man/father" for *kuma* "bear"). The attribution of human capacities to animals, often predicated with verbs of cognition, in this and other cases might be productively interpreted in relation to the perspectivist realization of human–animal relationships common to many cultures (Brightman, 1993; Descola, 2005; Viveiros de Castro, 1992).

3 A few caveats must be appended to this generalization. On the question of phonological avoidances, one conspicuous counter-example is the Lardil male-initiate language, Damin, in which novel phonological segments are employed and particular everyday phonological segments are avoided. This is an exception that nevertheless proves the rule; phonological replacements are limited to lexical roots of the avoidance repertoire and do not apply to the bound morphology (i.e., to morphemes that can only occur when "bound" to other morphemes), which is shared with everyday Lardil (Hale & Nash, 1997). Fleming (2017a) is an extended treatment of this exceptional case. On the question of grammatical morphemes, the suppression of transitive morphology in Bunaba mother-in-law language offers a counter-example to the generalization (Rumsey, 1982; see further discussion of this case in Chapter 2).

4 Much like the famous gender registers of Yana (Sapir, 1985, pp. 206–12), gender indexicality in Yanyuwa is better characterized asymmetrically as a "men's language." Historically, categorical gender indexicality in Yanyuwa was achieved via a pragmaticization of semantic gender distinctions. Male speakers employed non-human masculine noun-class markers when referring to other men. See Fleming (2015a) for a reconstruction. The current speaker-indexing function is limited to the specific gender status of post-initiation men.

2. Many to One: Lexicon Asymmetries in Avoidance Registers

1 This chapter is a substantially revised and expanded version of a paper originally published in the *Journal of Linguistic Anthropology* (Fleming, 2015b). My thanks to the anonymous reviewers of the manuscript and to the *JLA* for publication permissions.

2 Here I must highlight an important difference between activity-based avoidance registers and Aboriginal Australian mother-in-law languages. Activity-based registers are almost always composed of vocabulary borrowed from the everyday language. The word-forms are the same as everyday vocabulary, but their semantic denotations are extended or otherwise reworked in avoidance speech. Mother-in-law languages, contrastingly, are almost exclusively composed of lexical forms that are not employed in everyday speech. Drawing upon a terminological distinction that will be introduced in Chapter 3, mother-in-law vocabulary items are "sociopragmatically marked" – they occur only in (voicing) avoidance speech. One possible explanation for the difference is that the use of a sociopragmatically marked vocabulary performs a signalling function for

third parties, one that isn't necessary in contexts where activity-specific avoidance registers are employed. Because individuals employ a formally distinct vocabulary in the co-presence of taboo in-laws, other co-present individuals, whether or not they are attentively listening to what is said, can infer that the speaker is in the presence of an avoidance relation. This may help third parties to the affinal interaction to adjust their own comportment accordingly, avoiding, for instance, obscene or aggressive talk. The discursive patterns observed by Francesca Merlan for Mangarayi communities suggest the validity of such an analysis (see also Warner 1964, pp. 99–102):

> Talk regarded as indecent, and the offer in one's presence of physical violence towards one's avoidance category relative, are considered sufficient reason in the area I know for the offended hearing relative to engage in wild and berserk behaviour, usually towards the offender. Of such incidents people say that they were mightily ashamed to hear their avoidance relatives sworn at or treated in that way, and could not do otherwise but act crazily. If anyone begins to talk in a jesting or obscene manner to one in the presence of, or within earshot of, one's avoidance relative(s), there is a conventionalised form of utterance which one may use to tell the offender to stop immediately, and which means simply, "You are shaming me." (Merlan, 1997, pp. 105–6)

Use of a formally distinct vocabulary may function as an advertisement or beacon, alerting bystanders to the co-presence of an avoidance dyad and thus to the need for circumspection in the local context. In cases of activity-specific context-dependent registers, all discursive participants are normatively expected to employ the register. There is little potential for conflicting interpretations of vocabulary items which have different meanings in everyday and avoidance speech. The global context of the discursive event (e.g., everyday Kalam as used in a hamlet versus pandanus language as used in the forest) cues the appropriate interpretive frame. Nevertheless, the "invisible hand" (after N. Evans, 2003b) processes that are driving this difference remain to be determined.

3 This principle of maximal register cohesion of avoidance speech contrasts with, for instance, mixing of honorific speech-level vocabularies in Island Southeast Asia (e.g., Javanese, Madurese, Sundanese, Balinese, Sasak). See Fleming (2015b) and Chapter 8 for a fuller exploration of this comparison.

4 Another source of evidence for this inference is the widespread finding that avoidance vocabulary items are on average longer than everyday vocabulary items (Crowley, 1983; Dixon, 1990; McGregor, 1989). For Gooniyandi, more than 90% of non-verbal and 98% of verbal roots are minimally bisyllabic in the mother-in-law language, whereas only 70% of everyday

lexical roots have more than one syllable (McGregor, 1989, p. 639). In Uradhi, 57% of everyday roots have two or fewer syllables, while only 13% of mother-in-law language words are that short.

Crowley (1983) suggests the "possibility ... that many of the avoidance terms may in fact be diachronically (or even synchronically) polymorphemic" (p. 385). He observes that quite a number of nouns have final syllables in -βi and -ŋu, "suggesting that they are derived from comitative ... and nominalising suffixes ... respectively" (p. 386). Dixon (1990) makes similar observations for Jalnguy avoidance lexemes that are not reconstructed as borrowings from neighbouring languages. In everyday Dyirbal and Yidiny, 75–80% of lexical roots have two syllables, while the rest have more. But in the avoidance repertoires, 50% of original (i.e., non-borrowed) vocabulary has more than two syllables (p. 51). It is likely that the greater word length of avoidance vocabulary reflects the dependence upon derivational morphology, word compounding, and periphrasis in the derivation of novel avoidance vocabulary under conditions of limited lexical resources.

However, both the word-length data and the compositional character of "non-nuclear" avoidance idioms may also reflect the relative lack of historical depth of the specialized register repertoire items as compared to their everyday counterparts. A common finding in historical linguistics is that newly coined expressions are, on average, phonologically longer and more morphologically analyzable than words and expressions with greater historical depth (Campbell, 2004, p. 414; Sapir, 1985, p. 434). Over time, words and expressions may be re-analyzed as morphologically simplex and may become phonologically clipped or otherwise shortened.

5 Recall that Lévy-Bruhl (1910), among many others, erroneously saw linguistic patterns of this kind as signs of a "primitive mentality" prisoner to a phenomenal and subjective experience that it cannot abstract away from (cf. Lévi-Strauss, 2021).

6 Avoidance register data should be of interest to ethnobiological linguistics. In the authoritative account of Berlin (1992), lexical form – in particular, the distinction between monomial and polynomial lexical coding of folktaxa – is understood to be a direct reflection of the cognitive salience of the folk-rank of an ethnobiological taxon. Folk-generics are seen as being "psychologically basic or salient" (C.H. Brown, 1984, p. 4); it is for this reason that they are coded with monomial expressions. In avoidance repertoires, however, folk-generic taxa, if labelled at all, are typically coded for by minimally binomial expressions, while monomial expressions typically denote taxa of intermediate or life-form rank. Contra Berlin (1992; see McKnight 1999, p. 154), these data suggest that the difference between monomial and polynomial lexical coding does not reflect cognitive/

perceptual biases – the same speakers, after all, employ both systems. Rather, these differences are structural facts *par excellence*. Like Saussure's famous example of the difference in the denotational range of English *mutton* (which exclusively covers the dead animal) and French *mouton* (which denotes the animal, alive or dead), differences of semantic specificity of monomial expressions across register varieties reflect differences in the number of monomial terms that are structurally opposed in the semantic "space" of ethnobiological denotation (Saussure 1995). Folk-generic terms cannot be borrowed from the everyday language because they are taboo. Under these conditions, the small number of monomial terms already registered as avoidance terms for folk-generics in an early phase of the historical development of the avoidance register get leaned upon in creating polynomial, descriptive paraphrases to refer to closely related folk-generics. Through this process, these select monomial terms essentially get shifted up one taxonomic level and come to denote the class of folk-generics for which they serve as the head noun in complex polynomial expressions. Although the conclusions that I draw are quite different from those which he draws, I follow David McKnight's (1999, p. 154) lead in using the avoidance register data to critique Berlin's theory of ethnobiological taxonomy. The reader interested in pursuing this point should consult the Lá'bì glossary in Vidal (1976, pp. 313–39).

7 Classifiers are ubiquitous in sign languages, and this has appropriately been understood as related to the affordances of the manual-visual modality with respect to the oral-aural one (Meier et al., 2002). However, lexical classifiers (i.e., nuclear or hypernymic nouns and verbs) also appear to be commonly employed in restricted spoken languages, like avoidance registers, as well as early in the development of writing systems. This raises the possibility that lexical classifiers are more robustly attested in younger linguistic varieties, where already fashioned lexical resources are forced to bear a higher functional load. The sign languages that have been the focus of most intensive study are relatively young – certainly when compared to spoken languages. (French Sign Language, which dates to the eighteenth century, is often cited as the oldest sign language.) Perhaps the prevalence of classifiers in sign languages is not only a modality effect but also related to the greater youth of these linguistic varieties with respect to spoken languages.

8 Chapter 7 discusses other fashions of speaking which similarly involve an iconic but nonreferential relationship between semantic and social pragmatic meanings, between denotational and interactional textuality. See, in particular, the discussion of "semantic echoes."

9 The lexical economy of the avoidance register, Lá'bì, is not only achieved through polysemous one-to-many semantic correspondences between the

avoidance and everyday lexicons. Yves Moñino (1977) illustrates through a range of rich examples that it is also accomplished by means of homonymous one-to-many phonolexical correspondences. For instance, in everyday Gbaya-Kara, *wàr* ("bean") and *wàrà* ("hoe") are near-homophones. In Lá'bì they are both rendered with *mbìzò*. Similarly, everyday *tòré* ("scorpion") and *tòrò* ("reed") are both translated into Lá'bì with *ndòké*. The use of these oral rebuses in the Gbaya-Kara avoidance register is yet another fashion of speaking which reinforces the rich ideological understanding of the learning of this register as the revelation of an exclusively masculine esoteric knowledge. Understanding the intended meaning of the forms requires playfully and creatively decoding the rebuses – hearing the "scorpion" hidden behind the "reed" (Boyer, 1980).

As this example illustrates, a restricted repertoire of forms can be made to cover a wider denotational range by activating either latent semantic or phonological iconisms between elements of the positive and negative repertoires. (Signed rebuses are also robustly attested in the alternate sign languages employed by widows in central Australia [Kendon, 1988].) Notably, both of the strategies for bootstrapping a richer semantics from a limited lexicon – what we might call synonymy maximization and rebus maximization – are employed in the early development of logographic writing systems (see Boltz, 1994, on the use of both of these strategies in the development of Chinese writing). The origins of writing simulate the conditions of the development of avoidance registers. In both cases, the elements of a diachronically emerging lexical repertoire are denotationally extended in discursive (or orthographic) practice in order to communicate diverse meanings with limited semiotic resources. Again, it is this dialectical relationship between "contextualized usage" and "language structure" which drives lexicon asymmetry in the "early" development of language systems *ex nihilo*.

10 More specifically, the acquisition of Damin begins with the recitation of the names for fish species, followed by other animal species. This piscine priority likely relates to the myth of origin of Damin, which its speakers held "was developed in Dreamtime by *kaltharr*, [the] yellow trevally [fish]" (McKnight, 1999, p. 245). Just as yellow trevally was the first speaker of the language, so too are the names of fish species the first words spoken by initiates. In the case of Lá'bì, plant species performatively mediate the beginning and the end of the space-time of Lá'bì as an avoidance language. Immediately after their ritual scarification on their first day at the initiation camp, initiates are touched by their sponsors on the ears with a bundle of leaves tied with a vine: "après cela, les lá'bì mourraient s'ils parlaient une autre langue que celle de l'initiation [after this, the initiates would die if they spoke any other language than Lá'bì]" (Vidal, 1976,

p. 126). It is from this moment onward that Lá'bì is employed exclusively in the initiation camp. Each initiate is surrounded by a group of initiated men who show him leaves of different plant species and tell him the name of the species. The initiate should repeat these names back without error at pain of receiving lashes. The cessation of the period of the avoidance of the Gbaya language also has a botanical connection. During the initiation period, initiates are prohibited from eating the fruit of a particular species of night-shade (*Solanum*); once they return to the village, the ritual eating of this fruit allows the initiates to once again speak Gbaya (Vidal, 1976, p. 136). Plants, and names for plants, bookend the space-time of initiation, mediating the opening and closing of the ears and mouth to the everyday (Gbaya) and initiate (Lá'bì) languages.

3. Name Registers: A Sociolinguistic Kind

1 Genealogical product terms are employed as a shorthand for kinship relations. Standard abbreviations are as follows: B = brother, Z = sister, F = father, M = mother, H = husband, W = wife, S = son, D = daughter; lower case 'e' = elder, 'y' = younger (e.g., HeB = husband's elder brother).
2 Many referent-targeting honorific registers do operate in this way; honorific concrete nouns are employed to refer to objects possessed or employed by honoured referents. See, e.g., Koshal (1987) on Ladakhi.
3 Agha (2003, p. 234) makes a distinction between the set of individuals, or "the social domain," competent "to recognize" a register (i.e., its repertoire variants, stereotypic values, prototypic contexts of use, etc.) and the social domain of individuals possessing a "competence to speak it." This distinction arises in his discussion of British accent culture. This is a milieu in which socially contoured constraints on the acquisition of devilishly complex phonolexical repertoires clearly underwrite the class- and regionally based circulation of register variants and their "prestige" (or "stigmatized") values within the linguistic marketplace. That is, it is a sociolinguistic ecology in which competence to produce the register importantly conditions the social patterning of its use. Agha's (2003) analysis of "received pronunciation" (RP) in British English thus emphasizes the epistemic constraints (e.g., access to public schooling, circulation of printed pronunciation guides, etc.) that limit the social domain of users of the register. Here I modify Agha's analytic to better fit the data with which we are concerned. Unlike the case of RP-English, for avoidance registers, epistemic constraints are typically not as important in determining the patterning of the use of registers within local speech communities as are deontic (or normative) conditions; the social domain of actual producers is more constrained by the "shoulds" than the "coulds" of register

production. So, for instance, it is married (as opposed to unmarried) individuals who are normatively expected to employ avoidance vocabulary among the Sengseng and the Kaulong (Chowning, 1985; Goodale, 1980). But this does not mean that unmarried individuals are wholly incapable of using the forms employed by married individuals (e.g., in reported speech). Because of the importance of deontic constraints on the production of avoidance speech, when I describe the social domain of an avoidance register I will typically be making appeal to the social domain of individuals normatively expected to employ the register. Of course, competence to produce a register repertoire will always be a precondition on register production in any sociolinguistic setting. In terms of avoidance registers, one axis of asymmetry in epistemically conditioned competence to produce is between young and old. Aboriginal Australian mother-in-law registers, for example, are reportedly not acquired until later in adolescence or even adulthood (N. Evans, 2003b, p. 37). For name registers keyed to in-law relationship, the period directly after marriage may be one of sociolinguistic insecurity, as speakers may be unsure of the full dimensions of the phonolexical class of words that are tabooed as a function of the name of a relation (e.g., Chowning, 1985, p. 184; Treis, 2005, p. 298).

4 Tom Harrisson (1937) offered the following florid description of the "conspicuous ... coloured headdress" which women used in the 1930s to cover their faces in the presence of male affines: "[It is] a purple-stained strip of matting, decorated with surréaliste zag patterns and herring-bones, folded in piles on top of one another on the head. Both edges of the matting are left free unplaited, to cascade down the women's firm shoulders and back, to the waist—long purple hair. When the women see a strange man or tabu relative such as their husband's brother, they let out a little squeal, crouch on their heels by the narrow edge of the path, covering their faces with their false hair, so that from head to foot they are like some rock left hanging and wet with purple anemones and brown weed from the slob of a receded wave" (p. 397).

5 Chiefly power in Malekula (Vanuatu) was traditionally mediated by passage through a series of increasingly costly, ranked grades. Although V'ënen Taut chiefdoms were the most hereditary of those found in Vanuatu, chiefly power was still articulated by passage through an elaborate, exclusively-male, set of "ranked grades, entry into which is gained by the performance of ritual based on the sacrifice of pigs with artificially developed tusks, the transfer of payments for insignia and services, and the performance of elaborate dances" (Allen, 1984a, p. 33). These graded societies fused dimensions of Melanesian 'achieved' big-man systems with aspects of Polynesian 'ascribed' chiefly hierarchy by combining "the competitive egalitarian ethic commonly associated with big-man politics with an elaborate form of social hierarchy" (p. 34).

6 With respect to the non-linguistic enactment of respect, Harrisson (1937) suggests a generalized sex-biased honorific kinesic code: women "must never pass a man or be passed by a man with their heads and shoulders higher than or equal to the man's," so "in male company ... they squat" (p. 398). Guiart (1952, p. 182), while acknowledging the differential postural respect which women had to show, suggests that the vertical code was also obeyed by men and that it was linked specifically to the person of the chief ("Suivant que le chef est debout ou assis, on passe auprès de lui en s'écartant, le dos courbé, ou en marchant presque à quatre pattes. Les femmes se montrent encore plus 'serviles' ....") Note the similarities here to the verticality-based honorific gestures and postures found in Micronesian and Polynesian chiefdoms, where relative placement in vertical space is an emblem of relative status (e.g., Firth, 1969, for Tikopia). What is notable in the Solomon Islands and Vanuatu is how the same honorific resources found in Polynesia in the mediation of rank-hierarchy are employed in a markedly gendered fashion (see Pearce, 2015, p. 207, for Unua [Malekula]; Maranda, 2001, p. 98, for Lau [Malaita]; Simons, 1982, for Kwara'ae and To'abaita [Malaita]).

7 Irvine and Gal (2000, pp. 39–47) represents a pioneering treatment of similar, ideologically driven structural changes in the Nguni languages of southern Africa, again through the mediation of avoidance registers.

8 This is a common pattern in Northern California and the Pacific Northwest, where the names of deceased individuals are avoided in all contexts by close cognatic kin – a practice that often ends only when the name is re-entered into circulation through the baptism of a child with it. Additionally, non-kin are normatively expected to avoid saying the name in the co-presence of close kin of the deceased. Among the Tolowa, uttering the "dead name" of an interlocutor was classified as an act of swearing, whether it was intentional or not, and was punishable by a fine of up to 20 dollars (Drucker, 1937, p. 249). See also Bright (1958, p. 177, note 16) on name "swearing" or *pitaxyárih* among the Karok. For other representative examples of fining or even physical punishments for violations of interlocutors' name taboos in Northern California, see Du Bois (1935, p. 67) on Wintu; Foster (1944, p. 187) on Yuki; and Silver (1978, p. 216) on Shastan groups.

9 My thanks to Alice Mitchell for suggesting the relationship between true homophone avoidance and naming customs (cf. Herbert, 1990, p. 470). Further comparative research on the social circulation and semantic organization of proper nouns is needed (but see Ellen, 1983; Lévi-Strauss, 2021; de Pina-Cabral, 2010).

10 Maarten Mous (2001), who first characterized this phenomenon, uses the term "paralexification" to describe this structural property of

morphosyntactic isomorphy across register varieties (see Treis, 2005, for examples, and Storch, 2011, for further discussion).

11 Name registers are found in Australia, only there they are centred around the avoidance of the names of deceased individuals (Nash & Simpson, 1981). Whereas affinal name taboo is also broadly present in Australia, it does not condition – with the exception of Gooniyandi (McGregor, 1989, p. 632) – homophone avoidance in the way that post-mortem name taboos do. The lack of European cases may be partly a function of biases in my reading and research.

12 Fleming et al. (2019) provides a dedicated treatment of the daughter-in-law name and homophone avoidance registers of east and southern Africa (see also Fleming, 2014a, pp. 127–35, which unfortunately mischaracterizes Kambaata as having a sociolectal repertoire).

4. Rigid Performativity: Cross-Cultural Convergences in Name Registers

1 Parallel phenomena may occur in other linguistic modalities, as where logographs employed in the written name of the Chinese emperor were tabooed in written Chinese (Künstler, 1994).

2 The particular illocutionary "force" of the citational act of disseminating copies of the cartoons should be situated in the specifics of the *Jyllands-Posten* incident and its continuing aftermath. The re-publication of the Danish cartoons in 2008 played a crucial role in stabilizing the value of cartoon-citation as effective action. The first mass event of republication occurred one day after the discovery of a plot to kill the cartoonist Kurt Westergaard was made public. It thus reframed the act of re-publication from being one that purports to be neutral with respect to the effects of the images – one that would merely share information – into an "act of solidarity"; within the language of Austin, it reframed the reporting event from being a constative act that merely cites an earlier performative act into being an illocutionary act in its own right. Mass reprinting was followed by more protests in the Islamic world and by the bombing by al-Qaeda of the Dutch embassy in Pakistan. It is not only the fact of dissemination but also the size of the print run that is important here – the analogue as well as the digital signal. The *Charlie Hebdo* issue in November 2011, entitled *Charia Hebdo*, which led to the firebombing of the magazine's offices, was sold at twice the normal circulation. The print run of the issue with the crying Muhammad cover published the week after the massacre at the offices of *Charlie Hebdo* in 2015 was seven million plus. There are, again, two readings here – or rather, two effects. On the one hand, republication is a gesture of solidarity or defiance in the face of violence; on the other hand, and precisely because it has been framed as a performative

act, republication reinforces the value of Muhammad images as injurious images (cf. the British National Party's mass-printing of pamphlets in 2006 with the infamous bomb-in-the-turban image). This is simply to underscore that the perlocutionary effects of disseminations of Muhammad cartoons are not some automatic and pre-reflective Islamic conditioned-response to any and all images of the Prophet; they are mediated by a specific history of (re)circulations of these images (see Gruber, 2009, for a nuanced account of traditions and tropes of the visual representation of Muhammad). Even if the offence of Muhammad cartoons cannot be understood as a narrow question of the violation of a religious law or blasphemy, this does not mean that the cartoons are not hurtful for many Muslims (Asad, 2009). Mahmood (2009) argues that – at least for the urban Egyptian Muslims with whom she conducted field research – affective reactions to these and other derogatory or denigrating images of Muhammad reflect the particular mimetically grounded devotional practices and ethical dispositions that devout Muslims develop toward the Prophet.

3 The term "rigid performativity" was suggested to me by Michael Silverstein, yet another example of his inexhaustible intellectual generosity. The term captures the idea that name taboos stand at the intersection of two great themes of reflection on indexicality in twentieth-century analytic philosophy: speech-act performativity in the tradition of J.L. Austin and the rigid designation of personal names in the tradition of Saul Kripke. For further discussion, see Fleming (2011), from which this section has been adapted.

4 The term "fictive" here is inartful. In some languages-in-culture it is clear that name-sharing reflects an underlying ontological identity between referents (see, for instance, Nuttall, 1994, on homonymous kinship among Greenlandic Inuit).

5 "The respect [a Melpa-man] owes [his wife's] parents in particular a woman interprets for herself as well. A husband should not only refrain from using the ordinary names of his parents-in-law to their face, they having a right to demand compensation if he does, but out of consideration for his wife should never speak their name in her company.... Studied insults can utilize this: a husband roused to anger against his wife may refer to her parents by their ordinary names" (M. Strathern, 1972, p. 38). For another example of the intentional violation of an in-law name taboo in anger, see Taylor (1984, p. 133).

6 Similar considerations could be profitably invoked to explain the diachronic emergence of post-mortem and hierarchically based homophone avoidance. In name registers not tied to kinship, avoidance levels may invoke quite different sociocultural values, but they still achieve the same kind of functional grading. Take the example of Twana (Salishan; Pacific

Northwest) post-mortem name registers as described by William Elmendorf (1951). In Twana, avoidance levels index social status within a system of hierarchical ranks. Elmendorf reports that there was a normative proscription on uttering the "adult name" (*u' bat*) of a deceased individual. Though the "adult name" of all deceased individuals thus had an indefeasible performativity, not all individuals bore "adult names" – children, slaves, and low-class freemen did not bear them, and, correspondingly, post-mortem name taboo with respect to their names was not a community-wide practice. A further differentiation by rank was achieved at the top-and-centre of the social ladder: "Unlike the name taboo, which automatically operated on the death of anyone bearing an adult name, the word taboo [i.e., homophone avoidance] went into effect only on the initiative of the deceased's kin, involved sponsorship of a formal feast, and seems only to have been exercised in cases where the deceased was a prominent upper-class person" (p. 206). Homophone avoidance was by no means automatic; Elmendorf cites the case of a family of low status failing in their attempt to get a homophone of a dead relative's name prohibited (p. 207).

A classificatory framework of names and name transmission which bestowed powerful names only upon individuals of higher ranks served to exclude those of lower status within the society from even meriting respect-through-post-mortem-name-avoidance. Meanwhile, homophone avoidance augmented the respect enacted to the (kin of) deceased persons of highest statuses. Once again, distinct avoidance levels are functioning as analogue signs, only here of social status. The "word taboo" was a sign of the relatively high status of the deceased and of their kin. Indeed, quite costly potlatch-type feasts had to be sponsored by the family of the deceased in order to prohibit the use of a homophone (cf. Roth, 2008).

Scaling of post-mortem name avoidance seems to have served as an iconic-indexical of rank hierarchies throughout northern California and the Pacific Northwest. Among the Yurok, for instance, compensation paid to the family of the deceased upon violation of a post-mortem name taboo was increased the higher the rank of the deceased (Kroeber, 1925, pp. 38–9; see also Bright, 1979, on Karok).

5. Not on Speaking Terms: Closing and Rerouting Channels of Communication

1 My thanks to Costas Nakassis for this turn of phrase. The intertextual *renvoi* is to Saul Kripke's (1980) characterization of personal names as "rigid designators."

2 This is not to say that there are not signs of avoidance where the "sympathetic" (or iconic) aspect is not front and centre. With respect to avoidance relatives, most specifically those of adjacent generation, a Dhopadhola (Bantu) speaker should "not refer to sexual matters in their presence and because milk is said to be like semen he should not drink it at their homes" (Sharman, 1969, p. 104). As Stanley Tambiah (2017) so elegantly explained, the Frazerian binarism between iconic and indexical readings of "magical acts" fails to capture the ways in which both sign modes work in tandem in any given instance.

3 A channel-verifying query like "Can you hear *this*?" both presences the channel via the production of a signal that passes through the channel (indexical participation) and queries about the success of that very same signal in passing through the channel to the receiver (symbolic metalanguage). Think here of the mild uncanniness of calling out to your partner, "Are you home?," upon entering your home, only to discover that they are not. The question presupposes that the channel is open even as it poses the question of whether it is. Silence is not the same kind of response as "Yes!," even though they are paradigmatically opposed responses in this context.

4 A study of communicative infrastructures of kinship as these are contoured by relationship-keyed ethoses should be a desideratum for an interactionally grounded social anthropology. Small-scale societies are often reductively represented as homogeneous communities of intimate face-to-face interaction (see Stasch, 2009, for a critique). At the same time, literatures on demography and cumulative culture consistently treat "more" interconnectedness of networked nodes of human agents as "better" (e.g., Apicella et al., 2012, on Hadza social networks). But if joking-avoidance is "adaptive," as one imagines its global distribution would suggest to cultural evolutionists, clearly such a model is far too simplistic. It may be the way that joking-avoidance differentiates relations both within and between groups that is crucial here. Avoidance actively produces distant-"intimates" and close-"strangers," rather than letting these categories emerge "naturally" as a function of interactional histories. Avoidance between cross-sex siblings or cross-sex parent-child dyads sacrifices within-group closeness. But what is gained is the presupposition of "intimate" status with strangers (e.g., a classificatory father's father in Aboriginal Australia or a namesake among the Nharo). This dynamic is perhaps most apparent in societies where the social world is egocentrically bifurcated into joking and avoidance relations.

5 To be clear, Merlan (1997, pp. 111–22) frames the relationship between avoidance and exchange somewhat differently than I have presented it here. Bride service is often found in foraging societies, and it is correlated

with child-in-law/parent-in-law avoidance. Characteristic of bride service is "the continuous nature of obligation of in-laws throughout the marriage, and particularly that of the son-in-law to provide in recognition of what has been or will be given him" (p. 111). Merlan argues that in such contexts, interpersonal avoidance and associated feelings of shame may have an adaptive value. Because demands from avoidance kin cannot be refused, extreme timidity in interpersonal relations may have the effect of reducing the likelihood of the wife's family making too many demands upon the groom. On this account, reticence to engage in direct communication serves to buffer the exploitation of the son-in-law's labour:

> Though it may appear paradoxical, the ethnographic material warrants the conclusion that where social relationship is constituted and reproduced in terms of inculcated and strongly experienced obligation, there exist the strongest feelings and conventionalised manifestations of "shame," which among other things place limits on readiness to interaction and to make demands. This is partly reproduced by the limitation of interpersonal access and demand, familiarity by easy access and the possibility of regular demand. (p. 114)

Notably, patterns of in-law interaction are hedged around with the same "politeness strategies" that are commonly employed to mitigate and mute the force of requests and demands (P. Brown & Levinson, 1987), a point underscored by numerous Australianists (e.g., C. Goddard, 1992; Rumsey, 1982; cf. Rushforth, 1981). It would seem that by saturating the avoidance relationship with the feeling of shame, demands for goods and services may be inhibited. Gregor's (1974, p. 343) Mehinaku ethnography follows a similar line of analysis: The "period of brideservice is regarded as onerous and socially uncomfortable. To a degree it is made more bearable by a set of affinal taboos which strictly regulates a young man's interaction with his parents-in-law...." (Note the family resemblance to Radcliffe-Brown's theory of kinship avoidance as conflict mitigation.)

But a reversed perspective on the question of the relationship between shame/avoidance and exchange is also possible. Avoidance – especially in foraging societies – is a mutual and reciprocal experience. Just as shame may impede demand making on the part of the senior party to the relationship, it may serve to elicit the provisioning of more goods and services by the junior member. Exchange is often figured as a way of "buying the shame" (Wagner, 1986a, p. 57) associated with the avoidance relationship (e.g., Eves, 1998; Oliver, 1970, pp. 170–1). And because the shame of the relationship can never be fully expunged, the saturation of the relationship with this sentiment ensures the constant flow of goods and services.

Even more fundamentally, the onset of affinal avoidance is often explicitly and ritually linked to marriage exchange (i.e., betrothal and/or the provisioning of bride price). In this light, avoidance can be read as a form of paradoxical metacommunication that elicits exchanges by deferring them:

> What is the appropriateness of avoidance, per se, to marriage and affinal relationships? A link can be seen in the privilege of option, or preferment, the right (often bargained for) to marry a certain person. In this respect a bride, for instance, is given over as against the possibility of *not being given*. Avoidance, eliciting a relationship through not "relating" in certain respects – relating by demurral – is the opposite of preferment, and its appropriateness as a means of eliciting the affinal relationship (as against joking) is that of "marking" or encoding the favor of preferment within the relationship itself. By not speaking with, not imposing upon, not mentioning, or even totally avoiding the benefactors involved in the gesture of preferment, one elicits the spontaneity of granting the preferment again and again. (Wagner, 1986a, pp. 55–6)

More could and should be said about the complex relationship between interactional avoidance and exchange. See the Conclusion for more on the theme of shame.

6 In Eurasia, the mapping of joking/avoidance onto alternate/adjacent generations, a pattern robustly associated with forager societies cross-culturally, occurs in Munda societies (R. Parkin, 1988). Additionally, this pattern of alternate-generation joking versus adjacent-generation avoidance is present in a complex way in East Africa (see McGivney, 1993, and D. Parkin, 1988, on Mijikenda; cf. Wilson, 1951, on Nyakyusa). Khoe and San avoidance practices conform, as might be expected on grounds of social organization, to this egalitarian harmonic/disharmonic pattern rather than to the age- and gender-stratified one (e.g., Barnard, 1978a; R. Lee, 1986; Ōno, 2016; Silberbauer, 1981; see also the discussion of homonymous kinship in Chapter 4).

7 Hammock placement and treatment are an important idiom for signalling marital and affinal relationship in the Xingu River area. Among the Mehinaku, wives provide hammocks and hammock cords for their husbands (while husbands provide woven baskets, spindles, and shell jewellery to their wives). Young, unmarried men must barter with married men to acquire hammocks produced by their wives (Gregor, 1974, p. 335). Hammock placement is a conventionalized performative of marriage – a second marriage may be effected by "one of the bride's kinsmen who carries the groom's hammock to her house" (Gregor, 1977, p. 282). Hammock placement, as well as drinking manioc porridge from the same bowl and taking daily baths in the river together, are some of the most important "public expressions of marriage relationship" (Gregor, 1974, p. 340). Only

married couples – as opposed to lovers – hang their hammocks horizontally one above the other, tied to the same posts, with the husband's "slightly above his wife's. In this position they sleep with their heads just a few inches apart ... This is the most intimate of the hammock positions and it indicates a close marital relationship" (p. 340). Hammock positioning is a salient, public sign of marital status and relationship, easily visible in the large, internally undivided residences that house extended families. Various degrees of disalignment of hammocks and bodies can signal marital strife. By tying one of the hammock cords to a different post, the husband or wife may publically signal that there are problems in the relationship. Further, during periods of marital strain, a wife will position her head in line with her husband's feet – bodily disalignment, here, as a trope of an interpersonal disalignment (p. 344). As with the Kamayurá, Mehinaku parents-in-law and children-in-law should not touch each other's hammocks.

8 Shill address is sometimes taken one step further by means of a complementary trope of **sham reference**. Here not only address but reference to the taboo relation in displaced. The use of the mother-in-law register in Uradhi (Cape York Peninsula) is complemented by the use of this strategy: "Should one wish to communicate with one's spouse's family, one would speak to someone else within hearing distance of them, signalling the fact that one is not addressing that person but is in fact addressing an in-law by switching to the special style, which is always clearly marked from the everyday style. One would address the involved bystander in the second person, even though one is not actually speaking to him or her. Thus, for example, one might say to someone near a taboo relative: *uwunu anpaɲiyu* 'don't climb up.' (everyday style), and be ordering *that person* not to climb. But if one says instead: *uwunu ayankumari* 'don't climb up.' (avoidance style), to the same person, one is in fact telling one's in-law not to climb up" (Crowley, 1983, p. 314). Sham reference accompanies elaborate practices of speech intermediation in Akan courtly language (Yankah, 1991, 1995). An official orator or *okyeame* serves as Goffmanian animator, transmitting the king's speech. But he also serves as the king's proxy addressee, channeling communication from co-present non-royals to the king. Just as he occupies the role of addressee for the king on the interactional plane, so too may he occupy the role of referent for the king on the denotational one: "The Akan further ensure the sanctity of royal space through lexical avoidance: the use of euphemisms for certain words and concepts considered indecent in collocation with the chief, for example, death, sickness, or misdemeanor. In all such cases, the okyeame's name may be substituted for the chief's" (Yankah, 1991, p. 6). Here the *okyeame* stands in as the sham referent for the king (cf. Fisher, 1976, on "dropping remarks").

9 The cultivation of the attitude of forbearance means the joking relationship can be a privileged site for articulating social critique. Among Plains groups, joking relationships offered a unique site for articulating public criticism: "When a man has committed some reprehensible deed, e.g., married a clan mate, or shown jealousy, it was not the function of his fellows clansmen but of his *makutsati* [joking relative] to reprove him or make fun of him ... and he was obliged to take all this in good part as the prerogative of *makutsati*" (Lowie, 1917, p. 42, cited in Provinse, 1937, p. 357).
10 Thomas Gregor (1977) points to this ambiguity of "high jinx" in his analysis of Mehinaku cross-cousin joking relationships. The relationship incorporates a "degree of antagonism that can become both dramatic and blatant. In the *Jawarí* spear-throwing ritual, cross-cousins belonging to different tribes hurl wax-tipped spears at each other. Although the spears do not penetrate the skin, they leave nasty bruises and may, the villagers say, break a bone" (pp. 280–1).

6. Out of Touch: Sensory Avoidances and the Multimodality of Mutuality

1 The connection between marriageability and veiling may also be reflected in exceptions to the norm of veiling in the presence of unrelated adult males. In northern Yemen, elite women do not veil from members of the eminently unmarriageable and racialized *akhdam* "servant class," and these are the "only adult men who are allowed into women's gatherings" (Meneley, 2000, p. 66). At the same time, veiling practices often have second-order signaller-focal values as signs of caste or class rank (see, for example, Pastner, 1982, on Baluchistan).
2 Put in a more technical metalanguage: Sign interpreters are able to make specific "decontextualizable deductions" concerning the social characteristics of the origo of the index but not about the target of the index (i.e., they can deduce the marital status of the woman who covers but not of the persons before whom she covers). Because the sign provides specific social information about the origo but not the target of the index, it motivates the emergence of a "second-order indexical" reading of coverings as signaller-focal indexes of identity (after Silverstein, 1981, 2003, on "decontextualizable deducibility" and "indexical orders").
3 Lacking recordings or transcripts, it is difficult to generalize about these paralinguistic dimensions of the avoidance signal from ethnographic sources. Nevertheless, impressionistic descriptions suggest that volume, pitch, voice quality, and tempo can all be indexical of interpersonal respect. Western Apache father-in-law and son-in-law (unlike mother-in-law and son-in-law) may speak with each other, but conversation is "brief and to the point," and "they maintain a reserved manner and utter their words

slowly and carefully in moderated voice" and never raise their voices (G. Goodwin, 1942, p. 255). Paralinguistic features bear a high functional load in the Western Desert Language in-law respect register, *tjalpawang-kanyi* ("oblique speech"). This register does not involve lexical taboos, as in mother-in-law languages, but rather employs honorific morphology, avoidance of addressee-reference, as well as paralinguistic cues like "higher pitch, softer volume and slower tempo of delivery, often also with rising intonation" (C. Goddard, 1992, p. 99). Requests employing "oblique speech" may be "spoken rather quietly, slowly, at a higher pitch and with exaggerated rising intonation, almost as if to give the impression that the speaker is musing aloud in a somewhat disinterested way, rather than addressing another person" (p. 101). In the Wik-speaking Cape Keerweer community, mother-in-law language – when used in the co-presence of the target of avoidance – was accompanied by paralinguistic modulation of the speech signal; speakers "do not make sudden jumps of intonation, do not speak loudly, and speak very slowly, often in 'creaky voice'" (Sutton, 1978, p. 220). Gurindji *pirnti-ka* "on the side" speech, which is employed between a mother-in-law and child-in-law, is spoken in a "quiet voice, usually starting off with a higher pitch than is typical of ordinary speech" which falls in a pronounced manner at the end of the phrase, and with "creaky voice" (McConvell, 1982, p. 97). Guugu Yimidhirr say that *guugu dhabul* "taboo [kin] language" should be uttered in a "deliberately subdued voice, drawing out words and dropping into a near whisper" (Haviland, 1979b, p. 217). See also Sicoli (2010) on honorific voice registers.

4 For Chechen communities this period of silence is reportedly limited to the marriage celebrations themselves. Chechen brides had their modesty tested during the wedding ceremony. The bride was supposed to maintain her reserve even as the guests would try to get her to laugh or enter into their banter. Jaimoukha (2005, p. 128) claims that this ritual is "a watered-down version of the ancient custom of 'holding one's tongue,' in which the bride maintained a code of silence with respect to her older in-laws, which was only broken at the end of the wedding in a special ceremony."

5 The mouth cover appears to have been of different dimensions in different locales, sometimes covering only the mouth, at other times the mouth and nose. It is paired, in all cases, with a veil. The mouth cover emblematizes the external control over the mouth, the entrainment of silence that marriage and the presence of affines imposed on the new bride. In the mouth covering and other non-linguistic avoidances involving the mouth, the organs of vocal production become subject to taboos so hypertrophic as to extend beyond the proscriptions of audible speech, encompassing its visible source as well. Symbolically, the mouth cover functions as an auditory veil.

6 I was introduced to Karbelashvili's text and the case by Kendon (1988). My thanks to German Dziebel and Kevin Tuite for reading over the manuscript and giving me notes on it.

7. The Pragmatic Suspension of Semantic Distinctions: Honorific Pronouns in Kinship Avoidance

1 Here I depart from Silverstein's argument. He held that "the formal-functional analogy of [T-V systems] for speaker-hearer deference *is an exceptional case*" (Silverstein, 1976, 40–1, italics added). He was drawn to this conclusion, I think, because he saw the formal-functional analogy in pronominal honorification to be based upon the ways in which skewed number or person values metaphorically represent or "figure" social indexical meanings. As the name register data presented at the end of Chapter 4 already indicate, I see the formal-functional analogy between sign-avoidance and interpersonal-respect to be a more widespread phenomenon. This is because I privilege the way in which semantic skewing "disfigures" the language system as the kernel iconic-indexical meaning at play in the formal-functional analogy (see discussion in main text, below).

2 In Mijikenda, all pronominal usage is reciprocal – if A addresses B with V, then B addresses A with V. Indeed, kinship-restricted honorific registers often belie the Brown-and-Gilman–influenced claim of P. Brown and Levinson (1987, p. 178) that the discourse patterning of T-V systems always involves non-reciprocal honorific address or reference (King, 2001, p. 179). In the majority of kinship-restricted systems, use of V pronouns is reciprocal. This is an underappreciated but pivotal point for a would-be sociolinguistic typology of honorific systems. See Fleming (2023) for more on this topic.

3 In later writings, Silverstein offers a more culture-historically nuanced position: "[The] tropic reading [of the skewed semantic feature] is characteristic of a folk- or ethno-metapragmatic view of the indexical facts ... [that] interprets the indexical effect in terms of an interpretation of figuration ('metaphor,' etc.) at the denotational plane of function (though indexing deference is, of course, a nondenotational act) ... *Exactly what this essential tropic content is, depends on the language...*" (Silverstein, 2003, pp. 208–9; italics added).

4 "The concept of rhematization captures the way registers that are taken up as indexes of social personae [or social relationships] from one ideological perspective can also be construed as icons, or can be construed as icons in another ideological frame" (Gal, 2013, p. 34).

5 A potential counter-example to this overly clean distinction between semantic and pragmatic meaning in honorification might be the semantic

echo of the honorific plural in Pohnpeian. In Pohnpeian, a dedicated second-person pronoun (*komwa*), likely derived from the dual (*komwi*), is employed in respectful address. But for chiefs the still more respectful third-person plural (*ihr*) should be employed (both in addressee- and non-participant-reference). Elizabeth Keating (2000), drawing on extensive ethnographic field research in the village of Madloenihmw, sketches the cultural logics that likely rationalize this usage. Deities and ancestor spirits reside in the paramount chief's feast house (*nah*), only at a higher (i.e., more esteemed) and even more interior location within the *nah* than where the chief is seated. The third-person plural is employed to refer to the chief and chieftess because they "embody, speak for, and are authorized by these ancestral entities" (p. 308). Any reference to the chief in some sense includes his godly ancestors. "The Pohnpeian chief is addressed with the third person plural pronoun and a plural form is affixed to his address term because he embodies the authority of past chiefs, the ancestor spirits" (Keating & Duranti, 2006, p. 152). As with the namesakes identified through tropic kin-term use in Chapter 4, the metaphor has, in some sense, become real.

6 It is not widely appreciated that addressee-honorification in some languages is achieved by skewing of pronominal number not only in addressee-reference but also in (notionally singular) speaker-reference (see Fleming, 2017b, for a dedicated treatment of this topic). In the sample presented in Table 7.1, this occurs in Santali (1st.exclusive.dual = addressee$_{target}$ honorific; cf. the Kri son-in-law dual), Mijikenda (1st.plural = addressee$_{target}$ honorific), and Boazi (1st.plural = addressee$_{target}$ honorific). Although the royal *we* historically employed in some European languages might seem to make the speaker "count for more than one social individual" (Silverstein, 1976, p. 39), this reading is certainly not available in these languages where the use of first-person non-singular pronouns functions as an addressee-honorific. Therefore, these cases cannot be accounted for on the (iconic) figurational thesis that has been favoured in the literature. They are fully consistent with the (indexical) disfigurational account of honorific pronouns which I am presenting here.

7 Although kin relations are listed as genealogical products, it should be underscored that kinship relations in Manus cannot be reduced to genealogical products. Kin terms and honorific pronouns are employed to entail different footings of social relationship. Here, as elsewhere, avoidance registers are a semiotic resource that not only "presuppose" kinship relationality but can also be creatively employed to "entail" a particular relational kinship frame (Haviland, 1979a; Rumsey, 1982). Sometimes a wife's older sister (WoZ) or a husband's older brother (HoB) is tropically refigured as a mother-in-law or father-in-law, respectively. They will be referred to with

parent-in-law terms, and the full spectrum of heightened avoidance practices characteristic of the treatment of a cross-sex parent-in-law (including the use of the plural) will be adopted. Co-habitation conditions this fictive generational raising of elder cross-sex sibling: "The occupation of a house by two brothers, in which case the younger wife must avoid the older brother, as a titular 'father-in-law,' is a common situation" (Mead, 1934, p. 267). Just as with a mother-in-law, a man and his wife's elder sister should never be co-present; between a man and his wife's younger sister it is only eating in each other's presence that is taboo.

8 Note that the pronoun *gin*, which is employed in both addressee- and non-participant-reference to generationally senior affines, lacks the deictic selectivity (after Fleming & Sidnell, 2020, after Agha, 2007) of second-person pronouns – that is, *gin* is used for both second- and third-person plural reference in Jahai.

9 Examples include Tinrin (Austronesian; New Caledonia) (Osumi, 1995, pp. 140–1), Waorani (isolate; Ecuador) (Peeke, 1973; Rival, 2002), and Boumaa Fijian (Schmidt, 1988, with a tip of the hat to Corbett, 2000). From the description in Sah (2010, pp. 199–200), the Sino-Tibetan language Raji appears also to have a system of this kind. Examples are given of the dual being employed for siblings-in-law and the plural for parents-in-law. The Santali dialect described in MacPhail (1983) is also a system of this kind. The dual is employed (in both speaker- and addressee-reference) between children-in-law and parents-in-law, while the plural is employed between co-parents-in-law (cf. Choksi, 2021; Ghosh, 2008). Finally, for scaling over social contexts within the same relationship type, see Ozanne-Rivierre (1994, p. 219, after La Fontinelle): "En Nouvelle-Calédone (La Fontinelle 1971:268) 'une belle-fille peut se voir dans l'intimité tutoyée par la mère de son mari (qu'elle vouvoie au duel), mais elle sera vouvoyée au duel devant sa famille venue en visite et, toutes deux, belle-mère et belle-fille, utiliseront le pluriel [pour s'adresser l'une à l'autre] lors d'une grande cérémonie.' [In New Caledonia, a daughter-in-law may find herself addressed with the second singular pronoun by her mother-in-law (who she, in return, will address with the dual pronoun) when they are alone together, but she will be respectfully addressed in the dual by her mother-in-law when the daughter-in-law's family comes to visit, and both of them, the mother-in-law and the daughter-in-law, [will address one another] using the plural during important ceremonial occasions.]"

10 The use of the term *recursivity* should not lead readers to immediately equate the formal-functional diagrammatic structure that converts the full range of number distinctions in Manus into a graded honorific series with the ideological process theorized by Gal and Irvine (2019) and called "fractal recursivity." Three points are relevant here: (1) Here I am concerned

with the formal organization of semiotic repertoires of deference indexicals (i.e., with the organization of object signs). Fractal recursivity denotes the recursive application of an ideological operation (i.e., a metasemiotic operation) across distinct social or conceptual domains. (2) The kind of organization of object-signs that I am describing *must* have the appearance of a nested structure, while nesting in fractal recursivity is only one of many possible ways in which the same metasemiotic distinction can be instantiated across distinct domains (Gal & Irvine 2019, p. 130). (3) Fractal recursivity involves ideologies of differentiation, while the object-sign repertoires that I am discussing involve grading of a unitary indexical function (i.e., grading of signs that are deferential with respect to others that are even more deferential). See Fleming (2023) for more discussion of these points. Fractal recursivity and the nested suspension of semiotic variants are connected insofar as diagrammaticity appears to be a crucial structuring principle of "pragmatic grammar[s]" writ large (Silverstein, 1976; cf. Stasch, 2014).

8. Degrees of Unfreedom: From Pragmatic Structures to Intensities of Experience

1 Honorific "speech levels" are sometimes projections from purely text-level phenomena, as in Tibetan (Agha, 1998, p. 162, examples 2a-e). These "speech levels are ideological constructs ... that ... revalorize and essentialize infelicities of contextualization ... of deference coherence, as 'impurities' of sentence structure.... Thus one type of stereotypic construct, the lexical register, is used to MOTIVATE another, i.e. speech levels" (p. 191, note 6). In other languages, however, distinct lexical (or morphological) repertoires are graded by honorific function. In Javanese, for example, there is a triadic distinction made between non-honorific (*ngoko*), mid-honorific (*madya*) and high-honorific (*krama*) speaker$_{origo}$-addressee$_{target}$ honorific vocabularies. Person-referring human nouns and deictics appear always to be privileged shibboleths of honorific speech levels and are correspondingly sites of exaggerated lexical differentiation (Errington, 1988).
2 Suggesting a similar asymmetry of competency, use of the avoidance register among Bininj Gunwok speakers may be a means of rendering confidential the content of the conversation (N. Evans, 2003a; cf. Hoenigman, 2012, on Awiakay "mountain talk").
3 Bininj Gunwok is, however, an exception to this generalization. Unlike Gooniyandi, Mangarayi, Bunaba, or Djaru, where many everyday words were never substituted for in avoidance speech, every single Bininj Gunwok open-class term has an enregistered *kun-balak* "language for wife bestower" alternant (Evans, 2003a, p. 61). And yet Murray Garde (2013)

characterizes the discursive implementation of *kun-balak* in the following manner: "In most situations where *kun-kurrng* [in the sense of *kun-balak*] is used there is usually not a complete and exclusive switch to the marked register. Speakers can sprinkle *kun-kurrng* lexemes throughout their ordinary register usage or commence their discourse with *kun-kurrng* and quickly switch to normal register after they have indexically made their point" (p. 179). This case does not, therefore, conform to the model presented in Chapter 2 which links register cohesion, at the level of discourse practice, to large, semantically abstract avoidance lexicons, at the level of language structures. (A more pronounced use of honorific forms as a frame-setting device at the beginning of an interaction is also noted for Wik [Sutton, 1978, p. 222].)

4 The analytic of indexical (or deference) focus has received more cursory treatment already; see note 10 in the Introduction and the end of the opening section of Chapter 3 for these earlier discussions.

5 The cross-linguistic skewing of honorific systems toward referent-targeting indexical focus types reflects the referentialist bias of speaker metalinguistic awareness (Agha, 2007; Errington, 1985; Silverstein, 1979). This is to say that it is a finding in the typology of sociopragmatics that makes sense in the light of how folk-consciousness rationalizes the social significations of linguistic forms and structures. (For more on this, see the discussions of the sociopragmatics of naming in Chapter 3 and "referential telescoping" in Chapter 4.) Such rationalizations inform discursive practices which, in turn, come to (however partially or awkwardly) reify those rationalizations. Referential biasing of honorific language is produced by precisely the kind of feedback between ideology, structure, and practice that I have been concerned to study in this volume.

6 For more on this functional trade-off, see the discussion of honorific registers in Austronesian languages in Fleming (2016).

7 Kokatha avoidance registers were described by A.P. Elkin in an important series of articles on "Kinship in South Australia" published in *Oceania*. Though Elkin (1940, p. 348) expresses some doubts about his data, saying the "special vocabularies ... require further checking", he was certain that there were at least two distinct honorific vocabularies employed among Kokatha speakers. One vocabulary was employed in reference and address between *maradju*, classificatory brothers-in-law who additionally stand in the relationship of guardian and novice in initiation rites. ("In the case of two men who were *maradju* in circumcision, unless they know this vocabulary they can only speak to one another through a third person" [p. 345].) A second distinct repertoire was employed by a man when addressing, or referring to, a sister (a category that includes father's mother and mother's mother). There was, then, a minimally three-way division

between the "neutral" register and two kinship-keyed repertoires. A similar, but somewhat distinct, differentiation of sub-repertoires as a function of the kin relation between the origo and target of the index is also reported for Pintupi (Hansen & Hansen, 1974; Myers, 1991).

Mary Laughren's painstaking analysis of Ken Hale's field notes offers a fine-grained picture of how Warlpiri sub-repertoires are differentiated by the social categorization of the kinship relationship obtaining between the origo and the target of avoidance repertoires. The primary social categories targeted by Warlpiri avoidance are *makurnta-warnu* ["shame-associated"] kin – that is, kin of the other matrimoiety – as opposed to *makurnta-wangu* ["shame without"] – that is, kin of one's own matrimoiety (Laughren, 2001, p. 200). Just treating the speech of men, there are at least four distinct sub-repertoires. One repertoire is employed for male members of the kin class of which ego's father's mother is a member. This is the class from which ego's wife should ideally come, so this repertoire can be called the "brother-in-law" repertoire. (Women of this class – which include ego's wife – are addressed and referred to with everyday speech.) A second repertoire is employed specifically for the female members of the kin class of which ego's father's mother's mother is a member. This is "crucially ... the class to which *ego*'s spouse's mother belongs" (p. 201). This is the "mother-in-law/son-in-law" repertoire. A third, residual repertoire, is employed for all other members of the class containing ego's father's mother's mother (and her mother) as well as the class of kin containing ego's father's mother. Finally, "there is also a very extensive avoidance lexicon which is used by men to refer to all *makurnta-warnu* kinsmen except members of their father's subsection" (p. 205). All of these varieties contrast with a "neutral" vocabulary employed between other kin dyads.

8 Here I am drawing upon Erving Goffman's (1981) nomenclature for distinguishing participant roles. A quick review is therefore in order. Goffman decomposed the Speaker role into a number of more basic primitives (e.g., Author, Principal, Animator). For my purposes, the distinction between (represented) Speaker and (actual) Animator is the crucial one. The Speaker is the role associated with grammatical category of first person (in reflexively calibrated discourse) and the subject of verbs of speaking which represent discursive events (in reportively calibrated discourse). Animator, contrastingly, is a residual role associated with the phatic infrastructure of discursive communication – the "individual active in the role of utterance production," even if that utterance itself represents another utterance (p. 144). Analogously, Addressee – the role associated with the second person and the direct or indirect object of a verb of speaking – can be distinguished from speech Recipient: "Animator and recipient are part of the same level and mode of analysis, two terms cut from the same cloth,

not social roles in the full sense so much as functional nodes in a communication system" (p. 144).

9 Augmentative-diminutive morphology in native languages of California and the Pacific Northwest often involves systematic shifts in the pronunciation of vowels and consonants (Haas, 1970; Nichols, 1971; Sapir, 1985, pp. 179–96). These shifts may characterize the relative bigness/smallness of the denotatum. But the alternations can also index the speaker's stance (e.g., affection or contempt) toward the referent, and even other nonreferential effects (e.g., voicing particular animal characters in myth narration, indexing a physical deformity of addressee, etc.). For Wasco-Wishram Chinookan, Silverstein shows that the augmentative-diminutive distinction operates along a continuum or cline. To give only an impression of that very complex structure, take the example of voicing in stop consonants. In this series, voiced stops [augmentative function] contrast with unvoiced stops [neutral function], which, in turn, contrast with ejectives (as glottalized, and therefore maximally unvoiced stops) [diminutive function] (Silverstein, 1994, pp. 46–7). Similar effects are accomplished through a variety of other distinctive features as well as by means of shifts in the manner and the place of articulation. Further, these distinct phonetic-articulatory scales are complexly combined with one another, both on particular segments and across segments, expanding the spectrum of expressive effects. Observe that phonological features like voicing, nasalization, and glottalization are "normally subordinated to ... zero autonomous power with respect to reference-and-predication in the doubly articulated structure of language" (p. 42). As phonemic, distinctive features, they are "denotational diacritic" (Agha, 2007, p. 108) – they distinguish meaningful units of linguistic form but do not have meaning in themselves. The augmentative-diminutive alternations thus constitute a "'breakthrough' mode of semiosis" in which this series of distinctive and digital (on/off) features – contrasts that distinguish linguistic symbols – are transformed into an analogue (by-degrees) system of iconic-indexicals. This is a system in which the quantity of a given feature (form) corresponds with the intensity of speaker's affection/disgust for the referent (function). For another case of breakthrough structure in phonetic media, see Sicoli (2010).

10 As discussed above, elaboration of, and mastery over, honorific speech often becomes a second-order signaler-focal index of status (after Agha, 1998). In the Sidaama (Ethiopia) name register example, it was noted that highest-caste, Yemereero, women engaged in the most elaborate name-avoidance practices. Similarly, the practice of *purdah* (lit. "curtain") or *ghunghat* in South Asia was historically most exaggerated among highest-caste groups (e.g., Jacobson, 1982, p. 92). The second-order interpretation of avoidance as a status signal might be treated in terms of the model

of "conspicuous leisure" (Veblen, 1994) or "honest signaling" (A. Zahavi & Zahavi, 1997). Isolation curtails the range of possible tasks that a woman can perform outside of the house and thus presupposes a surplus labour force, like servants (see, for instance, Pastner, 1982, on the correlation between intensity of *purdah* practiced and caste rank in Baluchistan). On this account, hypertrophic veiling and social segregation are "honest signals" of economic resources (see Bliege Bird & Smith, 2005, for an introduction to "signaling theory"). This line of analysis might perhaps help explain why visual avoidance displays become most exaggerated in hierarchical societies. Scepticism is warranted, however. For instance, the reductive narrative of Chinese footbinding that correlated female constraint with social status has collapsed when subjected to close empirical scrutiny (Bossen & Gates, 2017).

11 Douglas, Turner, and Leach developed a perspective on taboo in the 1960s which interpreted it as a means of keeping cultural categories discrete and distinct. It was hybrid forms – "the betwixt and the between" – that were subject to taboo, and this in order to safeguard categorical discriminations. The critical engagement with this theory of taboo has been a remarkably productive site for theorizing the indexical anchoring of cultural structures. Valerio Valeri (2000), building upon work by Alfred Gell and Julia Kristeva, showed, *contra* Mary Douglas, that it is not just any categorical boundaries that must be safeguarded. It is the spectre of the dissolution of the corporeal and intercorporeal boundaries of the embodied subject which most often give rise to taboos and associated avoidance rituals. In a parallel critique of Leach, Stanley Tambiah's (1969) Thai ethnography showed that sexual and alimentary taboos make sense only when anchored to the lived spaces of the dwelling, settlement, paddy field, and surrounding forest. Silverstein (2004) builds upon Tambiah's work, elevating this argument concerning the indexical anchoring of structure to a theoretical principle.

12 "Thus obviation is the opposite of structuralism, for it makes the referential categories of convention peripheral to its ultimate realization of an encompassing image. 'Structure' is not singled out as the determinant of meaning, but rather *subsumed*, as orienting features of a landscape might be, within the coordinating binocular perspective that organizes detail into significance" (Wagner, 1986b, p. 131). (The term "binocular" reminds one of Bateson's [1980, 1982] description of human [and other animal] relationships by analogy with binocular vision. See the Conclusion.)

Conclusion: The Mutuality of Being Apart

1 My critical comments draw upon Stasch (2009, pp. 8–11). They also draw on Jacques Derrida's (1972, 1983) critique of "logocentrism." Derrida

argued that the Western philosophical tradition tended to reduce the truth of language to the act of speaking. In the self-presence of the spoken word, meaning seems to stand alone, to be fully present to itself and to us. Derrida valorized writing over speech for the way in which it allows one to think the relationship between signification and being as other than presence. Writing as a doubly displaced sign of the spoken comes to emblematize the meaning of language conceived otherwise. First, because all written signifiers refer themselves to spoken signifiers, the written involves a greater displacement and distance from any would-be final, signifieds. Second, writing involves a displacement between the participant frameworks of its production and reception – the author is not present when the reader reads. Citation (Nakassis 2013, 2016a) and intertextual allusion – meaning rooted in displacement – become prototypic of a linguistic signification that is always partial and multiple, always unstable, neither original nor final. Writing, not speech, captures our "thrown-ness" into meaning. A similar problem of presence seems to be at work in the "mutuality of being" formulation. Much as with the determination of the truth of language in speech, the truth of kinship (relationship) is ultimately located in the purported transparency of "direct" and "unmediated" interpersonal contact. If the analogy holds, one might ask: What counts as the "writing" of kinship? How does the avoidance dyad "inscribe" its relationship? Is there any relating that does not leave its "trace"?, etc.

2 "If you want to talk about, say, pride, you have to talk about two persons, and what happens between them. 'A is admired by B' and 'B's admiration is conditional and may turn to contempt' and so on. You have to gather up the contingency patterns of the relationship. Similarly, with dependency, courage, passive-aggressive behaviour, fatalism, and all characterological attributes. These should all be expanded, in their definitions at least, to the patterns of interchange in combinations of double description" (Bateson, 1982, p. 5).

3 The intimate connection between character, relationship, and interaction was a theme that informed Bateson's work from the very start of his career. In his path-breaking ethnography of the Iatmul (Papua New Guinea), Bateson offered a preliminary account of the connection between interpersonal relationship and characterological attribute. He designated this connection with the concept of "ethos," which he defined as "the expression of a culturally standardised system of organisation of the instincts and emotions of the individuals" (Bateson, 1958, p. 118). An ethos is not a static repertoire of stereotyped behaviours and feelings. Rather, ethoses are coupled, mutually motivating, ways of being that stimulate and foster one another. In order to model the interactional back-and-forth of relationship,

Bateson (1972) coined another neologism, "schismogenesis," to describe positive feedback loops in interpersonal interactional sequences. He distinguished between two types: "(*a*) *symmetrical schismogenesis*, where the mutually promoting actions of A and B were essentially similar, *e.g.*, in cases of competition, rivalry, and the like; and (*b*) *complementary schismogenesis*, where the mutually promoting actions are essentially dissimilar but mutually appropriate, *e.g.*, in cases of dominance-submission, succoring-dependence, exhibitionism-spectatorship, and the like" (p. 109). Bateson's concept of schismogenesis suggests both the dialogic mutuality of relationship – the way one comportment "triggers" another – and the idea that these dynamics may involve the progressive amplification of a relational quality across a sequence of interactional pair-parts or events.

4 Escalating intensification is often apparent in interactional sequences characteristic of joking relationships. Take, for instance, the following sequences that Suzette Heald (1990) describes for Gisu (Uganda) joking relatives:

> The [*bukulo* joking] relationship is developed by the reciprocal "snatching" – known by the special term, *xutubuta* – of each other's property. These thefts begin with small items, such as pots or chickens, and progress to goods of higher value, the aim being to snatch a cow from each other. Such snatching is done strictly by turn, with one man initiating the exchange and then waiting until his partner retaliates by taking an item of equivalent value. The way is then open to snatching items of greater value, and so on, with the taking of cattle effectively ending the cycle of escalation. Any further snatching between the two is then said to begin anew with the taking of chickens. (p. 383)

This sequence conforms fairly well to the symmetrical schismogenesis model (see note 3 for definitions). The snatching of a chicken elicits not a claim of theft but a reciprocal action of similar kind. This in turn elicits the snatching of an object of "higher value." The legibility of each move one step "up" in the escalatory pattern implicitly relies upon a framework of commensurability (here a framework of relative values of portable possessions). The escalatory pattern plateaus with "the taking of cattle" – the paradigmatic objectification of value for the Gisu – at which point the sequence can be re-initiated. Note how the schismogenetic sequence involves a dynamic flipping back and forth of perspectives. At any given turn in the sequence, the same action is considered a provocation (by one interactant) and a response to a provocation (by the other).

5 Drawing on his own personal experience, Tylor (1889, p. 246) had suggested that "a reason readily presents itself [for affinal avoidance], inasmuch as the ceremony of not speaking to and pretending not to see some well-known person close by, is familiar enough to ourselves in the social rite which we call 'cutting' [i.e. 'cutting off contact with someone']. This,

indeed, with us implies aversion, and the implication comes out even more strongly in objection to utter the name ('we never mention her,' as the song has it)."

6 To be fair to Parsons, her analysis clearly acknowledges that avoidance is mediated by conventions. These newcomers, "as strangers ... are ... embarrassing or disconcerting; and so the family, in self-protection, – notably its senior members, – makes rules for their conduct, particularly rules against seeing too much of them or seeing them at awkward moments" (Parsons, 1916, p. 288). The question remains: If the rules are meant to circumvent the embarrassment, why should the embarrassment be felt all the more intensely when the rules are followed?

7 So, for instance: "The native explanation for [Gurindji, Australia] mali [i.e., wife's mother-daughter's husband] avoidance is minyirri 'shame, embarrassment.' The less strict form of avoidance is called mapu-mapu 'little bit of shame' (mapu is the word for 'shame' in the adjoining Mudbura language)" (McConvell, 1982, p. 94).

8 Although shame is conceptualized and symbolized differently in different language communities, it has biological bases that stabilize its cross-cultural expression. Shame displays have deep phylogenetic roots and were likely adaptive in human evolution (Fessler, 2004). The same stereotyped shame displays are attested across different cultures – in particular, the aversion to, and withdrawal from, social interaction and downturned eye gaze. And these displays are analogous to "appeasement" displays in nonhuman primates (Keltner et al., 1997, after de Waal, 1986). Appeasement displays are well understood as evolved signals of (acceptance of) subordinate status. Their adaptive value derives from their role in conflict mitigation; if low-ranked individuals signal acceptance of their subordination, high-ranked individuals have no incentive to engage in costly conflicts with them to establish or assert their dominance. Distinguishing it from guilt, shame in humans conserves this necessarily intersubjective and social signalling function – shame displays signal ego's acceptance of the (actual or imagined) social disapproval of other members of the social group (Maibom, 2010; cf. Goffman, 1956, on embarrassment). In the human context, there is thus a paradoxical meta-communicative dimension to shame displays. Ashamed individuals voluntarily remove themselves from the social scene. However, in so doing, they enact respect for the very social norms the adherence to which is indexical of group membership. Ashamed individuals thus signal their membership in the group in and by symbolically removing themselves from it.

9 Freud's interpretation of kinship avoidance as an intensified or generalized form of incest restrictions had an important influence on

mid-twentieth-century American anthropology. Psychology seemed capable of grounding a positivistic and comparative science of the human. Avoidance customs, from this perspective, were the "outer" (social and collective) form of a repression of sexual instincts that was its "inner" (psychological and individual) content. In his magnum opus, *Social Structure*, G.P. Murdock (1967) treated avoidance in a chapter entitled "The Regulation of Sex." (See the Introduction for a critique of Murdock's comparative methodology.) Individual psychology provided the universalizing framework within which Murdock could frame the problem of avoidance. Subscribing to the Freudian interpretation, Murdock hypothesized that kinship avoidances were necessary where incest taboos were not sufficiently integrated into the unconscious psychology of the individual. (See Stephens, 1962, for the fullest development of this position; see McCurdy, 1959, for an empirical refutation of the hypothesis as concerns brother–sister avoidance.) In Murdock's view, kinship avoidance is a prosthetic/supplement that fills in the gaps where personal psychology has failed to sufficiently regulate the individual. "*Our* own society" does not require elaborate avoidance restrictions, "so thoroughly do *we* instill *our* sex mores in the consciences of individuals that *we* feel quite safe in trusting *our* internalized sanctions" (Murdock, 1967, p. 273; italics added). Frontal comparison – marked by the switch to first-person plural pronouns – projects psychological deviance onto the other by identifying the first-person perspective (of the author/reader of Murdock's positivistic social scientific tract) with the "normally" developed individual (see Candea, 2019, on "frontal" [us/them] vs. "lateral" [them/them] comparison in anthropology).

10 As an example, take the cross-sex sibling avoidance so widespread in island Melanesia and Polynesia. Avoidance between siblings raised together is typically the most intense and ritualized, with fade-out with more "distant" classificatory cross-sex siblings. Importantly, onset of avoidance is not from birth but usually at or around puberty – that is, after the period of early childhood exposure to the other. Among Birao speakers of Guadalcanal, "as soon as a boy is about 10 years old he ceases to sleep in the family dwelling but goes instead to the men's house" (Hogbin, 1937, p. 68). From that time onward he and his sister avoid ever being alone together, ever eating together, or mentioning each other's names or the everyday words from which they are derived. Here, as elsewhere, the sexual theme is highly salient: "Sexual matters are expressly forbidden as topics in conversation, and it is said that before a person makes any remark with a sexual significance he is careful to glance around to see whether a pair of brothers, or a brother and sister, are present" (p. 68).

If we take the Westermarck effect seriously, it is clear that cross-sex sibling avoidance does not arise from a need to repress incestuous relationships. On the contrary, brother–sister avoidance draws upon this biological priming in symbolizing social relationship (cf. Sperber, 1985). Just as the natural world is a resource for *bricolage* in totemic imaginaries (Lévi-Strauss, 2021), biologically primed human nature (*qua* evolved psychological biases) provides a palette that cultural orders draw upon in symbolizing the social. Far from reducing the sexual element in the brother–sister relationship, cross-sex sibling avoidance works to fosters the conscious and reflexive consideration of it – it forces the individual to think the unthinkable. Avoidance plays off of, or tropes upon, the biologically primed disinclination to experience a childhood companion as an object of sexual desire. The terror that Mandak or Lelet express about the possibility of sexual desire for a cross-sex sibling suggests that such a desire is experienced as doubly unnatural (Clay, 1977, p. 94; Eves, 1998, p. 130).

11 See also Gregory's (2011) concept of "skinship." Unfortunately, I came across his important article only after having completed the major revisions for this manuscript, so I have not been able to do justice to his empirical materials or the conclusions that he draws from them.

References

Aberle, D.F. (1961). Navaho. In D. Schneider & K. Gough (Eds.), *Matrilineal kinship* (pp. 96–101). University of California Press.

Abu-Lughod, L. (1986). *Veiled sentiments: Honour and poetry in a Bedouin society*. University of California Press.

Abu-Lughod, L. (2015). *Do Muslim women need saving?* Harvard University Press.

Adane, D. (2014). Social deixis in Hadiyya. *International Journal of Language and Linguistics*, 2(5), 301–4. http://doi.org/10.11648/j.ijll.20140205.12

Adeney-Risakotta, F. (2005). *Politics, ritual and identity in Indonesia: A Moluccan history of religion and social conflict*. Prima Center.

Adriani, N. (1893). *Sangireesche spraakkunst*. A.H. Adriani.

Agha, A. (1993). Grammatical and indexical convention in honorific discourse. *Journal of Linguistic Anthropology*, 3(2), 131–63. http://doi.org/10.1525/jlin.1993.3.2.131

Agha, A. (1998). Stereotypes and registers of honorific language. *Language in Society*, 27(2), 151–93. http://doi.org/10.1017/S0047404598002012

Agha, A. (2000). Register. *Journal of Linguistic Anthropology*, 9(1–2), 216–19. http://doi.org/10.1525/jlin.1999.9.1-2.216

Agha, A. (2003). The social life of cultural value. *Language & Communication*, 23(3–4), 231–73. http://doi.org/10.1016/S0271-5309(03)00012-0

Agha, A. (2005). Voice, footing, enregisterment. *Journal of Linguistic Anthropology*, 15(1), 38–59. http://doi.org/10.1525/jlin.2005.15.1.38

Agha, A. (2007). *Language and social relations*. Cambridge University Press.

Aikhenvald, A.Y. (2016). *How gender shapes the world*. Oxford University Press. https://doi.org/10.1093/acprof:oso/9780198723752.001.0001

Aikhenvald, A. (n.d.) *Names and naming in Papuan languages of New Guinea*. Unpublished manuscript.

Alia, V. (2007). *Names and Nunavut: Culture and identity in Arctic Canada*. Berghahn Books.

Allen, M.R. (1984a). Elders, chiefs, and big men: Authority legitimation and political evolution in Melanesia. *American Ethnologist*, *11*(1), 20–41. https://doi.org/10.1525/ae.1984.11.1.02a00020

Allen, M.R. (1984b). Ritualized homosexuality, male power and political organization in North Vanuatu: A comparative analysis. In G.H. Herdt (Ed.), *Ritualized homosexuality in Melanesia* (pp. 83–127). University of California Press. https://doi.org/10.1525/9780520341388-003

Alpher, B. (1991). *Yir-Yoront lexicon: Sketch and dictionary of an Australian language*. Mouton de Gruyter. https://doi.org/10.1515/9783110872651

Alpher, B. (1993). Out-of-the-ordinary ways of using language. In M. Walsh & C. Yallop (Eds.), Language and culture in Aboriginal Australia (pp. 97–106). Australian Aboriginal Studies Press.

Ameka, F. (2004). Grammar and cultural practices: The grammaticalization of triadic communication in West African Languages. *Journal of West African Languages*, *30*(2), 5–28.

Anderson, J.W. (1982). Social structure and the veil: Comportment and the composition of interaction in Afghanistan. *Anthropos*, *77*(3–4), 397–420.

Apicella, C.L., Marlowe, F.W., Fowler, J.H., & Christakis, N.A. (2012). Social networks and cooperation in hunter-gatherers. *Nature*, *481*, 497–501. https://doi.org/10.1038/nature10736

Arghynbaev, Kh.A. (1984). Kinship system and customs connected with the ban on pronouncing the personal names of elder relatives among the Kazakhs. In T. Dragadze (Ed.), *Kinship and marriage in the Soviet Union: Field studies* (pp. 40–59). Routledge & Kegan Paul.

Armstrong, W.E. (1928). *Rossel Island: An ethnological study*. Cambridge University Press.

Asad, T. (2009). Free speech, blasphemy, and secular criticism. In T. Asad, W. Brown, J. Butler, & S. Mahmood, *Is critique secular? Blasphemy, injury, and free speech* (pp. 20–63). University of California Press.

Austin, J.L. (1962). *How to do things with words*. Harvard University Press.

Bakhtin, M.M. (1981). Discourse in the novel. In M. Holquist (Ed.), *The dialogical magination* (pp. 259–422). University of Texas Press.

Bala, M., & Koul, O.N. (1989). *Modes of address and pronominal usage in Punjabi: A sociolinguistic study*. Central Institute of Indian Languages.

Ball, C. (2015). Avoidance as alterity stance: An Upper Xinguan affinity chronotope. *Anthropological Quarterly*, *88*(2), 337–72. https://doi.org/10.1353/anq.2015.0027

Bamford, S., & Leach, J. (2009). Introduction: Pedigrees of knowledge: Anthropology and the genealogical method. In S. Bamford & J. Leach (Eds.), *Kinship and beyond: The genealogical method reconsidered* (pp. 1–23). Berghahn Books. https://doi.org/10.1515/9781845458966-002

Banfield, A. (1993). Where epistemology, style, and grammar meet literary history: The development of represented speech and thought. In J.A. Lucy (Ed.), *Reflexive language: Reported speech and metapragmatics* (pp. 339–64). Cambridge University Press. https://doi.org/10.1017/CBO9780511621031.018

Barakat, R. (1975). *The Cistercian sign language: A study in non-verbal communication*. Cistercian Publications.

Barnard, A. (1978a). The kin terminology system of the Nharo Bushmen. *Cahiers d'études africaines*, 18(72), 607–29. https://doi.org/10.3406/cea.1978.2370

Barnard, A. (1978b). Universal systems of kin categorization. *African Studies*, 37(1), 69–82. https://doi.org/10.1080/00020187808707509

Barnes, R.H. (1980). Hidatsa personal names: An interpretation. *Plains Anthropologist*, 25(90), 311–31. https://doi.org/10.1080/2052546.1980.11909001

Baron-Cohen, S. (1997). *Mindblindness: An essay on autism and theory of mind*. MIT Press.

Basso, E.B. (1975). Kalapalo affinity: Its cultural and social contexts. *American Ethnologist*, 2(2), 207–28. https://doi.org/10.1525/ae.1975.2.2.02a00010

Basso, E.B. (2007). The Kalapalo affinal civility register. *Journal of Linguistic Anthropology*, 17(2), 161–83. https://doi.org/10.1525/jlin.2007.17.2.161

Basu, D.N. (1975). A socio-linguistic study of the Bangla kinship terms. *Indian Linguistics*, 36, 217–26.

Bateson, G. (1958). *Naven*. Stanford University Press. https://doi.org/10.1515/9781503621138

Bateson, G. (1972). *Steps to an ecology of mind*. Chandler.

Bateson, G. (1980). *Mind and nature: A necessary unity*. Bantam.

Bateson, G. (1982). Difference, double description, and the interactive designation of the self. In F. Hanson (Ed.), *Studies in symbolism and cultural communication* (pp. 3–8). University of Kansas.

Bean, S.S. (1970). Two's company, three's a crowd. *American Anthropologist*, 72(3), 562–4. https://doi.org/10.1525/aa.1970.72.3.02a00080

Bean, S.S. (1978). *Symbolic and pragmatic semantics: A Kannada system of address*. University of Chicago Press.

Beidelman, T.O. (1997). *The cool knife: Imagery of gender, sexuality, and moral education in Kaguru initiation ritual*. Smithsonian Institution Press.

Bell, F.L.S. (1962). Kinship avoidance and linguistic evasion in Tanga, New Ireland. *Mankind*, 5(11), 477–9. https://doi.org/10.1111/j.1835-9310.1962.tb00278.x

Bellman, B.L. (1984). *The language of secrecy: Symbols and metaphors in Poro ritual*. Rutgers University Press. https://doi.org/10.36019/9781978816800

Benet, S. (1974). *Abkhasians: The long-living people of the Caucasus*. Holt, Rinehart and Winston.

Benjamin, G. (1967). Temiar kinship. *Federation Museums Journal*, 12, 1–25.

Benjamin, G. (1968). Temiar personal names. *Bijdragen tot de Taal-, Land- en Volkenkunde, 124*(1), 99–134. https://doi.org/10.1163/22134379-90002886

Benjamin, G. (1999). *Temiar kinship terminology: A linguistic and formal analysis.* Academy of Social Sciences (AKASS).

Benveniste, É. (1971). *Problems in general linguistics* (M. Meek, Trans.). University of Florida Press.

Berberian, H. (2004). Armenian women and women in Armenian religion. In S. Joseph & A. Najmabadi (Eds.), *Encyclopedia of women and Islamic cultures, Vol. II* (pp. 10–14). Brill.

Berberian, H. (2008, 28 July). Armenian women in the late 19th- and early 20th-century Persia. *Encyclopædia Iraenica.* Updated 12 August 2011, from https://www.iranicaonline.org/articles/armenia-ii-women

Berezkin, Y., & Duvakin, E. (2016). The captive khan and the clever daughter-in-law. *Folklore, 64,* 33–56. https://doi.org/10.7592/FEJF2016.64.khan

Bergsland, K., & Vogt, H. (1962). On the validity of glottochronology. *Current Anthropology, 3*(2), 115–53. https://doi.org/10.1086/200264

Berlin, B. (1992). *Ethnobiological classification: Principles of categorization of plants and animals in traditional societies.* Princeton University Press. https://doi.org/10.1515/9781400862597

Bickel, B., Bisang, W. & Yādava, Y.P. (1999). Face vs. empathy: The social foundation of Maithili verb agreement. *Linguistics, 37*(3), 481–518. https://doi.org/10.1515/ling.37.3.481

Bird-David, N. (2017). *Us, relatives: Scaling and plural life in a forager world.* University of California Press. https://doi.org/10.1525/california/9780520293403.001.0001

Birtalan, Á. (2003). Oirat. In J. Janhunen (Ed.), *The Mongolic languages* (pp. 210–28). Routledge.

Blackwood, B. (1935). *Both sides of Buka passage: An ethnographic study of social, sexual, and economic questions in the North-Western Solomon Islands.* Clarendon.

Bliege Bird, R., & Smith, E.A. (2005). Signaling theory, strategic interaction, and symbolic capital. *Current Anthropology, 46*(2), 221–48. https://doi.org/10.1086/427115

Bloch, M., & Sperber, D. (2002). Kinship and evolved psychological dispositions: The mother's brother controversy reconsidered. *Current Anthropology, 43*(5), 723–34. https://doi.org/10.1086/341654

Blom, J.-P., & Gumperz, J. (1972). Code-switching in Norway. In J. Gumperz & D. Hymes (Eds.), *Directions in sociolinguistics* (pp. 407–34). Holt, Rinehart and Winston.

Blythe, J. (2013). Preference organization driving structuration: Evidence from Australian Aboriginal interaction for pragmatically motivated grammaticalization. *Language, 89*(4), 883–919. https://doi.org/10.1353/lan.2013.0057

Blythe, J. (2018). Genesis of the trinity: The convergent evolution of trirelational kinterms. In P. McConvell, P. Kelly, & S. Lacrampe (Eds.), *Skin, kin and clan: The dynamics of social categories in Indigenous Australia* (pp. 431–72). ANU Press. https://doi.org/10.22459/SKC.04.2018.13

Boas, F. (1911). Introduction. In *Handbook of American Indian languages, 1*, 1–83. Bureau of American Ethnology.

Boltz, W.G. (1994). *The origin and early development of the Chinese writing system*. American Oriental Society.

Bongela, K.S. (2001). *Isihlonipho among AmaXhosa* [Unpublished doctoral dissertation]. University of South Africa.

Bossen, L., & Gates, H. (2017). *Bound feet, young hands: Tracking the demise of footbinding in village China*. Stanford University Press. https://doi.org/10.2307/j.ctvqsdshq

Bourdieu, P. (1979). *La distinction : critique sociale du jugement*. Les éditions de minuit.

Bowen, J.R. (2007). *Why the French don't like headscarves: Islam, the state, and public space*. Princeton University Press.

Boyer, P. (1980). Les figures du savoir initiatique. *Journal des africanistes, 50*(2), 31–57. https://doi.org/10.3406/jafr.1980.2002

Boyer, R.M., & Gayton, N.D. (1992). *Apache mothers and daughters: Four generations of a family*. University of Oklahoma Press.

Bradley, J. (1988). Yanyuwa: "Men speak one way, women speak another." *Aboriginal Linguistics, 1*, 126–34.

Bright, W. (1958). Karok names. *Names, 6*(3), 172–9. https://doi.org/10.1179/nam.1958.6.3.172

Bright, W. (1979). Toward a typology of verbal abuse: Naming dead kin in northwestern California. *Maledicta, 3*, 177–80.

Brightman, R. (1993). *Grateful prey: Rock Cree human-animal relationships*. University of California Press.

Brosius, J.P. (1995). Signifying bereavement: Form and context in the analysis of Penan death-names. *Oceania, 66*(2), 119–46. https://doi.org/10.1002/j.1834-4461.1995.tb02540.x

Brosius, J.P. (1996). Father dead, mother dead: Bereavement and fictive death in Penan Geng society. *Omega, 32*(3), 197–226. https://doi.org/10.2190/WH9X-CCK2-BTL7-BQ8G

Brown, C.H. (1984). *Language and living things: Uniformities in folk classification and naming*. Rutgers University Press. https://doi.org/10.36019/9781978815711

Brown, P. (1980). How and why are women more polite: Some evidence from a Mayan community. In S. McConnell-Ginet, R. Borker, & N. Furman (Eds.), *Women and language in literature and society* (pp. 111–36). Praeger.

Brown, P., & Levinson, S.C. (1987). *Politeness: Some universals in language usage*. Cambridge University Press. https://doi.org/10.1017/CBO9780511813085

Brown, R., & Ford, M. (1961). Address in American English. *Journal of Abnormal and Social Psychology*, 62(2), 375–85. https://doi.org/10.1037/h0042862

Brown, R., & Gilman, A. (1960). The pronouns of power and solidarity. In T.A. Sebeok (Ed.), *Style in language* (pp. 253–76). MIT Press.

Bruce, S.G. (2007). *Silence and sign language in medieval monasticism: The Cluniac tradition, c. 900–1200*. Cambridge University Press. https://doi.org/10.1017/CBO9780511496417

Buber, M. (1970). *I and thou*. Simon & Schuster.

Bull, W.E. (1960). *Time, tense, and the verb*. University of California Press.

Bulmer, R. (1967). Why is the cassowary not a bird? A problem of zoological taxonomy among the Karam of the New Guinea highlands. *Man*, 2(1), 5–25. https://doi.org/10.2307/2798651

Burenhult, N. (2005). *A grammar of Jahai*. Pacific Linguistics.

Burrows, E. (1936). *Ethnology of Futuna*. Bernice P. Bishop Museum.

Busse, M. (2005). "We will exchange sisters until the world ends": Inequality, marriage and gender relations in the Lake Murray-Middle Fly Area, Papua New Guinea. In C. Gross, H.D. Lyons, & D.A. Counts (Eds.), *A polymath anthropologist: Essays in honour of Ann Chowning* (pp. 79–88). University of Auckland.

Butler, J. (1997). *Excitable speech: A politics of the performative*. Routledge.

Campbell, L. (2004). *Historical linguistics: An introduction*. MIT Press.

Candea, M. (2019). *Comparison in anthropology: The impossible method*. Cambridge University Press. https://doi.org/10.1017/9781108667609

Carsten, J. (1995). The substance of kinship and the heat of the hearth: Feeding, personhood, and relatedness among Malays in Pulau Langkawi. *American Ethnologist*, 22(2), 223–41. https://doi.org/10.1525/ae.1995.22.2.02a00010

Carsten, J. (Ed.). (2000). *Cultures of relatedness: New approaches to the study of kinship*. Cambridge University Press.

Carruthers, A.M. (2017a). Grading qualities and (un)settling equivalences: Undocumented migration, commensuration, and intrusive phonosonics in the Indonesia-Malaysia borderlands. *Journal of Linguistic Anthropology*, 27(2), 124–50. https://doi.org/10.1111/jola.12153

Carruthers, A.M. (2017b). "Their accent would betray them": Clandestine movement and the sound of "illegality" in Malaysia's borderlands. *Sojourn: Journal of Social Issues in Southeast Asia*, 32(2), 221–59. https://doi.org/10.1355/sj32-2a

Caton, S.C. (1986). *Salāam tahīyah*: Greetings from the highlands of Yemen. *American Ethnologist*, 13(2), 290–308. https://doi.org/10.1525/ae.1986.13.2.02a00060

Cauquelin, J. (2004). *The Aborigines of Taiwan—The Puyuma: From headhunting to the modern world*. Routledge. https://doi.org/10.4324/9780203498590

Chandralal, D. (2010). *Sinhala*. John Benjamins. https://doi.org/10.1075/loall.15

Cheesman, L.E. (1933). The island of Malekula, New Hebrides. *The Geographical Journal, 81*(3), pp. 193–207. https://doi.org/10.2307/1784034

Chirikba, V.A. (2015). Abkhaz personal names. *Iran and the Caucasus, 19*(4), 343–56. https://doi.org/10.1163/1573384X-20150405

Choksi, N. (2010). The dual as honorific in Santali. In *Proceedings of the 32nd all India Conference of Linguists* (pp. 125–30). University of Lucknow.

Choksi, N. (2021). Structure, ideology, distribution: The dual as honorific in Santali. *Journal of Linguistic Anthropology, 31*(3), 382–95. https://doi.org/10.1111/jola.12343

Chowning, A. (1980). Culture and biology among the Sengseng of New Britain. *The Journal of the Polynesian Society, 89*(1), 7–31.

Chowning, A. (1985). Rapid lexical change and aberrant Melanesian languages: Sengseng and its neighbours. In A. Pawley & L. Carrington (Eds.), *Austronesian linguistics at the 16th Pacific Science Congress* (pp. 169–98). ANU Press.

Clay, B.J. (1977). *Pinikindu: Maternal nurture, paternal substance*. University of Chicago Press.

Clendon, M. (2014). *Worrorra: A language of the north-west Kimberley coast*. University of Adelaide Press. https://doi.org/10.20851/worrorra

Clyne, M., Norrby, C., & Warren, J. (2009). *Language and human relations: Styles of address in contemporary language*. Cambridge University Press. https://doi.org/10.1017/CBO9780511576690

Codrington, R.H. (1957). *The Melanesians: Studies in their anthropology and folklore*. HRAF Press. (Original work published 1891)

Collier, J., & Rosaldo, M.Z. (1981). Politics and gender in simple societies. In S. Ortner & H. Whitehead (Eds.), *Sexual meanings: The cultural construction of gender and sexuality* (pp. 275–329). Cambridge University Press.

Collins, J.T. (1989). Notes on the language of Taliabo. *Oceanic Linguistics, 28*(1), 75–95. https://doi.org/10.2307/3622975

Comrie, B. (1976). Linguistic politeness axes: Speaker-addressee, speaker-referent, speaker-bystander. *Pragmatics Microfiche, 1*(7), 1–12.

Comrie, B. (2000). Language contact, lexical borrowing, and semantic fields. In D.G. Gilbers, J. Nerbonne, & J. Schaeken (Eds.), *Languages in contact* (pp. 73–86). Rodopi. https://doi.org/10.1163/9789004488472_008

Corbett, G.G. (2000). *Number*. Cambridge University Press. https://doi.org/10.1017/CBO9781139164344

Corbett, G.G. (2012). Politeness as a feature: So important and so rare. *Linguistik Online, 51*(1), 9–27. https://doi.org/10.13092/lo.51.302

Crowley, T. (1983). Uradhi. In R.M.W. Dixon & B.J. Blake (Eds.), *Handbook of Australian languages, vol. 3* (pp. 306–428). John Benjamins.

Crowley, T., & Bowern C. (2010). *An introduction to historical linguistics*. Oxford University Press.
Csordas, T.J. (2008). Intersubjectivity and intercorporeality. *Subjectivity*, 22, 110–21. https://doi.org/10.1057/sub.2008.5
Cysouw, M. (2003). *The paradigmatic structure of person marking*. Oxford University Press. https://doi.org/10.1093/oso/9780199254125.001.0001
Da Matta, R. (1982). *A divided world: Apinayé social structure* (A. Campbell, Trans.). Harvard University Press. https://doi.org/10.4159/harvard.9780674419094
Das, S.K. (1968). Forms of address and terms of reference in Bengali. *Anthropological Linguistics*, 10(4), 19–31.
Dasgupta, S. (1986). *Caste kinship and community: Social system of a Bengal caste*. Universities Press.
Davies, J. (1991). Marked pronouns and verbs for marked social relationships in a Chadic and a Papuan language. In A. Pawley (Ed.), *Man and a half: Essays in Pacific anthropology and ethnobiology in honour of Ralph Bulmer* (pp. 397–405). Polynesian Society.
Davies, W.N.G., & Quinche, C. (1933). AmaNdebele taboos and etiquette. *Bantu Studies*, 7(1), 277–84. https://doi.org/10.1080/02561751.1933.9676322
Dawson, J. (1881). *Australian Aborigines: The languages and customs of several tribes of Aborigines in the western district of Victoria, Australia*. George Robertson.
Deacon, T. (1998). *The symbolic species: The co-evolution of language and the brain*. W.W. Norton.
Dean, M. (2011). *From darsan to tirusti: "Evil eye" and the politics of visibility in contemporary South India* [Unpublished doctoral dissertation]. University of Pennsylvania.
Deger, J. (2008). Imprinting on the heart: Photography and contemporary Yolngu mournings. *Visual Anthropology*, 21(4), 292–309. https://doi.org/10.1080/08949460802156318
Delaporte, Y. (2009). La langue des signes des moines trappistes : de la norme aux usages réels. In A. Herrou & G. Krauskopff (Eds.), *Moines et moniales de par le monde : la vie monastique au miroir de la parenté* (pp. 91–102). L'Harmattan.
Dench, A. (1987). Kinship and collective activity in the Ngayarda languages of Australia. *Language in Society*, 16(3), 321–39. https://doi.org/10.1017/S0047404500012410
Dench, A. (1991). Panyjima. In R.M.W. Dixon & B.J. Blake (Eds.), *Handbook of Australian languages*, vol. 4 (pp. 124–243). Oxford University Press.
de Pina-Cabral, J. (2010). Xará: Namesakes in southern Mozambique and Bahia (Brazil). *Ethnos*, 75(3), 323–45. https://doi.org/10.1080/00141844.2010.516837
Derrida, J. (1972). *De la grammatologie*. Les éditions de minuit.

Derrida, J. (1983). *Margins of philosophy* (A. Bass, Trans.). University of Chicago Press.

Descola, P. (2005). *Par-delà nature et culture*. Gallimard.

de Waal, F.B.M. (1986). The integration of dominance and social bonding in primates. *The Quarterly Review of Biology*, 61(4), 459–79. https://doi.org/10.1086/415144

Diffloth, G. (1980). To taboo everything at all times. *Berkeley Linguistics Society*, 6, 157–65. https://doi.org/10.3765/bls.v6i0.2141

Dixon, R.M.W. (1971). A method of semantic description. In D.D. Steinberg & L.S. Jakobovits (Eds.), *Semantics: An interdisciplinary reader in philosophy, linguistics, and psychology* (pp. 436–71). Cambridge University Press.

Dixon, R.M.W. (1972). *The Dyirbal language of north Queensland*. Cambridge University Press. https://doi.org/10.1017/CBO9781139084987

Dixon, R.M.W. (1980). *The languages of Australia*. Cambridge University Press.

Dixon, R.M.W. (1982). *Where have all the adjectives gone? And other essays in semantics and syntax*. Mouton. https://doi.org/10.1515/9783110822939

Dixon, R.M.W. (1984). *Searching for Aboriginal languages*. University of Queensland Press.

Dixon, R.M.W. (1990). The origin of "mother-in-law vocabulary" in two Australian languages. *Anthropological Linguistics*, 32(1/2), 1–56.

Dixon, R.M.W., & Aikhenvald, A.Y. (2002). *Word: A cross-linguistic typology*. Cambridge University Press. https://doi.org/10.1017/CBO9780511486241

Dowdy, S. (2015). Reflections on a shared name: Taboo and destiny in Mayong (Assam). *South Asia Multidisciplinary Academic Journal*, 12, 1–26. https://doi.org/10.4000/samaj.4027

Dowling, T. (1988). "Hloniphani bafazi!"/"Women, respect!" Isihlonipho sabafazi – The Xhosa women's language of respect – The oral transmission of sexism? In E. Sienart & A.A. Bell (Eds.), *Catching winged words: Oral tradition and education* (pp. 177–81). Natal University Oral Documentation and Research Center.

Driver, H.E. (1966). Geographical-historical versus psycho-functional explanations of kin avoidances. *Current Anthropology*, 7(2), 131–82. https://doi.org/10.1086/200690

Drucker, P.A. (1937). The Tolowa and their southwest Oregon kin. *University of California Publications in American Archaeology and Ethnology*, 36(4), 221–300.

Drucker-Brown, S. (1982). Joking at death: The Mamprusi grandparent-grandchild joking relationship. *Man*, 17(4), 714–27. https://doi.org/10.2307/2802042

Du Bois, C. (1935). Wintu ethnography. *University of California Publications in American Archaeology and Ethnology*, 36(1), 1–158.

Dyen, I. (1963). Lexicostatistically determined borrowing and taboo. *Language*, 39(1), 60–6. https://doi.org/10.2307/410762

Dziebel, G.V. (2007). *The genius of kinship: The phenomenon of human kinship and the global diversity of kinship terminologies.* Cambria Press.

Eck, D. (1985). *Darsan.* Columbia University Press.

Eilberg-Schwartz, H., & Doniger, W. (1995). Off with her head! The denial of women's identity in myth, religion, and culture. University of California Press. https://doi.org/10.1525/9780520915312

Eggan, F. (1937). The Cheyenne and Arapaho kinship system. In F. Eggan (Ed.), *Social anthropology of North American tribes* (pp. 35–95). University of Chicago Press.

El Guindi, F. (1999). *Veil: Modesty, privacy and resistance.* Berg.

Elkin, A.P. (1940). Kinship in South Australia. *Oceania, 10*(3), 295–349. https://doi.org/10.1002/j.1834-4461.1940.tb00295.x

Elkin, A.P. (1950). Ngirawat, or the sharing of names in the Wagaitj tribe, northern Australia. In I. Tönnies (Ed.), *Beiträge zur Gesellungs- und Völkerwissenschaft* (pp. 67–81). Gebrüder Mann.

Ellen, R.F. (1983). Semantic anarchy and ordered social practice in Nuaulu personal naming. *Bijdragen tot de Taal-, Land- en Volkenkunde, 139*(1), 18–45. https://doi.org/10.1163/22134379-90003454

Elmendorf, W.W. (1951). Word taboo and lexical change in Coast Salish. *International Journal of American Linguistics, 17*(4), 205–8. https://doi.org/10.1086/464130

Enfield, N.J. (Ed.). (2002). *Ethnosyntax.* Oxford University Press.

Enfield, N.J. (2022). Asymmetries in the system of person reference in Kri, a language of upland Laos. In D.N. Djenar & J. Sidnell (Eds.), *Signs of deference, signs of demeanour: Interlocutor reference and self-other relations across Southeast Asian speech communities* (pp. 27–43). NUS Press. https://doi.org/10.2307/jj.285053.6

Enfield, N.J., & Sidnell, J. (2017). *The concept of action.* Cambridge University Press. https://doi.org/10.1017/9781139025928

Enfield, N.J., & Stivers, T. (Eds.). (2007). *Person reference in interaction: Linguistic, cultural and social perspectives.* Cambridge University Press. https://doi.org/10.1017/CBO9780511486746

Errington, J.J. (1985). On the nature of the sociolinguistic sign: Describing the Javanese speech levels. In E. Mertz & R.J. Parmentier (Eds.), *Semiotic mediation: Sociocultural and psychological perspectives* (pp. 287–310). Academic Press. https://doi.org/10.1016/B978-0-12-491280-9.50018-2

Errington, J. (1988). *Structure and style in Javanese: A semiotic view of linguistic etiquette.* University of Pennsylvania Press. https://doi.org/10.9783/9781512815764

Evans, I.H.N. (1970). *Studies in religion, folk-lore & custom in British north Borneo and the Malay peninsula.* Frank Cass & Co.

Evans, N. (1992). Multiple semiotic systems, hyperpolysemy, and the reconstruction of semantic change in Australian languages. In G.

Kellermann & M.D. Morrissey (Eds.), *Diachrony within synchrony: Language history and cognition* (pp. 475–508). Peter Lang.

Evans, N. (2003a). *Bininj Gun-wok: A pan-dialectal grammar of Mayali, Kunwinjku and Kune.* Australian National University.

Evans, N. (2003b). Context, culture, and structuration in the languages of Australia. *Annual Review of Anthropology, 32,* 13–40. https://doi.org/10.1146/annurev.anthro.32.061002.093137

Evans, N. (2006). Dyad constructions. In K. Brown (Ed.), *Encyclopedia of language and linguistics* (pp. 24–8). Elsevier. https://doi.org/10.1016/B0-08-044854-2/00188-7

Evans, N. (2013). Language diversity as a resource for understanding cultural evolution. In P.J. Richerson & M.H. Christiansen (Eds.), *Cultural evolution: Society, technology, language, and religion* (pp. 233–68). MIT Press. https://doi.org/10.7551/mitpress/9780262019750.003.0013

Eves, R. (1998). *The magical body: Power, fame and meaning in a Melanesian society.* Harwood.

Feinberg, R., & Ottenheimer, M. (Eds.). (2001). *The cultural analysis of kinship: The legacy of David M. Schneider.* University of Illinois Press.

Fessler, D. (2004). Shame in two cultures: Implications for evolutionary approaches. *Journal of Cognition and Culture, 4*(2), 207–62. https://doi.org/10.1163/1568537041725097

Finlayson, R. (1995). Women's language of respect: Isihlonipho sabafazi. In R. Mesthrie (Ed.), *Language and social history: Studies in South African sociolinguistics* (pp. 140–53). Philip.

Firth, R. (1937). *We, the Tikopia.* American Book Company.

Firth, R. (1969). Postures and gestures of respect. In P. Maranda & J. Pouillon (Eds.), *Exchange and communication: Mélanges Lévi-Strauss* (pp. 230–24). Mouton.

Fisher, L.E. (1976). *dropping remarks* and the Barbadian audience. *American Ethnologist, 3*(2), 227–42. https://doi.org/10.1525/ae.1976.3.2.02a00040

Fleck, D.W. (2013). *Panoan languages and linguistics.* American Museum of Natural History.

Fleming, L. (2011). Name taboos and rigid performativity. *Anthropological Quarterly, 84*(1), 141–64. https://doi.org/10.1353/anq.2011.0010

Fleming, L. (2012). Gender indexicality in the Native Americas: Contributions to the typology of social indexicality. *Language in Society, 41*(3), 295–320. https://doi.org/10.1017/S0047404512000267

Fleming, L. (2014a). Australian exceptionalism in the typology of affinal avoidance registers. *Anthropological Linguistics, 56*(2), 115–58. https://doi.org/10.1353/anl.2014.0006

Fleming, L. (2014b). Negating speech: Medium and modality in the development of alternate sign languages. *Gesture, 14*(3), 263–96. https://doi.org/10.1075/gest.14.3.01fle

Fleming, L. (2015a). Speaker-referent gender indexicality. *Language in Society*, 44(3), 425–34. https://doi.org/10.1017/S0047404515000251

Fleming, L. (2015b). Taxonomy and taboo: The (meta)pragmatic sources of semantic abstraction in avoidance registers. *Journal of Linguistic Anthropology*, 25(1), 43–65. https://doi.org/10.1111/jola.12073

Fleming, L. (2016). Of referents and recipients: Pohnpeian humiliatives and the functional organization of Austronesian honorific registers. *Berkeley Linguistics Society*, 42, 293–312.

Fleming, L. (2017a). Artificial language, natural history: Speech, sign, and sound in the emergence of Damin. *Language & Communication*, 56, 1–18. https://doi.org/10.1016/j.langcom.2017.01.001

Fleming, L. (2017b). Honorific alignment and pronominal paradigm: Evidence from Mixtec, Santali, and Dhimal. *Berkeley Linguistics Society*, 43, 95–120.

Fleming, L. (2022). Social indexicality. In S. Völkel & N. Nassenstein (Eds.), *Approaches to language and culture* (pp. 237–74). De Gruyter. https://doi.org/10.1515/9783110726626-010

Fleming, L. (2023). Dispensing with Europe: A comparative linguistic anthropology of honorific pronouns. *Journal of Linguistic Anthropology*, 33(1), 25–50. https://doi.org/10.1111/jola.12386

Fleming, L., & Lempert, M. (2011). Introduction: Beyond bad words. *Anthropological Quarterly*, 84(1), 5–14. https://doi.org/10.1353/anq.2011.0008

Fleming, L., Mitchell, A., & Ribot, I. (2019). In the name of the father-in-law: Pastoralism, patriarchy, and the sociolinguistic prehistory of eastern and southern Africa. *Sociolinguistic Studies*, 13(2–4), 171–92. https://doi.org/10.1558/sols.37860

Fleming, L., & Sidnell, J. (2020). The typology and social pragmatics of interlocutor reference in Southeast Asia. *Journal of Asian Linguistic Anthropology*, 1(1), 1–20. https://doi.org/10.47298/jala.v1-i1-a1

Fleming, L., & Slotta, J. (2018). The pragmatics of kin address: A sociolinguistic universal and its semantic affordances. *Journal of Sociolinguistics*, 22(4), 375–405. https://doi.org/10.1111/josl.12304

Flom, G.T. (1925). Noa words in North Sea regions: A chapter in folklore and linguistics. *The Journal of American Folklore*, 38(149), 400–18. https://doi.org/10.2307/535238

Florey, M.J., & Bolton, R.A. (1997). Personal names, lexical replacement, and language shift in Eastern Indonesia. *Cakalele*, 8, 27–58.

Foley, W.A. (1986). *The Papuan languages of New Guinea*. Cambridge University Press.

Forge, A. (1970). Learning to see in New Guinea. In P. Mayer (Ed.), *Socialisation: The approach from social anthropology* (pp. 269–92). Tavistock.

Fortes, M. (1953). The structure of unilineal descent groups. *American Anthropologist*, 55(1), 17–41. https://doi.org/10.1525/aa.1953.55.1.02a00030

Fortes, M. (1969). *Kinship and the social order*. Routledge & Kegan Paul.
Foster, G.M. (1944). A summary of Yuki culture. *Anthropological Records*, 5(3), 155–244.
Fox, H. (1996). An honorific sub-dialect among Big Nambas women. In J. Lynch & F. Pat (Eds.), *Oceanic studies: Proceedings of the first international conference on Oceanic linguistics* (pp. 375–82). Pacific Linguistics.
Fox, J.J. (Ed.). (1988). *To speak in pairs: Essays on the ritual languages of eastern Indonesia*. Cambridge University Press. https://doi.org/10.1017/CBO9780511551369
François, A. (2001). *Contraintes de structures et liberté dans l'organisation du discours : une description du Mwotlap, langue océanienne du Vanuatu* [Unpublished doctoral dissertation]. Université Paris-IV Sorbonne.
Franklin, K.J. (1967). Names and aliases in Kewa. *Journal of the Polynesian Society*, 76(1), 76–81.
Franklin, K.J. (1972). A ritual pandanus language of New Guinea. *Oceania*, 43(1), 66–76. https://doi.org/10.1002/j.1834-4461.1972.tb01197.x
Franklin, K.J., & Stefaniw, R. (1992). The "pandanus languages" of the Southern Highlands Province, Papua New Guinea: A further report. In T. Dutton (Ed.), *Culture change, language change: Case studies from Melanesia* (pp. 1–6). Pacific Linguistics.
Frazer, J.G. (1958). *The golden bough: A study in magic and religion*. The Macmillan Company.
Freud, S. (1918). *Totem and taboo*. Moffat Yard & Company.
Friedrich, P. (1986). Social context and semantic feature: The Russian pronominal usage. In J.J. Gumperz & D. Hymes (Eds.), *Directions in sociolinguistics: The ethnography of communication* (pp. 270–300). Blackwell.
Fuchs, T. (2013). The phenomenology and development of social perspectives. *Phenomenology and the Cognitive Sciences*, 12(4), 655–83. https://doi.org/10.1007/s11097-012-9267-x
Gal, S. (2013). Tastes of talk: Qualia and the moral flavor of signs. *Anthropological Theory*, 13(1/2), 31–48. https://doi.org/10.1177/1463499613483396
Gal, S., & Irvine, J. (2019). *Signs of difference: Language and ideology in social life*. Cambridge University Press. https://doi.org/10.1017/9781108649209
Garde, M. (1996). *Saying nothing: The language of joking relationships in Aboriginal Australia* [Unpublished Master's thesis]. Northern Territory University.
Garde, M. (2008a). Person reference, proper names and circumspection in Bininj Kunwok conversation. In I. Mushin & B. Baker (Eds.), *Discourse and grammar in Australian languages* (pp. 203–32). John Benjamins. https://doi.org/10.1075/slcs.104.11gar
Garde, M. (2008b). The pragmatics of rude jokes with grandad: Joking relationships in Aboriginal Australia. *Anthropological Forum*, 18(3), 235–53. https://doi.org/10.1080/00664670802429362

Garde, M. (2013). *Culture, interaction and person reference in an Australian language: An ethnography of Bininj Gunwok communication*. John Benjamins. https://doi.org/10.1075/clu.11

Gáspár, C. (2003). A preliminary study on women's language in Mongolian languages. *Annales Universitatis Scientiarum Budapestinensis de Rolando Eötvös Nominatae: Sectio Linguistica, 26*, 227–36.

Gell, A. (1996). Reflections on a cut finger: Taboo in the Umeda conception of the self. In M. Jackson (Ed.), *Things as they are: New directions in phenomenological anthropology* (pp. 115–127). Indiana University Press.

Gell, A. (1998). *Art and agency: An anthropological theory*. Clarendon. https://doi.org/10.1093/oso/9780198280132.001.0001

Ghosh, A. (2008). Santali. In G.D.S. Anderson (Ed.), *The Munda languages* (pp. 11–98). Routledge.

Gibson, J.J. (1962). Observations on active touch. *Psychological Review, 69*(6), 477–91. https://doi.org/10.1037/h0046962

Gibson, J.J. (1966). *The senses considered as perceptual systems*. George Allen & Unwin.

Gifford, E.W. (1922). Californian kinship terminologies. *University of California Publications in American Archaeology and Ethnology, 18*, 1–285.

Gilbert, W.H. (1937). Eastern Cherokee social organization. In F. Eggan (Ed.), *Social anthropology of North American tribes* (pp. 285–340). University of Chicago Press.

Goddard, C. (1992). Traditional Yankunytjatjara ways of speaking: A semantic perspective. *Australian Journal of Linguistics, 12*(1), 93–122. https://doi.org/10.1080/07268609208599472

Goddard, I. (1979). The languages of south Texas and the lower Rio Grande. In L. Campbell & M. Mithun (Eds.), *The languages of Native America* (pp. 355–89). University of Texas Press. https://doi.org/10.7560/746244-008

Goffman, E. (1956). Embarrassment and social organization. *American Journal of Sociology, 62*(3), 264–71. https://doi.org/10.1086/222003

Goffman, E. (1963). *Behaviour in public places*. Free Press.

Goffman, E. (1979). Footing. *Semiotica, 25*(1/2), 1–29. https://doi.org/10.1515/semi.1979.25.1-2.1

Goffman, E. (1981). *Forms of talk*. University of Pennsylvania Press.

Goffman, E. (1986). *Stigma: Notes on the management of spoiled identity*. Simon & Schuster.

Golla, V. (2011). *California Indian languages*. University of California Press. https://doi.org/10.1525/9780520949522

Goodale, J. (1980). Gender, sexuality and marriage: A Kaulong model of nature and culture. In C.P. MacCormack & M. Strathern (Eds.), *Nature, culture, and gender* (pp. 119–42). Cambridge University Press.

Goodale, J. (1995). *To sing with pigs is human: The concept of person in Papua New Guinea*. University of Washington Press.

Goodwin, G. (1942). *The social organization of the Western Apache*. University of Chicago Press.

Goodwin, M.H. (2017). Haptic sociality: The embodied interactive constitution of intimacy through touch. In C. Meyer, J. Streeck, & J.S. Jordan (Eds.), *Intercorporeality: Emerging socialities in interaction* (pp. 73–102). Oxford University Press. https://doi.org/10.1093/acprof:oso/9780190210465.003.0004

Goody, J. (1959). The mother's brother and the sister's son in West Africa. *Journal of the Royal Anthropological Institute of Great Britain and Ireland, 89*(1), 61–88. https://doi.org/10.2307/2844437

Gregor, T. (1974). Publicity, privacy, and Mehinacu marriage. *Ethnology, 13*(4), 333–49. https://doi.org/10.2307/3773050

Gregor, T. (1977). *Mehinaku: The drama of daily life in a Brazilian Indian village*. University of Chicago Press. https://doi.org/10.7208/chicago/9780226150338.001.0001

Gregory, C. (2011). Skinship: Touchability as a virtue in East-Central India. *HAU: Journal of Ethnographic Theory, 1*(1), 179–209. https://doi.org/10.14318/hau1.1.007

Grice, H.P. (1975). Logic and conversation. In P. Cole & J. Morgan (Eds.), *Syntax and semantics 3: Speech acts* (pp. 41–58). Academic Press. https://doi.org/10.1163/9789004368811_003

Grimes, B.D. (1997). Knowing your place: Representing relations of precedence and origin on the Buru landscape. In J.J. Fox (Ed.), *Poetic power of place: Comparative perspectives on Austronesian ideas of locality* (pp. 115–30). Australia National University.

Grimes, C.E., & Maryott, K.R. (1994). Named speech registers in Austronesian languages. In T. Dutton & D.T. Tryon (Eds.), *Language contact and change in the Austronesian world* (pp. 275–319). Mouton de Gruyter. https://doi.org/10.1515/9783110883091.275

Gruber, C. (2009). Between logos (*kalima*) and light (*nūr*): Representations of the Prophet Muhammad in Islamic painting. *Muqarnas, 26*, 229–62. https://doi.org/10.1163/ej.9789004175891.i-386.66

Guemple, D.L. (1965). Saunik: Name sharing as a factor governing Eskimo kinship terms. *Ethnology, 4*(3), 323–35. https://doi.org/10.2307/3772991

Guiart, J. (1952). L'organisation sociale et politique du Nord Malekula. *Journal de la Société des océanistes, 8*, 149–259. https://doi.org/10.3406/jso.1952.1740

Guiart, J. (1953). Native society in the New Hebrides: The Big Nambas of Northern Malekula. *Mankind, 4*(11), 439–46. https://doi.org/10.1111/j.1835-9310.1953.tb00198.x

Haas, M. (1970). Consonant symbolism in northwestern California: A problem in diffusion. In E. Swanson (Ed.), *Languages and cultures of western*

North America: Essays in honor of Sven S. Liljeblad (pp. 86–96). Idaho State University Press.

Hafford, J.A. (2015). *Wuvulu grammar and vocabulary* [Unpublished doctoral dissertation]. University of Hawai'i at Manoa.

Hage, P. (1969). A Guttman scale analysis of Tikopia speech taboos. *Southwestern Journal of Anthropology, 25*(1), 96–104. https://doi.org/10.1086/soutjanth.25.1.3629470

Hale, K.L. (1966). Kinship reflections in syntax: Some Australian languages. *Word, 22*(1–3), 318–24. https://doi.org/10.1080/00437956.1966.11435458

Hale, K.L. (1982). The logic of Damin kinship terminology. In J. Heath, F. Merlan, & A. Rumsey (Eds.), *The languages of kinship in Aboriginal Australia* (pp. 31–7). University of Sydney.

Hale, K.L., & Nash, D. (1997). Damin and Lardil phonotactics. In D. Tryon & M. Walsh (Eds.), *Boundary rider: Essays in honour of Geoffrey O'Grady* (pp. 247–59). Pacific Linguistics.

Hallpike, C.R. (1972). *The Konso of Ethiopia: A study of the values of a Cushitic people*. Clarendon Press.

Hamayon, R. (1979). Le pouvoir des hommes passe par la « langue des femmes » : variations mongoles sur le duo de la légitimité et de l'aptitude. *L'Homme, 19*(3/4), 109–39. https://doi.org/10.3406/hom.1979.368000

Hamayon, R., & Bassanoff, N. (1973). De la difficulté d'être une belle-fille. *Études Mongoles, 4*, 7–74.

Handelman, D., & Kapferer, B. (1972). Forms of joking activity: A comparative approach. *American Anthropologist, 74*(3), 484–517. https://doi.org/10.1525/aa.1972.74.3.02a00180

Handman, C. (2010). Events of translation: Intertextuality and Christian ethnotheologies of change among Guhu-Samane, Papua New Guinea. *American Anthropologist, 112*(4), 576–88. https://doi.org/10.1111/j.1548-1433.2010.01277.x

Hansen, K.C., & Hansen, L.E. (1974). *Pintupi dictionary*. SIL, AAB.

Harkness, N. (2013). Softer soju in South Korea. *Anthropological Theory, 13*(1/2), 12–30. https://doi.org/10.1177/1463499613483394

Harkness, N. (2015). The pragmatics of qualia in practice. *Annual Review of Anthropology, 44*, 573–89. https://doi.org/10.1146/annurev-anthro-102313-030032

Harris, J. (1970). Gunkurrng, a mother-in-law language. In S. Wurm & D. Laycock (Eds.), *Pacific studies in honor of Arthur Capell* (pp. 783–89). Pacific Linguistics.

Harrisson, T. (1937). *Savage civilisation*. Victor Gollancz.

Hart, C.W.M. (1930). Personal names among the Tiwi. *Oceania, 1*(3), 280–90. https://doi.org/10.1002/j.1834-4461.1930.tb01650.x

Haugen, J.D., & Philips, S.U. (2010). Tongan chiefly language: The formation of an honorific speech register. *Language in Society, 39*(5), 589–616. https://doi.org/10.1017/S004740451000062X

Haviland, J. (1979a). Guugu Yimidhirr brother-in-law language. *Language in Society*, 8(2-3), 365-93. https://doi.org/10.1017/S0047404500007600

Haviland, J. (1979b). How to talk to your brother-in-law in Guugu Yimidhirr. In T. Shopen (Ed.), *Languages and their speakers* (pp. 161-239). Winthrop.

Haviland, J. (1986). "Con buenos chiles": Talk, targets and teasing in Zinacantán. *Text*, 6(3), 249-82. https://doi.org/10.1515/text.1.1986.6.3.249

Haviland, J. (1996). Projections, transpositions, and relativity. In J.J. Gumperz & S. Levinson (Eds.), *Rethinking linguistic relativity* (pp. 271-323). Cambridge University Press.

Haxthausen, A. von. (1854). *Transcaucasia*. Chapman & Hall.

Head, B.F. (1978). Respect degrees in pronominal reference. In J.H. Greenberg, C.H. Ferguson, & E.A. Moravcsik (Eds.), *Universals of human language, vol. 3* (pp. 151-212). Stanford University Press.

Heald, S. (1990). Joking and avoidance, hostility and incest: An essay on Gisu moral categories. *Man*, 25(3), 377-92. https://doi.org/10.2307/2803709

Helmbrecht, J. (2005). Politeness distinctions in pronouns. In M. Haspelmath, M.S. Dryer, D. Gil, & B. Comrie (Eds.), *The world atlas of language structures* (pp. 186-9). Oxford University Press.

Herbert, R.K. (1990). *Hlonipha* and the ambiguous woman. *Anthropos*, 85(4-6), 455-73.

Héritier, F. (1994). *Les deux soeurs et leur mère : anthropologie de l'inceste*. Odile Jacob.

Hiatt, L.R. (1984). Your mother-in-law is poison. *Man*, 19(2), 183-98. https://doi.org/10.2307/2802276

Hickey, R. (2003). The German address system: Binary and scalar system at once. In I. Raavitsainen & A. Jucker (Eds.), *Diachronic perspectives on address form systems* (pp. 401-25). John Benjamins. https://doi.org/10.1075/pbns.107.16hic

Hill, J.H., & Hill, K.C. (1978). Honorific usage in modern Nahuatl: The expression of social distance and respect in the Nahuatl of the Malinche Volcano area. *Language*, 54(1), 123-55. https://doi.org/10.2307/413001

Hoenigman, D. (2012). From mountain talk to hidden talk: Continuity and change in Awiakay registers. In N. Evans & M. Klamer (Eds.), *Melanesian languages on the edge of Asia: Challenges for the 21st century* (pp. 191-218). University of Hawai'i Press.

Hogbin, H.I. (1937). The hill people of north-eastern Guadalcanal. *Oceania*, 8(1), 62-89. https://doi.org/10.1002/j.1834-4461.1937.tb00406.x

Hogbin, H.I. (1969). *A Guadalcanal society: The Kaoka speakers*. Holt, Rinehart & Winston.

Holden, C.J., & Mace, R. (2003). Spread of cattle led to the loss of matrilineal descent in Africa: A coevolutionary analysis. *Proceedings of the Royal Society B: Biological Sciences*, 270(1532), 2425-33. https://doi.org/10.1098/rspb.2003.2535

Honigmann, J.J. (1956). Notes on Sarsi kin behavior. *Anthropologica*, 2, 17–38.
Hoskins, J. (1993). Violence, sacrifice, and divination: Giving and taking life in eastern Indonesia. *American Ethnologist*, 20(1), 159–78. https://doi.org/10.1525/ae.1993.20.1.02a00080
Howell, R.W. (1973). Teasing relationships. *Addison-Wesley Module in Anthropology*, 46, 3–22.
Hui, J., Cashman, T., & Deacon, T. (2008). Bateson's method: Double description. What is it? How does it work? What do we learn? In J. Hoffmeyer (Ed.), *A legacy for living systems: Gregory Bateson as precursor to biosemiotics* (pp. 77–92). Springer. https://doi.org/10.1007/978-1-4020-6706-8_6
Humphrey, C. (1974). Inside a Mongolian tent. *New Society*, 30, 273–5.
Humphrey, C. (1978). Women, taboo, and the suppression of attention. In S. Ardener (Ed.), *Defining females: The nature of women in society* (pp. 89–108). Croom Helm.
Hunn, E.S., & Brown, C.H. (2011). Linguistic ethnobiology. In E.N. Anderson, D.M. Pearsall, E.S. Hunn, & N.J. Turner (Eds.), *Ethnobiology* (pp. 319–34). Wiley-Blackwell. https://doi.org/10.1002/9781118015872.ch19
Hunter, M. (1936). *Reaction to conquest: Effects of contact with Europeans on the Pondo of South Africa*. Oxford University Press.
Huntsman, J.W. (1971). Concepts of kinship and categories of kinsmen in the Tokelau Islands. *Journal of the Polynesian Society*, 80(3), 317–54.
Hvoslef, E.H. (2001). The social use of personal names among the Kyrgyz. *Central Asian Survey*, 20(1), 85–95. https://doi.org/10.1080/02634930123251
Irons, W. (1975). *The Yomut Turkmen: A study of social organization among a Central Asian Turkic-speaking population*. University of Michigan, Museum of Anthropology. https://doi.org/10.3998/mpub.11394884
Irvine, J.T. (1992). Ideologies of honorific language. *Pragmatics*, 2(3), 251–62. https://doi.org/10.1075/prag.2.3.02irv
Irvine, J.T. (2009). Honorifics. In G. Senft, J.-O. Östman, & J. Verschueren (Eds.), *Culture and language use* (pp. 156–72). John Benjamins. https://doi.org/10.1075/hoph.2.15irv
Irvine, J.T. (2011). Leaky registers and eight-hundred-pound gorillas. *Anthropological Quarterly*, 84(1), 15–39. https://doi.org/10.1353/anq.2011.0011
Irvine, J.T., & Gal, S. (2000). Language ideology and linguistic differentiation. In P.V. Kroskrity (Ed.), *Regimes of language: Ideologies, polities, and identities* (pp. 35–84). School of American Research Press.
Jackson, G. (1975). *The Kopon: Life and death on the fringes of the New Guinea Highlands* [Unpublished doctoral dissertation]. University of Auckland.
Jackson, G. (1991). Is taboo alive? The uses and parameters of Kopon taboo. In A. Pawley (Ed.), *Man and a half: Essays in Pacific anthropology and ethnobiology in honour of Ralph Bulmer* (pp. 265–76). Polynesian Society.

Jacobson, D. (1982). Purdah and the Hindu family in central India. In H. Papanek & G. Minault (Eds.), *Separate worlds: Studies of purdah in South Asia* (pp. 81–109). Chanakaya Publications.

Jaimoukha, A.M. (2005). *The Chechens: A handbook*. Routledge. https://doi.org/10.4324/9780203356432

Jakobsen, J. (1897). *The dialect and place names of Shetland*. T. & J. Manson.

Jakobson, R. (1960). Concluding statement: Linguistics and poetics. In T. Sebeok (Ed.), *Style in language* (pp. 62–94). MIT Press.

Jakobson, R. (1971). Shifters, verbal categories, and the Russian verb. In *Selected writings II: Word and language* (pp. 130–47). Mouton. https://doi.org/10.1515/9783110873269.130

Janhunen, J. (Ed.). (2003). *The Mongolic languages*. Routledge.

Kanwisher, N., McDermott, J., & Chun, M.M. (1997). The fusiform face area: A module in human extrastriate cortex specialized for face perception. *The Journal of Neuroscience*, 17(11), 4302–11. https://doi.org/10.1523/JNEUROSCI.17-11-04302.1997

Karbelashvilli, D. (1935). *Ruchnaija rech' na Kavkaze*. Research Institute of Caucasian Studies, Academy of Sciences of the USSR.

Karp, I. (1978). *Fields of change among the Iteso of Kenya*. Routledge & Kegan Paul.

Keane, W. (2003). Semiotics and the social analysis of material things. *Language & Communication*, 23(3–4), 409–25. https://doi.org/10.1016/S0271-5309(03)00010-7

Keating, E. (1998). *Power sharing: Language, rank, gender and social space in Pohnpei, Micronesia*. Oxford University Press. https://doi.org/10.1093/oso/9780195111972.001.0001

Keating, E. (2000). Moments of hierarchy: Constructing social stratification by means of language, food, space, and the body in Pohnpei, Micronesia. *American Anthropologist*, 102(2), 303–20. https://doi.org/10.1525/aa.2000.102.2.303

Keating, E., & Duranti, A. (2006). Honorific resources for the construction of hierarchy in Pohnpei and Samoa. *Journal of the Polynesian Society*, 115(2), 145–72.

Keen, I. (2014). Language in the constitution of kinship. *Anthropological Linguistics*, 56(1), 1–53. https://doi.org/10.1353/anl.2014.0000

Keenan, E.O. (1973). A sliding sense of obligatoriness: The poly-structure of Malagasy oratory. *Language in Society*, 2(2), 225–43. https://doi.org/10.1017/S0047404500000725

Keesing, R., & Fifi'i, J. (1969). Kwaio word tabooing in its cultural context. *Journal of the Polynesian Society*, 78, 154–77.

Keltner, D., Young, R.C., & Buswell, B.N. (1997). Appeasement in human emotion, social practice, and personality. *Aggressive Behavior*, 23(5), 359–74. https://doi.org/10.1002/(SICI)1098-2337(1997)23:5%3C359::AID-AB5%3E3.0.CO;2-D

Kendon, A. (1988). *Sign languages of Aboriginal Australia: Cultural, semiotic and communicative perspectives*. Cambridge University Press.

Kendon, A. (1990). Signs in the cloister and elsewhere. *Semiotica, 79*(3–4), 307–29.

Kern, H. (1893). Woordverwiselling in het Galelareesch. *Bijdragen tot de Taal-, Land- en Volkenkunde, 42*, 120–28. https://doi.org/10.1163/22134379-90000155

Khiba, Z.K. (1980). A contribution to Abkhaz lexicography: The secret language of the hunters. *Bedi Karthlisa, 38*, 269–77.

Kim, U. (2018a). *Ethical management of speech among Kazak nomads in the Chinese Altai* [Unpublished doctoral dissertation]. University of Michigan.

Kim, J.-B., & Sells, P. (2007). Korean honorification: A kind of expressive meaning. *Journal of East Asian Linguistics, 16*(4), 303–36. https://doi.org/10.1007/s10831-007-9014-4

Kim, U. (2018b). Grammar of respect and disrespect: Honorific register formation in Altai Kazak. *Sociolinguistic Journal of Korea, 26*(4), 23–55. https://doi.org/10.14353/sjk.2018.26.4.02

Kimenyi, A. (1992). Why is it that women in Rwanda cannot marry? In K. Hall, M. Bucholtz, & B. Moonwomon (Eds.), *Locating power: Proceedings of the second Berkeley women and language conference*, Vol. 2 (pp. 300–11). Berkeley Women and Language Group.

King, J.T. (2001). The affinal kin register in Dhimal. *Linguistics of the Tibeto-Burman Area, 24*(1), 163–82.

Kintz, D. (1986). Ce que disent les anthroponymes peuls. *Langage et Société, 36*, 27–40. https://doi.org/10.3406/lsoc.1986.2052

Kirton, J. (1971). Complexities of Yanyula nouns: Inter-relationship of linguistics and anthropology. *Papers in Australian Linguistics, 5*, 15–70.

Kirton, J., & Timothy, N. (1982). Some thoughts on Yanyuwa language and culture. *Work Papers of SIL-AAB (Series B), 8*, 1–18.

Knight, C. (2007). *The bear as barometer: The Japanese response to human-bear conflict* [Unpublished doctoral dissertation]. University of Canterbury.

Knight, C. (2008). The Moon Bear as a symbol of *Yama*: Its significance in the folklore of upland hunting in Japan. *Asian Ethnology, 67*(1), 79–101.

Knooihuizen, R. (2008). Fishing for words: The taboo language of Shetland fishermen and the dating of Norn language death. *Transactions of the Philological Society, 106*(1), 100–13. https://doi.org/10.1111/j.1467-968X.2007.00202.x

Kobayashi, H., & Kohshima, S. (2001). Unique morphology of the human eye and its adaptive meaning: Comparative studies on external morphology of the primate eye. *Journal of Human Evolution, 40*(5), 419–35. https://doi.org/10.1006/jhev.2001.0468

Kockelman, P. (2003). The meanings of interjections in Q'eqchi' Maya: From emotive reaction to social and discursive action. *Current Anthropology, 44*(4), 467–79. https://doi.org/10.1086/375871

Kockelman, P. (2006). Residence in the world: Affordances, instruments, actions, roles, and identities. *Semiotica, 162,* 19–71. https://doi.org/10.1515/SEM.2006.073

Kockelman, P. (2010). *Language, culture, and mind: Natural constructions and social kinds.* Cambridge University Press. https://doi.org/10.1017/CBO9780511711893

Kockelman, P. (2013). The anthropology of an equation: Sieves, spam filters, agentive algorithms, and ontologies of transformation. *HAU: Journal of Ethnographic Theory, 3*(3), 33–61. https://doi.org/10.14318/hau3.3.003

Kockelman, P. (2016a). Grading, gradients, degradation, grace. Part 1: Intensity and causality. *HAU: Journal of Ethnographic Theory, 6*(2), 389–423. https://doi.org/10.14318/hau6.2.022

Kockelman, P. (2016b). Grading, gradients, degradation, grace. Part 2: Phenomenology, materiality, and cosmology. *HAU: Journal of Ethnographic Theory, 6*(3), 337–65. https://doi.org/10.14318/hau6.3.022

Kolbusa, S. (2000). *Ingamwana: Nyakyusa-Schwiegermeidung* [Unpublished Master's thesis]. University of Bayreuth.

Komori, J. (1999). Analysis of women's words in Kerewe (Tanzania): A language aspect of the avoidance relationship. *Journal of Asian and African Studies, 58,* 343–63. [In Japanese]

Koshal, S. (1987). Honorific systems of the Ladakhi language. *Multilingua, 6*(2), 149–68. https://doi.org/10.1515/mult.1987.6.2.149

Krader, L. (1953). *Kinship systems of the Altaic-speaking peoples of the Asiatic steppes.* [Unpublished doctoral dissertation]. Harvard University.

Krifka, M. (2019). Honorific and affiliative uses of dual and paucal number in Daakie. *SIL Language and Culture Documentation and Description, 45,* 62–76.

Kripke, S. (1980). *Naming and necessity.* Harvard University Press.

Kroeber, A.L. (1925). *Handbook of the Indians of California.* Smithsonian Institution.

Kruspe, N., & Burenhult, N. (2019). Pronouns in affinal avoidance registers: Evidence from the Aslian languages (Austroasiatic, Malay Peninsula). In P. Bouissac (Ed.), *The social dynamics of pronominal systems: A comparative approach* (pp. 289–314). John Benjamins. https://doi.org/10.1075/pbns.304.12kro

Kulick, D. (2003). No. *Language & Communication, 23*(2), 139–51. https://doi.org/10.1016/S0271-5309(02)00043-5

Kunene, D.P. (1958). Notes on *hlonepha* among the Southern Sotho. *African Studies, 17*(3), 159–82. https://doi.org/10.1080/00020185808707057

Künstler, M.J. (1994). Taboo and the development of periphrasis in Chinese. *Rocznik Orientalistyczny, 49*(2), 129–38.

Lake, H., & Kelsall, H.J. (1894). The camphor tree and camphor language of Johore. *Journal of the Straights Branch of the Royal Asiatic Society, 26,* 35–56.

Landes, R. (1937). *Ojibwa sociology*. Columbia University Press.
Laughren, M. (2001). What Warlpiri "avoidance" registers do with grammar. In J. Simpson, D. Nash, M. Laughren, P. Austin, & B. Alpher (Eds.), *Forty years on: Ken Hale and Australian languages* (pp. 199–225). Pacific Linguistics.
Laycock, D. (1972). Towards a typology of ludlings. *Linguistic Communications*, 6, 61–113.
Lee, B. (1997). *Talking heads: Language, metalanguage and the semiotics of subjectivity*. Duke University Press. https://doi.org/10.1515/9780822382461
Lee, R. (1986). !Kung kin terms, the name relationship and the process of discovery. In M. Biesele, R. Gordon, & R. Lee (Eds.), *The past and future of !Kung ethnography: Critical essays in honour of Lorna Marshall* (pp. 77–102). Buske.
Lee, R. (1993). *The Dobe Ju/'hoansi*. Harcourt Brace College.
Lempert, M. (2018). On the pragmatic poetry of pose: Gesture, parallelism, politics. *Signs and Society*, 6(1), 120–46. https://doi.org/10.1086/695425
Levinson, S.C. (1983). *Pragmatics*. Cambridge University Press. https://doi.org/10.1017/CBO9780511813313
Levinson, S.C. (2006). Parts of the body in Yélî Dnye, the Papuan language of Rossel Island. *Language Sciences*, 28(2–3), 221–40. https://doi.org/10.1016/j.langsci.2005.11.007
Levinson, S.C. (2008). Landscape, seascape and the ontology of places on Rossel Island, Papua New Guinea. *Language Sciences*, 30, 256–90. https://doi.org/10.1016/j.langsci.2006.12.032
Lévi-Strauss, C. (1958). *Anthropologie structurale*. Plon.
Lévi-Strauss, C. (2021). *Wild thought* (J. Mehlman & J. Leavitt, Trans.). University of Chicago Press. https://doi.org/10.7208/chicago/9780226413112.001.0001
Lévy-Bruhl, L. (1910). *Les fonctions mentales dans les sociétés inférieures*. Librairie Félix Alcan.
Lindblom, G. (1920). *The Akamba in British East Africa: An ethnological monograph*. Appelbergs boktryckeri aktiebolag.
Llewellyn-Jones, L. (2003). *Aphrodite's tortoise: The veiled woman of Ancient Greece*. The Classical Press of Wales. https://doi.org/10.2307/j.ctv1n357p0
Lockwood, W.B. (1955). Word taboo in the language of the Faroese fishermen. *Transactions of the Philological Society*, 54(1), 1–24. https://doi.org/10.1111/j.1467-968X.1955.tb00287.x
Loeb, E.M. (1926). Pomo folkways. *University of California Publications in American Archaeology*, 19(2), 149–405.
Lomas, G.C.J. (1989). The Huli language of Papua New Guinea [Unpublished doctoral dissertation]. Macquarie University.
Lowie, R.H. (1917). *Notes on the social organization and customs of the Mandan, Hidatsa, and Crow Indians*. The American Museum of Natural History.
Lowie, R.H. (1920). *Primitive society*. Liveright.

Lucy, J.A. (1985). Whorf's view of the linguistic mediation of thought. In E. Mertz & R.J. Parmentier (Eds.), *Semiotic mediation: Sociocultural and psychological perspectives* (pp. 73–97). Academic Press. https://doi.org/10.1016/B978-0-12-491280-9.50010-8

Luzbetak, L.J. (1951). *Marriage and the family in Caucasia: A contribution to the study of North Caucasian ethnology and customary law*. St. Gabriel's Mission Press.

Lyons, J. (2002). *Linguistic semantics: An introduction*. Cambridge University Press.

MacPhail, R.M. (1983). *Introduction to Santali*. Firma KLM Private Ltd.

Mahmood, S. (2009). Religious reason and secular affect: An incommensurable divide? In T. Asad, W. Brown, J. Butler, & S. Mahmood, *Is Critique Secular? Blasphemy, Injury, and Free Speech* (pp. 64–100). University of California Press.

Majnep, I.S., & Bulmer, R. (1977). *Birds of my Kalam country*. Auckland University Press.

Makhlouf, C. (1979). *Changing veils: Women and modernization in North Yemen*. Croom Helm.

Madan, T.N. (1989). *Family and kinship among the Pandits of rural Kashmir*. Oxford University Press.

Maibom, H.L. (2010). The descent of shame. *Philosophy and Phenomenological Research, 80*(3), 566–94. https://doi.org/10.1111/j.1933-1592.2010.00341.x

Malsch, D.L. (1987). The grammaticalization of social relationship: The origin of number to encode deference. In A. Giacalone-Ramat, O. Carruba, & G. Bernini (Eds.), *Papers from the 7th international conference on historical linguistics* (pp. 407–18). John Benjamins. https://doi.org/10.1075/cilt.48.30mal

Mandelbaum, D.G. (1986). Sex roles and gender relations in north India. *Economic and Political Weekly, 21*(46), 1999–2004.

Mandelbaum, D.G. (1988). *Women's seclusion and men's honor*. University of Arizona Press.

Manning, P. (2012). *The semiotics of drink and drinking*. Continuum.

Maranda, P. (2001). *The double twist: From ethnography to morphodynamics*. University of Toronto Press. https://doi.org/10.3138/9781442681125

Marshall, L. (1957). The kin terminology system of the !Kung Bushmen. *Africa, 27*(1), 1–25. https://doi.org/10.2307/1156363

Martyna, W. (1980). The psychology of the generic masculine. In S. McConnell-Ginet, R. Borker, & N. Furman (Eds.), *Women and language in literature and society* (pp. 69–78). Praeger.

Mathews, R.H. (1905). *Ethnological notes on the Aboriginal tribes of New South Wales and Victoria*. F.W. White. https://doi.org/10.5962/p.359439

Mauss, M. (1926). Parentés à plaisanteries. *École pratique des hautes études : section des sciences religieuses, 36*, 3–21.

Maybury-Lewis, D. (1984). Name, person, and ideology. In E. Tooker & B. Conklin (Eds.), *Naming systems* (pp. 1–10). Proceedings of the American Ethnological Society.

Mayfield, R. (1987). *Central Cagayan Agta texts*. Linguistic Society of the Philippines and Summer Institute of Linguistics.</bok>

Mbaya, M. (2002). Linguistic taboo in African marriage context: A study of the Oromo Laguu. *Nordic Journal of African Studies*, 11(2), 224–35.

McAllister, J.G. (1937). Kiowa-Apache social organization. In F. Eggan (Ed.), *Social anthropology of North American tribes* (pp. 99–172). University of Chicago Press.

McConvell, P. (1982). Neutralisation and degrees of respect in Gurindji. In J. Heath, F. Merlan, & A. Rumsey (Eds.), *The languages of kinship in Aboriginal Australia* (pp. 86–106). Oceania Publications.

McCurdy, D. (1959). *A cross-cultural study of brother-sister avoidance* [Unpublished Master's thesis]. Stanford University.

McDowell, N. (1976). Kinship and exchange: The *kamain* relationship in a Yuat River village. *Oceania*, 47(1), 36–48. https://doi.org/10.1002/j.1834-4461.1976.tb01262.x

McGivney, J. (1993). "Is she a wife or a mother?" Social order, respect, and address in Mijikenda. *Language in Society*, 22(1), 19–39. https://doi.org/10.1017/S0047404500016900

McGregor, W. (1989). Gooniyandi mother-in-Law "language": Dialect, register, and/or code? In U. Ammon (Ed.), *Status and function of language and language varieties* (pp. 630–56). Mouton de Gruyter.

McGregor, W. (2012). Kin terms and context among the Gooniyandi. *Anthropological Linguistics*, 54(2), 161–86. https://doi.org/10.1353/anl.2012.0009

McKnight, D. (1999). *People, countries, and the Rainbow Serpent: Systems of classification among the Lardil of Mornington Island*. Oxford University Press.

McWhorter, J. (2014). *The language hoax: Why the world looks the same in any language*. Oxford University Press.

Mead, M. (1934). *Kinship in the Admiralty Islands*. American Museum of Natural History.

Meier, R.P., Cormier, K., & Quinto-Pozos, D. (Eds.). (2002). *Modality and structure in signed and spoken languages*. Cambridge University Press. https://doi.org/10.1017/CBO9780511486777

Meneley, A. (2000). Living hierarchy in Yemen. *Anthropologica*, 42(1), 61–73. https://doi.org/10.2307/25605958

Meneley, A. (2008). Oleo-signs and quali-signs: The qualities of olive oil. *Ethnos*, 73(3), 303–26. https://doi.org/10.1080/00141840802324003

Merlan, F. (1982a). "Egocentric" and "altercentric" usage of kin terms in Mangarrayi. In J. Heath, F. Merlan, & A. Rumsey (Eds.), The languages of kinship in Aboriginal Australia (pp. 125–40). Oceania Publications.

References

Merlan, F. (1982b). *Mangarayi*. North-Holland.

Merlan, F. (1997). The mother-in-law taboo: Avoidance and obligation in Aboriginal Australian society. In F. Merlan, J.A. Morton, & A. Rumsey (Eds.), *Scholar and sceptic: Australian Aboriginal studies in honour of L. R. Hiatt* (pp. 95–122). Aboriginal Studies Press.

Meyer, C., Streeck, J., & Jordan, J.S. (Eds.). (2017). *Intercorporeality: Emerging socialities in interaction*. Oxford University Press. https://doi.org/10.1093/acprof:oso/9780190210465.001.0001

Michael, L. (2014). Social dimensions of language change. In C. Bowern & B. Evans (Eds.), *Handbook of historical linguistics* (pp. 484–502). Routledge. https://doi.org/10.4324/9781315794013

Miller, D. (2007). What is a relationship? Is kinship negotiated experience? *Ethnos*, 72(4), 535–54. https://doi.org/10.1080/00141840701768334

Miller, J. (1998). Tsimshian ethno-ethnohistory: A "real" Indigenous chronology. *Ethnohistory*, 45(4), 657–74. https://doi.org/10.2307/483299

Mitchell, A. (2015). Words that smell like father-in-law: A linguistic description of the Datooga avoidance register. *Anthropological Linguistics*, 57(2), 195–217. https://doi.org/10.1353/anl.2016.0004

Mitchell, A. (2018). Allusive references and other-oriented stance in an affinal avoidance register. *Journal of Linguistic Anthropology*, 28(1), 4–21. https://doi.org/10.1111/jola.12174

Mithun, M. (1988). Lexical categories and number in Central Pomo. In W. Shipley (Ed.), *In honor of Mary Haas* (pp. 517–37). Mouton de Gruyter. https://doi.org/10.1515/9783110852387.517

Moñino, Y. (1977). Conceptions du monde et langue d'initiation lábì des Gbaya-Kara. In G. Calame-Griaule (Ed.), *Langage et cultures africaines* (pp. 115–47). Librairie Françoise Maspero.

Mooney, J. (1898). *Calendar history of the Kiowa Indians*. Bureau of American Ethnology.

Moore, R.E. (1988). Lexicalization versus lexical loss in Wasco-Wishram language obsolescence. *International Journal of American Linguistics*, 54(4), 453–68. https://doi.org/10.1086/466097

Moriguchi, T. (1995). Linguistic and anthropological analysis of avoidance in Bunun, Taiwan. *Tokyo University Linguistics Papers*, 14, 23–47.

Mous, M. (2001). Paralexification in language intertwining. In N. Smith & T. Veenstra (Eds.), *Creolization and contact* (pp. 113–23). John Benjamins. https://doi.org/10.1075/cll.23.05mou

Murdock, G.P. (1967). *Social structure*. The Free Press.

Murdock, G.P. (1971). Cross-sex patterns of kin behavior. *Ethnology*, 10(3), 359–68. https://doi.org/10.2307/3772922

Murphy, R.F. (1964). Social distance and the veil. *American Anthropologist*, 66(6), 1257–74. https://doi.org/10.1525/aa.1964.66.6.02a00020

Murphy, R.F., & Quain, B. (1955). *The Trumaí Indians of central Brazil*. University of Washington Press.

Myers, F.R. (1991). *Pintupi country, Pintupi self: Sentiment, place, and politics among Western Desert Aborigines*. University of California Press.

Nadel, S.F. (1947). *The Nuba: An anthropological study of the hill tribes in Kordofan*. Oxford University Press.

Nakassis, C.V. (2013). Citation and citationality. *Signs and Society*, 1(1), 51–78. https://doi.org/10.1086/670165

Nakassis, C.V. (2016a). *Doing style: Youth and mass mediation in south India*. University of Chicago Press. https://doi.org/10.7208/chicago/9780226327990.001.0001

Nakassis, C.V. (2016b). Linguistic anthropology in 2015: Not the study of language. *American Anthropologist*, 118(2), 330–45. https://doi.org/10.1111/aman.12528

Nash, D., & Simpson, J. (1981). "No name" in central Australia. In C. Masek, R. Hendrick, & M. Miller (Eds.), *Papers from the parasession on language and behavior* (pp. 165–77). Chicago Linguistic Society.

Nayacakalou, R.R. (1971). The Fijian system of kinship and marriage. In A. Howard (Ed.), *Polynesia: Readings on a culture area* (pp. 133–57). Chandler.

Needham, R. (1954). The system of teknonyms and death-names of the Penan. *Southwestern Journal of Anthropology*, 10(4), 416–31. https://doi.org/10.1086/soutjanth.10.4.3628836

Needham, R. (1980). *Reconnaissances*. University of Toronto Press. https://doi.org/10.3138/9781487577865

Newman, S. (1944). *Yokuts language of California*. Viking Fund.

Nichols, J. (1971). Diminutive consonant symbolism in western North America. *Language*, 47(4), 826–48. https://doi.org/10.2307/412159

Nozawa, S. (2015). Phatic traces: Sociality in contemporary Japan. *Anthropological Quarterly*, 88(2), 373–400. https://doi.org/10.1353/anq.2015.0014

Nozawa, S. (2020, 20 April). Effacement. In *Japanese media and popular culture: An open-access digital initiative of the University of Tokyo*. https://jmpc-utokyo.com/keyword/effacement/

Nussbaum, M.C. (2006). *Hiding from humanity: Disgust, shame, and the law*. Princeton University Press.

Nuttall, M. (1994). The name never dies: Greenland Inuit ideas of the person. In A. Mills & R. Slobodin (Eds.), *Amerindian rebirth: Reincarnation belief among North American Indians and Inuit* (pp. 123–35). University of Toronto Press. https://doi.org/10.3138/9781442670761-011

Oberg, K. (1953). *Indian tribes of northern Mato Grosso, Brazil*. Smithsonian Institution.

O'Connor, M.C. (1990). Third-person reference in northern Pomo conversation: The indexing of discourse genre and social relations.

International Journal of American Linguistics, 56(3), 377–409. https://doi.org/10.1086/466164

Oliver, D.L. (1970). *A Solomon Island society: Kinship and leadership among the Siuai of Bougainville*. Beacon Press.

Oliver, D.L. (2002). *Polynesia in early historic times*. Bess Press.

Ōno, H. (2016). Is same sex sibling avoidance or joking? *African Study Monographs, 52*, 105–118.

Opler, M.E. (1937). An outline of Chiricahua Apache social organization. In F. Eggan (Ed.), *Social anthropology of North American tribes* (pp. 173–239). University of Chicago Press.

Opler, M.E. (1941). *An Apache life-way: The economic, social, and religious institutions of the Chiricahua Indians*. University of Chicago Press.

Opler, M.E. (1947). Rule and practice in the behavior between Jicarilla Apache affinal relatives. *American Anthropologist, 49*(3), 453–62. https://doi.org/10.1525/aa.1947.49.3.02a00060

Opler, M.E., & Bittle, W.E. (1961). The death practices and eschatology of the Kiowa Apache. *Southwestern Journal of Anthropology, 17*(4), 383–94. https://doi.org/10.1086/soutjanth.17.4.3628949

Opler, M.E., & Hoijer, H. (1940). The raid and war-path language of the Chiricahua Apache. *American Anthropologist, 42*(4), 617–34. https://doi.org/10.1525/aa.1940.42.4.02a00070

Osumi, M. (1995). *Tinrin grammar*. University of Hawai'i Press.

Ozanne-Rivierre, F. (1994). L'expression de la personne : quelques exemples océaniens. *Faits de langues, 3*, 211–19. https://doi.org/10.3406/flang.1994.926

Panian, A.E. (1969). The new life of the Kolkhozniks of the village of Mrgavan, Artashat Raion, Armenian SSR. *Soviet Anthropology and Archeology, 8*(2), 123–44. https://doi.org/10.2753/AAE1061-19590802123

Pans, A.E.M.J. (1998). The mother-in-law taboo. *Ethnology, 37*(1), 71–97. https://doi.org/10.2307/3773849

Papanek, H. (1973). Purdah: Separate worlds and symbolic shelter. *Comparative Studies in Society and History, 15*(3), 289–325. https://doi.org/10.1017/S001041750000712X

Parkin, D. (1988). The politics of naming among the Giriama. *The Sociological Review, 36*(S1), 61–89. https://doi.org/10.1111/j.1467-954X.1988.tb03326.x

Parkin, R. (1988). Marriage, behaviour and generation among the Munda of Eastern India. *Zeitschrift für Ethnologie, 113*(1), 67–85.

Parkin, R. (1993). The joking relationship and kinship: Charting a theoretical dependency. *Journal of the Anthropological Society of Oxford, 24*(3), 251–63.

Parkin, R. (2013). Relatedness as transcendence: On the renewed debate over the meaning of kinship. *Journal of the Anthropological Society of Oxford, 5*(1), 1–26.

Parmentier, R.J. (1994). *Signs in society: Studies in semiotic anthropology*. Indiana University Press.

Parsons, E.C. (1916). Avoidance in Melanesia. *Journal of American Folklore*, 29(112), 282–92. https://doi.org/10.2307/534488

Pastner, C.M. (1982). Gradations of Purdah and the creation of social boundaries on a Baluchistan oasis. In H. Papanek & G. Minault (Eds.), *Separate worlds: Studies of purdah in South Asia* (pp. 164–89). Chankya Publications.

Paulston, C.B. (1976). Pronouns of address in Swedish: Social class semantics and a changing situation. *Language in Society*, 5(3), 359–86. https://doi.org/10.1017/S004740450000717X

Pawley, A. (1992). Kalam pandanus language: An old New Guinea experiment in language engineering. In T. Dutton, M. Ross, & D. Tryon (Eds.), *The language game: Papers in memory of Donald C. Laycock* (pp. 313–34). Pacific Linguistics.

Peirce, C.S., & Welby, V. (1977). *Semiotic and significs: The correspondence between Charles S. Peirce and Victoria Lady Welby* (C.S. Hardwick, Ed.). Indiana University Press.

Pearce, E. (2015). *A grammar of Unua*. De Gruyter Mouton. https://doi.org/10.1515/9781614516590

Peeke, M.C. (1973). *Preliminary grammar of Auca*. Summer Institute of Linguistics.

Pike, K. (1954). *Language in relation to a unified theory of the structure of human behavior*. Summer Institute of Linguistics.

Pillai, M.S. (1972). Address terms and the social hierarchy of the Tamils. *Proceedings of the first all India conference of Dravidian linguists*, 1, 424–32.

Platz, S. (1996). Armenians. In P. Friedrich & N. Diamond (Eds.), *Encyclopedia of world cultures, volume 6: Russia and Eurasia/China* (pp. 27–31). G.K. Hall.

Potts, C. (2005). *The logic of conventional implicatures*. Oxford University Press. https://doi.org/10.1093/acprof:oso/9780199273829.001.0001

Provinse, J.H. (1937). The underlying sanctions of Plains Indian culture. In F. Eggan (Ed.), *Social anthropology of North American tribes* (pp. 341–76). University of Chicago Press.

Pullum, G.K. (1991). *The great Eskimo vocabulary hoax, and other irreverent essays on the study of language*. University of Chicago Press.

Putnam, H. (1996). The meaning of "meaning." In A. Pessin & S. Goldberg (Eds.), *The twin Earth chronicles: Twenty years of reflection on Hilary Putnam's "The meaning of 'meaning'"* (pp. 3–52). M.E. Sharpe.

Radcliffe-Brown, A.R. (1924). The mother's brother in South Africa. *South African Journal of Science*, 21, 542–55.

Radcliffe-Brown, A.R. (1940). On joking relationships. *Africa*, 13(3), 195–210. https://doi.org/10.2307/1156093

Radcliffe-Brown, A.R. (1949). A further note on joking relationships. *Africa*, 19(2), 133–40. https://doi.org/10.2307/1156517

Rampton, B. (2018). Goffman: Key concepts in exploration of the interaction order. *Working Papers in Urban Language & Literacies* #239.

Raum, O.F. (1973). *The social functions of avoidances and taboos among the Zulu*. De Gruyter. https://doi.org/10.1515/9783110832884

Reesink, G.P. (1987). *Structures and their functions in Usan*. John Benjamins. https://doi.org/10.1075/slcs.13

Rice, K. (2015). *"Most of them, they just want someone to under them": Gender, generation, and personhood among the Xhosa* [Unpublished doctoral dissertation]. University of Toronto.

Rijkhoff, J. (1998). Bystander deixis. In Y. Matras (Ed.), *The Romani element in non-standard speech* (pp. 51–67). Harrassowitz.

Rijnberk, G. van (1954). *Le langage par signes chez les moines*. North-Holland.

Rival, L. (2002). *Trekking through history: The Huaorani of Amazonian Ecuador*. Columbia University Press. https://doi.org/10.7312/riva11844

Rivers, W.H.R. (1914). *The history of Melanesian society*. Cambridge University Press.

Robbins, J. (1994). Equality as a value: Ideology in Dumont, Melanesia and the West. *Social Analysis*, 36, 21–70.

Robinson, S. (2011). *Split intransitivity in Rotokas, a Papuan language of Bougainville* [Unpublished doctoral dissertation]. Radboud University Nijmegen.

Roscoe, J. (1902). Further notes on the manners and customs of the Baganda. *The Journal of the Anthropological Institute of Great Britain and Ireland*, 32, 25–80. https://doi.org/10.2307/2842903

Roscoe, J. (1965). *The Baganda: An account of their native customs and beliefs*. Cass.

Roth, C. (2008). *Becoming Tsimshian: The social life of names*. University of Washington Press.

Roughsey, D. (1971). *Moon and rainbow: The autobiography of an Aboriginal*. A.H. & A.W. Reed.

Rousseau, J. (1978). The Kayan. In V.T. King (Ed.), *Essays on Borneo societies* (pp. 78–91). Oxford University Press.

Rumsey, A. (1982). Gun-Gunma: An Australian Aboriginal avoidance language and its social functions. In J. Heath, F. Merlan, & A. Rumsey (Eds.), *The languages of kinship in Aboriginal Australia* (pp. 160–81). Oceania Linguistic Monograph, No. 24.

Rumsey, A. (1990). Wording, meaning, and linguistic ideology. *American Anthropologist*, 92(2), 346–61. https://doi.org/10.1525/aa.1990.92.2.02a00060

Rumsey, A. (2000). Bunuba. In R.M.W. Dixon & B. Blake (Eds.), *The handbook of Australian languages, volume 5* (pp. 35–152). Oxford University Press.

Rushforth, S. (1981). Speaking to "relatives-through-marriage": Aspects of communication among the Bear Lake Athapaskans. *Journal of Anthropological Research*, *37*(1), 28–45. https://doi.org/10.1086/jar.37.1.3629513

Russell, K. (2020). Facing another: The attenuation of contact as space in Dhofar, Oman. *Signs and Society*, *8*(2), 290–318. https://doi.org/10.1086/708145

Ryan, D. (1958). Names and naming in Mendi. *Oceania*, *29*(2), 109–16. https://doi.org/10.1002/j.1834-4461.1958.tb02946.x

Sah, K.K. (2010). Raji pronouns. *Nepalese Linguistics*, *25*, 197–207.

Sahlins, M. (1962). *Moala: Culture and nature on a Fijian island*. University of Michigan Press. https://doi.org/10.3998/mpub.9690566

Sahlins, M. (2013). *What kinship is—and is not*. University of Chicago Press. https://doi.org/10.7208/chicago/9780226925134.001.0001

Salmon, M.T. (1927). Linguistique et histoire : quelques commentaires. *Le Bulletin de la Société des Études océaniennes*, *20*, 260–71.

Sanford, M.S. (1971). Present day death practices and eschatology of the Kiowa Apache. *University of Oklahoma Papers in Anthropology*, *12*, 81–134.

Sapir, E. (1910). *Yana texts*. University of California Press.

Sapir, E. (1921). *Language*. Harcourt, Brace & Company.

Sapir, E. (1985). *Selected writings of Edward Sapir in language, culture and personality* (D.G. Mandelbaum, Ed.). University of California Press.

Sartre, J.-P. (2003). *Being and nothingness: An essay in phenomenological ontology* (H.E. Barnes, Trans.). Routledge.

Saussure, F. de (1995). *Cours de linguistique générale*. Éditions Payot & Rivages.

Scheffler, H.W. (1965). *Choiseul Island social structure*. University of California Press. https://doi.org/10.1525/9780520323605

Schlücker, B., & Ackermann, T. (2017). The morphosyntax of proper names: An overview. *Folia Linguistica*, *51*(2), 309–39. https://doi.org/10.1515/flin-2017-0011

Schmidt, A. (1988). *Language in a Fijian village: An ethnolinguistic study* [Unpublished doctoral dissertation]. Australian National University.

Schneider, D.M. (1968). *American kinship: A cultural account*. Prentice-Hall.

Schneider, D.M. (1984). *A critique of the study of kinship*. University of Michigan Press. https://doi.org/10.3998/mpub.7203

Schneider, D.M., & Homans, G.C. (1955). Kinship terminology and the American kinship system. *American Anthropologist*, *57*(6), 1194–208. https://doi.org/10.1525/aa.1955.57.6.02a00100

Scott-Phillips, T.C. (2015). *Speaking our minds: Why human communication is different, and how language evolved to make it special*. Palgrave Macmillan.

Seeger, A. (1981). *Nature and society in central Brazil: The Suya Indians of Mato Grosso*. Harvard University Press. https://doi.org/10.4159/harvard.9780674433038

Seigelshifer, V., & Hartman, T. (2011). From *tichels* to hair bands: Modern orthodox women and the practice of head covering. *Women's Studies International Forum, 34*(5), 349–59. https://doi.org/10.1016/j.wsif.2011.05.006

Seki, L. (1983). Observações sobre variação sociolinguïstica em Kamaiurá. *Cadernos de Estudos Lingüísticos, 4*, 73–87.

Seki, L. (2000). *Gramática do Kamaiurá: Língua Tupi-Guarani do alto Xingu*. Imprensa Oficial.

Shapiro, J. (1982). "Women's studies": A note on the perils of markedness. *Signs, 7*(3), 717–21. https://doi.org/10.1086/493911

Shapiro, W. (1970). Local exogamy and the wife's mother in Aboriginal Australia. In R. Berndt (Ed.), *Australian Aboriginal anthropology* (pp. 51–69). University of Western Australia Press.

Shapiro, W. (1979). *Social organization in Aboriginal Australia*. ANU Press.

Shapiro, W. (2008). What human kinship is primarily about: Toward a critique of the new kinship studies. *Social Anthropology, 16*(2), 137–53. https://doi.org/10.1111/j.1469-8676.2008.00038.x

Sharma, U.M. (1978). Women and their affines: The veil as a symbol of separation. *Man, 13*, 218–33. https://doi.org/10.2307/2800246

Sharman, A. (1969). "Joking" in Padhola: Categorical relationships, choice and social control. *Man, 4*(1), 103–17. https://doi.org/10.2307/2799268

Sharp, J. (2004). *Nyangumarta: A language of the Pilbara region of western Australia*. Pacific Linguistics.

Sibree, J. (1892). Curious words and customs connected with chieftainship and royalty among the Malagasy. *The Journal of the Anthropological Institute of Great Britain and Ireland, 21*, 215–30. https://doi.org/10.2307/2842548

Sicoli, M.A. (2010). Shifting voices with participant roles: Voice qualities and speech registers in Mesoamerica. *Language in Society, 39*(4), 521–53. https://doi.org/10.1017/S0047404510000436

Sidnell, J. (2009). Participation. In S. D'hondt, J.O. Östman, & J. Verschueren (Eds.), *Pragmatics of interaction*, (pp. 125–56). https://doi.org/10.1075/hoph.4.08sid

Silberbauer, G.B. (1981). *Hunter and habitat in the central Kalahari desert*. Cambridge University Press.

Silver, S. (1978). Shastan peoples. In W.C. Sturtevant & R.F. Heizer (Eds.), *Handbook of North American Indians, volume 8, California* (pp. 211–24). Smithsonian Institution.

Silverstein, M. (1976). Shifters, linguistics categories, and cultural description. In K. Basso & H. Selby (Eds.), *Meaning in anthropology* (pp. 11–55). University of New Mexico Press.

Silverstein, M. (1979). Language structure and linguistic ideology. In P.R. Clyne, W.F. Hanks, & C.L. Hofbauer (Eds.), *The elements: A parasession on linguistic units and levels* (pp. 193–247). Chicago Linguistic Society.

Silverstein, M. (1981). The limits of awareness [Sociolinguistic Working Paper, No. 84]. Southwest Educational Development Laboratory.

Silverstein, M. (1985). Language and the culture of gender: At the intersection of structure, usage, and ideology. In E. Mertz & R.J. Parmentier (Eds.), *Semiotic mediation: Sociocultural and psychological perspectives* (pp. 219–53). Academic Press. https://doi.org/10.1016/B978-0-12-491280-9.50016-9

Silverstein, M. (1987a). The three faces of "function": Preliminaries to a psychology of language. In M. Hickmann (Ed.), *Social and functional approaches to language and thought* (pp. 17–38). Academic Press.

Silverstein, M. (1987b). Cognitive implications of a referential hierarchy. In M. Hickmann (Ed.), *Social and functional approaches to language and thought* (pp. 125–64). Academic Press.

Silverstein, M. (1993). Metapragmatic discourse and metapragmatic function. In J.A. Lucy (Ed.), *Reflexive language: Reported speech and metapragmatics* (pp. 33–58). Cambridge University Press. https://doi.org/10.1017/CBO9780511621031.004

Silverstein, M. (2003). Indexical order and the dialectics of sociolinguistic life. *Language & Communication*, 23(3–4), 193–229. https://doi.org/10.1016/S0271-5309(03)00013-2

Silverstein, M. (2004). "Cultural" concepts and the language-culture nexus. *Current Anthropology*, 45(5), 621–52. https://doi.org/10.1086/423971

Silverstein, M. (2010). "Direct" and "indirect" communicative acts in semiotic perspective. *Journal of Pragmatics*, 42(2), 337–53. https://doi.org/10.1016/j.pragma.2009.06.003

Silverstein, M. (2013). Worora kinship and "parenteral" relationships. *Anthropological Theory*, 13(1/2), 89–103. https://doi.org/10.1177/1463499613483402

Simmons, D.R., Robertson, A.E., McKay, L.S., Toal, E., McAleer, P., & Pollick, F.E. (2009). Vision in autism spectrum disorders. *Vision Research*, 49(22), 2705–39. https://doi.org/10.1016/j.visres.2009.08.005

Simons, G.F. (1982). Word taboo and comparative Austronesian linguistics. In A. Halim, L. Carrington, & S.A. Wurm (Eds.), *Papers from the Third International Conference on Austronesian Linguistics*, Vol. 3. (pp. 157–226). Pacific Linguistics.

Skeat, W.W., & Blagden, C.O. (1906). *Pagan races of the Malay Peninsula*, Vol. 2. Macmillan.

Slotta, J. (2012). On the receiving end: Cultural frames for communicative acts in post-colonial Papua New Guinea [Unpublished doctoral dissertation]. University of Chicago.

Slotta, J. (2015). The perlocutionary is political: Listening as self-determination in a Papua New Guinean polity. *Language in Society*, 44(4), 525–52. https://doi.org/10.1017/S0047404515000421

Slotta, J. (2020). Pragmatics. In A. Agha & J. Sidnell (Eds.), *The international encyclopedia of linguistic anthropology* (pp. 1–16). John Wiley. https://doi.org/10.1002/9781118786093.iela0323

Slotta, J. (2023). *Anarchy and the art of listening: The politics and pragmatics of reception in Papua New Guinea*. Cornell University Press. https://doi.org/10.7591/cornell/9781501770005.001.0001

Smith, I., & Johnson, S. (1986). Sociolinguistic patterns in an unstratified society: The patrilects of Kugu Nganhcara. *Journal of the Atlantic Provinces Linguistic Association, 8*, 29–43.

Smith, I., & Johnson, S. (2000). Kugu Nganhcara. In R.M.W. Dixon & B. Blake (Eds.), *Handbook of Australian languages*, Vol. 5 (pp. 357–489). Oxford University Press.

Sommer, B.A. (2006). *Speaking Kunjen: An ethnography of Oykangand kinship and communication*. Pacific Linguistics.

Sperber, D. (1985). Anthropology and psychology: Towards an epidemiology of representations. *Man, 20*(1), 73–89. https://doi.org/10.2307/2802222

Sperber, D., & Wilson, D. (1995). *Relevance: Communication and cognition*. Blackwell.

Stasch, R. (2002). Joking avoidance: A Korowai pragmatics of being two. *American Ethnologist, 29*(2), 335–65. https://doi.org/10.1525/ae.2002.29.2.335

Stasch, R. (2003). Separateness as a relation: The iconicity, univocality and creativity of Korowai mother-in-law avoidance. *Journal of the Royal Anthropological Institute, 9*(2), 317–37. https://doi.org/10.1111/1467-9655.00152

Stasch, R. (2008). Referent-wrecking in Korowai: A New Guinea abuse register as ethnosemiotic protest. *Language in Society, 37*(1), 1–25. https://doi.org/10.1017/S0047404508080019

Stasch, R. (2009). *Society of others: Kinship and mourning in a West Papuan place*. University of California Press. https://doi.org/10.1525/9780520943322

Stasch, R. (2014). Linguistic anthropology and sociocultural anthropology. In N.J. Enfield, P. Kockelman, & J. Sidnell (Eds.), *The Cambridge handbook of linguistic anthropology* (pp. 604–21). Cambridge University Press. https://doi.org/10.1017/CBO9781139342872.030

Stephens, W.N. [with R.G. D'Andrade]. (1962). *The Oedipus complex: Cross-cultural evidence*. Free Press of Glencoe.

Storch, A. (2011). *Secret manipulations: Language and context in Africa*. Oxford University Press. https://doi.org/10.1093/acprof:oso/9780199768974.001.0001

Storch, A. (2017). Typology of secret languages and linguistic taboos. In A.Y. Aikhenvald & R.M.W. Dixon (Eds.), *The Cambridge handbook of linguistic typology* (pp. 287–321). Cambridge University Press. https://doi.org/10.1017/9781316135716.010

Strathern, A. (1970). Wiru penthonyms. *Bijdragen tot de Taal-, Land- en Volkenkunde, 126*(1), 59–74. https://doi.org/10.1163/22134379-90002824

Strathern, A. (1989). Flutes, birds, and hair in Hagen. *Anthropos, 84*, 81–7.

Strathern, M. (1972). *Women in between: Female roles in a male world*. Seminar Press.

Strathern, M. (1985). Kinship and economy: Constitutive orders of a provisional kind. *American Ethnologist, 12*(2), 191–209. https://doi.org/10.1525/ae.1985.12.2.02a00010

Strathern, M. (1988). *The gender of the gift: Problems with women and problems with society in Melanesia*. University of California Press. https://doi.org/10.1525/california/9780520064232.001.0001

Strathern, M. (1992). *After nature: English kinship in the late twentieth century*. Cambridge University Press.

Strawson, P.F. (1966). Review of Wittgenstein's *Philosophical Investigations*. In G. Pitcher (Ed.), *Wittgenstein: The philosophical investigations* (pp. 22–64). Anchor Books.

Suárez, J. (1971). A case of absolute synonyms. *International Journal of American Linguistics, 37*(3), 192–5. https://doi.org/10.1086/465160

Subrahmanian, K. (1978). My Mrs. is Indian. *Anthropological Linguistics, 20*(6), 295–6.

Sutton, P.J. (1978). *Wik: Aboriginal society, territory and language at Cape Keerweer, Cape York Peninsula, Australia* [Unpublished doctoral dissertation]. University of Queensland.

Tambiah, S.J. (1969). Animals are good to think and good to prohibit. *Ethnology, 8*(4), 423–59. https://doi.org/10.2307/3772910

Tambiah, S.J. (2017). Form and meaning of magical acts. *HAU: Journal of Ethnographic Theory, 7*(3), 451–73. https://doi.org/10.14318/hau7.3.030

Tarlo, E. (1996). *Clothing matters: Dress and identity in India*. Hurst.

Taylor, P.M. (1984). Tobelo kin, spouses, and in-laws. *Maluku & Irian Jaya, 3*(1), 119–46.

Taylor, P.M. (1990). *The folk biology of the Tobelo people: A study in folk classification*. Smithsonian Institution Press. https://doi.org/10.5479/si.00810223.34.1

Teferra., A. (1987). Ballishsha: Women's speech among the Sidama. *Journal of Ethiopian Studies, 20*, 44–59.

Thomas, G. (1931). Customs and beliefs of the natives of Buka. *Oceania, 2*(2), 220–31. https://doi.org/10.1002/j.1834-4461.1931.tb01667.x

Thompson, C. (1981). A sense of sharm: Some thoughts on its implications for the position of women in a village in central India. *South Asia Research, 1*(2), 39–53. https://doi.org/10.1177/026272808100100206

Thomson, D.F. (1935). The joking relationship and organized obscenity in north Queensland. *American Anthropologist, 37*(3), 460–90. https://doi.org/10.1525/aa.1935.37.3.02a00100

Tomasello, M. (2019). *Becoming human: A theory of ontogeny*. Harvard University Press. https://doi.org/10.4159/9780674988651

Tonkinson, R. (1978). *The Mardudjara Aborigines: Living the dream in Australia's desert*. Holt, Rinehard and Winston.

Trawick, M. (1996). *Notes on love in a Tamil family*. Oxford University Press.

Treis, Y. (2005). Avoiding their names, avoiding their eyes: How Kambaata women respect their in-laws. *Anthropological Linguistics, 47*(3), 292–320.

Tsunoda, T. (1981). *The Djaru language of Kimberley, Western Australia*. Pacific Linguistics.

Tuite, K., & Schulze, W. (1998). A case of taboo-motivated lexical replacement in the indigenous languages of the Caucasus. *Anthropological Linguistics, 40*(3), 363–83.

Tylor, E.B. (1889). On a method of investigating the development of institutions; applied to laws of marriage and descent. *The Journal of the Anthropological Institute of Great Britain and Ireland, 18*, 245–72. https://doi.org/10.2307/2842423

Valenzuela, P.M. (2003). *Transitivity in Shipibo-Konibo grammar* [Unpublished doctoral dissertation]. University of Oregon.

Valeri, V. (2000). *The forest of taboos: Morality, hunting, and identity among the Huaulu of the Moluccas*. University of Wisconsin Press.

van der Tuuk, H.N. (1971). *A grammar of Toba Batak*. (J. Scott-Kemball, Trans.). Martinus Nijhoff. (Original work published 1865–7)

van Gennep, A. (1908). Essai d'une théorie des langues spéciales. *Revue des études ethnographiques et sociologiques, 1*, 327–37.

Veblen, T. (1994). *The theory of the leisure class*. Dover.

Verguin, J. (1957). Deux systèmes de vocabulaire parallèle à Madagascar. *Word, 13*(1), 153–6. https://doi.org/10.1080/00437956.1957.11659632

Vidal, P. (1976). *Garçons et filles : le passage à l'âge d'homme chez les Gbaya Kara*. Laboratoire d'ethnologie et de sociologie comparative.

Villa, S.H., & Matossian, M.K. (1982). *Armenian village life before 1914*. Wayne State University Press.

Viveiros de Castro, E. (1992). *From the enemy's point of view: Humanity and divinity in an Amazonian society* (C.V. Howard, Trans.). University of Chicago Press. https://doi.org/10.7208/chicago/9780226768830.001.0001

Viveiros de Castro, E. (2009). The gift and the given: Three nano-essays on kinship and magic. In S.C. Bamford & J. Leach (Eds.), *Kinship and beyond: The genealogical model reconsidered* (pp. 237–68). Berghahn. https://doi.org/10.1515/9781845458966-012

Vogelsang-Eastwood, G., & Vogelsang, W. (2008). *Covering the moon: An introduction to Middle Eastern face veils*. Peeters.

Volkova, N. (1994). The Udis. In P. Friedrich & N. Diamond (Eds.), *Encyclopedia of world cultures, volume 6: Russia and Eurasia/China* (pp. 375–78). G.K. Hall.

Vreeland, H.H. (1962). *Mongol community and kinship structure*. HRAF Press.

Wagner, R. (1967). *The curse of Souw: Principles of Daribi clan definition and alliance in New Guinea*. University of Chicago Press.

Wagner, R. (1972). Incest and identity: A critique and theory on the subject of exogamy and incest prohibition. *Journal of the Royal Anthropological Institute*, 7(4), 601–13. https://doi.org/10.2307/2799952

Wagner, R. (1977). Analogic kinship: A Daribi example. *American Ethnologist*, 4(4), 623–42. https://doi.org/10.1525/ae.1977.4.4.02a00030

Wagner, R. (1981). *The invention of culture*. University of Chicago Press.

Wagner, R. (1986a). *Asiwinarong: Ethos, image, and social power among the Usen Barok of New Ireland*. Princeton University Press. https://doi.org/10.1515/9781400861033

Wagner, R. (1986b). *Symbols that stand for themselves*. University of Chicago Press.

Wallace, J.M. (1969). Katu phonemes. *Mon-Khmer Studies*, 3, 64–73.

Warner, W.L. (1964). *A black civilization: A social study of an Australian tribe*. Harper & Row.

Webster, A. (1998). "One did not just say anything": Chiricahua Apache warpath vocabulary as linguistic ideology. *Kroeber Anthropological Society Papers*, 83, 102–6.

Webster, A. (2008). A note on Plains Apache warpath vocabulary. *International Journal of American Linguistics*, 74(2), 257–61. https://doi.org/10.1086/587706

Webster, A. (2021). Anthropology at the water's edge: Morris Opler among the Apaches. *Journal of the Southwest*, 63(3), 468–505. https://doi.org/10.1353/jsw.2021.0011

Weiner, J.F. (1988). *The heart of the pearl shell: The mythological dimension of Foi sociality*. University of California Press. https://doi.org/10.1525/9780520336933

Whittier, P.R. (1981). *Systems of appellation among the Kenyah Dayak of Borneo* [Unpublished doctoral dissertation]. Michigan State University.

Whorf, B.L. (2000). *Language, thought and reality* (J.B. Carroll, Ed.). MIT Press.

Wilkins, D.P. (1997). Handsigns and hyperpolysemy: Exploring the cultural foundations of semantic association. In D. Tryon & M. Walsh (Eds.), *Boundary rider: Essays in honour of Geoffrey O'Grady* (pp. 413–44). ANU.

Williams, F.E. (1930). *Orokaiva society*. Oxford University Press.

Willie, M. (1991). *Navajo pronouns and obviation* [Unpublished doctoral dissertation]. The University of Arizona.

Wilson, M. (1951). *Good company: A study of Nyakyusa age-villages*. Oxford University Press.

Witherspoon, G. (1977). *Language and art in the Navajo universe*. The University of Michigan Press. https://doi.org/10.3998/mpub.9705

Wojtylak, K.I. (2015). Fruits for animals: Hunting avoidance speech style in Murui (Witoto, Northwest Amazonia). *Berkeley Linguistics Society*, *41*, 545–62. https://doi.org/10.20354/B4414110007

Wolf, A.P. (2004). Introduction. In A.P. Wolf & W.H. Durham (Eds.), *Inbreeding, incest, and the incest taboo: The state of knowledge at the turn of the century* (pp. 1–23). Stanford University Press. https://doi.org/10.1515/9780804767415-002

Yankah, K. (1991). Power and the circuit of formal talk. *Journal of Folklore Research*, *28*(1), 1–22.

Yankah, K. (1995). *Speaking for the chief: Okyeame and the politics of Akan royal oratory*. Indiana University Press.

Young, R.W., & Morgan, W. (1980). *The Navajo language: A grammar and colloquial dictionary*. University of New Mexico Press.

Zahavi, A., & Zahavi, A. (1997). *The handicap principle: A missing piece of Darwin's puzzle*. Oxford University Press. https://doi.org/10.1093/oso/9780195100358.001.0001

Zahavi, D. (2012). Self, consciousness, and shame. In D. Zahavi (Ed.), *The Oxford handbook of contemporary phenomenology* (pp. 304–23). Oxford University Press. https://doi.org/10.1093/oxfordhb/9780199594900.013.0016

Zuckerman, C.H.P. (2016). Phatic violence? Gambling and the arts of distraction in Laos. *Journal of Linguistic Anthropology*, *26*(3), 294–314. https://doi.org/10.1111/jola.12137

Zuckerman, C.H.P. (2020). Phatic, the: Communication and communion. In A. Agha & J. Sidnell (Eds.), *The international encyclopedia of linguistic anthropology*. John Wiley. https://doi.org/10.1002/9781118786093.iela0311

Zuckerman, C.H.P., & Enfield, N.J. (2023). Limits of thematization. *Linguistic Anthropology*, *33*(3), 234–63. https://doi.org/10.1111/jola.12399

Index

Note: The letter *f* following a page number denotes a figure; the letter *t*, a table.

Abkhaz, 63, 100, 112, 181, 278n2
Abu-Lughod, Lila, 173, 262
Achumawi, 196*t*
address: and addressivity, 153, 212, 236; avoidance of, 153–4, 209–10, 213, 237*t*; negated, 157, 183, 232; shill, 72, 155–8, 227, 237, 293n8
affordances, 139, 163–5, 184–5, 282n7
Agha, Asif: on deference/indexical focus, 85–6, 94, 229; on honorific registers of person deixis, 192, 194; on indexical orders, 302n10; on metasemiotic typification, 142; on register cohesion, 61; on semiotic range, 139; on semiotic/speech registers, 15, 35; on social domain of a register, 284n3; on speech levels, 224–5, 299n1
Agta (Cagayan), 167
Akan, 293n8
Anderson, Jon, 173–4, 178–9
Anishinaabe, 140, 186
Apache: Chiricahua, 3, 16–19, 168, 172, 288n9; Jicarilla, 23; Kiowa, 92, 113–14, 116–17; raiding registers 56; Western, 147–8, 294n3

Armenian, 177, 181–4
Austin, John L., 108, 287n2, 288n3
avoidance levels, 18–24, 275n12. *See also* speech levels
avunculate, 6–7, 21
Awiakay, 40, 299n2

Baganda, 167, 186
Baluchistan, 294n1, 303n10
Barakat, Robert, 68
Barok (Usen), 160, 257–9, 263
Bateson, Gregory: on double description, 256–7, 303n12, 304n2; on logical types, 163; on metacommunication, 144, 158–9, 186–7; on the pattern which connects, 217; on schismogenesis, 304n3
Bear Lake Dene, 147, 197
Benjamin, Geoffrey, 209
Berlin, Brent, 65, 67, 281n6
betrothal, 175, 208, 257, 275n11
Big Nambas. *See* V'ënen Taut
Bininj Guwok, 61, 164, 196, 232–3, 299nn2–3
Birao, 195*t*, 307n10
Bird-David, Nurit, 14, 254–5

Blythe, Joe, 93, 233
Boazi, 195*t*, 202, 297n6
bride price, 148–9, 208, 258
bride service, 147–9, 154, 259, 261, 275n11, 290n5
Brosius, Peter, 114–17
Brown, Penelope, and Stephen Levinson, 54, 275n10, 277n1, 291n5, 296n2
Brown, Roger, and Albert Gilman, 94, 149, 192, 296n2
Buka, 177*t*, 186
Bunaba, 54, 61, 73–5, 77, 279n3
Buru, 39–41, 44, 58–9

calibration type, 119–21, 235
Carsten, Janet, 13, 254
Caucasus, 110, 112, 151, 181–4
causal theory of reference, 118
Chechen, 295n4
Chinook, 302n9
Choiseul Islanders, 166
Choksi, Nishaant, 194
Chowning, Ann, 90–1, 107
Clay, Brenda Johnson, 262
commensurability/commensuration, 24–5, 27, 129, 133, 223, 240, 276n17
communicative infrastructure, 143–52, 290n4
comparative linguistic anthropology, 31, 184
Corbett, Greville, 224, 298n9
Crowley, Terry, 62, 156, 281n4
Csordas, Thomas, 166

Daakie, 195*t*
Dalabon, 196, 233
Damin. *See* Lardil
Daribi, 7, 177*t*, 257, 259
Datooga, 97*t*, 101
Dean, Melanie, 171
defeasance conditions, 108–11, 129*f*

deference focus. *See* indexical focus
deictic selectivity, 298
Derrida, Jacques, 303n1
Dhopadhola, 290n2
diagrams (indexical-icons), 72, 74, 129*t*, 205–6, 215–17, 240–2
differentially enregistered. *See* sociopragmatically marked
Dixon, R.M.W., 39, 51–3, 63–4, 233, 239, 281n4
Djaru, 74, 195*t*, 230
Dyirbal, 38–9, 51–2, 61, 63–4, 232, 239, 281n4

Eggan, Fred, 10
Elkin, A.P., 300n7
Elmendorf, William, 289n6
emblems (iconic-indexicals), 85, 140–1, 202–3, 241, 247*t*, 248–9
Enfield, N.J., 197
Errington, Joe, 94, 229, 275n12
ethnobiological taxonomy, 65–8, 281n6
Evans, Nicholas, 233, 280n2
Eves, Richard, 169, 264, 267

Faroese, 277n2
fashions of speaking, 70–5, 198–201
Fifi'i, Jonathan, 48, 92
Fijian, 155–6, 215
Firth, Raymond, 21–2, 191, 198–9, 276n15
Foi, 175, 179
Fortes, Meyer, 8, 14
Fox, Helen, 87–9
Frazer, J.G., 29, 86, 290n2
Freud, Sigmund, 265, 306n9

G|ui, 195*t*, 197
Gal, Susan, 286n7, 296n4, 298n10
Garde, Murray, 24, 170, 299n3
Gbaya(-Kara), 66*t*, 76–8, 283nn9–10

generation (alternating/adjacent), 104, 124–6, 268t, 292n6
Gilman, Albert. *See* Brown, Roger
Gisu, 160, 305n4
Goffman, Erving, 15, 139, 144, 181, 301n8
Goodale, Jane, 8–9, 90–1
Goodwin, Greville, 147–8
Gooniyandi, 54–5, 195t, 227, 231, 237–8, 280n4, 287n11
Guiart, Jean, 286n6
Gujarati, 242–4
Gun-gunma. *See* Bunaba
Gurindji, 72, 158, 177t, 231, 295n3
Guugu Yimidhirr, 46–7, 52–3, 60, 66t, 67, 73, 158–9, 225, 232, 239–40, 295n3

Hadiyya, 97t, 220
Hage, Per, 21–3
Handman, Courtney, 169, 273n3
Harrisson, Tom, 177t, 285n4, 286n6
Haviland, John, 46, 52t, 60, 158–9, 225
Heald, Suzette, 305n4
Hidatsa, 97t
Hindi, 146t, 263
honorific pronouns. *See* registers, of personal deixis
honorifics. *See* registers
Huli, 40
Humphrey, Caroline, 83–4

iconic-indexicals. *See* emblems
ideology: in relation to iconicity and indexicality, 276; in relation to structure and usage, 25–7, 49–50, 70–80, 197–201, 300n5; performativist, 48, 60, 79, 164; phatic, 152; referentialist, 121–4
indexical focus: fluid, 228–33; relational vs. absolute, 275n10;
indexical origo/target, 85–6, 233–9, 274n10. *See also* interactional roles
indexical icons. *See* diagrams
indexical orders, 86–93, 243, 294n2
interactional roles: addressee (vs. recipient/bystander) as, 233–9, 301n8 (*see also* address avoidance); speaker (vs. animator) as, 108, 233–9, 301n8; referent (vs. nonparticipant) as, 85–6
Inuit, 92, 127, 288n4
Irons, William, 244–6
Irvine, Judith, 85, 286n7, 298n10

Jackson, Graham, 23–4, 248
Jacobson, Doranne, 150, 179, 243
Jahai, 195t, 211f, 298n8
Jakobson, Roman, 45, 119, 184, 273n3
Jalnguy. *See* Dyirbal
Javanese, 229, 233, 275n12, 280n3, 299n1
joking relationships: and categorical identification, 104–6, 127; and extreme license, 6, 137, 276n15; as paradoxical metacommunication, 160–1, 294n10; and schismogenesis, 258, 305n4
Ju|'hoan, 124–6, 195t, 247f

Kalam, 40–1, 56–7
Kalapalo, 95t, 97t, 263, 265, 276n17
Kalmucks, 97t
Kamayurá, 97t, 153–5, 196t
Kamba, 97t, 101
Kambaata, 47, 95, 97t, 102, 107, 143, 287n12
Karok, 286, 289
Kashmiri Pandits, 151–2
Kaulong, 8–9, 90–1, 97t, 105, 266, 285n3
Kazak, 97t, 98–9

Keating, Elizabeth, 297n5
Keesing, Roger, 48–9, 92–3
Kerewe, 97*t*
Kewa, 56–8
kinship: categorical differences/ identities of, 104–6, 268*t*; as elicited relationship, 256–9; definition of, 267–71; studies of, 12–14, 254–6
Kinyarwanda, 97*t*
Kobon, 23–5, 195*t*, 204–5
Kodi, 278n2
Korowai, 4, 15, 166, 171, 195*t*, 208, 276n14
Kri, 195*t*, 197, 297n6
Kripke, Saul, 118, 120–1, 288n3, 289n1
Kugu Nganhcara, 156, 226–7
Kunjen, 72, 227, 231, 236–7
Kwaio, 48, 92–3
Kwara'ae, 286n6
Kyrgyz, 97*t*, 99

Lá'bi. *See* Gbaya(-Kara)
Ladakhi, 228
Landes, Ruth, 140
Lardil, 41, 65–8, 75–8, 279n3
Lau, 286n6
Laughren, Mary, 301n7
Lee, Richard, 124–6
Lelet, 140, 169, 195*t*, 264, 267
Lempert, Michael, 225
Levinson, Stephen. *See* Brown, Penelope
Lévi-Strauss, Claude, 7–8, 124, 251
lexicon asymmetry, 51–60
Li Garan. *See* Buru

Madhya Pradesh, 150, 179, 243, 263
Maithili, 212
Malagasy, 86, 110
Mandak, 262–3, 267
Mandan, 97*t*

Mangarayi, 110–11, 195*t*, 215, 226, 231, 234–5, 280n2
Manus, 37, 171–2, 175, 177*t*, 205–8, 214*f*, 297n7
many-to-one. *See* lexicon asymmetry
Marshall, Lorna, 124
Matagi, 278n2
Mehinaku, 95*t*, 259–60, 265, 291n5, 292n7, 294n10
Melpa, 18, 56, 164, 288n5
Mendi, 177*t*, 179–80
Merlan, Francesca: on univocality of avoidance speech, 4–6, 202, 240, 280n2; on bride service and in-law avoidance, 148, 290n5
metapragmatics, 17, 21, 91, 101, 142, 187, 194, 199–200, 223, 225, 229, 249, 296n3; definition of, 44; and linguistic proscription, 43–9, 53; referential biasing of, 94, 120–2, 127; self-negating, 73, 75, 157, 159 (*see also* paradoxical meta-communication)
Mijikenda, 195*t*, 197, 296n2, 297n6
Mitchell, Alice, 86, 286n9
Mongolian, 83–5, 98–100, 176
mother-in-law languages. *See* registers
Motuna, 221–2
Mous, Maarten, 286n10
Murdock, George Peter, 10–12, 103, 273n4, 274n5, 307n9
Murui, 35–6
mutuality: and intercorporeality, 165–8; and kinship, 13–14, 254–6
Mwotlap, 97*t*, 195*t*

Nakassis, Constantine, 289n1
names: and homonymous kinship, 124–7; and homophone avoidance, 83–102, 131–4, 219–22; and namesakes, 100, 111–12; as proper

nouns, 122; and referential telescoping, 122–4; as rigid designators, 120–1
Navajo, 157, 274n6, 274n8
Ndebele, 97t
Nharo, 124
Nyakyusa, 8, 97t, 101, 137–8, 170
Nyangumarta, 172, 230

Ojibwa. *See* Anishinaabe
Oliver, Douglas, 221
Opler, Morris, 3, 17, 19t, 23, 113, 168, 274n9
Ordos, 97t
Orokaiva, 176
Oromo, 97t

Panyjima, 72, 227, 232
paradoxical meta-communication, 144, 157, 159–61, 181, 179, 292n5, 306n8
Parkin, Robert, 13, 137–8
Parsons, Elsie Clews, 259–60, 306n6
Pashto, 173, 178–9
Pawley, Andrew, 40, 57t
Peirce, C.S., 15, 184
Penan, 114–17
performativity: indefeasible, 28, 108–12; rigid, 117–21
person (grammatical): fourth, 14, 274n8; skewing of, 211–13. *See also* negated address
phatic communication: and the anti-phatic function, 143–5 (*see also* address, avoidance of; address, negated; communicative infrastructure); definition of, 273n3; and the senses, 163–71
Pohnpeian, 297n5
Pomo: Central 196t; Northern, 117
prosopagnosia, 170
Puyuma, 278n2

Radcliffe-Brown, Alfred, 6, 7, 10, 103, 145, 291n5
Raji, 195t, 298n9
registers: avoidance, 36–9, 279n2; brother-in-law, 46, 52t; daughter-in-law, 98–102; definition of, 15–16, 35–6; honorific, 85–6, 274n10, 275n12; initiate, 65, 75–8, 282n9, 283n10; kinship, 14–16; mother-in-law, 38, 51–5, 228–40; name, 83–96; pandanus, 40, 56–8; of person deixis, 191–215
repertoires: anti-phatic, 139–40; definition of, 15–16, 35–6; idiolectal/sociolectal, 86–9; negative/positive, 20, 37, 43, 60–1
rhematization: definition of, 296n4; and semantic echoes, 198–201, 274n6, 296n5
Rice, Kathleen, 178
Rotokas, 195t
Rumsey, Alan, 54–5, 72, 77
Rushforth, Scott, 147

Sahlins, Marshall, 13–14, 155, 254–5
Sangir, 278n2
Santali, 195t, 197, 202, 292n6, 298n9
Sapir, Edward, 45
Sarsi. *See* Tsúùtínà
Sartre, Jean-Paul, 5, 264
Schneider, David, 12–13, 254–7
self-negating metapragmatics. *See* paradoxical meta-communication
Semai, 278n2
Sengseng, 90–1, 97t, 105, 107
sense of hearing, 163–5, 180–1. *See also* sign languages
sense of sight, 165, 168–171. *See also* technologies of visual avoidance
sense of touch, 165–8. *See also* sex

sex: as cause of avoidance, 10, 265, 306n9; as symbolically opposed to avoidance, 167, 265–7
shame, 160–1, 258–65, 306n8
Shasta, 286n8
Shipibo-Konibo, 156–7
Sidaama, 97*t*, 100, 128*t*, 149–50, 219–21, 302n10
sign languages, 68–9, 181–4, 282n7, 283n9
Silverstein, Michael: on the body, 139, 143; on breakthrough semiosis, 241, 302n9; on calibration types, 119; on formal-functional analogy in honorific pronouns, 192–3, 198, 216, 296nn1,3; on interactional negation, 156, 158; on structure-usage-ideology dialectics, 26, 50, 53, 72; on metalinguistic awareness, 94, 123; on ritual performativity, 249, 303n11
Siuai. *See* Motuna
skin, 142, 165–7, 250, 267, 269, 271
Slotta, James, 71–2, 93–4, 219, 273n3
social domain, 86–93, 284n3
sociopragmatically marked, 60, 86–93, 279n2
Sommer, Bruce, 10, 227, 236, 237*t*
Southern Sotha, 97*t*
speech intermediation, 145–52, 155–8
speech levels, 224–5, 275n12, 280n3, 299n1. *See also* avoidance levels
Stasch, Rupert: on the hierarchy of sensory modes of avoidance, 142, 164, 166; on kinship avoidance and the interaction order, 15; on uncanny iconicity, 116; on the univocality of avoidance, 4–6
Storch, Anne, 96, 287n10

Tahitian, 86–7
Tambiah, Stanley, 249, 290n2, 303n11
Tamil, 97*t*, 100, 107, 120, 128*t*
Tarlo, Emma, 242–4
technologies of visual avoidance, 171–80, 242–6, 295n5
Temiar, 195*t*, 209–10
Thompson, Catherine, 263
Tikopia, 21–3, 191, 195*t*, 198–200, 247*t*, 276n15
Tinrin, 298n9
To'abaita, 286n6
Toba Batak, 195*t*
Tolowa, 286n8
Tonkinson, Robert, 10
Treis, Yvonne, 47, 101
triadic communication. *See* speech intermediation
Tsúùtínà, 146*t*, 147, 170
Turkmen, 244–6
T-V systems. *See* registers, of person deixis
Twana, 288n6
Tylor, E.B., 6, 259, 262, 305n5

Udi, 182
Unua, 286n6
Uradhi, 66*t*
Usan, 195*t*

V'ënen Taut, 87–90, 128*t*, 177*t*, 285n5, 286n6
Valeri, Valerio, 167–8, 303n11
veiling. *See* technologies of visual avoidance

Wagner, Roy, on affinal avoidance, 292n5; on joking relationships, 160; on the elicitation of kinship, 255, 257–9, 270; on the incest taboo, 103; on the obviation of structure, 251, 303n12

Wailiki, 197
Waorani, 298n9
Warlpiri, 112, 215, 230–1, 301n7
Wauja, 95t, 97t
Westermarck effect, 265–6, 308n10
Western Desert Language, 10, 72, 159, 295n3; Kokatha, 230, 300n7; Pintupi, 230, 301n7
Whorf, Benjamin Lee, 40, 71
Wik, 54, 73, 112, 159, 176, 215, 226–7, 295n3, 300n3
Wilson, Monica, 8, 137–8, 170
Winda Winda, 72, 175
Wintu, 286n8
Wiru, 163–4
Worora, 75, 158

Wurrung, 73, 159, 177t, 232
Wuvulu, 195t

Xhosa, 97t, 101, 140–1, 177–8
Xingu River, 95, 98, 153, 197, 292n7

Yana, 196t, 279n4
Yélî Dnye, 44, 277n1
Yemeni, 179, 224, 294n1
Yidiny, 281n4
Yir-Yoront, 215, 231
Yokuts, 199–200
Yuki, 286n8
Yurok, 112, 289n6

Zulu, 97t, 131–3, 150, 274n10